D1522941

Bamboo World

Front Cover: Nastus elatus
Back Cover: Growing, working with and producing from bamboo

Bamboo World : The Growing and Use of Clumping Bamboos

First published in Australia in 1999 by Kangaroo Press
an imprint of Simon and Schuster (Australia) Pty Limited
20 Barcoo Street, East Roseville NSW 2069

A Viacom Company
Sydney New York London Toronto Tokyo Singapore

National Library of Australia
Cataloguing-in-Publication data

Cusack, Victor.
Bamboo world: the growing and use of clumping bamboos.

   Bibliography.
   Includes index.
   ISBN 0 86417 934 0.

   1. Bamboo. 2. Bamboo work. I. Stewart, Deirdre.
   II. Title.

   584.9

Cover and internal design: Vivien Valk
Illustrator: Victor Cusack
Photographer: Deirdre Stewart

Set in Leawood 7.5pt
Printed by Kyodo Printing Co. (S'pore) Pte Ltd

10 9 8 7 6 5 4 3 2 1

Bamboo World

The Growing and Use of Clumping Bamboos

WRITTEN AND ILLUSTRATED BY VICTOR CUSACK
PHOTOGRAPHS BY DEIRDRE STEWART

KANGAROO PRESS

Contents

■ **1.G** Gigantochloa ridleyi *plantation with a Balinese sleeping platform*

Author's Note
and Dedication

Recording my 50 years of passion for bamboo has been both fascinating and satisfying. I am not a scientist, but my past careers and education have made me cautious of accepting information unless it is either proven by my own experience, or verifiable preferably from more than one scientifically based text. Most of the more scientific books available are presented in concise language covering a certain spectrum of the subject. The object of this book, however, is to communicate knowledge, both scientific and practical, of the fabulous clumping bamboos of the world. Most important also is the need to raise awareness that these sympodial bamboos are non-invasive and predictable in growth.

I could perhaps be accused of being a little unfair in my bias against monopodial running bamboos, but that bias arises from the large number of phone calls that I receive from people who have a rapidly expanding problem with monopodial bamboos. Many are either reluctant to use, or banned from using, chemical sprays on their estate and they face expensive machinery bills or weeks of hard labour to tackle the problem, which often recurs annually to some degree in spite of their best efforts.

This book offers a new perspective. It tries to impart a broad spectrum of soundly based information on how to make your own bamboo furniture, or musical instruments, or fences and screens, or buildings, or paper, or water toys. It explains how to grow edible bamboo shoots for the kitchen and how to develop plantations for marketing.

Being a designer of steel structures and mechanisms, I found it a natural extension of my love of bamboo

to write to Dr Jules Janssen in the late 1970s. I was immediately excited by the calculations and photos of trusses under test loads he kindly sent me (and had similar experiences with Dr Tewari and Professor Walter Liese). Most of what we all learn has originally been sourced from someone who has had the passion to discover it before us, but each simple new thing man learns has to be communicated in many forms before it becomes available and usable for mankind; hence this book!

To collaborate with my wife, Deirdre, who has produced the beautiful photography of this book has been a fascinating adventure in itself, the marvel being that we are still together and having fun! I also owe much to individuals like Marek Fluteman, Jo Quin and Jim Wertz from Australia, Dr Songkram Thammincha (Thailand), Professor Zhang Guangchu, Professor Fu Maoyi and Lou Yiping from China, all whose specialised, often broad, knowledge I respect immensely.

I dedicate this book to Walter Liese (Professor Emeritus of Hamburg University). He is deservedly respected as one of the world's grand old men of bamboo, whose years of passion, accumulated knowledge and ground-breaking research on bamboo has contributed so much, and been given freely so often, to the cause of underprivileged people of many races. Professor Liese will support me in also dedicating the book to the grandeur and beauty of the plant bamboo, and to the task of informing people from cultures not familiar with bamboo about these little-known and much-misunderstood clumping bamboos of the world.

Victor Cusack, 1999
Bamboo World

Introduction

■ **1.A** Dendrocalamus sikkimensis, *newly emerging shoot*

■ **1.B** Bambusa oldhamii *showing two- to three-month-old leafless culms on a three-year-old clump*

Each year during the shoot season, we stand spellbound in our beautiful botanical garden, gazing in awe at the newly emerging shoots of tropical giant bamboos. They thrust the earth aside in great clods as they heave their mighty bulk from beneath the earth. *Dendrocalamus* species like *asper*, *brandisii* and *sikkimensis* create exotically decorated, upwardly mobile cones of life, up to 300 mm across the base. They are clothed in fur-covered, curving culm leaf overlays of velvet-black or purple tinged bronze, each overlay with two rows of dark bladed frills descending like the fins of a sea creature emerging from the deep. Within eight to ten weeks, these giant shoots will rocket into the air to within 90 per cent of their ultimate height, to become fledgling culms, still without leaves or roots of their own to nurture that great thrust of energy. Is it any wonder that we are fascinated and captivated by these extraordinary sub-tropical and tropical sympodial giants!

My romance with bamboo started when I was a ten-year-old child. Fascinated with the tall, straight, tube structure of this obviously different plant, I made flutes by burning finger and mouth holes (and my fingers) with red-hot pokers. I made pan flutes by tying cut-off sections of different lengths together, wonderfully straight pea shooters, spear shafts with delicately heat-hardened, hand-carved barbs to take into the sea with me to catch octopus, and light strong bows-and-arrows, all superior to and lighter than my efforts with conventional wood.

As a teenager I travelled up the east coast of Australia and gazed in awe at the massive old neglected clumps of *Bambusa balcooa* planted mostly for windbreaks and cattle fodder between 1850 and 1950, and now common in the area. However, it wasn't until the seventies when I started travelling extensively in Asia that I finally saw and came to understand the grandeur and importance of these wonderful clumping (sympodial) species, and their importance to the people of those areas.

Approximately fourteen million hectares of the earth's surface are covered with bamboo, most of it in Asia, with China being the country with the majority of species and largest growing areas. With such vast areas of quickly renewable biomass existing, it is obviously making a significant contribution to the photosynthesis and air purification process necessary for the earth's survival. About 20 million tonnes are harvested every year, primarily for local use in papermaking, building, furniture, edible shoots, and a multitude of other uses (Tewari, 1989). The annual global revenue generated from bamboo is estimated to be about US$4500 million (Liese, 1988).

Few people in the Western world have had sufficient contact with the clumping bamboos of the tropical and subtropical regions to realise how truly magnificent and useful these valuable plants can be. Travellers to Asian cities rarely encounter the plant itself, but many return with tales of amazing scaffolding structures, apparently (but not really) holding up complete skyscrapers under construction.

Those amazing scaffolding structures (in Hong Kong and Guangzhou) are constructed usually from the superior, non-invasive sympodial bamboos of central Asia and southern China. The (relatively) inferior and invasive running (monopodial) bamboos that most people in Australia and the USA recognise are only used for such tasks when the stronger sympodial bamboos are not available. The Shanghai/Hangzhou area uses moso because it is readily available. It is too cold to grow the stronger and often larger clumpers. Even in Japan, moso is used mostly for chopsticks, laminated floorboards, split blind manufacture, utensils, etc. (Oshima Jinsaburo, 1931). Most of China's moso is used for papermaking, with lesser amounts for craft, laminated floorboards and so on. Most of the scaffolding in Hong Kong and Guangzhou is constructed from the clumping bamboos *Bambusa tuldoides* and *B. bambos* (with a small amount of moso imported from northern areas because of its low cost and abundance).

Most of the useful superior species of clumping bamboos are akin to giant rainforest plants: huge, beautiful, powerful grasses so much in demand that in some countries the indigenous bamboo resources are being destroyed by insensitive selfish harvesting. As an example, India harvests nearly ten million tonnes/year of bamboo (Adkoli, 1995), approximately 80 per cent of which is used by local people, and 2.2 million tonnes by the pulp and paper industry. Dr D.N.Tewari, recently retired Director General of India's huge forest research establishment at Dehra Dun, says, 'The increased demand from traditional users and a disproportionate level of consumption by the pulp and paper industry have created a serious resource shortage and a rise in prices... many sources near mills are exhausted.' According to Tewari, the same shortages have appeared in China and Bangladesh. In the Philippines, overharvesting of *Bambusa blumeana* has led to some furniture factories importing culm stock from Vietnam. It is illogical, when one considers the dependence that many Asian races have on the plant. Governments and people are letting this degradation occur in spite of bamboo being the fastest growing woody plant in the world, and capable of giving an annually renewable harvest of such diversity.

A prime example of the prevailing Western cultural blind spot exists to this day in Australia. When the British

■ **1.D** *Bamboo scaffolding on a temple in Thailand*

Bamboo is the fastest growing, most versatile woody plant in the world, and is annually renewable if harvested in an intelligent way. This extraordinary plant is part of the everyday life and culture of most of Asia, yet strangely, the Western world remains relatively uninterested and uneducated about it. This is partly because there are no indigenous bamboo species in any part of Europe, or the Middle East, and whilst very superior clumping bamboos abound in South America, the USA has only one rather inferior southern runner (known as 'canebrake').

■ **1.C** Dendrocalamus giganteus *clump in Bogor Botanical Gardens, Indonesia*

migrated to Australia, they brought their favourite garden plants with them. Almost all the bamboos were northern Chinese genera such as the well-known, very invasive *Phyllostachys aurea* (golden bamboo). Those running bamboos have very rapidly become such a nuisance that some local government bodies, without a broader understanding of alternative genera, have banned all bamboos. Even now, 90 per cent of Australians reject the very idea of considering bamboo as a garden plant because so few know or can accept that there are dozens of very beautiful non-invasive clumping bamboos. The irony is that Australia is located in the South-East Asian region, has more than one million people (more than 5 per cent) of Asian origin, and claims to be part of this area that abounds in the wonderful clumping bamboos.

Few people are aware that Australia itself has at least three and possibly five indigenous species, all of the clumping type. According to Peter Bindon, an archeologist, Aboriginal people were making didgeridoos from *Bambusa arnhemica* long before they made them from hollowed out branches of gum trees (issues 5 and 6 of the magazine *Australian Bamboo Network*).

Unlike the very invasive, cold-climate, running varieties, these clumping bamboos will not attack your neighbour, are easy to maintain, and have dozens of practical uses. Many of the clumping varieties, particularly

some of the spectacular southern Chinese varieties, are also very cold climate tolerant.

In Asia, millions of dollars are spent on bamboo research each year. In Thailand alone there was a budget of US$40 million for research and plantation establishment (Thammincha, 1995) and even the Costa Rican government in Central America has invested heavily in bamboo timber plantations and a massive earthquake-proof house construction program (Janssen, 1995).

The Western world, however, is not yet taking this useful plant seriously. Most Asian countries treat this fastest growing, annually renewable resource with great reverence. Bamboo feeds them, houses them, graces and shades their environment. It is used to make their musical instruments, cooking and eating utensils, furniture, hunting weapons, and ceremonial artifacts. It even provides the reinforcement for their concrete (the best clumpers are as strong as mild steel in tension). Bamboo provides their carrying and storage baskets, lamps and lampshades, ropes and strings, roof tiles, hats, and has hundreds of other practical and spiritual uses.

Using modern technology, Asia is now producing bamboo plywood superior in strength to that produced in the Western world, composite beams laminated from strips machined from high strength bamboos, elegant, precision-made floorboards of superior strength, and many other value-added products available now in Australia. A large part of both India's and China's paper is made from bamboo fibre, which, with the right technology, is capable of producing a higher strength and quality of paper than that from wood pulp (the finest and most highly valued art paper in China is made from very young, still leafless culms).

I have striven to distil simple practical advice on using bamboo for a wealth of applications. I have drawn on both traditional village technology and modern scientific research, accumulated over many years of travel, practice, research, growing, and association with village communities and scientists from several countries. Many of those I have learned from I now know as friends. I have also attempted to dispel many of the inadequate technological myths still being aired, mostly spawned by romantic, well-meaning Western world 'alternatives' trying to come to terms with a strange medium without experience, resources or knowledge.

This book is not intended to be a taxonomical reference book, but it will help people select and grow the non-invasive clumping bamboos most suited to their environment, be it cool or warm, wet or dry. I hope also it may help you recognise some of the lovely species that you will increasingly come across as the plants become more accepted and inevitably popular. The day of the palm tree is over!

■ **1.F** Bambusa arnhemica, *showing its iridescent green shoot, and the bright orange colour of the older sun-exposed culms*

1 The Advantages of Clumping over Running Bamboos

Few people in the USA or Australia seem to be aware of the existence of the clumping bamboos. In northern America, there is more excuse because of the cold climate extremes, but for most of Australia this doesn't apply. There are approximately 1500 species of bamboo in our world. Roughly half are running (monopodial) bamboos, but I suspect there are actually more clumping species than runners. New species are being found every year, so we're far from knowing the exact number of each. Clumping bamboos of the genera *Gigantochloa* and *Schizostachyum* are frequently being 'discovered', mostly in Indonesia, many of them useful bamboos with local names that the indigenous people have been using for centuries (so much for being 'discovered' or 'named'!).

■ SKETCH **1.2** *A typical clumping bamboo culm and shoot*

■ **1.H** Thyrsostachys siamensis *(monastery bamboo) clumps in a regularly spaced row in Thailand, showing their tight clumping habit*

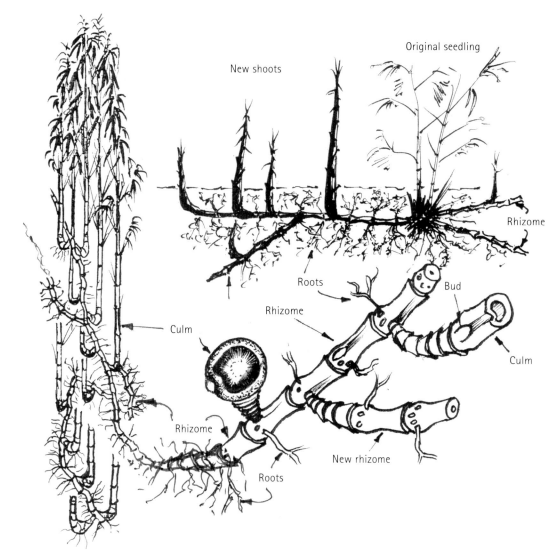

■ SKETCH **1.1** *Monopodial (running) rhizomes (shown with the culms and rhizomes cut off). Note that each single rhizome can develop many new culms when matured, is capable of travelling a considerable distance, and of producing many rhizomes.*

The Chinese are still discovering and taxonomically ordering new species, both clumping and running, on a regular basis.

Basically, sympodial (clumping) bamboos are shallow-rooted, rainforest-type plants. Whilst they will grow in total sunlight, most will also grow comfortably, some even better, in a total canopy environment. Their growth area is limited by the fact that each rhizome produced develops into a single culm or pole (Sketches 1.2 and 3.1) located very close to its mother culm, making the plant predictable and genetically non-invasive (see Chapter 3 for a more detailed plant description). The majority of clumping species tend to be more tropical or subtropical than the running bamboos, but many are still very cold-tolerant, some few originating in the high mountain country of northern China and surviving temperatures of -20°C (panda bear food).

Monopodial (running) bamboos are very different to clumping bamboos in many ways, in fact so much so that it would be better if they were treated as a different plant.

Runners are naturally dominant monoculture forest plants, certainly not suited to a rainforest canopy environment. They all originate from the very cold parts of the world, mainly northern China, Japan and Korea, with at least one from the USA. The rhizomes of monopodial bamboos (Sketch 1.1) are usually long, outgoing, adventurous, solid or semi-solid underground canes (up to 60 mm diameter on large species) that support a dense fine root system. These rhizomes, similar in appearance to a knobbly bamboo culm section, develop buds at almost every internode. Because each bud develops into either another rhizome or a culm (pole) it means that a single rhizome is capable of producing many culms plus many rhizomes over a period of some years.

New rhizomes on most runners such as moso—the famous edible shoot bamboo grown in cool parts of China and Japan—spend three years developing their bulk and producing more rhizomes before they are able to have significant shoots and culms. Three-year-old rhizomes then produce their first significant shoots, and do so for two or three years, then retire aged five to six to become starch and energy storage conduits for feeding the progression of younger rhizomes they have already produced. With an active rhizome life of only about five years, the plant must keep producing rhizomes reaching out into new territory in order to survive. Eventually, the oldest part of the growing area becomes choked with old 'storage' rhizomes no longer capable of producing culms, and that section of the forest loses vigour and deteriorates, producing fewer and only stunted rhizomes. The same applies to a runner in a concrete garden retainer or a pot—it will eventually fill the contained area with tangled rhizomes circling desperately around the periphery trying to break out.

The majority of monopodial bamboos grow quite happily in cold, temperate, subtropical, or sometimes even tropical areas, but most seem very vigorous in temperate/sub-tropical areas (ours went berserk, so we chose to dig them up to avoid the high maintenance costs fast approaching). I hear complaints from UK bamboo fans that they can't get runners to perform 'like they do in Sydney'. The vigour of their spread also depends on the soil and water conditions, which accounts for the odd runner that never gets to spread.

The problem is that many countries, Australia amongst them, have inherited these originally northern Asian, cold-climate, monopodial bamboo species from European settlers who didn't know of the existence of the clumping species. The spreading habit of running bamboo has caused a strong prejudice to develop against all bamboos. This prejudice is such that some local government authorities in Australia have banned, or are considering banning, the planting of all bamboo species (without even knowing of the existence of the sympodial species with their very different growth habit)!

Running (monopodial) species can be very beautiful plants if planted in a controlled environment, but in most cases a sympodial species can be substituted with none of the problems one must expect with runners. In most cases, the qualities of the plant chosen will be superior.

Comparison of Running and Clumping Bamboos

Clumping bamboos grow faster when young. Clumpers invest their energy into taller clumps and above-ground vegetation. They develop mature-sized culms in about half the time taken by runners (usually within four years as opposed to eight years for runners). Each short-necked, clumping rhizome produces a single shoot that develops into a culm in the same year or season that it grows from the bud.

■ **1.1** Nastus elatus—*an energetic 2½-year-old clump*

Running bamboos grow more slowly when young. About 75 per cent of a running bamboo's energy goes into creating their underground rhizome system to ensure the ultimate spread of the whole forest, rather than into the development of the individual plant. The visual display of mature, larger culms and vegetation happens when the rhizome is three years old (rather than the same year, as with a clumper). Above-ground growth, for runners, is a lower priority to the long-term conquest of taking over the area.

■ **1.J** *Phyllostachys nigra-boriana—an out-of-control forest of the invasive runner in NSW, now covering more than two hectares*

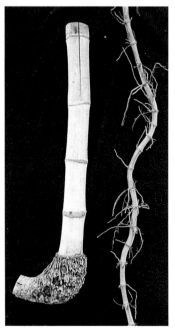

■ **1.K** *Rhizomes—sympodial (on the left) and monopodial (on the right)—note that each clumping rhizome is short and supports one culm only, whereas the many buds on the long running rhizome can produce many culms*

Running bamboos are invasive. Most people know of locations where monopodial bamboos have popped up from under the fence next door. A number of people in Sydney, NSW, have recently successfully sued their neighbour for damage or intrusion by unwanted bamboo. Near our Bamboo World botanical gardens in northern NSW (and near Bellingen), I have seen huge areas of out-of-control *Phyllostachys aurea* (golden bamboo) the most common culprit, covering tens of hectares of valuable land. I know of similar large areas of *P. nigra* (black bamboo), *P. nigra-boriana*, *Pleioblastus simonii* and other monopodial species out of control and still running. Our local Council (Kyogle, NSW) has a major problem from *P. simonii* rhizomes broken at flood-time from the creek bank and washed downstream, where it has re-infested the creek sides for considerable distances.

Running bamboos should be contained or controlled. Running bamboos should never be planted without having a soundly based management system in place prior to planting, and never where they can run amongst other plant species worth preserving. To contain a monopodial bamboo, there must be an adjacent, regularly used road, a river or creek that has water ponded or running for at least four months of each year, or an impervious barrier of concrete or rubber buried in the ground to a depth commensurate with that particular monopodial species. That depth can be anything from 1.2 m for moso, about 0.6 m for golden bamboo and somewhat less for some smaller species. Constant mowing, slashing, or cattle eating new shoots and tramping on rhizomes will help, but the area around can be so damaged by the bamboo's efforts to break out of its defined area that the soil, totally clogged with frustrated rhizomes multiplying underground, cannot reasonably support other growth. Burying galvanised iron is not completely effective because the rhizomes find the joins and wriggle through, and the iron eventually rusts, allowing the plant to escape.

Running bamboo cannot survive in an undamaged rainforest canopy. Fortunately, runners are not suited to the environment beneath a rainforest canopy (thank goodness for small mercies). They do their best to destroy other plants (and usually ultimately succeed) but like lantana and many other weeds, they don't grow in total shade.

Runners are dominant, monoculture forest-forming plants. Running bamboo will invade sclerophyll eucalypt forest. Their shallow roots show little respect for the already established deep-rooted trees. I have seen areas of sparse eucalypt forest slowly strangled out by *Phyllostachys aurea* and other species. For this reason, runners are very unsuitable as permaculture plants.

Running bamboos are hard to eradicate. Once established, runners are very expensive and difficult to eradicate, requiring either hand digging or bulldozing of all rhizomes (runners propagate only from rhizome sections, not from roots, branches or culm sections). An alternative is to cut off all culms late in winter and spray Roundup on the leaf matter that later appears for some consecutive years until it finally stops popping up. I'm told that filling cut ends with 50 per cent Roundup helps, but I haven't tried it, and I prefer to minimise chemical usage. (We have small *Pleioblastus simonii* shoots still appearing occasionally from our relatively successful attempt at eradicating the species fourteen years ago, but we are still spraying.)

Clumping bamboos are non-invasive. The ultimate maximum size and shape of any sympodial species can be predicted, and they cannot self-propagate beyond where they are planted except in the very rare situation where they flower and produce fertile seed. (See Chapter 4.)

Clumpers grow beautifully with eucalypts or in rainforests or in a permaculture environment. Clumping bamboos tend to grow taller and straighter in such environments, subject to there being enough water.

Most clumping bamboos require minimal clump maintenance. Many of the smaller or medium decorative clumpers require no maintenance other than what is given to other plants in that environment. Simple clump management techniques applied to some of the larger or more vigorous clumping bamboos will benefit both the owner and the plant, but they *will* remain where they were planted, and cannot self-propagate from roots or rhizomes (see Chapters 5 and 9).

Running bamboos are structurally inferior. The anatomical structure of running bamboos is of a vascular bundle and cell arrangement containing fewer fibre bundles, with shorter fibres, generally of an inferior type to those of the superior clumping (sympodial) bamboos commonly used for structures (W. Liese, 1995). This also results in most monopodial culms generally being thinner-walled than most species of sympodial bamboo. (For further details and exceptions, see Chapter 3.)

The giant clumping species grow larger than running species. There are plenty of clumping bamboos that produce straight small diameter culms (e.g. *Thyrsostachys siamensis, Bambusa tuldoides, B. nana, B. malingensis, Gigantochloa albociliata,* etc.) comparable in size but superior in strength to the running bamboos. The largest of the monopodial bamboos considered to be of an acceptable structural quality (*Phyllostachys bambusoides,* known as 'madake') grows rarely, in Japan, to a maximum diameter of 120 mm and 22 m high (and never that big according to the Chinese). The largest of all the runners is moso (*Phyllostachys hetracycla pubescens*), normally up to 120 mm diameter (but occasionally 160 mm) and 26 m high, but moso's attractive straight wood is considered to be structurally inferior, even amongst runners, because of its short fibre length. Many of the clumping bamboos are capable, in ideal conditions, of producing massively strong 300 mm diameter culms over 30 m tall, and demonstrably superior.

Assessing the age of running bamboo culms is difficult. There is no dependable logical pattern to the position of monopodial culms with respect to their age, because new rhizomes often double back into already established areas. Identifying culm age is necessary when harvesting both clumping and running species in order to ensure that you are not harvesting sapwood (see Chapters 9 and 11). On the other hand, clumping culms can be aged more easily. It is possible, even though sometimes difficult, to track back from the branchless young culm to the mother culm, grandmother culm and so on, via each short-necked rhizome. Often the signs of age are more evident on clumping culms, making it easier to select mature wood.

■ **1.L** Dendrocalamus brandisii—*a young clump growing in a very vertical form in a rainforest environment*

■ **1.M** Bambusa textilis *'Glabra', mature and untouched, showing its tight vertical clumping habit and naturally exposed lower leafless culms*

Harvesting shoots from running bamboos is more labour-intensive. The best edible running bamboo shoots are normally dug from underground rather than cut off close to ground level as for most clumping shoots. (See Chapter 10.)

Many running bamboos are more cold-tolerant. While this observation appears to argue in favour of the running bamboos, there are a reasonable number of beautiful cold-tolerant clumping bamboos (see Chapter 5 for expanded comment on this important item).

When we originally started planting bamboos at Bamboo World (1984–85), I planted about 20 runners. Within two to three years I dug most of them out. They had been totally out-performed by the clumpers, growing side by side in the same environment and time period. Within two years of planting we had beautiful clumpers like *Dendrocalamus asper*, *D. latiflorus*, *Nastus elatus*, *Bambusa tuldoides*, *B. textilis* and many others more than 6 m high growing as distinctive, luxurious plants. During this time, the runners were still busy reaching out their underground rhizomes, producing a fairly rapidly spreading proliferation of small diameter culms, the maximum being less than 2.5 m high at the original planting location. A major maintenance problem was developing.

I have to agree that a (properly contained) forest of running bamboo can be a very beautiful place. Walking through a moso forest is quite inspiring, but the same can be said when walking through the beautiful clumping bamboo forests of Java, Thailand or China. One can achieve the same awe-inspiring effect by planting a plantation of beautiful clumping bamboos, of either the same or mixed species. As an extra benefit, you will not have the hassle of containing your forest within reasonable boundaries.

I have retained about three beautiful running species. They are on parole and under observation, so to speak, but the question I ask myself and others is:

Why bother to plant an inferior species that takes longer to develop and will give you nothing but trouble to maintain when it is possible to plant a beautiful superior non-invasive alternative? The clumping bamboos are preferable to the running bamboos on every possible comparison except where winter temperatures are extreme.

■ **1.E** Dendroclamus giganteus *culm that emerged as a shoot only four months earlier*

■ **1.N** Phyllostachys heterocycla pubescens, *the beautiful runner (known as 'moso' in Japan) growing as a plantation in a Chinese forest*

2 General Comment and Taxonomy

■ **2.A** Bambusa multiplex *cv. 'Fernleaf', a small garden species with mostly solid culms*

The first serious attempt to tackle the identification of bamboos was compiled well before the word 'taxonomist' existed. A 'Bamboo Chart' classifying some of China's 500 species, from 39 genera, was compiled by Dai Kaizhi during the Jin Dynasty (AD 317–420). It described 61 bamboo species (G. Bojie and W. Zhengping, 1993).

Bamboo was originally classified as a woody member of the grass family, Gramineae (Aschersen et Graebner, 1902). It is a monocot rather than a dicot, which means that it has no cambium layer or bark. Some taxonomists and botanical scientists have expressed unease at this original classification, considering that it is sufficiently different from grass that it should be classified as a family of its own, Bambusaceae (Link, 1815)—but the original classification remains at present. Bamboos form the tribe Bambuseae of the sub-family Bambusoideae. They have distinguishing features in common that set them apart from grass, such as comprehensive branch systems

and petiolate (stalk form) leaves, and, mostly but not always, hollow culm structures divided into progressive compartments by internode diaphragms. Whoever heard of a 300 mm diameter grass stalk 36 m high?

Interestingly, not all bamboos are hollow, in fact some of the strongest, medium-sized clumping bamboos have either completely solid culms, or almost so for about half their height (e.g. *Bambusa nana*, *B. tulda*, *B. polymorpha* and *Dendrocalamus strictus*). There are also a number of solid small species (e.g. *Bambusa multiplex* cv. 'Fernleaf' and cv. 'Golden Goddess', etc.) that are a useful substitute for rattan cane when making solid baskets. People often confuse bamboo (particularly bamboo with no hole) with cane or rattan, which is actually a solid but more flexible member of the palm tree family (Palmae). Like bamboo, rattan is also used to make furniture, and is often used split into strips to bind the joints of bamboo furniture.

■ **2.B** Bambusa lako *(Widjaja), recently taxonomically reclassified; sold in Australia until 1998 as* Gigantochloa *sp.* *'Timor Black', and before that, mistaken for* Gigantochloa atroviolacea

There are about 1500 existing species of bamboo divided into about 80 different genera. No book has ever fully covered the subject of bamboo and probably never will, particularly with new species being discovered or identified every year. This identification (taxonomical) problem is also confused by a number of issues:

a) Over the years, few taxonomists have been able to devote enough time to the species.

b) Earlier this century, there was a lack of university educated Asian taxonomists, let alone Europeans prepared to spend long periods in tropical Asia.

There was also a tendency for Europeans to be more interested in cold-tolerant monopodial bamboos (runners) that survive more comfortably in the European climate, resulting in taxonomical effort being biased towards monopodial bamboos. This combination has resulted in a considerable lack of knowledge and understanding about the very existence of the beautiful sympodial bamboos of southern China, India, South-East Asia, the Pacific Islands and South America. There were, however, occasional superb efforts from a few early scientists who did devote as much of their time as possible, people like Munro (1868), Kurz (1876), Gamble (1896),

Camus (1923), Holttum (1958) and McClure (1966). These days, whilst still not enough is being done, there has been increased effort by a dedicated few, with significant taxonomical contributions from W. Lin, E. Widjaja (Indonesia), S. Dransfield (an Indonesian working at Kew Gardens, UK), C. Stapleton (Kew Gardens, UK), D. Tewari (India) and magnificent anatomical work by W. Liese (Hamburg, Germany). There has been engineering work by J. Janssen (Holland) and S.Surjokusumo (Bogor, Indonesia), and architectural work by O. Hidalgo Lopez, S. Velez (Columbia) and others, but a huge task remains unresolved as a challenge to those with the skill and energy.

c) The Latin-based botanical naming system, originally developed by the Swedish botanist Linnaeus, relies heavily on the description of the flower and its associated support (panicle) to classify plants into genus and species. Unfortunately, most bamboos rarely flower, some only every 100 years or so (see Chapter 4), which gives the eager taxonomist the daunting problem of staying alive long enough to see it in flower, often in its indigenous, probably remote country! Bamboos are quite often re-classified or renamed by taxonomists when a rare flowering takes place, or after a more accurate scientific effort has been made to re-look at obscure, older identifications. This is why some bamboos have different scientific names in different countries, and sometimes have one or more synonym, a confusing situation that cannot be easily solved. Two recent examples still being confused in nurseries are *Bambusa glaucescens* (Willd.) Sieb. now called *Bambusa multiplex* (Lour.) Raeusch., and *Bambusa arundinacea* (Retz.) Willd. now called *Bambusa bambos* (L.) Voss. If you consider that there have been 130 different genera named, but now only about 80 accepted and in common usage, it will give you some clue to the magnitude of the taxonomical problems that have, and still do, exist.

From about 1930 onwards, the Chinese began making serious contributions to bamboo taxonomy using Linnaeus's Latin-based identification system, and particularly since the mid-1970s, have made major taxonomical advances. This is appropriate, because China has more species than any other country. It seems reasonable to concede them the right to straighten out the misnaming of the past (within the discipline of taxonomical practice), and to name their own new cultivars, variations or species. Examples are abundant in the recently published

A Compendium of Chinese Bamboo, which moves the well-known *Bambusa oldhamii* and *B. beecheyana* into the genus *Dendrocalamopsis* (*oldhamii* and *beecheyana*), which is different again from the common genus of *Dendrocalamus*. It will be happening still 50 years from now because there is so much work left to be done.

Whilst taxonomists have been busy classifying (naming) bamboos for the last 150 years or so, those same bamboos were known for thousands of years by the local people, who still have their own names and uses for them. When botanically classified and named, those bamboos are merely being 'discovered' by the scientific world (e.g. *Gigantochloa manggong* named in 1995 by Widjaja). Synonyms cause problems for visiting enthusiasts trying to identify bamboos by 'local' vernacular names because the same species often grows in different areas or countries under a different local name. Asia has many local words for 'bamboo' (as the prefix to the species' local name), some being 'pring', 'bambu', 'jajang', 'awi', 'buloh', 'buluh', 'phai', 'tiying', and so on. Some are used as a general term for 'bamboo', and some signify that it belongs to a special group with similar characteristics (like a genus).

All this is now being further complicated by scientists creating new crossed species by artificial insemination, conceiving new and hopefully super bamboos by introducing pollen from one superior species into flowers of another. The work of Professor Zhang Guangchu in creating such superior bamboos for timber and superior edible shoots is a very significant step forward that will affect both productivity and quality in the near future (Zhang Guangchu, 1997).

Bamboo occurs naturally in most countries within the broad belt between the Tropics of Cancer and Capricorn, including Madagascar, Africa, South America, Pacific Islands and Australia. Some cold-climate species, mostly running bamboos and a few cold-hardy clumpers (e.g. *Fargesia* genus in China), grow north of the Tropic of Cancer into China, Korea, Japan, India and USA, and also south of the Tropic of Capricorn in South America (e.g. *Chusquea* genus). Bamboo is not indigenous to Europe or the Middle East, where it has now become a popular garden plant. Various species grow between sea level and 4000 m elevation (even some clumpers in the Himalayas), with the majority of the sympodial bamboos growing below 1500 m elevation (*Dendrocalamus asper* grows to 1500 m).

My curiosity has become as vigorous as the plant. Bamboo covers such a vast and interesting field that it will maintain me in constant discovery for my lifetime!

■ **2.c** Dendrocalamus asper, *the main edible shoot species for Thailand (pai tong), and the major large structural bamboo for Indonesia (bambu betung)*

3 Plant Description

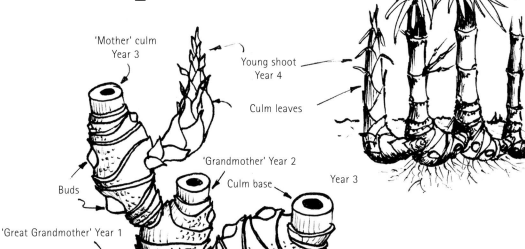

Foliage or vegetative leaves

'Mother' culm Year 3

Young shoot Year 4

Culm leaves

'Grandmother' Year 2

Culm base

Year 3

Buds

'Great Grandmother' Year 1

Rhizome

Year 4

Roots

Rhizome neck

■ SKETCH **3.1** *Sympodial (clumping) rhizomes (shown with the culm cut off). Note that each new rhizome develops only one culm, and can travel only the length of the short rhizome neck. Whilst rhizomes have multible buds to produce future rhizomes, they also can reach out only a very short distance, which causes the plant to 'clump' or remain in a tight predictable circle.*

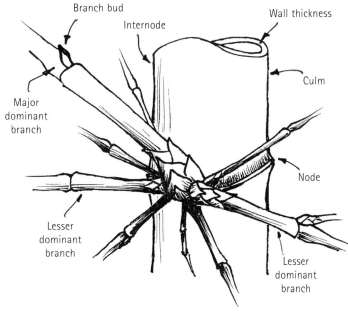

Branch bud

Internode

Wall thickness

Culm

Major dominant branch

Node

Lesser dominant branch

Lesser dominant branch

■ SKETCH **3.2** *A typical* Bambusa *genus three-branch dominant node structure*

My object is to impart knowledge and a passion for the little-known sympodial (clumping) bamboos. Whilst some of the 'do-it-yourself' technology in this book can be applied to both clumping and running species, monopodial bamboos are not described in great detail in this chapter. The most fundamental difference between runners and clumpers is their totally different growth habit resulting from very different rhizome systems, described in Chapter 1 and Sketches 1.1, 1.2 and 3.1.

I have chosen to use 'sympodial' for the clumping bamboo rhizome form rather than 'parchymorph' or 'unicaespitose', because of its more common usage. Similarly I have used 'monopodial' for running bamboo rhizomes instead of 'leptomorph' or 'diffuse'. For the rarer long-necked rhizome encountered on *Guadua* and some other clumpers, I have used 'modified caespitose', an important fact to identify because those rarer clumpers need more room for their well-spaced culms.

Where possible, I have avoided using botanical words not likely to be part of most people's vocabulary. I have explained a word if it is useful or necessary.

Each pole generated by a bamboo clump is called a **culm** (Sketch 3.1). It is generally (but not always) a hollow, woody, round section divided into compartments by diaphragms called **nodes** (Sketch 3.2). The lengths between nodes, called **internodes** (Sketch 3.2), vary in length according to the species and diameter of the culm. Most large structural bamboos have internodes varying between about 200 and 600 mm long, but some smaller species with culms up to 30 mm diameter develop internodes up to a metre long. Two fascinating examples are *Schizostachyum jaculans*, commonly used to make hunting blowpipes in Malaysia, and a similar bamboo called *S*. sp. 'Murray Island' found on Australia's northern islands and some South Pacific islands, as yet not taxonomically named.

The wall thickness of culms varies with different genera and species, but within any species also decreases in thickness from the base to the top. *Bambusa*, *Dendrocalamus*, *Gigantochloa* and *Guadua* genera are mostly heavy-walled and often very good for structural use. *Schizostachyum* culms are mostly thin-walled and are often split for making screens (Sketch 16.2) and baskets. The thick or thin wall is a function of their cellular structure (explained later in this chapter). The structural inferiority of runners is because of their generally thin walls and shorter fibre particles.

Some bamboo species have such heavy wall thicknesses that the hole disappears or almost disappears, and the culm becomes virtually solid for all or part of the culm length (e.g. *Bambusa tulda*, *B. polymorpha* and *Dendrocalamus strictus*). Such bamboos, when green, can be bent by heating and steaming, then holding in place until cool. Their solid structure prevents collapse during the bending process.

Each new culm on a sympodial bamboo develops from a single **shoot** which projects vertically upward from a single **rhizome** which has developed from a bud on the 'mother' rhizome and culm (Sketch 3.1). The new rhizome and its projecting shoot depend entirely on the mother culm, grandmother culm, and the clump's mature rhizome system to supply virtually its total needs throughout its development to almost full height. The rhizome, like the trunk of a tree, forms the only joining link bretween the different parts of the plant (culm, branches, leaves) and is the supporting foundation, the link between roots and culms. New culms usually reach 90 per cent of full height within two months of emerging from the ground as a shoot, with larger species taking about three months. Some reach a growth rate of up to a metre a day during the mid-height maximum acceleration period, so you can almost watch them shooting into the air! The last 10 per cent of culm growth takes about twelve months longer.

■ **3.A** Dendrocalamus giganteus *is a much valued large diameter powerful structural bamboo.*

The culms are without **vegetative leaves** or foliage (Sketches 3.1 and 3.3) or **branches** (Sketch 3.2) until after they reach this 90 per cent full height stage. Branch structures and leaves then develop from the top down, often quite slowly. New culms on some species take up to two years or longer to develop their *full* consignment of branches and leaf. The newly developed culm then joins the other mature culms within the community of culms we know as a **clump**, building up starch and sap to feed the new crop of rhizomes and culms due to appear during the summer season. In contrast, monopodial running bamboos have their shooting period in the springtime and can produce many shoots in a single year from each long rhizome. A mature sympodial rhizome generally has only one new rhizome and attached shoot per year, but can have two or more. This accounts for the multiplication of culms in a young clump, and the multiplicity of shoots produced by a clump being managed specifically for shoot production (see Chapter 21).

The fragile **shoot** (Sketches 3.1 and 10.1) when it first emerges from the ground, is actually a stack of integrated nodes, which rapidly develop internodes separating each node from the other, telescoping the culm as it shoots upwards. The telescoping internode extensions begin with the lower node separations, the last telescoping action taking place in the top part of the culm.

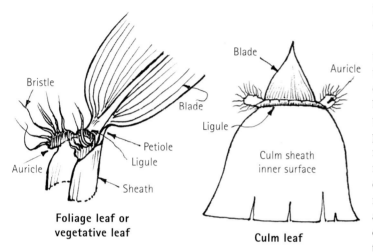

Foliage leaf or vegetative leaf

Culm leaf

■ SKETCH **3.3** *Typical culm leaf and foliage leaf structure*

(PHOTO: PROF. WALTER LIESE)

■ **3.B** Dendrocalamus asper—*a young culm shedding its no longer required culm leaf*

Growth rates are often spectacular in a single year. Given close to ideal conditions, they always follow the same pattern of development. Each yearly generation of culms is larger than the last year's culms. The diameter is usually twice, and sometimes more than, that of the previous year, until the plant reaches its full culm diameter potential for the conditions and site. This is usually within four to five years. Tall bamboos are also capable of more than doubling their height each year for the first two years, as one would expect with such large culm diameter increases.

The **rhizome** (Sketches 3.1, 10.1 and Photo 1K) is the bulbous, woody section joined by a tapering neck to its mother rhizome where its bud has swelled and developed. Each rhizome carries a number of dormant buds which can be activated in later seasons, or sometimes in the same season. The culm, growing as the projection of the shoot that develops out of the top of the rhizome, emerges from the ground already virtually the maximum diameter that it will achieve, and sometimes even larger (e.g. *Dendrocalamus asper*). Both the final maximum wall thickness and the final maximum diameter are achieved during those first couple of months as the developing culm catapults into the air. The culm wall thickness usually reduces with height, but some species do produce culms that are slightly smaller in diameter and with shorter internodes near the base of the culm, and then actually increase in diameter and lengthen their internodes as they climb higher. All culms eventually taper to a small, thinner walled diameter with a reducing leafy apex, some erect, some pendulous.

Young culms are virtually 98 per cent water and initially have no fibre or strength to resist snapping. During this frail period, they are tightly bound in a strong wrapping of **culm leaves** (Sketch 3.1) which remain alive and viable only until the culm develops sufficient fibre to become self-supporting, the fibre developing from the bottom upwards. These culm leaves progressively die, also from the bottom upwards, and mostly drop off the culm once they have served their purpose. On some few species, such as *Thyrsostachys siamensis* and *Gigantochloa apus*, the culm leaves die but remain attached to the culm, becoming one of the distinctively decorative features of those species. (Very handy for identification!)

Culm leaves vary in shape and size according to their location on the length of the culm, but also vary distinctively according to species. For this reason many taxonomists use the culm leaf as one of the major identification tools for different species. A typical culm leaf is shown in Sketch 3.3, but as this is not intended to be a taxonomical book, there is no description of the varying culm leaf shapes of individual species. I recommend *Bamboos* edited by well known taxonomists E. Widjaja (Herbarium Bogoriense, Indonesia) and S. Dransfield (Kew Gardens, UK) and published by PROSEA (Plant Resources of South-East Asia) to anyone wanting to study the detailed taxonomy of these bamboos.

The anatomical structure of sympodial bamboos, as mentioned earlier, is superior in strength to the monopodial bamboos. W. Liese (1995) describes four different types of **vascular bundle**, Type 1 and Type 4 being divided into two subtypes. In terms of increasing strength, one could grade them from Type 1 to Type 4. The monopodial bamboos fall into Type 1 and Type 2. *Melocanna baccifera*, a sympodial bamboo with extremely long rhizome necks (sometimes described as modified unicaespitose), together with the sympodial *Schizostachyum* genus, fall into Type 2 and Type 3. This accounts for the fact that some of the *Schizostachyum* clumping bamboos have very thin (but quite strong) culm walls, often used for splitting and basket making. Type 3 and/or Type 4 anatomical structures are inevitably present in powerful sympodial structural genera such as *Gigantochloa* (Type 3 only), and *Bambusa*, *Dendrocalamus* and *Guadua* (Types 3 and 4). The Types 3 and 4 cellular structures have isolated **fibre bundles** with longer fibres (2.3 to 4 mm long) located like satellites positioned outside and in addition to the fibre bundles normally attached to the vascular bundles. This makes them much stronger than Type 1 with vascular bundles which also have shorter fibres (1.3 to 2.5 mm long). The stronger isolated fibre bundles often form a polylamellate structure with alternating directional layers of micro fibrils building massively strong fibre structures (a little like tubular plywood). This, together with the extremely long fibre length of bamboo compared to even the best of hardwoods, results in tensile strengths far in excess of timber, and approaching that of mild steel.

The fibre bundles within the structure, like the culm diameter itself, have already established their maximum outer diameter shortly after the bamboo culm climbs into the air. The difference is that the wall thickness of the culm remains the same during its life, but the wall thickness of the fibre tubes within increases as they age, reducing the fibre hole as the culm grows older and stronger. It takes three to four years to reach a reasonable mature strength, which is one reason why bamboo culms should not be harvested until they have been standing for at least that long.

Earlier research (Liese, 1995) and published data (Cusack, 1997) indicated that bamboo reached its maximum strength at about three to four years, which is the age when Indonesians harvest their culms for structures and furniture. More recent research (Liese, 1997), on culms grown on to confirm their exact age, indicates that culms continue to develop (more slowly) in strength, unless damaged, for some years, even up to seven years. Much of the strength increase after four years is due to the **parenchyma** (the fill-in tissue between fibres) becoming tougher and drier with age, which makes it harder to split older culms. Older bamboo, perhaps from ten years onwards, slowly deteriorates in strength in spite of the fibre wall thickness continuing to increase, because of the general aging process and deterioration of the culm's ability to feed every part of its structure. Each time a culm

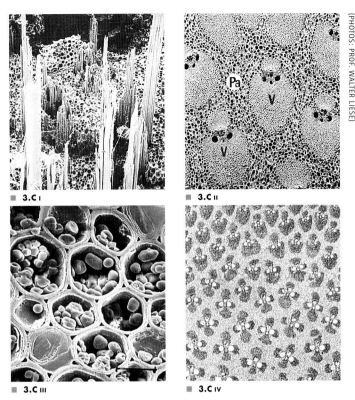

(PHOTOS: PROF. WALTER LIESE)

■ **3.C I** *A tensile fracture of a Dendrocalamus latiflorus internode, showing the torn apart fibre bundles standing free of the matrix of parenchyma*

■ **3.C II** *Vascular bundles (marked 'V') supported in their matrix of parenchyma (marked 'Pa'). The major portion of the vascular bundles is made up from a multiplicity of tubular fibre bundles formed by overlapping javelin-shaped individual fibres, varying from approximately 1.3 mm to 2.5 mm long for Type 1, to between 2.3 mm and 4.0 mm long for Types 3 and 4 vascular bundles.*

■ **3.C III** *Parenchyma cells showing stored starch in the form of tiny round deposits, waiting ready to feed the system during the next shoot season*

■ **3.C IV** *Vascular bundles showing increase in bundles and fibre density as they approach the culm surface, and a decrease in their ability to carry moisture*

is damaged slightly (for example, being rubbed against another culm by wind) it produces a gelatinous matter that blocks off the moisture conducting cells as a natural protective device against loss of moisture and evaporation. A series of such events over years closes down on a culm's ability to feed itself adequately, until it eventually dies of clogged arteries and general deterioration (just like the rest of us!) when it is about twelve to fifteen years old (sometimes a little older).

With smaller species bamboos, this culm death is not noticeable, probably because the dead culms disappear due to fungus attack fairly quickly. With some larger species, particularly vigorous bamboos like *Bambusa balcooa*, ancient untended clumps can become very messy and clogged with dead timber unless the maturing live timber is harvested regularly, and the young shoots likely to cause congestion are removed (cook and eat them!)

■ **3.E** Bambusa chungii, *a beautiful garden species that retains its spectacular white culm bloom*

before they grow into culms. This becomes apparent when you look at any of the old *B. balcooa* clumps well established on the east coast of Australia. The clump literally dies in the middle, the outer ring becoming a tangle of both dead and live culms. The new culms must bend and twist their way upwards to get around the low branches and various impediments. It's a great pity because *B. balcooa* will normally produce beautiful, straight, strong culms suitable for structural work if the clump is managed and properly harvested, and that species is so far the only large structural species reasonably abundant in Australia.

The maximum size a clumping species will grow is predictable. The culms of these sympodial bamboos remain within a defined, predictable growth pattern (see Sketch 3.1). All their rhizomes remain located within the tight circle formed by the new outer culms projecting out of those rhizomes at ground level. Each mature rhizome, however, feeds itself by sending out long, fine roots that reach out in a large circle to feed the clump. Whilst the root circle is often up to three or four times the diameter of the clump itself, these fine roots are definitely not capable of propagating new plants. The roots are known to have the beneficial effect of loosening and aerating heavy or compacted soil (Janssen, 1997), and they do effectively bind the soil together, which is why sympodial bamboos are so effective for soil erosion or river bank erosion.

Because of the clumping bamboos' tightly contained rhizome structure, it is extremely difficult for a rhizome

section to be broken out and relocated by nature to form a new clump. Even then the clump would be non-invasive. When monopodial (running) bamboos are used to hold river banks together, all the rhizomes reaching invasively out and along the bank of a river are capable of reproducing the monopodial plant. This would happen if a small piece of rhizome were broken off in a flood and washed ashore further downstream.

In Indonesia, amongst the volcanic mountain country, the first job after bulldozing a new road in a steep hillside is to plant clumping bamboos as the road is formed. The steep sides are bound together in the form of a matted buttress, and the bamboo becomes available for harvesting by the local people.

As culms mature, their moisture content drops from nearly 98 per cent when first being formed to about 50 to 60 per cent (150 per cent relative moisture content) when about 12 months old, evenly distributed throughout the sappy, relatively weak wood. The percentage moisture of live culms also varies with the time of the year, dropping after the mature culms have supplied much of their starch and sap to the quickly growing shoot. Moisture content is also higher at the bottom, thicker walled end of a culm, becoming less as it climbs higher. This is logical, as the lower part of the culm has a greater percentage of water-carrying vessels (and a smaller percentage of fibre) in order to deliver the moisture to the top part of the culm and the foliage.

As an example, a healthy three-year-old *Dendrocalamus asper* culm, measured in the wet season, can have 50 per cent moisture at the base and 40 per cent in the upper culm. The upper culm can reduce to as low as 20 per cent in the dry or dormant season. If harvested mature and properly dried, the moisture content drops to about 12 per cent, which is much the same as seasoned hardwood.

Interestingly, the relative percentage of fibre compared to water-carrying cells, that is, less lower down and more higher up, means that the strength per unit area of a bamboo culm increases as the wall thickness gets thinner higher up. This partly compensates for the strength reduction due to decrease in diameter and wall thickness.

There is also a denser concentration of fibre bundles around the outer periphery of the culm wall mass than within the inner wall mass because the moisture-carrying system is more concentrated in the inner culm wall thickness. This resultant concentration of fibre bundles towards the outside of the culm's wood also results in a stronger structural section, because the culm (as a beam) is more effective with its strength fibres located as far away from its central axis as possible (maximising its radius of gyration). Nature is a masterful designer!

When the spring and early summer rains come, bamboo culms again rapidly build up their moisture content ready to feed the new shoots that come in late summer. And so the cycle continues, constantly renewing, and sustainable on an annual basis.

Commonly Available Genera of Bamboo

The most important sympodial genera are listed below, with accompanying broad descriptive notes—necessarily broad since a description to fit all the species within each genus is not possible.

Bambusa

This is the most common genus, with dozens of very variable species ranging from very small (*B. multiplex* var. *riviereorum*—1.5 m high with 10 mm diameter culm) to quite large (*B. bambos*—25 m high with 200 mm diameter culms). It contains many of the most beautiful bamboos in the world: *B. textilis*, the graceful very erect Chinese weaver's bamboo; *B. tuldoides*, the most used bamboo for scaffolding in Hong Kong and Guangzhou; the fabulous straight timber bamboos *B. nana* and *B. nutans*; the beautiful white-culmed *B. chungii*; and the wonderful cold-tolerant Chinese hedge bamboo family, *B. multiplex*.

Many species belonging to this genus are extensively utilised for structures and a multitude of other uses. Most are both beautiful and edible, some very high quality eating (e.g. there are five million *B. oldhamii* growing in plantations in the Fujian province of China where it is too cold to grow *D. latiflorus*) and others quite bitter (e.g. *B. tulda* and *B. vulgaris*). Many *Bambusa* species originated in southern China, and tend to be more cold-tolerant clumpers than some of the other genera, some growing where temperatures reach -15°C.

They always have three dominant branches projecting from a developed culm node (Sketch 3.2), the mid-branch of the three being considerably larger than the other two. They in turn are larger than any other minor branches projecting from that node.

Both foliage and culm leaves vary greatly from species to species, some with very fine leaves and others with medium leaves. None of the *Bambusa* genus have the huge leaves of some other genera described below.

Dendrocalamus

This is a tropical genus with about 40 species (I read and believed that there were less than 20 species until I spent time investigating the amazing *Dendrocalamus* species in China). They are mostly huge strong bamboos, with some medium-sized representatives. Amongst this genus are the largest bamboos known to man, *D. giganteus*, *D. brandisii*, the beautifully grotesque *D. sinicus*, and the magnificent giant *D. asper*, which is the most used large bamboo for structures in Indonesia, and for huge edible plantation shoots in Thailand (up to 10 kg each). Only slightly smaller but just as productive of shoots and

■ **3.F** Dendrocalamus sinicus, *grotesquely beautiful and one of the largest bamboos in the world*

timber is the huge-leafed *D. latiflorus*, grown in southern China and Taiwan for its edible shoots averaging 4 kg each. The smaller drought-hardy species, *D. strictus*, is the main bamboo harvested for paper production in India. Most members of this genus produce high quality, edible shoots, some highly valued like the huge-leafed *D. hamiltonii*, but *D. asper* and *D. latiflorus* are the proven clumping species grown in the huge plantations of China, Thailand and Taiwan.

Like the *Bambusa* genus, *Dendrocalamus* also has the dominant three-branch pattern at developed nodes, but the dominant mid-branch is often more swollen where it leaves the culm. The swollen branch base forms a shape almost like a sympodial rhizome with its small neck attached to the node, and complete with buds under the heavy culm-leaf-like covering. The larger species have very powerful foliage leaf sheaths wrapped around the outer ends of the branches supporting the alternatively arranged petiole and its vegetative leaf blade (Sketch 3.3). They are usually, but not always, very large-leafed fairly erect bamboos, two exceptions being the fine-leafed pendulous *D. strictus* (which has bitter shoots) and the beautiful elegant fine-leafed *D. membranaceus*. None are happy growing in areas where temperatures fall below about -4°C.

Dendrocalamopsis

The Chinese have recently reclassified a number of bamboos into this classification, some known before as *Bambusa* and some as *Dendrocalamus*. Amongst them are well-known bamboos such as (*Bambusa*) *oldhamii* and (*Dendrocalamus*) *beecheyana*.

The characteristics of these bamboos are (still) similar to the *Dendrocalamus* genus.

■ **3.6** Gigantochloa pseudoarundinacea, *a large beautifully striped, straight species valued for its timber and edible shoots*

Gigantochloa

This is another tropical species of great beauty and diversity of use. There are approximately 30 taxonomically described *Gigantochloa* species, but there are obviously a large number of interesting undescribed cultivars existing in Indonesia. Some of these may ultimately be defined as new species rather than a cultivar or variation of an existing species. We have most of the identified species and some of the interesting variations growing in our Botanical Display Garden at Bamboo World.

These very strong durable *Gigantochloa* are mostly a mixture of medium to big, large-leafed species, 70 to 150 mm diameter, but they are not as huge as most *Dendrocalamus* species. *Gigantochloa pseudoarundinacea* (syn. *G. maxima*) reaches 30 m height with relatively slender culms, and *G. levis* has stout 180 mm culms but is not a tall species.

The branch and leaf structure is very similar to *Dendrocalamus*, and identification is more to do with individual species' characteristics than any obvious describable factors, although *Gigantochloa*'s vegetative leaves often feel rougher and drier than *Dendrocalamus* or *Bambusa*. They are almost all very superior structural bamboos with straight durable wood, said to be fairly resistant to powder beetle if harvested properly. Many produce fine eating shoots, particularly *G. atter*, *G. albociliata*, *G. levis*, *G. robusta* and *G. pseudoarundinacea* (syn. *G. maxima*), and are vigorous growers in a reasonable environment, most tolerating an occasional light frost.

Gigantochloa apus is easily identified by its retained black-haired culm leaves on slightly rough, dark grey-green culms and large leaves. It is the bamboo most used in Indonesia for basket splits, rope and string making, roof ties for the blady grass roofing, and for roof rafters, because of its extremely long overlapping fibre structure, and its capacity to produce long straight culms with little change in diameter over a considerable length. Others such as *G. atter* and *G. pseudoarundinacea* are probably the most sought after medium-sized structural bamboos in Indonesia. *Gigantochloa albociliata*, a beautiful

■ **3.H** Guadua angustifolia, *a large superior structural bamboo from South America. Note the distance between culms, caused by the long-necked (modified unicaespitose) rhizomes.*

■ **3.I** Schizostachyum brachycladum, *the beautiful erect golden bamboo considered sacred in Bali*

smaller species with pendulous tips, produces very solid culms much valued for structures or for bending under heat for furniture making.

The *Gigantochloa* species are the most important and widely planted bamboos in Indonesia, with different areas valuing different species or even variations on those species. They are valued there as being the strongest of the medium-sized structural bamboos (as *D. asper* is valued as a larger structural species).

Guadua

This genus is indigenous from Mexico down to the South American continent. Distinctively different in appearance to the earlier genera described, it contains some 30 varied species, the large *Guadua angustifolia* being one of the great structural bamboos of this world. It is a spectacular, erect species growing 25 m high and 200 mm diameter. It is easily identified by short internodes, and bright white internode collars (about 25 mm wide) contrasting against dark green smooth-surfaced culms that climb 5 or 6 m into the air without a branch or leaf. It is truly an impressive sight.

Another species, *Guadua amplexifolia*, is the only sympodial bamboo I know that produces upward-pointing leaves. Our *G. paniculata* is one of the most delicate, pendulous bamboos I have seen, but beware its thorns!

Guadua species are generally thorny, some with powerful nodal thorns either side of their single, often zigzag branches. Some species develop a secondary branch, particularly on slightly higher nodes, and occasional smaller tertiary branches mostly on the upper nodes. *Guadua* culms are usually spaced apart, less dense than most other sympodial bamboos because of their long-necked, modified unicaespitose rhizome system.

The Columbian architects O. Hidalgo Lopez and S. Velez are very advanced in the way they are using this bamboo to produce modern buildings, having built more than 40 buildings ranging from houses and factories to shopping arcades. *Guadua* has been quoted as being more resistant to powder beetle and fungal rot than other species (Farrelly, 1984), but I was assured by Oscar Hidalgo that it is still desirable to treat this bamboo, even though its resistance may be greater than many other species. Costa Rica has established plantations of *G. angustifolia* to support a successful government program encouraging the construction of earthquake-proof bamboo houses (Janssen, 1995).

Schizostachyum

This genus, with more than 40 taxonomically described species and many more yet to be taxonomically ordered, varies considerably in size and appearance. It is a thin to very thin-walled, more delicate species, generally not considered suitable as a structural bamboo. The thin-walled culms occur because its fibre structure is mainly Type 2 (Liese,1995).

The *Schizostachyum* branching system is easily recognised by the star-like explosion of prolific branches of roughly the same size projecting from each developed node.

The largest of the species is the spectacular *Schizostachyum brachycladum*, up to 15 m high and 100 mm diameter but normally smaller, and probably the most beautiful, decorative bamboo in the world. With very close-packed, absolutely vertical, ivory yellow, green-striped culms and huge sometimes yellow-striped leaves on the upper half of the culms only, it is not surprising that it is considered to be sacred in Bali.

Schizostachyum species are much used as musical instruments (flutes, pan flutes and bamboo xylophones). The long internode thin walls also split easily into superb long flexible flats suitable for weaving fences, screens and baskets. A number of the smaller species (*S. jaculans* and *S.* sp. 'Murray Island') have very thin walls and spectacular straight internodes up to a metre long, *S. jaculans* being used in Malaysia to make hunting blowpipes with poison tipped darts.

Thyrsostachys

Two known species, both very erect beautiful fine-leafed bamboos. *Thyrsostachys siamensis* (syn. *T. regia*), is called 'monastery bamboo' because it is often planted as a tranquil barrier around temples. Its larger even more attractive brother *T. oliveri* has smooth green exposed erect culms. Both are valued for their strong wood.

There are many other sympodial genera, but none as diverse or as useful as those listed above. The following gives a few attractive examples.

Cephalostachyum

About eleven described species distributed from Himalayas to Thailand, with the beautiful upright *C. pergracile*, known as tinwa bamboo, being the most popular and useful species. The young culms are filled with spiced rice and coconut milk, and cooked over a fire to create 'skin rice'. It produces particularly straight, very strong wood, bare of lower leaves but with spectacular orange culm leaves with large cup-shaped blades—hence its species name of *pergracile. Cephalostachyum virgatum* is also an attractive garden plant, vertical but smaller.

■ **3.J** Thyrsostachys siamensis *showing its typical mature form*

■ **3.K** Cephalostachyum pergracile, *a spectacular garden species, also showing its decorative shoot and culm leaf*

Chusquea

A very small to small (2 m to 12 m) South American genus. Usually cold-tolerant, its small leaves are arranged on clusters of fine branches like florets that almost circle the culm. Unusual and sometimes quite beautiful. Unfortunately, we have been unable to get any of them to grow successfully (we are still trying) in our Australian sub-tropical climate. It may be better suited to some parts of Tasmania.

Dinochloa

An interesting, rainforest climbing bamboo with not many species, the best known species being *D. maclellandii*, *D. morheadii* and *D. scandens*. It has been suggested that the indigenous climbing bamboo growing prolifically on the edges of north Queensland's rainforests is *D. morheadii*, but the jury is out and one taxonomist believes it may be a species distinct to Australia (*D. morheadii* grows in Indonesia).

Drepanostachyum

Very small cold-tolerant Himalayas bamboo. We are successfully growing the beautifully decorative *D. falcatum*, an elegant garden species.

Fargesia

Very small cold-tolerant Chinese bamboos that are popular in USA and UK gardens. They are slow, indifferent performers in our sub-tropical climate, but could do well in Tasmania or other cool climates.

Melocanna

A genus with one very important useful species, much used for structures, food and weaving in Bangladesh. It has a large plum-like fruit said to be good eating. Unfortunately, the clone in Australia is a very poor performer (we have two slow growers).

Nastus

About fifteen species of often exotically attractive bamboos, mostly from Indonesia, New Guinea and Madagascar. Tropical, reasonably drought-tolerant and often high altitude bamboos, the best known species are *N. elegantissimus* and *N. elatus* (the latter produces tender non-bitter shoots that can be eaten raw).

Neohouzeaua

Two known species of small tropical lowlands bamboo indigenous from Thailand to Bangladesh. We are successfully growing the very attractive *N. mekongensis*.

■ **3.L** Nastus elatus, *elegant and valued for its non-bitter edible shoot*

Otatea

Attractive Mexican drought-tolerant bamboos, the two best known being *O. acuminata aztecorum* (Mexican weeping bamboo) and *O. acuminata acuminata*. They both grow well in our environment.

Thamnocalamus

Small cold-tolerant Indian/Himalayan bamboos. We find *T. spathaceus* an attractive performer here. There is confusion between this genus and *Fargesia* on some species (including *F. murieliae*) that the Kew Gardens taxonomist Chris Stapleton is working towards clarifying.

There are many other genera, and even new ones suggested, but the above section covers the most important sympodial (clumping) bamboos. I have no doubt that this book will some day be somewhat out-of-date because of the constantly changing picture, but that's life.

4 The Flowering Cycle Phenomenon

The most extraordinary phenomenon of bamboo is its flowering and seeding cycle, which often causes chaos, death and destruction amongst a complete species almost simultaneously around the world. It is a complex phenomenon with much variation between species, sometimes even within species.

There are three basic flowering patterns that appear, dependent on genera and species.

1. **Annual flowering cycle.** Bamboos following this pattern flower every year, don't die, but rarely produce a viable seed.

2. **Sporadic flowering cycle.** These bamboos flower occasionally, suffer temporarily from stress but don't die, and produce very little viable seed.

3. **Gregarious flowering cycle.** Bamboos representing this pattern produce masses of viable seed, and mostly die of exhaustion in the process.

■ **4.A** Gigantochloa hasskarliana *in the midst of a sporadic flowering which produced a leafless culm dedicated to flower panicles, as well as flowers on older culm branches*

Annual flowering cycle

A small number of bamboos flower very frequently, usually every year. Most of the *Schizostachyum* genus fall into this category (e.g. *S. brachycladum*). The flowering spikelets appear from mature branches on healthy culms, and generally cause very little stress to the plant unless the season is dangerously dry, which often causes a heavier flowering. Annually flowering bamboos rarely produce viable seed, but you can find a rare viable seed occasionally if you spend enough time looking for seed casings that feel full and hard rather than hollow (viable seeds on *S. brachycladum* have a long projecting tail). They rarely produce culms dedicated to flowers only.

Sporadic flowering cycle

More numerous than the annual flowering bamboos, sporadically flowering bamboos flower in an irregular pattern within localised areas. Bamboos of the same species in different geographic areas are not affected, and don't flower.

An example of this occurred with *Bambusa balcooa* in 1996, where it flowered on the north coast of NSW, Australia, but the original parent plant established early this century in Sydney's Royal Botanic Gardens didn't flower, and nor did *B. balcooa* in other areas of Australia flower at that time. (It flowered some years ago further south in the Rollands Flat area.)

As with annually flowering bamboos, sporadically flowering bamboos rarely produce viable seed, but if one spends hours searching, it is possible to find one or two. Some sporadically flowering species do produce more viable seed than others, *Dendrocalamus latiflorus* being one example. We recently had *Gigantochloa hasskarliana* from Thailand sporadically flowering here in Australia, and I found a small number of seeds (from the thousands it produced) that did germinate. In some areas of Thailand, some clumps of *G. hasskarliana* flower sporadically almost every year, and because the species is valuable for timber, the locals go to great pains to collect viable seed. In a single year they managed to collect only 532 grams (half a kilo), a good result because with 23 other sporadically flowering species they only managed to find between 10 and 60 grams in the same year (A. Anantachote, 1985).

Most of the sporadic flower panicles appear from mature branches on healthy culms, but sometimes they produce a culm without leaves, dedicated to flowers only (as do gregariously flowering bamboos). The frequency of a sporadic flowering in a single species or clone doesn't appear to follow a definite pattern, seeming almost accidental, or more related to weather conditions, or stress, rather than to genetics. Sometimes bamboos recently planted or transplanted, or brought in from another country, suddenly succumb. Sporadic flowering does put the bamboo under stress, causing it to look a little down-at-heel, but generally the plant recovers quickly.

Records dating back more than 100 years suggest that *Dendrocalamus latiflorus* is a sporadically flowering bamboo (see Chapter 21 for details).

Gregarious flowering cycle

This strange phenomenon applies to most bamboo species (both sympodial and monopodial), and appears to be linked to a genetic time clock within the bamboo. Most gregarious bamboos have a flowering cycle of between 30 and 120 years. For most species, their cycle remains predictable within a reasonably small time variation, but for others the cycle can halve or double in time (e.g. *Bambusa tulda*'s cycle in India varies between 30 and 60 years—Liese, 1985).

When a particular variation or cultivar of a species flowers gregariously, it does so all over the world virtually simultaneously (within the parameters of season, etc.). Gregariously flowering bamboos produce huge volumes of viable seeds, in fact they produce numerous culms dedicated to nothing but flowers and seed spikelets. The flowering process, which can take up to two years, puts great stress on the plant, and many, usually most, of the flowering plants actually die of exhaustion. Those that don't die eventually produce small new culms, and re-build their strength over some seasons.

An example of this was *Fargesia murieliae*, which flowered simultaneously starting three years ago (1995) all around the world, including UK, Sweden, USA, etc. The very stressed plants I saw in Kew Gardens, UK were possibly in the process of dying.

Another example with a devastating financial impact was the flowering of approximately 40 000 hectares of *Dendrocalamus asper* in the edible shoot plantations of Thailand. The initial estimate of loss in the first year was US$80 million, which will continue in a reduced amount until the plantations are re-established (Thammincha, 1995). The few plants of the same Thai cultivar (pai tong keo) planted years ago in Australia flowered the same year as their Thai brothers. In effect, seedlings from that Thai cultivar should not flower again for more than 100 years, but vegetative cuttings or transplants from the four other Thai cultivars, and both the Indonesian cultivars of *D. asper*, are liable to flower and die at any time in the not-too-distant future.

Gregariously flowering bamboos normally produce huge masses of viable seed, which is unfortunately not viable for very long (two months to two years depending on species and cool storage technique). Existing culms become prematurely aged during the gregarious flowering process, becoming brittle and unsuitable for structural use. They are often harvested as soon as it is realised they are about to gregariously flower.

Gregariously flowering bamboos sometimes sporadically flower. It appears that the fairly widespread sporadic flowering of a known gregariously flowering species, together with a marked reduction in shoot production during a season, is an indication that the species may gregariously flower within the next two seasons.

Bamboo flowers are small, unspectacular and straw-coloured to greenish in colour, developing usually into seeds which look like wheat, or even smaller grass seed. The seed is edible and very nourishing. In fact, millions of people in India were said to have been saved from starvation when *Dendrocalamus strictus* flowered gregariously during a critical drought some years ago. There are a few rare exceptions to flower and seed shape. *Melocanna baccifera* has a large plum-shaped fruit weighing 150 to 300 gm, sweet and apparently good to eat. *Ochlandra* and *Dinochloa* species are somewhat similar.

Research is being done in a number of countries to avoid the phenomenon of bamboos actually dying of exhaustion when they gregariously flower. One system showing some promise involves cutting off all of the culms in a clump, both flowering and otherwise, and applying high levels of nitrogen-rich fertiliser. Otherwise, one has to wait for the seedlings inevitably produced by gregarious flowering to grow again into a mature clump.

What an amazingly unique plant is bamboo! And how little we know of its extraordinary flowering cycle, so powerful that it causes plants of the same species to die in different countries, even different hemispheres, almost simultaneously! Or even how its fatal time clock works!

■ **4.B** Dendrocalamus asper *cv. 'Pai Tong Keo'—this cultivar which gregariously flowered in Thailand in 1994 caused the destruction of 40 000 hectares of plantation.*

5 Growing Conditions and Management

With such a diversity of plants and environments, it is impossible to come up with a single formula for management that suits every sympodial bamboo. I can specify general criteria that will suit most bamboos, and make specific qualifications later for fragile species or harsh environments.

Clumping (sympodial) bamboos are basically akin to a rainforest plant. They grow happily amongst rainforest trees, are used to sharing a shallow-rooted environment, and will fight their way up towards the canopy more aggressively than most rainforest plants (which tend to wait for a hole in the canopy before growing).

Being shallow-rooted plants, they also grow successfully in forest country amongst tall, deep-rooted trees (e.g. sclerophyll eucalypt forest) and live as under-cover plants without taking too much from the existing plants. Their periphery of fine roots radiate out and form a close knit circular mat around the rhizome/culm circle, loosening and aerating heavy soils, and mulching the ground with their roots (Janssen, 1997).

Whilst they all tend to thrive in semi-shade, most of them will grow happily in full sunlight. Growing amongst trees in a shaded environment usually causes them to grow taller and straighter, in fact very rapidly if they have sufficient food and water to keep up with their growth potential. We have one two-year-old *Dendrocalamus asper* 'Hitam', a beautiful black bamboo, which is producing shoots almost 300 mm diameter and very tall, absolutely

■ **5.A** Schizostachyum funghomii *(background) in an ideal pond bank growing environment and* Dendrocalamus stenoaurita *(foreground, hanging leaves)*

■ **5.B** Dendrocalamus asper *cv. 'Hitam' (two years old),* *the beautiful vigorous black cultivar, growing vertically in a* *shaded environment*

■ **5.C** Dendrocalamus latiflorus *cv. 'Mei Nung', lichen-covered and growing happily in a rainforest*

straight vertical culms. It's a good practice to choose that environment if you want to grow some structural bamboos for their timber culms. In this sense, clumping bamboos are ideal permaculture plants that will grow happily in a profusion of other species, and produce a renewable diversity of food and timber. In some cases, growing the bamboo in a rainforest environment causes fundamental changes in the appearance of the plant, an example being *Bambusa multiplex* cv. 'Alphonse Karr'. It normally grows 4 m high and 20 mm diameter in a very tight, fairly erect clump with culms almost touching when planted in full sunlight; however, when planted in jungle it produces 10 m long culms, 35 mm diameter, each culm individually spaced from the other, and forms a larger base diameter. Also, bamboos grown in a rainforest environment often become encrusted with lichen, making identification sometimes difficult.

There *are* species that are fragile in full sunlight, some always so and some only until they are established. These include a number of the *Schizostachyum* species including *S. brachycladum*, *S. glaucifolium*, the Australian species, *S.* sp. 'Murray Island' and *Bambusa forbesii*, also *Cephalostachyum pergracile* and the climbing bamboos of

the *Dinochloa* genus, all of which prefer a well-watered spot with some shade rather than hot dry sunlight. When grown in warmer climates, all of the high altitude sympodial bamboos of the genera *Fargesia*, *Thamnocalamus*, *Himalayacalamus* and *Chusquea* will only prosper if grown in a very shady, cool environment.

With few exceptions, the majority of sympodial bamboos are very tough plants. Our first 20 bamboos were planted in 1984. We were not living on the property to care for them until 1993. They survived grass competition, full sunlight, a succession of droughts, and wallaby attack. One was accidentally slashed off to ground level and still survived! The sites we chose on Bamboo World's 34 hectares were not always ideal. Some we planted on the crown of an extremely windy, very dry hill. During that initial ten-year period, they received absolutely no fertiliser or hand watering, and yet none of them died! They all looked healthy. What was interesting was their actual growth compared to their potential growth. Bamboos planted in dry, poorer soil looked perfectly healthy, but they had bonsaid themselves to some extent, an example being a *Bambusa multiplex* cv. 'Alphonse Karr' only 2 m high with 10 mm diameter culms in one place, and one

■ **5.D** Bambusa multiplex *growing in full subtropical sunlight. This plant has never been watered or fertilised in its fourteen-year life.*

concurrently planted 4 m high with 20 mm diameter culms in a better spot. Another example was a very exposed hilltop *Bambusa oldhamii*, lacking water, that reached 8 m high and 30 mm diameter over eight years, and proceeded to double its height and diameter during the next three years because we were available to water, mulch and feed it. One can use this phenomenon to advantage. If you want a large species but don't have the space, plant it in a poor spot and ignore it after it's established, and it won't grow as big!

Unless you live in a dry area lacking summer rain (or you are expecting a viable crop performance from your bamboo), it is not normally necessary to water your sympodial bamboos once established. We tend to water our Botanic Garden bamboos during droughts only or, with adolescent plants, in periods where there has been no rain at all for some time. Remember, however, that I am defining survival limits. If you want them to grow more quickly, the answer is water and more water.

Given enough water, most species don't drop lots of leaf, but they tend to be partially deciduous during droughts, or during their dormant season if it is dry (mid-winter to mid-spring). They replenish their leaves when rain arrives, or in late spring. Some few species (e.g. *Bambusa tulda*) tend to be more deciduous than others.

Most, but not all bamboos, do like water, and will grow fastest in damp (not constantly soggy) semi-shaded forest conditions in company with other trees; however,

they will not grow, in fact they will die, if planted in a permanently soggy environment. Some bamboos survive in very dry conditions once established (e.g. *Dendrocalamus strictus* and *Otatea acuminata aztecorum*), but many that can survive prolonged wet conditions will also survive prolonged dry conditions. *Nastus elatus* will die quickly if planted in an area subject to flooding, whereas *Bambusa ventricosa* (Buddha's belly bamboo) or *B. multiplex* (Chinese hedge bamboo), planted in a river bank to prevent soil erosion, will emerge virtually intact and undamaged (with the river bank intact!) after being completely covered by a roaring torrent. Additionally, they will survive in appallingly dry, cold conditions.

How Fast Do They Grow?

Sympodial bamboos will grow even faster if you feed and mulch them, but will mostly survive if you don't. We fertilised the more than 200 different sympodial species now growing in our Bamboo World Botanical Display Garden in order to accelerate the mature development of each plant. The results were spectacular in most cases. Most bamboos will achieve the full diameter and height of culm (that one can expect of that species in that environment) within four years for the small to medium bamboos (up to 100 mm diameter), and within six to seven years for larger species. This must be qualified by the fact that each species has an ideal growing environment, and its potential growth and size become less as the environment becomes less ideal. As an example, the growth rate and size of *Dendrocalamus giganteus* and *D. brandisii*, which happen to be two of the largest species known to man when grown in their normally very tropical environment, do not seem to reach either the rate of growth or size when grown in Australia, even in Cairns which is a fairly tropical environment. On the other hand, our *D. asper* produced 300 mm diameter shoots only 30 months after being planted as a 2 mm diameter plant. *D. asper* is generally grown in the high altitude, cooler areas of Java and Bali, and seems to thrive in a more temperate climate, along with *D. latiflorus* and many of the sympodial species indigenous to Southern China.

Dendrocalamus asper is also grown in tropical lowland country in Thai plantations, where it doesn't seem to reach the height and diameter of those in the Java highlands. I don't know whether this is because of the heat or because shoot production places the plant under stress. More likely it is because it is a different cultivar. Except in extremes, most bamboos will grow and look good, but their potential size is reduced as the environment becomes less ideal.

Obviously some species grow faster than others in the initial stages. Species like *Bambusa oldhamii*, *B. tulda*, *B.*

textilis, *B. tuldoides*, *B. malingensis*, *Nastus elatus* and many others will usually grow 2 m high within the first year (during their first full shoot season), up to 7 m high within two years, and achieve full potential height for that site within four or five years, depending on environment and care. Larger species like *Dendrocalamus asper*, *D. latiflorus*, *Gigantochloa atter*, *Bambusa balcooa* and some others will exceed the above growth rate in the first years, again depending on care and conditions. Some took a while longer to settle in on our site (e.g. *Thyrsostachys siamensis* and some of the *Schizostachyum* genus), accelerating their growth after sitting about for close to 12 months.

If you compare those growth rates with other plants, however, most bamboos outgrow any other species known to man. In the shoot season, my wife and I walk amongst our 'babies' every day, looking for shoots that thrust the earth open in their haste. We are constantly amazed at the accelerating charge into the sky of a new developing culm, at some stages climbing up to a metre higher each day that we look. We enjoy this aspect very much, as we have less time available to wait as we grow older.

How Tough Are They?

Bamboos will grow successfully in a desert environment if they get enough water. I read a report from an enthusiastic outback grower (350 km north-east of Alice Springs, on the edge of the Simpson Desert) who has quite a few species established and thriving on bore water with a 1200 ppm salt content.

Many bamboos are reasonably salt-tolerant. I know of an enthusiast growing a large range of species on the banks of low-lying river flat country close beside a NSW mid-coast saltwater river. Located less than a kilometre from a surfing beach, they must be swept from time to time by salt-laden air, and the roots of the larger species must be into a brackish water table. His species include *Bambusa balcooa*, *B. blumeana*, *B. longispiculata*, *B. malingensis*, *B. multiplex*, *B. oldhamii*, *B. textilis*, *B. tulda*, *B. ventricosa*, *Dendrocalamus asper*, *Gigantochloa apus*, *Nastus elatus* and many others. Another enthusiast reported *D. latiflorus* on a bank just above tidal flats and mangroves, and I know of *B. balcooa*, *B. multiplex* and *B. oldhamiii* clumps growing very close to the shores of Sydney Harbour.

Whilst most clumping bamboos are considered to be subtropical plants, many of them will survive surprisingly cold winter climates reaching well below zero, or in protected microclimate environments in areas where temperatures get well below their normal tolerance range. These species, together with recommendations on how to nurture them, are described in detail in Chapter 6.

Planting Procedure

Remember that adolescent and mature clumping bamboos have their very vigorous, often spectacular growth period once per year. It commences about January in the southern hemisphere, or July in the northern hemisphere, sometimes a little earlier (e.g. *Bambusa malingensis*) or later (e.g. *Dendrocalamus latiflorus*, *B. oldhamii* and *B. multiplex*), depending on the species and the season.

Their shoots begin to appear in midsummer, and can extend into autumn and even winter. Mostly, individual mature clumps have all their shoots within about six to twelve weeks of the first one appearing. There are exceptions to that normal expectation as follows:

1. Given enough TLC, newly planted young bamboos, in their early bid for survival, often have such amazing energy that they will often have shoots out of season; in fact all year long. Planted even in midwinter in a frost-free environment, they often produce new shoots and vegetative leaves, and built up a strong root system that enables them to produce even larger shoots and culms when the summer shoot season eventually arrives.

2. If you harvest all the earlier shoots for eating, or for aesthetic reasons, the clump will keep on generating replacement shoots because it is still full of energy and the desire to produce full-sized culms. The shoot season can be extended, even up to six months, if this practice is followed (see Chapter 21 on plantation management).

3. Young plants planted out after the shoot season has begun often work hard building up roots, small culms and vegetation until close to midwinter (depending on the environment). They often then produce a single large culm before going into their dormant period, until the next shoot season.

4. Other newly planted youngsters manage to have one decent-sized culm early in the shoot season, and put all their energy into developing the roots and leaves on that culm, which can be six times the height of the original plant: then months later in the season, the plant will suddenly produce an even bigger taller culm than the first.

Winter shoots (those breaking ground after June in the southern hemisphere) rarely appear on a mature plant. When they do, they usually stop growing after breaking the ground, and die.

Planting a sympodial bamboo is no different to planting a tree in that same location. Our soil at Bamboo World is mostly black or chocolate basalt, with some red basalt. We generally tractor-rip a cross (about 450 mm deep) on a flat site, or a 2 m long contour rip on a sloping site, and plant our bamboo in the middle of the rip lines with the bagged or potted plant's soil level 25 to 50 mm below ground level. If ripping is impractical, dig a hole larger than the bag and loosen the surrounding soil with a crowbar.

After preparing the hole to the correct depth for the plant's soil height, lay the bagged plant on its side. Avoiding the roots, cut the bottom free from the bag sides until it forms a flap lying on the ground. Place the flat of your hand on the soil exposed at the bottom, lift the bag by its still intact sides and, dragging the flap behind, place the bare soiled bottom in the prepared hole with the bamboo leaf faces pointing northeast. Pour friable soil around the still intact bag sides (except onto the flap), then pull the bag upwards over the leaves and branches and off the bamboo plant. Finish the soil placement, fertilise lightly around but not in contact with the bamboo, mulch heavily with grass slashings or straw, then flood water the plant and surrounding area. Planting this way eliminates disturbance to the roots.

If your soil is really poor, it will pay to spend more time in preparation. Remember that bamboo is a shallow rooted plant. It is therefore quicker and easier to suitably modify poor quality soils than it would be for a deep-rooted plant. Rip or dig the area more extensively and work straw, mulch matter and organic fertiliser (manure) into the area for a 1 m radius. Then prepare your planting hole, position the bamboo in the hole as earlier described, and fill around the bamboo with good quality friable soil or potting mix. This should give the plant a good start, and look after its needs until future mulching, fertilising, and the natural action of the bamboo's roots and leaf mulch modify the soil environment.

Our pH is 5.2, which is adequate. If it is less, add lime to sweeten the soil, but we hear of many instances of bamboo growing comfortably in soil with a pH of 4.5. Bamboos are also very tolerant of clay soils, but if it looks too harsh and heavy, add gypsum, which breaks the clay down beautifully.

Try and keep newly planted bamboos well watered at least until they have survived their first summer season, and you will get accelerated growth. Kangaroos and wallabies can be a problem, eating small developing shoots and leaves. We place a wire screen over or around some newly planted bamboos. If cattle and horses are present, the protection needs to be very strong as grazing animals love bamboo leaves (which are almost 20 per cent crude protein content). If the nights are still very cold, or if they are not quite sun-hardened during hot weather (most nursery plants are fragile), it helps to clip on a temporary sun screen, for instance a cut fertiliser bag, over, or frost shield around, the wire screen.

If you are planting tropical bamboos in areas where the temperatures get down close to their tolerance limit, don't plant out until springtime. Choose a site amongst trees if you expect heavy frost. One site in Queensland subject to heavy frost (ground temperatures of -6°C and

■ **5.E** Dendrocalamus minor *var.* amoenus, *a beautiful striped bamboo*

-8°C) lost many tropical bamboos initially, but has now succeeded in growing those species in sclerophyll forest. It also pays to apply high mineral fertiliser similar to that used for roses or citrus plants about four weeks before you expect sub-zero temperatures. The salt content of the sap is raised, which gives the plant a greater cold-tolerance (salt water freezes at a lower temperature than fresh).

Don't despair if your young plant loses all or almost all its leaves initially. It happens fairly frequently, but they usually shoot new green leaves fairly quickly. Bamboos under drought stress can lose all their leaves, which reappear miraculously the moment it rains again. Except for the sun-tender species, they are capable of surviving severe heat waves. We see our bamboos roll up their leaves every time the temperature tops 35°C only to roll them open again when the cool of night descends.

■ **5.F** Bambusa textilis, *cold-tolerant to -12˚C, located ideally in a protected environment*

Mature Clump Maintenance

Bamboo clumps suffer from 'motherhood'. Even though still handsome, our bamboos look their worst during our dry season, usually during autumn. This is partly because we don't water them.

The new late summer culms stand initially leafless, progressively trying to generate roots, leaves and branches during the dry season, weaning themselves from relying on the relatively exhausted more mature culms now depleted of sap and energy. The older culms often shed leaves as they partly sacrifice themselves to the younger developing culms and leaves. Sometimes the

strong August/September winds even strip leaves from windward culms, but the bared branches quickly develop new leaves when reasonable rain arrives. With young plants late in autumn, you often see the older 'mother' culm leaf system looking slightly stressed. The young, larger diameter, newly created culms with their first vegetative leaves, still rely partially on the mature (smaller) culm system and their fully developed root feeder system for sustenance.

Being voracious feeders, bamboos benefit from more frequent applications of fertiliser, say every three months, rather than larger, annual applications (except in the case of plantations—see Chapter 21). Fertiliser gets to the shallow root system very quickly. I've seen bamboos killed or produce grotesquely misshapen shoots by heavy applications of urea type fertiliser that can burn the sensitive fine root tips. This is not to say that they will not benefit from chemical fertilisers used in smaller more frequent doses, but they certainly thrive on organic type fertiliser and mulch as well.

In plantation conditions it is more practical and economical to use a mixture of organic and chemical fertilisers than to try and supply the plant's full needs from organic fertiliser only; however, this is a choice available to be decided by the grower. For our garden species, we tend to apply slashed mulch, poultry manure (aged natural or processed pelletised), blood and bone, and some NPK fertiliser. Bamboos are known to like some potash and a little silicon added to their environment (good for timber fibres but not so good for non-fibrous edible shoots), and a little gypsum will help loosen very heavy clay soil. As a fertiliser guide, you can apply up to 300 kg per hectare of total nitrogen content, which is about 1.5 kg per clump, or 10 kg per clump of 15:15:15 NPK for large clumping species such as *D. asper*. Alternate yearly with 40 kg per clump of 'manure' (unspecified origin). Forty kg would be satisfactory for a fully mature, large bamboo like *D. asper* but should be reduced according to the size of the bamboo (e.g. 6 kg/clump for a *Bambusa multiplex* cv. 'Fernleaf' or 20 kg for a mature *Bambusa tuldoides*). Apply 90 per cent of the fertiliser outside the rhizome area within the root circle, scattering the remainder amongst the rhizome/culm circle.

Don't apply fertiliser in large quantities from four to six weeks prior to the commencement of the shoot season for the next six months, or your edible shoots will be soft and lacking in crisp texture.

In Indonesia and in the Chinese *D. latiflorus* plantations, the farmers sometimes cut three trenches like intermittent slots around the clump about 1.5 m outside the outer rhizome ring, each about 1 to 1.5 m long on large bamboos, thus partially severing the roots to the depth of the trench. By filling the trench with mulch and fertiliser, new roots soon generate and grow into the 'feed-trough'. The ideal time would be two months before the shoot season (November, southern hemisphere).

Mulching

Bamboos become self-mulching to some degree. The fine, shallow, radiating feeder roots retard other growth near the rhizome and culm system. It also helps to condition the soil and retain soil moisture if the area inside and immediately outside the rhizome system is lightly mulched and composted. This is more something you would do in a plantation seeking maximum perfor-

■ **5.G** Bambusa vulgaris *cv. 'Wamin' with its extraordinary bulging culms, a large Buddha's belly-type decorative species*

■ **5.H** Bambusa vulgaris *cv. 'Vittata' with its beautiful green-striped golden culms*

mance than something that is necessary. Mulch inside the rhizome circle lightly only, or the bamboo will be encouraged to climb higher out of the ground, a natural phenomenon caused by the new shoot buds being located on the sides of the mother rhizome, causing each progressive rhizome to be located slightly higher.

Pruning or Harvesting Timber

Pruning requirements of bamboo vary with the species, and with what you want to achieve. Small species and many dense decorative bamboos require no work at all. Our nine cultivars of *Bambusa multiplex*, mostly fourteen-year-old bamboos, have never been touched. Most sympodial bamboos planted in the Western world never receive maintenance, but within Asian communities where good species are valued for their multitude of uses (e.g. China and Indonesia), the mature culms are mostly harvested, cured and stored under cover ready for use.

With most larger species, the minimum maintenance would be to remove any dead and dying culms. It also pays to thin out new shoots if the clump is becoming too crowded, or the growing culm is going to be so close to others that it will be unable to climb into the air without having to twist and turn. Cut them off before they develop into culms, cook them up and eat them!

Many of the superior large species remain in a very tight clump, and don't develop into very large diameter clumps. As an example, I have seen beautiful mature clumps of the very large species *Dendrocalamus asper*, *D. brandisii*, *D. sikkimensis*, *Gigantochloa atter*, and *G. apus*, all about eighteeen years old in Queensland, none of which are more than about 2 to 2.5 m across the base. Even specimens of the giant ancient *D. giganteus*, more than 30 m high in Bogor Gardens, Indonesia, are not more than 3 to 4 m across the base. All these elegant erect giants have no leaves for some metres from ground level and are a delight to the eye.

Some pruning maintenance is beneficial to some species for aesthetic reasons. As an example, we remove most of the young shoots (and eat them) from *Bambusa ventricosa* (Buddha's belly bamboo) leaving only well-spaced, larger culms. We then clip the branch buds off the remaining new culms as they develop, up to a height of about 2 m. The result is a display of spectacular, bulging internoded culms each separate from the other. It makes a spectacular garden piece. If *B. ventricosa* (or many others) is only being grown for its superb landslip/riverbank/erosion/hedge/windbreak qualities, there is no need to follow the above procedure unless considered aestheti-cally desirable. (We started removing shoots from our Buddha's belly bamboo when it was 12 years old and 2 m across the base.) We use exactly the same procedure on the much larger Buddha's belly-type bamboo, *Bambusa vulgaris* cv. 'Wamin', which has bulging culms up to 125 mm diameter, and its close relative, the green-striped yellow *B. vulgaris* cv. 'Vittata', with spectacular visual results in both cases. All these bamboos can be maintained as very small clumps by using this shoot removal procedure, and the shoots are very easy to cut off.

When your clumps are three years old, it pays to cut the smallest of the older culms off close to ground level, leaving the larger culms only. This encourages large shoot and culm generation from the larger culms retained. If you want to use the timber, remember that bamboo culms should only be harvested in the 'dry' or dormant season (normally late winter, early spring), and you should cut off only culms that have been standing for at least three or four years (see Chapter 11 for a detailed explanation). Cut the culms above ground level to avoid damage to the attached rhizome, close to but above a node to minimise decay from water lying inside the cut-off culm (Liese, 1985). In timber plantations all the mature (three- to four-year-old) culms are removed each year, and as many shoots as possible are left intact, cutting (and eating or selling) only those that will cause future congestion or twisting culm growth (see Chapter 11). This not only maximises the quality of the timber harvested, but also the quantity and straightness of future timber.

From the above maintenance options you can see that you may choose to do almost nothing with most species, or you can choose a management system appropriate for your intended use. Large bamboos worked primarily for producing timber tend to look better than those worked for shoot production, where the bamboo is deliberately placed under stress to increase the number of shoots at the expense of culms and leaves, however you can strike an attractive balance between the two crops.

If your larger species clump gets to a size that you enjoy, and you don't want it to grow any larger, cut all the shoots off each year (and eat them) except one or two that you choose to grow on into mature culms. Leave small diameter shoots to grow on if you want to minimise growth, or large diameter shoots if you want height or stature. Later the same year, cut down the same number of culms that you have left as shoots to grow on, choosing only the oldest culms to cut. The clump will remain the same size as long as you maintain it in that way. You can also prevent it from growing in any direction you want by using the same technique.

I have given minimum and maximum maintenance options, and indicated how easy most species are to get on with. I strongly recommend that the large and vigorous species *Bambusa balcooa*, common on the east coast of Australia, should definitely be planted only if one is prepared to follow the above timber culling maintenance procedure diligently every year. Many clumps of this very vigorous bamboo were established more than 50 years ago and have remained untouched. Many are huge and full of dead timber which becomes a fire hazard. It

has become almost impossible to harvest good quality straight wood because of the twisted mass of elevated timber that the new shoots have to negotiate to reach full height. It also has a powerful intermingling branch system beginning virtually at ground level, branches so strong that they prevent cut-off culms from falling or being extracted easily from the clumps. Properly managed, it produces very straight strong timber, but it doesn't compare in quality or ease of maintenance with most of the other large superior timber species, some of them even reaching a culm base diameter of 15 m and an overhanging drip line of 3 m. It is just too vigorous. This problem is not experienced with any of the great structural bamboos of the *Dendrocalamus* or *Gigantochloa* genera, which are low maintenance plants.

On the whole these beautiful bamboos tend to be very easily maintained, strong performers even in diverse conditions, and a joy to live with. The little maintenance required is a small price to pay for the elegance of their dancing in a breeze, performed for us to the tranquil accompaniment of their gently rubbing culms—an enormous natural cello creaking dignified frictional music.

■ **5.1** Bambusa balcooa (*a very old clump*), *the vigorous, difficult to control 'rogue' sympodial clumping bamboo, not recommended for planting*

6 Species Selection and Uses

Until relatively recently, very few non-invasive (clumping) species were available in Australia, and the situation appears to have been much the same in the USA. It was actually an American migrant to Australia, Jim Wertz, who fell in love with bamboo about eighteen years ago and began bringing into this country as many species as he could lay his hands on, concentrating primarily on sympodial species. His beautiful rainforest property on the edge of a northern Queensland World Heritage area now abounds with wonderful mature clumps scattered amongst fruit trees and rainforest.

We purchased our first 20 sympodial bamboos from Jim in 1984, and have since increased our collection to include more than 2000 bamboos. More than 200 are the different species or varieties or cultivars of sympodial bamboo represented in our Bamboo World Botanical Gardens on the north coast region of NSW (near Murwillumbah). We have now established seven hectares of bamboo plantation for producing edible shoots and timber at a planting density of between 200 and 277 plants per hectare, depending on species. Building our botanical collection involves travelling overseas into the backblocks of Java, Bali, Thailand, China and the Philippines to seek out and introduce new species to Australia. Importing plants is a tricky business involving huge losses due to the stress of bare-rooting the plants before import and praying that they will survive the quarantine process of fumigation with methyl bromide on arrival (we have lost more than 8000 plants in the last eighteen months). We have our own Government-approved quarantine house to ensure they receive maximum TLC but some species are very susceptible to the gas, and many die in spite of our best efforts.

Len Muller, an avid collector of Indonesian bamboos, has dozens of taxonomically unidentified *Gigantochloa*, *Dendrocalamus* and *Schizostachyum* genus bamboos now growing on his beautiful farm, Mount Mirinjo, near Cairns in northern Queensland. Many of these bamboos may one day prove to be either distinctly different cultivars of existing species, or even new species. Len's specialist knowledge has made a significant contribution to our understanding of Indonesia's bamboos and the ancient symbiotic relationship of the people with their bamboo. Much of his writing on the subject has been published in the American Bamboo Society magazines between 1995 and 1998.

Our collection of more than 200 species of sympodial bamboo becomes more accessible to more enthusiasts

■ **6.A** Schizostachyum funghomii, *a very beautiful erect garden species*

as we find ways of propagating these often difficult-to-reproduce plants. These non-invasive species include everything from miniature bamboos that never exceed a metre in height (ideal for a small garden or pot) to exotic giant structural bamboos that can tower more than 35 m. Depending on the species you choose, many will provide you with high quality eating shoots, or can be used as material for buildings, exotic fencing, weaving splits, furniture making, fishing rods, musical instruments, kitchen utensils, or a multitude of other imaginative uses. Any one of those potential uses could influence your species choice.

Few people realise that, if bamboo suddenly disappeared off the face of the earth, about 10 per cent of the people in South-East Asia would be homeless, an important nourishing food source (bamboo shoots)

■ **6.B** Dendrocalamus latiflorus, *with the author holding the huge leaf used to wrap seafood and rice balls in cooking*

■ **6.C** Gigantochloa atter, *which produces straight superior timber and high quality eating shoots*

common names, a description of that bamboo's characteristics, and a list of its more common uses.

I have suggested a 'recommended selection procedure' later in this chapter to make your task of choosing easier, but before you select your bamboo, consider the following possible uses that may tempt you or influence your decisions.

contributing close to two million tonnes of vegetable per year would need to be replaced, and (as we all know) the pandas and possibly even some elephants in Thailand would perish. A good enough excuse to plant some!

Chapter 7 lists more than 200 species of sympodial bamboo, the majority of which are available in Australia, and many in the USA (which seem to be short on the *Gigantochloa* species from South-East Asia, judging by the American Bamboo Society species availability lists). All are growing here in our Botanical Garden, but some rarer species haven't produced enough mature wood to propagate and make them readily available (a process that can takes three years or more). Each species description gives the height and culm diameter that species can achieve under ideal conditions, the minimum survival temperature, the botanical name, botanical synonyms, some

Colourful and Unique Species

Each species has its distinctive features, be it the huge leaves of *Dendrocalamus latiflorus* (used to wrap and cook rice balls), the fine leaves of *Thyrsostachys siamensis* (Photo 3J) or *T. oliveri*, the long thin elegant drooping leaves of *Nastus elatus* (Photo 1I) or *Otatea acuminata aztecorum*. Also distinctive are the chocolate/black culms of *Bambusa lako* (Photo 2B), the sooty black culms of *Gigantochloa atroviolacea* and the giant *Dendrocalamus asper* cv. 'Hitam' (Photo 5B) or the dark red/black culms of *Otatea acuminata aztecorum* (Mexican weeping bamboo). Or consider the bulging internodes of *Bambusa ventricosa* or *B. vulgaris* cv. 'Wamin' (Photo 5G), the small variegated leaves of *Gigantochloa* sp. 'Malay Dwarf Variegated', or

■ **6.D** Bambusa multiplex *cv. 'Alphonse Karr', a superb hedge bamboo and garden species with attractively striped golden culms*

just the verdant lush green beauty of many less adorned species like *Bambusa oldhamii* (Photo 1B), *Dendrocalamus asper* (Photo 2C) or *Gigantochloa atter* (Photo 6C).

The colours and shapes of the shoots contribute to the visual impact in quite a spectacular way, with delicate pink/green striped shoots on *Bambusa multiplex* cultivars 'Alphonse Karr' (Photo 6D) and 'Silverstripe', pink shoots on *Thyrsostachys siamensis* and green-striped shoots on many such as *Bambusa lako*. Or there are the mysterious

exotic black velvet shoots on *Dendrocalamus sikkimensis* (Photo 1A), and red velvet on *Otatea acuminata aztecorum*, and the grotesque dark primeval creations thrust from the earth by *Bambusa bambos*. The shapes and colours of the shoots and their powerful but dignified eruption from within the earth are a constant source of excitement and amazement for us; a significant part of the joy we experience in our bamboo environment!

Bamboos with exotically coloured culms also make spectacular garden features, some examples being listed below:

Bambusa arnhemica—orange-tinted mature culms (Photo 5H).
Bambusa vulgaris cv. 'Vittata'—bright green stripes on golden yellow culms.
Bambusa longispiculata—ivory stripes on light green culms.
Bambusa eutuldoides—fine white lines on young light green culms.
Bambusa multiplex cv. 'Alphonse Karr'—green stripes on gold/yellow culms.
Bambusa multiplex cv. 'Stripestem Fernleaf'—yellow/green culms with lighter stripes.
Bambusa viridi-vittata—bright green stripes on golden yellow culms.
Dendrocalamus latiflorus cv. 'Mei Nung'—dark green stripes on light green culms (Photo 5C).

■ **6.E** Bambusa longispiculata, *with its attractively striped, well-spaced culms*

Dendrocalamus minor var. *amoenus*—mid green stripes on pale green culms (Photo 5E).

Dendrocalamus sikkimensis—orange-tinted culms.

Gigantochloa albociliata—cream stripes on light grey/green culms.

Gigantochloa ligulata—cream stripes on medium green culms.

Gigantochloa rostrata—cream stripes on dark green culms.

Gigantochloa pseudoarundinacea—cream stripes on medium green culms (Photo 3G).

Gigantochloa robusta—bright ivory stripes on verdant green culms.

Schizostachyum brachycladum—striped leaves and green stripes on ivory gold culms (Photo 3I).

Schizostachyum glaucifolium—bright dark green stripes on light lime green culms.

Shapes or Shaping Clumps

Many species grow naturally without leaves or branches on the lower part of the clump after they reach maturity as if to deliberately reveal the finery of their decorative vertical culm structures. Some of those are smaller bamboos like *Bambusa multiplex* cv. 'Alphonse Karr' (Photo 6D), others medium-sized like the beautiful *Cephalostachyum pergracile* (Photo 3K), *Bambusa textilis* cv. 'Gracilis', *Thyrsostachys siamensis* (monastery bamboo) and Bali's sacred beauty *Schizostachyum brachycladum* (Photo 3I). Others are beautiful giants like *Dendrocalamus asper* (Photo 2C), *D. latiflorus* (Photo 6B), *D. giganteus* (Photo 1C), *D. brandisii* (Photo 11B), *Gigantochloa apus* (Photo 11A), *G. levis*, *G. pseudoarundinacea*, and many others, revealing massive exposed vertical culms under their exotic, higher leaf cover.

Some small to medium bamboos are so naturally dense in their clumping form that, whilst you may want to cut wood and use it, you would not normally consider removing culms for aesthetic reasons (e.g. all the *Bambusa multiplex* family, *B. textilis*, *Gigantochloa wrayi*, *Thyrsostachys siamensis* and many others). If you plant them in the space they require as a mature plant, those bamboos require little or no maintenance (see Chapter 5), and some provide strong wood and tasty, edible shoots as well (e.g. *T. siamensis*, *B. textilis*, *B. tuldoides*).

Some species can be pruned to achieve a modified decorative effect, removing the lower branch buds (or branches) up to head height to reveal the coloured culms (or dramatically bulging culm shapes). This leaves only a limited number of selected culms to grow on (remove and eat most of the shoots) to create a spectacular 'designed' appearance, like a full-sized bonsai (e.g. *B. ventricosa* known as Buddha's belly, or *B. vulgaris* 'Wamin', or 'Vittata'). With others, nature shapes the bamboo into

■ **6.F** Gigantochloa wrayi, *a delicate smaller garden species*

a beautiful form for us (e.g. *B. textilis*, *T. siamensis*).

If you want to make furniture with your bamboo, remember that after harvesting and curing, all of the striped bamboos lose their stripes to become the same familiar attractive 'bamboo' straw colour, except the black bamboos, which all retain their beautiful black colouring (very much valued for furniture making). Bamboos with a medium wall thickness are best suited for most furniture making, so that you can cut holes to fit one culm into another.

Bamboos for Cold Climates

The most important factor in selecting the bamboo species you want for your environment is climate. As mentioned earlier, some but not all the sympodial bamboos tend to be tropical or semi-tropical, whereas others are distinctly temperate, or even cold climate. If you live in a colder area, don't simply give up and plant a inferior monopodial running bamboo that will survive the cold climate, or it may become the bane of your and your neighbour's life. Select a sympodial bamboo carefully and intelligently, and plant it on a site within your environment that suits the species. These tough sympodial plants will give you great pleasure and usefulness.

The list following these comments highlights some of the cold-tolerant bamboos described in the species descriptions of Chapter 7. Bamboo, like any other plant, will reach its full potential in terms of size only if the environment is ideal. If conditions are not optimum, the bamboo will still thrive and look healthy so long as the actual growing conditions are within those specified for that species. Even if the conditions in your area are a little beyond those specified for the species, it will often survive and eventually flourish if you select a protected site within that environment and give it special attention whilst it is small. Sometimes the bamboo may be a little smaller or slower to reach maturity, particularly where hours of daylight sunshine are reduced, but it will mostly look just as beautiful. There are clumps of *Bambusa balcooa* growing in open frosty valleys all along the east coast of NSW. Those in extreme conditions look frost-burned around the lower branches during winter and tend to be about 60 per cent of the height and culm diameter of those growing in optimum conditions, but they recover

quickly and look green and luxurious during the warmer, wetter months.

Many of the magnificent tropical bamboos have a low temperature tolerance of -2°C to -4°C, species such as *Dendrocalamus asper* (Photo 2C), *D. latiflorus* (Photo 6B), *D. strictus*, *Bambusa lako* (Photo 2B), *Gigantochloa apus*, *G. atter* (Photo 6C), and others. In terms of beauty and usefulness these are superb bamboos well worth trying to establish. One site I know of, subject to minimum ground temperatures of -6°C to -9°C every winter, had those species burned off by frost for three years running. The rhizomes, still alive and well, continued to try and produce new shoots as summer approached. Those same plants were shifted into a shallow, tree-covered creek depression 100 m away, and protected with a plastic surround for one winter. They are now rocketing into the air, thriving with spectacular good health. By growing them amongst trees with some lower shrub growth to protect them from wind chill factor and the worst of the frost, they are able to survive in an area where the general conditions exceed their normal limit. One site recorded -6°C in the field and +1°C in a canopy 20 m away!

There are a whole group of beautiful, very cold-hardy bamboos that will survive where temperatures reach -9°C and more, species such as *Bambusa oldhamii* (-9°C), *B. tuldoides* (-9°C), *B. textilis* (-12°C), *B. ventricosa* (-9°C), all the *B. multiplex* cultivars (-12°C) and others. The following lists a range of very cold-tolerant species:

Bambusa balcooa (-5°C)
Bambusa blumeana (- 7°C)
Bambusa eutuldoides (-9°C)
Bambusa malingensis (-7°C)
Bambusa multiplex (-12°C)
Bambusa multiplex cv. 'Albo-striata' (-15°C)
Bambusa multiplex cv. 'Alphonse Karr' (-12°C)
Bambusa multiplex cv. 'Fernleaf' (-12°C)
Bambusa multiplex cv. 'Golden Goddess' (-12°C)
Bambusa multiplex cv. 'Silverstripe' (-12°C)
Bambusa multiplex cv. 'Stripestem Fernleaf' (-12°C)
Bambusa multiplex cv. 'Willowy' (-12°C)
Bambusa multiplex var. *riviereorum* (-12°C)
Bambusa nana (-9°C)
Bambusa oldhamii (-9°C)
Bambusa textilis (-15°C)
Bambusa textilis var. 'Glabra' (-12°C)
Bambusa textilis var. 'Gracilis' (-12°C)
Bambusa tuldoides (-9°C)
Bambusa ventricosa (-9°C)
Chusquea genus—all species—(-4°C to -6°C)
Dendrocalamopsis beecheyana (-9°C)
Dendrocalamus strictus (-9°C)
Drepanostachyum falcatum (-9°C)
Fargesia murieliae (-12°C)
Fargesia nitida (-20°C)
Fargesia spathacea (-20°C)
Otatea acuminata aztecorum (-9°C)

■ **6.G** Dendrocalamus strictus *produces a tight clump with willowy upper culms.*

Two interesting experiences growing clumping bamboos in cold climates may further encourage you. John Isaachsen in Auckland, New Zealand has succeeded in encouraging significant plantings of clumping bamboos over there. His stated philosophy and comment about current day NZ is:

> *From bad choice and neglect,* Phyllostachys aurea *has followed* Pseudosasa japonica *as the too-wide-spread 'menaces', giving bamboo generally unfavourable publicity and reputation, in error! We recommend more responsible emphasis: Choosing carefully, using and publicising species that cannot run (clumpers),* B. oldhamii *(in NZ since 1920),* B. textilis, B. multiplex, *etc. for screens.* Drepanostachyum falcatum *still leads smaller ornamentals' popularity.* D. latiflorus *(-4°C) since about 1955 is the spectacular biggest.*

He was quoted some years ago as saying, 'The worst thing any persons can do to the worldwide or local reputation of bamboos, is to plant or distribute running species carelessly'. Isaachsen's NZ property and nursery regularly experiences -5°C of frost, but he has distributed bamboos to areas considerably colder than that, and is obviously pleased at the extremely cold climates where clumping bamboos of his supply have succeeded in growing.

The second contribution is from Robert Perry of Sunset Nursery in Tampa, Florida. He observed that in a number of unusually severe freezes in Florida there were complete citrus groves frozen to death. He records 'Mile after mile of them ... ' but '... interspersed are healthy groves undamaged or only slightly damaged by the cold'. He goes on to point out that the citrus that survived had been fertilised, and that those that died were not being fertilised because of the depressed price of oranges. The connection, later verified and advocated by the University of Georgia, is he says a function of '...simple physics. Soluble salts, which are essentially what fertiliser is, lower the level at which damage from cold occurs. Going into and during winter you should use fertilisers. Not high nitrogen mixes but those such as rose or citrus formulation to induce cold hardiness! It's that simple! The fertiliser "soluble salts" are in the cells of the plant. This is in effect adding anti-freeze to your plants!' His comment on the recorded low temperature of bamboos in the wild is 'if the chart says 25°F (-4°C) ... and no lower, think about it. In the wild where temperature lows are garnered, realise the plants have not had fertilisers! In your garden use plenty of mulch! Fertilise lightly and frequently and you will probably find the temperamental bamboo may surprise you by withstanding several more degrees of cold with little or no damage. If well fed and the bamboo does lose foliage or even have culm injury it will bounce back quickly.' His nursery is one of the more advanced in the United States and his experienced advice and enthusiasm are worth following.

Privacy Hedges, Windbreaks, Noise and Dust Barriers

Being the fastest growing woody plant in the world, sympodial species (capable of reaching full height and diameter much faster than the spreading monopodial types of similar size), make the best and quickest of all windbreaks. Each plant stays where you plant it, so you achieve a hedge or windbreak effect by planting a number in a row. One can select the species to suit the required height, or even plant alternating different species for effect. There is even a group of about ten very different cultivars of *Bambusa multiplex*, nicknamed 'Chinese hedge bamboos' for that very reason. I know of one nursery hedge nearly half a kilometre long in northern NSW, planted only six years ago, that has reached its full potential height of 18 m. It is only 1 m wide, and presents

■ **6.H** Bambusa oldhamii *(five years old) used as a hedge and windbreak, only a metre across the base and about 500 metres long*

6.I Bambusa multiplex *var.* riviereorum *trimmed as a hedge in Hong Kong*

6.K Bambusa ventricosa, *the common Buddha's belly bamboo, grown in a pot to limit its size*

visually as a beautiful, vertical, verdant green wall of vegetation (*Bambusa oldhamii*, see Photo 6H). That hedge produces, as a by-product, hundreds of high quality eating shoots and hundreds of useful straight timber culms up to 100 mm diameter *every year*, much to its owner's delight (he claims you can light a cigarette in a cyclone whilst standing behind it). In very severe winds, large leaves tend to tear, but are soon replaced, whereas fine leaves survive well.

Most bamboos suitable for hedges are very fast-growing species. They are easily propagated by digging pieces out to replant further along the hedge row if one can't immediately obtain or purchase the number of plants required for the appropriate spacing (see Chapter 8 for propagation techniques). Remember that, being a sympodial bamboo, it is non-invasive and will not spread along the length of the hedge, nor deviate or extend its width from the line of the hedge without your help. The height and ultimate width is dictated by the species you choose (see Chapter 7 for species descriptions) and the growing conditions. If you think your hedge is too tall, cut the tops of the existing culms to the desired height, and then cut the tops of the new emerging culms (they are still soft) each year when they are about six to eight weeks old (before they develop leaves). The leaves will bush out up to the height you have cut, but the cut culm will not re-grow its tip!

Such windbreaks also reduce wind soil erosion with their virtually impenetrable dense leaf structure, and create wonderful sound or dust barriers when placed along a highway or dirt road.

Topiarising Bamboo

There are infinite variations of man-made distortions to bamboo's natural shape in Asia. In Hong Kong, many of their parks have neatly trimmed hedges of *Bambusa multiplex* var. *riviereorum* (Photo 6I) no more than 700 mm high, dense and box-shaped, simply clipped that way each year after the new crop of shoots has reached close to full height. I have seen *Thyrsostachys siamensis* cut off about 2 m high and clipped with a perfect dome-shaped top (Photo 6J), and both *Bambusa ventricosa* and *B. vulgaris* 'Wamin' (two Buddha's belly-type bamboos) cut off at a chosen height (say 2 or 3 m) to form a bushy top. The emerging new shoots are removed each year and the lower buds taken off to reveal the bulging culm internodes. The result looks more like a bushy-topped palm tree than a bamboo, but the effect is very decorative (commonly used in the streets of Kuala Lumpur).

6.J Thyrsostachys siamensis *topiarised into round-topped decorations*

Stock Control Hedges

If you want to keep cattle or horses out or in, the very elegant erect giant *Bambusa bambos* (giant thorny bamboo) with its sharp nail-like spines on a tangle of low strong branches will make an impenetrable hedge. It also produces superb edible shoots and superior timber, if you are prepared to brave the thorns to harvest them! (We clip the lower branches of our demonstration clump, but we leave the thorny branches on the fifty odd we planted as a cattle hedge.) It is one of the most beautiful and elegant of the tall bamboos in spite of its thorns, and is one of the main larger diameter bamboos used as scaffolding for skyscraper construction in Asia.

Indoor or Outdoor Pot-plants

You can use the fact that bamboos are unhappy about growing in pots to your advantage! They will grow, but they don't grow as large, either in height or culm diameter. Both *Bambusa ventricosa* (Buddha's belly bamboo) and all the *B. multiplex* cultivars make very attractive indoor plants that will only grow to about 20 per cent of their normal height in a large pot; in fact *B. ventricosa* is the main bamboo used in Japan and China for bonsai. Even the beautiful *Bambusa lako*, or *Cephalostachyum pergracile*, will grow to a limited controllable height in a large well-lit, indoor site if well-fed and watered. (*Bambusa lako* grows to about 3 m high and 20 mm diameter in bags, in our heavily shaded well watered nursery.)

■ **6.L** Bambusa multiplex *cv.* *'Fernleaf', pot-grown* *to limit its size*

Security Hedges

If you want to keep people from either seeing or trespassing, the dense fine-leafed *Bambusa blumeana* with its masses of small thorns will certainly discourage human intruders. Planted at 3 m or eventually even 4 m centres it

would be impossible to penetrate. It also produces high quality edible shoots, and superior strong wood. *Bambusa blumeana* is so much in demand in the Philippines for furniture that they are now importing it from Vietnam to make up their shortfall! (It produces twisted wood with beautiful shapes.) Ours contains dozens of finch nests constructed amongst the fine leaves and thorns.

Many other sympodial bamboos will make an impenetrable person hedge without thorns. Depending on the height and width you require, close-planted *Bambusa multiplex* (Photo 5D) or its shorter more upright cultivar 'Alphonse Karr' (Photo 6D), or the taller upright *B. textilis* (Photo 5F) would be quite impossible to climb through because of their close packed strong culms. They are all very fast growing species that can be propagated by digging pieces out to replant further along the hedgerow (see Chapter 8 for propagation techniques).

Soil Slips, Erosion and Riverbank Erosion

Sympodial bamboos make superb soil erosion or riverbank erosion plants. The clump base itself may be small but the very fine web of shallow roots that radiates outwards for three to six times the rhizome base diameter binds the earth in a stocking-like network of great strength, and the bamboo remains just where you planted it! Sympodial bamboos definitely cannot propagate from roots and they will not spread into areas remote from where you plant them. Throughout Asia these bamboos are planted to prevent slips in the roadside banks of steep mountain country immediately after the roads are bulldozed.

Tough species like *Bambusa ventricosa* (Buddha's belly bamboo) or *B. multiplex* will survive river bank floods, drought, cold, wind, extremes of heat, and still hold nature together, as well as providing an attractive landscape piece, good shoots to eat and useful wood for a multitude of purposes. Again, you can choose a species or size to suit height or needs.

Unlike running rhizome sections, it is extremely difficult for a part of a clumping bamboo rhizome to be torn from the bamboo by nature in such a way that it will propagate at a point remote from the parent plant. All sympodial rhizomes are powerfully interconnected within the clump, and clumping bamboos cannot propagate from root matter only.

For creek banks already heavily eroded, I would recommend planting the smaller *B. multiplex* cultivars ('Fernleaf' or 'Alphonse Karr') in the heavily eroded collapsed part of the bank (below flood level) at about 2.5 m centres or wherever you can get a section flat enough to plant. Then plant the parent *multiplex* or *B. ventricosa* about 1.5 to 2 m back from the edge of the collapsed section along the top (at about 5 m centres). The bamboos will survive going underwater and, once the shallow meshed roots spread, they will prevent further collapse and erosion. With a heavily eroded river, I would plant larger bamboos like *B. ventricosa* directly into the eroded area below the flood line, and even larger bamboos along the top, the species depending on that environment's lowest temperature.

I saw one *B. ventricosa* north of Cairns that went underwater during 43 inches of rain in 24 hours, but it sprang to attention afterwards, and the paddocks it was designed to protect at the junction of two creeks remained intact. I know of a *Bambusa balcooa* that has survived for many years well below the flood level of Terrania Creek (at The Channon in northern NSW) that regularly goes underwater and survives.

There are also the massive clumps of *Bambusa vulgaris* cv. 'Vittata' along the banks and below flood level on the river at Lismore, NSW, which have held the banks safe from erosion for generations in the town area despite a succession of massive floods.

The only instance I know where nature became powerful enough to defeat clumping bamboo was in the Northern Territory, Australia, where they had huge monsoonal floods that changed the complete course of rivers, and sent millions of tonnes of earth and river bank to sea. The indigenous species *Bambusa arnhemica* growing along the river was in some cases washed away, together with trees, in complete clumps with all rhizomes still joined and intact. In some cases a number of clumps with their fine webs of roots still entangled, complete with earth, washed out to change the course of nature. I guess now and again, nature reminds us of 'who's boss'.

Dam Wall Consolidation and Wind Erosion

For country people, planting sympodial bamboos in the outer face of dam walls solves a number of problems. The shallow roots bind the surface of the dam wall together and prevent washaway in heavy rain overrun situations. The fine shallow roots will not penetrate through, or deep into, the wall—unlike large tree roots that rot and tend to cause leaks. Sympodial bamboo roots form a very fine strong shallow mat only. The bamboos also provide shade to reduce dam water evaporation, shoots to eat, timber to harvest, and they beautify the site. They are ideal for reducing either wind or water soil erosion.

Edible Shoots, Structural or Furniture Timber, Weaving, Musical Instrument Making

Each bamboo that you select will have useful characteristics, described in detail in the Chapter 7 species descriptions. Further species recommendations are made in the various specialist use chapters.

Recommended Selection Procedure

1. **Establish your lowest cold-climate parameter.** Check whatever climate records you have (for your specific property) for the lowest annual temperature. Climate is the most important factor when selecting your species and your site. Temperature information can be deceptive if interpreted as applying to a wide area. In open fields, ground temperatures can drop two to four Celsius degrees below general air temperatures, light frost often being a good indication of this. Higher locations in low-altitude country, or timber-covered country with some undercover, are usually warmer and less prone to heavy frost. We often see frost in the valley below us that never seems to reach us. If the low temperature expected is close to the lower temperature tolerance of the chosen bamboo, choose your site carefully. From this survey, eliminate the bamboos that won't survive on your property, or choose your microclimate site carefully.

2. **Establish your major reason for planting.** It could be for a hedge, a garden decoration, structure, edible shoots, etc. Look at the usage data and eliminate the ones that don't suit your climate.

3. **Decide on the shape and size you want.** Make a decision as to what can be accommodated in the proposed setting. Different sympodial bamboos develop into a multitude of different shapes, from vertical and erect to pendulous, weeping, mushroom-shaped, flat-lying or climbing.

Air space, ground space, and height are the major deciding factors. Very erect medium/large bamboos such as *Bambusa oldhamii* or the elegant *Dendrocalamus membranaceus* (that can both produce vertical 100 mm culms up to 18 m high) can take up less air space than many lovely smaller pendulous species such as *Bambusa multiplex* cv. 'Fernleaf' (Photo 2A). These are usually only 3 m high but with a drooping culm profile that spreads sideways to cover a 5 m circle. Remember, your choice needs to be planted half its ultimate air space diameter from your neighbour's fence to avoid overhanging, or you will need to remove shoots on that side every year, and occasionally trim off offending culms.

Beautiful willowy bamboos like *Dendrocalamus strictus* or the pendulous *Gigantochloa albociliata* develop very small diameter bases but their air space can be as big as a gum tree.

Small to medium vertical bamboos such as *Gigantochloa wrayi*, *Bambusa textilis*, *Schizostachyum brachycladum*, *Thyrsostachys siamensis*, *Schizostachyum jaculans*, *Bambusa multiplex* cv. 'Alphonse Kerr' and others take up very little ground space, and have relatively smaller upper diameters than most bamboos, making them suitable for even suburban gardens. *Thyrsostachys siamensis* (Photos 1H, 3D, 3J) can even be used a feature in the centre of a courtyard because its very vertical, tightly bunched culm clump is so small, and its delicate fine leafy top is well above head height. Very small elegant species like *Bambusa multiplex* var. *riviereorum* normally grow only 1.5 m high and are quite vertical in profile, taking up very little of any garden space.

Large species such as *Dendrocalamus asper*, *D. latiflorus*, *Gigantochloa atter* or *Bambusa bambos* are all just a little big for most suburban gardens, and can take up to 3 m with their culm and rhizome circle and three times that for air space. However they will never take up the air or ground space that the lusty *Bambusa balcooa* demands (Photo 5I). I have seen rhizome circles of 15 m diameter on massive clumps at least 60 years old, that take up air space of about 30 m diameter because of the species' overhanging mushroom shape. It is often quite beautiful and awe-inspiring, but also a tangled mess of prolific, enthusiastic, and untended growth.

4. **Look at the local rainfall statistics.** Most species are quite drought-tolerant if they get good rain before and during the summer shoot season. Many clumping bamboos are accustomed to survival in a monsoonal climate, where they get heavy rain for half of the year and almost none for the other half. If your annual rainfall is below 600 mm, you'll have to water your mature clumps from time to time (or plant near a pond or greywater outlet from your house). You can choose very drought-hardy species such as *Dendrocalamus strictus*, *Otatea acuminata aztecorum*, *Bambusa bambos*, *B. multiplex* or *B. ventricosa*, or even *Bambusa oldhamii* once established.

5. **Check your chosen species' tolerance to sunlight.** Some more delicate species prefer part or even full shade (see Chapter 5).

■ **6.M** *Dendrocalamus membranaceus, above and right, showing its beautiful fine leaves, normally erect form, and the white bloom still showing on the younger culms*

With so many choices available the elimination process can be pleasurable although initially daunting. However, if you persevere, the choice you make will be worth the effort. You can not only enjoy the beauty and whispers of your choice, but it will most likely provide you with food and timber. It will happen so quickly after planting and in such a spectacular way that it will keep you entertained for many years.

If you get stuck for choice or want to check your decision or the cost, contact a specialist nursery (such as Bamboo World in northern NSW) for advice. Most nurseries know next to nothing about clumping bamboos (or even running bamboos for that matter), and planting the wrong species in the wrong environment can be a costly mistake.

7 Species Descriptions, Identification and Availability

The following species descriptions are not scientific in content, but designed to give the reader a feel for the shape, size and features of the bamboo. Taxonomical jargon and esoteric descriptions of culm leaf shape (valuable to the expert) have been mostly avoided simply because it would take the reader longer to learn the terminology than it would to read this book. The Reference List will give you taxonomical texts of value if you want to expand your knowledge beyond the scope of this book (e.g. PROSEA, McClure, Tewari, etc.).

I have tried to describe some unique aspects of most species that will help the reader to attempt identification. When you live with these beautiful plants, their distinguishing features, some obvious and some subtle, become instinctively identifiable, but describing these differences to an untrained bamboo fan is sometimes esoteric rather than specific. Two examples, *Dendrocalamus latiflorus* and *Gigantochloa atter* are both large, visually similar erect green bamboos. The internode of *D. latiflorus* is smooth (glabrous) whereas the top half of *G. atter*'s internodes are rough (non-glabrous) from fine hairs growing near the node. The large leaves of *G. atter* are a slightly yellowish green and not quite as large or as dark green when compared with the leaves of *D. latiflorus*. The young shoots of *D. latiflorus* are gold/green and almost hairless, whereas the shoots produced by *G. atter* are darker and hairy. An interesting difference exists between *D. latiflorus* and *Bambusa oldhamii*, which is visually a smaller version of *D. latiflorus* complete with smaller leaves. Interestingly, the most recent Chinese taxonomical book seems to have reclassified *B. oldhamii* as *Dendrocalamopsis oldhamii*. (If the experts are still arguing, what hope has the reader got?)

The descriptions are alphabetical, and list genus and species name and cultivar (cv.) if applicable. The description gives maximum achievable height, maximum achievable culm diameter, the minimum temperature the species will normally tolerate (where that is known), its origin, the common name (if applicable), synonyms if any, the bamboo's characteristics (often with clues on how to identify it), the young shoot's shape and colour and whether it's edible, and the bamboo's common uses. Sketches showing the shape of the mature clump of various species are presented in the Guide to Species Shape (page 220). These can be used as a scale to judge the clumps' probable mature diameter (by comparing the stated maximum height with the proportions of the sketch). The text gives references to photographs.

Except in exceptional cases, rather than comment on each bamboo's suitability for edible shoots, structural purposes or furniture making, I have recommended suitable species in those relevant chapters (10, 11 and 14).

All these clumping bamboos are growing at Bamboo World's Botanical Garden at various stages of maturity, as well as many newer acquisitions. In many instances,

■ **7.A** Bambusa bambos *(syn. B arundinacea)—shoots and young culms*

examples of an obviously different cultivar or variation of the same species, often from a different location are available. About two-thirds of those described were available at the time of writing (September, 1998); others are currently being established or propagated in our on-site tissue culture laboratory, or propagated in our nursery, and should be available before long (when the wood is mature enough to propagate).

Sympodial Bamboo Species Descriptions

Bambusa affinis (Munro). 8 m x 5 cm
A new import. Solid (no hole) culms at the base, very erect, with fine leaves.

Bambusa arnhemica. 8 m x 10 cm, to +5°C. (Photo 1F)
ORIGIN: Australia. This beautiful, thick-walled substantial bamboo is only found in NT, Australia. There are two clones that differ sufficiently to be separate cultivars, one having pale iridescent green shoots and delicate, small leaves, and the other dark striped shoots and a longer leaf. The thick-walled sappy culms turn vivid orange as they mature. Each cultivar grows in a region distinct from the other, their delicate pendulous clumps growing in profusion along watercourses. They are partly deciduous in the monsoonal dry periods. It has been used for thousands of years by our Aborigines (various uses include didgeridoo making, long before hollowed eucalypt logs were used by more southern populations). Its sappy quality makes me doubt its quality as a superior structural bamboo, and it would probably suffer higher shrinkage than many other species, but no figures are available. The fairly small shoots are harvested and eaten in spite of their relatively inferior quality and the crocodile-infested National Park monsoonal wetland where they are harvested. (I thought it was illegal to remove plant matter from National Parks!)

Bambusa balcooa (Roxb.). 25 m x 15 cm, to -5°C. (Photo 5I)
COMMON NAMES: baluka or balku bans, syn. Dendrocalamus balcooa. ORIGIN: Indian sub-continent. A very large, very vigorous, attractive structural/furniture making bamboo commonly seen on the NE coast of NSW. It needs space. Grey green culms with aerial root rings around lowest nodes. Strong almost horizontal branching and dark shiny medium leaves almost to ground level make this bamboo difficult to harvest. Large green dark hair-covered shoots are edible only if prepared properly.

Bambusa bambos (Voss). 30 m x 20 cm, to −2°C. (Photo 7A)
COMMON NAME: giant thorny bamboo, syn. B. arundinacea. ORIGIN: South-East Asia, where it is a major source for

superior structural culms and paper making. Forms an enormous impenetrable thorny cattle-proof hedge when planted close together. A superior structural bamboo of great beauty with graceful upright culms and slightly nodding tops. Shining bright green culms and fine light-green leaves. Huge excellent edible shoots, hairless but grotesque with their distorted culm leaf blades and contrasting dark and light colouring.

Bambusa basihirsuta (McClure). New import.

Bambusa beecheyana (Munro). See Dendrocalamopsis beecheyana.

Bambusa bicicatricata (Lin). New import.

Bambusa blumeana (Schult). 18 m x 10 cm, to -7°C.
COMMON NAME: lesser thorny bamboo, syn. B. spinosa. ORIGIN: South-East Asia. A medium vigorous bushy bamboo with attractive sprays of very fine leaves and numerous small hooked thorns. An ideal small stock or person barrier if planted as a hedge or windbreak. The strong dark green culms, thick-walled and sometimes bent or zig-zagged, are much in demand for furniture in the Philippines, which now imports some from Vietnam because of shortage. Produces extraordinary dark purple-tinged shoots with prominent bulging leaf blades. A superior edible shoot.

Bambusa boniopsis (McClure). 4 m x 2 cm, to -7°C.
An attractive smaller vivid green small-leafed Chinese bamboo, bushy to the base and spreading a little higher up.

Bambusa burmanica (Gamble). 15 m x 4 cm, to +5°C.
COMMON NAME: thaikawa. ORIGIN: Thailand/Burma/India/Malaysia. A very strong, mostly solid (holeless) dark green culm with medium large leaves. Used for roofing construction and, when split, thatching and basket making. Similar to B. tulda.

Bambusa cerosissima (McClure). 6 m x 5 cm, to (possibly) -9°C.
Syn. Lingnania cerosissima. Very erect, straight, vivid light green culms without lower branching, then large leaves hanging from drooping tops. Yellowish shoots covered in light hairs. Used in China for weaving.

Bambusa chungii (McClure). 10 m x 6 cm, to -4°C. (Photo 3E)
ORIGIN: China. This very erect beautiful bamboo has thin-walled white-powdered culms exposed for 3 m or more. A truly spectacular garden plant, used for weaving and handicrafts.

Bambusa corniculata (Chai et Fung). New import.

Bambusa dissemulator (McClure). 10 m x 5 cm, to -9°C. New import.

Bambusa dissemulator cv. 'Albinodia' (McClure). 10 m x 5 cm, to -9°C.
ORIGIN: China. Long fine leaves with dark green culms and a white ring at the node, sometimes with white stripes on lower internodes. Shoots light green and gold with darker top.

Bambusa dolichomerithalla. 11 m x 6 cm, to -2°C. Identity not confirmed.
Leafless vivid green culms with prominent creamy white stripe below a head of medium/fine leaves. Shoots light green with cream stripes.

Bambusa edulis (Keng). Syn. *Dendrocalamopsis edulis*.

Bambusa emeiensis (Fu Chaia et Ng). A new import.

Bambusa emeiensis var. 'Viridifavus' (Hsuen et Yi). A new import.

Bambusa eutuldoides (McClure). 12 m x 5 cm, to -9°C.
ORIGIN: China. COMMON NAME: dai ngan bamboo. Very dense and erect with strong straight fine-leafed almost solid culms useful for structures, farm tools and split weaving. Internodes 30–40 cm long. A strong useful smaller timber variety.

Bambusa eutuldoides var. 'Basisiriata' (McClure). A new import.

Bambusa forbesii (Ridley). 5 m x 3 cm, to +5°C. (Photo 7B)
ORIGIN: A native of Queensland, New Guinea and South-East Asia. COMMON NAME: Iron Range bamboo. This very attractive Australian native bamboo, possibly a misidentified *Schizostachyum*, is tight-clumping, vertical and leafless on the lower culm sections, and with very large, vivid green leaves on pendulous overhanging culms. Used for making arrow heads, water pipes, traditional handicrafts and casual drinking vessels in New Guinea. Prefers tropical, damp, semi-shade.

Bambusa gibboides (Lin). A new import.

Bambusa heterocycla (Munro). See *Gigantochloa* sp. 'Malay Dwarf'.

Bambusa intermedia (Hsueh et Yi). A new import.

Bambusa lako (Widjaja). 20 m x 10 cm, to -3°C. (Photos 7C, 18F, 2B)
Syn. *Gigantochloa*. sp. 'Timor Black'. COMMON NAME: au lako, or au meta in the Timor Islands where it is commonly found. This beautiful black bamboo has been sold for many years as *G.* sp. 'Timor Black', and also confused with the very similar *Gigantochloa atroviolacea*. It was taxonomically named only in 1997. The main differences are *B. lako* ('Timor Black') has light green

■ **7.B** Bambusa forbesii *exhibiting its large green leaves*

hairless striped (edible) shoots plus shiny chocolate black culms with an occasional peppermint green stripe, whereas *G. atroviolacea* has sooty black culms and dark hairy stripe-free (also edible) shoots, and slightly wider leaves. One of the world's most beautiful bamboos, its straight erect initially green culms turn chocolate black with age, retaining that colour after harvesting. Valuable for furniture and musical instruments. Spectacular leafless lower culms support a dense profusion of long thin vertically hanging pale green leaves (a little thinner than *G. atroviolacea* leaves). Very highly recommended.

Bambusa lapidea (McClure). A new import.

Bambusa longispiculata (Gamble). 18 m x 10 cm, to +5°C. (Photo 6E)
ORIGIN: Bangladesh/India. COMMON NAME: mitenga (Bengal) and thaikwa (Burma). Forms beautiful open clumps with well-spaced (modified unicaespitose) straight ivory-striped greyish green culms. Large decorative leaves. Structurally good. Spectacular edible shoots are light blue green with unusual cupped blade shape.

Bambusa maculata (Widjaja). 20 m x 12 cm, to -3°C.
COMMON NAME: pring tutul. Recently taxonomically identified as *Bambusa maculata*, it is somewhat confusing, as it was originally known as *B. vulgaris* var. *maculata*, a name later abandoned, now reinstated as a species. This bamboo is as beautiful growing alive as it is after harvesting and ageing. The live culms are an attractive cream striped green; however, the dried culm develops a mottled pattern of rich brown marks scattered generously over its surface. Highly prized as a furniture bamboo in Java and Bali.

■ **7.C** Bambusa lako *with its dark chocolate culms*

Bambusa malingensis (McClure). 10 m x 5 cm, to -7˚C.
ORIGIN: China. COMMON NAME: maling bamboo. Forms tight erect clumps with attractive small-leafed nodding tips. Dark green culms, powder-covered when young, are straight except for an occasional minor zig-zag near base. Edible shoots bronze and light green. Much used in China for shed, tool construction and basketry because of the thick-walled strong wood. Internodes up to 45 cm. Very vigorous growth when young. Plants grown from wild Queensland clumps of this bamboo have been misidentified and sold under various names such as *B.* 'Kennilworth', Mrs Small's bamboo, etc. but we are fairly confident that it is the same species being sold as *B. malingensis* in Australia.

Bambusa multiplex (Lour). 10 m x 4 cm, to -12˚C. (Photo 5D)
ORIGIN: China. The parent cultivar of a very elegant family of bamboos (catalogued immediately following), known as oriental hedge bamboo. Syn. *B. glaucescens*. This one's feathery nodding culms lean outwards from a small dense base to form a mobile puffball that dances in the wind. Leaves are medium-fine light green with blue tinged backs. (All multiplex cultivars have glaucous, or bluish, leaf backs.) Makes a beautiful, fast-growing, cold-tolerant windbreak, or for creek bank or steep hill landslip control. Strong profuse smaller culms make good garden stakes. Extensively used for screens, basketry and various handicrafts when split. All the *multiplex* family have edible shoots if properly prepared. Highly recommended.

***Bambusa multiplex* cv. 'Albo-striata'**. See *B. textilis* cv. 'Albo Striata'.

***Bambusa multiplex* cv. 'Alphonse Karr'**. Normally 4 m but to 10 m x 3.5 cm, to-12˚C. (Photo 6D)
ORIGIN: China. More erect than *multiplex*, it has spectacular bright yellow culms striped with green. The edible young shoots and culms are a delicate green striped pink. The lower third remains relatively leafless, presenting a tight fairly erect clump that bursts into a cap of fine distinctively arranged leaves. A beautiful, smaller (4 m) bamboo for a garden setting, and very popular as a suburban hedge because of its relatively erect form and moderate height. It reaches its full potential height (10 m) only when grown in a dense rainforest canopy.

***Bambusa multiplex* cv. 'Fernleaf'**. 4 m x 1.5 cm, to -12˚C. (Photos 2A, 6L)
ORIGIN: China. Starburst clusters of ten or more small leaves on each twig distinguish this cultivar from its brothers. The willowy outward-reaching form is delicately beautiful, particularly after rain when the extra weight flattens the form into a sparkling cascade. The strong mostly solid culms are used when young for 'cane' woven basket making. A garden piece.

***Bambusa multiplex* cv. 'Golden Goddess'**. 4 m x 1.5 cm, to -12˚C.
ORIGIN: China. Virtually indistinguishable from cv. 'Fernleaf' except for a slightly smaller leaf and culms that mature to a golden colour when growing in full sunlight.

Bambusa multiplex* var. *riviereorum. 2 m x 1 cm, to -12˚C. (Photo 6I)
ORIGIN: China. COMMON NAME: Chinese goddess bamboo. A dwarf variety with very tiny fern-like leaves and golden culms if exposed to full sunlight. This delicate very erect solid-culmed ornamental also does well as a potted plant or a bonsai specimen. A great small garden plant.

***Bambusa multiplex* cv. 'Silverstripe'**. 13 m x 4 cm, to -12˚C.
ORIGIN: China. Has fine white stripes on many of its leaves, and exotic edible pink striped shoots that fade with age. Usually grows 5 m high with cascading culms, except when grown under canopy. A strikingly beautiful plant.

***Bambusa multiplex* cv. 'Stripestem Fernleaf'**. 4 m x 1.5 cm, to -12˚C.
ORIGIN: China. Indistinguishable from 'Fernleaf' except for its fresh culms, which are first pink to yellow and later striped with green.

***Bambusa multiplex* cv. 'Willowy'**. 3 m+ x 2 cm, to -12˚C.
ORIGIN: China. Similar to cv. 'Fernleaf' except for having very fine leaves and arching willowy culms. A striking smaller ornamental.

Bambusa nana (Roxb.). 5 m x 4 cm, to -9˚C. (Photos 7D, 18J)
ORIGIN: China/Asia. Listed sometimes as a synonym of *B. multiplex*, but it is quite different. This very strong,

extremely vertical, attractive fine-leafed bamboo has solid, very straight culms (no hole) with no lower branches or leaves. It grows in a very tight clump tending to be pendulous at the top. It is a very important smaller diameter structural bamboo in Thailand, where it is grown in large plantation areas.

Bambusa nutans (Wall). 12 m x 8 cm, to maybe -5°C.
Erect, strong, green, thick-walled culms, branchless initially, but with leafy pendulous tops. Nodes have a white, sometimes hair-fringed ring. Large dull green leaves with blue tinted (glabrous) backs. Its high quality edible dark green shoots have scattered black hairs. A graceful garden species with strong straight useful poles.

Bambusa oldhamii (Munro). 18 m x 10 cm, to -9°C.
(Photos 1B, 6H)
ORIGIN: Southern China. Syn. *Dendrocalamopsis oldhamii.* This superbly erect, rapid-growing, straight-culmed bamboo takes up less space than most smaller bamboos. With its medium-sized, broad-leafed, dark green clean appearance, it's an ideal slightly larger suburban garden bamboo. Delicious shoots are light green and hairless except for a darker area being revealed by lower culm leaf. A white powder covers the shoots and the normally vivid green relatively thin-walled young culms, which later turn gold in strong sunlight. Beautiful straight timber, much used for furniture making, and light structures. Large plantings exist in China and Taiwan for shoot production in cooler climates, but crop yields are much less than *D. asper* and *D. latiflorus*. Used in NZ and

northern NSW for tall orchard and nursery windbreaks. A cold-tolerant 'must' for any collector. It is commonly known as Oldham's bamboo, and sometimes giant timber bamboo, which is a misnomer because it is not 'giant' and is a poor structural bamboo because of its thin culm walls from about 1 m height onwards.

Bambusa oliveriana. 10 m x 5 cm, to 0°C.
COMMON NAME: wapgusan. ORIGIN: Burma and India. A very pretty, moderate-sized, dense clumping bamboo with thick-walled, strong, straight, glossy green culms that turn golden with age. Makes superior fishing poles. Smallish very pointed delicate leaves. Edible shoots are purple tinged green sporting black hairy stripes on the blades.

Bambusa parchinensis (Hayata). 10 m x 6 cm, to -5°C.
Dark green culms, somewhat powdery when young. Shoots have a hair-covered leathery appearance.

Bambusa pervariabilis (McClure). 15 m x 6 cm, to 0°C.
ORIGIN: Guangdong Province, China. COMMON NAME: punt(ing) pole bamboo (in common with *B. tuldoides*, which it resembles). Its thick-walled, small-leafed, erect green culms are marked with cream stripes on the basal nodes, but turn gold with age. Shoots are purple tinged with light green stripes. Much used in China for farm tool handles, light pole structures, fishing rods, furniture and barge poles because of its strength. We have recently imported a fresh example of the species into Australia because we are of the opinion that the plant sold as *B. pervariabilis* here is actually a clone of *B. eutuldoides*. It is considered by the

■ **7.D** Bambusa nana *plantation in Thailand*

Chinese as a superior bamboo for small structures and edible shoots. It was recently crossed with *Dendrocalamus latiflorus* (we have the cross growing at Bamboo Garden) in an attempt to produce a superior bamboo with the productivity of *D. latiflorus* and the qualities of *B. pervariabilis*.

Bambusa polymorpha (Munro). 20 m x 10 cm, to 5°C. (Identity to be confirmed.)
ORIGIN: Bengal and Burma. Elegantly decorative timber variety with mostly solid (no hole) greyish green culms that have no lower branches in a mature stand. Fine light green leafy top of outstanding beauty if grown in a damp place. Edible slightly bitter shoots are cream striped dark green with purple-tipped, spoon-shaped blades.

Bambusa remotiflora (Kuntze). A new import.

Bambusa ridleyi. 5 m x 2.5 cm, to +5°C.
ORIGIN: Malaysia. This bamboo (different to *Gigantochloa ridleyi*) forms a very attractive, erect, pendulous-topped clump with internodes up to 45 cm. Used for weaving splits.

Bambusa rigida (Keng et Keng). A new import.

Bambusa rutila (McClure). A new import.

Bambusa sinospinosa (McClure). 24 m x 14 cm, to +2°C.
ORIGIN: China. COMMON NAMES: Chinese thorny bamboo or spiny bamboo. A very dense fine-leafed thorny bamboo ideal as a person- or cattle-proof fence and windbreak. Strong timber is hard to harvest. Edible shoots are often pickled.

Bambusa sp. 'Bengal Thorny'. A new introduction. There appear to be many slight variations of *B. bambos* in different areas, this being one of them.

Bambusa surrecta (Q H Dai). A new import.

Bambusa textilis (McClure). 12 m x 6 cm, to -15°C. (Photo 5F)
ORIGIN: China. COMMON NAME: weaver's bamboo (six cultivars). Spectacular very dense straight strong thin-walled almost vertical culms with long (40 to 60 cm) internodes. Younger dark green culms turn gold in the sun when mature. No leaves or branches on the lower half, followed by masses of long green pointed leaves, makes this a striking bamboo. Edible pale green hairless shoots with long pointed culm leaf blade contrast with initially white powdered culms that darken as it grows. Prized for its strong weaving splits and for general handicraft, flute and furniture uses. Very cold-tolerant.

Bambusa textilis cv. 'Albo-Striata'. I believe this is actually a mistaken identity for *Bambusa multiplex* 'Silverstripe', sometimes also called *B. multiplex* cv. 'Albo-Striata'.

Bambusa textilis var. *fasca* (McClure). (Photo 1M)
Differs from *B. textilis* only in that the culm sheaths have a light scattering of brown hair and a shorter blade, and the culms lack the initial white powdery appearance.

Bambusa textilis var. *glabra* (McClure). Differs from *B. textilis* above only in that it has a smoother (glabrous) hairless culm and sheath. A magnificent looking bamboo.

Bambusa textilis var. *gracilis* (McClure). 6 m x 4 cm, to -12°C.
ORIGIN: Subtropical China. COMMON NAME: slender weaver's bamboo. Again, almost identical to *B. textilis*, but smaller in height and culm diameter. This is an ideal graceful suburban garden plant (or hedge to block out the construction next door) because of its very erect form.

Bambusa textilis cv. 'Maculata'. Differs from *B. textilis* only in that the culms have purple brown-coloured stripes.

Bambusa textilis cv. 'Purpurescens'. Differs from *B. textilis* only in that the culms are either a mid dark purple brown colour.

Bambusa tulda (Roxb.). 25 m x 8 cm, to -2°C.
ORIGIN: India, where it is a major source of paper pulp. COMMON NAME: Bengal bamboo. A fast-growing, often deciduous, superior structural bamboo (tensile strength tested at 52 000 psi). It has large leaves on upper branches and fewer smaller leaves lower down. Fairly straight very smooth dark green culms with no hole or almost no hole in the lower part of the culm. Edible slightly bitter shoots (often pickled) have spectacular bulging blue-green blades and contrasting black hairs scattered over the upper sheath. Used extensively for furniture, basket making and a wide range of household utensils, and as concrete reinforcing. The sacred flute called 'eloo' used by the priests of Arunachal Pradesh is made from *B. tulda*. It was exported to UK as Calcutta cane for split constructed fishing rods. Grows very erect straight culms if planted in a forest environment.

Bambusa tuldoides (Munro). 12 m x 6 cm, to -9°C.
ORIGIN: China. COMMON NAME: punt pole bamboo. Attractive thick-walled, very strong, very straight, nearly erect, dark green culms. Edible shoots, light green with bronze blade, and with occasional white stripes. A frost-resistant, vigorous grower. Tensile strength tests exceed 40 000 psi. It is the main smaller diameter structural bamboo used in Hong Kong and Guangdong Province. Highly recommended.

Bambusa tuldoides cv. 'Swolleninternode' (Xia). A new import, similar to the parent, but with swollen internodes that look quite different in shape to *B. ventricosa*.

Bambusa variostriata (Lin). A new import.

Bambusa ventricosa (McClure). 17 m x 5 cm, to -9°C.
(Photo 6K)

ORIGIN: China. COMMON NAME: Buddha's belly bamboo. The lower internodes become short and swollen like a Buddha's belly, and are valued for their furniture making and decorative uses. Dark green culms turn gold when mature. Well-suited as an indoor potted plant or bonsai variety. Grows well in poor soil, and dry areas for wind-break or creek erosion. Makes an impenetrable hedge. Leaves are high protein fodder. Edible shoots are pointed and green/gold.

Bambusa viridi-vittata (Lin). A new striped import.

Bambusa vulgaris (Schrader). 25 m x 15 cm, to -2°C.

ORIGIN: uncertain. The most common species in the world, but rare in Australia. Good in wet places for soil erosion. Has attractive, dark green culms and long thin leaves. Bitter edible shoots with unusual cupped blades. Commonly used for structures in Asia, but is inferior because its high starch content makes it prone to powder beetle destruction.

***Bambusa vulgaris* cv. 'Vittata'**. 15m x 12 cm, to -2°C.
(Photos 5H, 20C)

COMMON NAME: painted bamboo. Syn *Bambusa vulgaris* Schrader. This spectacular decorative bamboo is a must for those with the space available. Its bright yellow culms are randomly striped with dark green, and the distinctive leaf formations cling glove-like to the culm forms. The bitter edible peppery shoots, prized by Vietnamese people, are spectacular with green gold colours and black hair patches, with protruding cup-shaped culm leaf blade shapes. Commonly used for structures, but inferior due to high starch content. Fairly drought-resistant, but very vigorous with adequate water.

***Bambusa vulgaris* cv. 'Wamin'**. 15 m x 12 cm, to -2°C.
(Photos 5G, 8C, 22B)

A larger and even more spectacular giant Buddha's belly-type bamboo. Verdant green with long narrow green leaves, the large diameter culm internodes develop a powerful bulging form on the lower 2 or 3 m of the culms, accentuated by the absence of lower leaf growth. Harsh conditions cause more spectacular distorted foreshortened internodes. Very bitter edible shoots somewhat similar in shape to *B. vulgaris*.

Cephalostachyum pergracile (Munro). 10 m x 5 cm, to +4°C. (Photo 3K)

ORIGIN: Asian Pacific. COMMON NAME: tinwa bamboo. Syn. *Schizostachyum pergracile*. This very attractive garden specimen has very straight, erect, lower leafless, light green culms covered with a white bloom when young. The unusual bronze/orange culm leaf is covered in dark hairs near the base, and has a cupped orange blade, prominent amongst the branchless leafless lower culms.

Widely used for light construction and as a flavour-imparting 'skin rice' cooking bamboo. Also valued for mats, weaving and basketry due to its splitting ability. A prized garden specimen in Asia.

Cephalostachyum virgatum (Kurz). 10 m x 8 cm, to -2°C.

ORIGIN: Burma/Thailand. This very vertical long-leafed bamboo with its pale green vertically hanging leaves is a particularly attractive garden or hedge species. It has no culm leaves for the first 2 m when mature. Also used for rafters and weaving.

Chusquea coronalis. 7 m x 2.5 cm, to -6°C.

ORIGIN: Mexico. This unusual stunning bamboo has tiny leaves in dense clusters. A spectacular decorative bamboo, it doesn't grow well in our subtropical climate.

Chusquea liebmannii. 8 m x 2 cm, -4°C.

ORIGIN: South America. This beautiful bamboo has florets of leaves distinctly spaced along arching culms.

Chusquea pitteri. 15 m x 5 cm, to -4°C.

ORIGIN: Mexico. This equally unusual bamboo has fine-leafed culms that climb into the air and arch over to hang down unless it can find a handy tree to climb through and upwards.

Dendrocalamopsis beecheyana (Munro). See *B. beecheyana*.

Dendrocalamopsis oldhamii (Munro). See *B. oldhamii*.

Dendrocalamopsis stenoaurita (Lin). 12 m x 8 cm, to -2°C. (Photo 9A)

ORIGIN: China. A beautiful straight, vertical green bamboo with leafless lower culms. High quality edible shoots and good timber.

Dendrocalamus asper (Back). (Indonesian sourced) 30 m x 30 cm, to -5°C. (Photos 2C, 21C)

ORIGIN: SE Asia. This ex-Indonesia clone is not recommended for plantation use. COMMON NAME: bamboo betung. A magnificent giant, it is the most important large diameter structural and furniture making clumping bamboo in Asia, and is used when split as reinforcing in concrete. It's a close relative of the most important clumping edible shoot producer (see *D. asper* 'Thai Green' below), with huge plantations in Thailand. A mature clump is a truly awesome sight with its huge relatively straight furry grey-green lower culms framed in dense very large-leafed upper growth. Lower culm nodes mostly have aerial roots. It has huge, delicious, dark brown purple-tinged hairy shoots. Very highly recommended.

***Dendrocalamus asper* cv. 'Hitam' Widjaja**. 30 m x 30 cm, to -5°C. (Photo 5B)

ORIGIN: Central Java. The world's largest black bamboo.

COMMON NAME: betung hitam (Indonesia). Identical to the above Indonesian variety except for having black culms that retain their colour after curing. Extremely valuable as a large furniture making culm.

***Dendrocalamus asper* cv. 'Thai Green'.** 30 m x 30 cm, to -5°C. (Photos 4B, 7B, 10A, 21A, 21B, 21E, 21I, 21J, 21P, 21V, 21W)
COMMON NAME: pai tong keo. This is the only *D. asper* clone that is suitable for edible shoot plantations, because it is not vulnerable to death by gregarious flowering for at least 100 years. (We are also tissue culturing this bamboo in plantation quantities for that reason, and to make it available at reduced prices.) The recent origin of this clone is Thailand, which had 54 000 hectares of *D. asper* growing in plantations. See Chapter 21 for details.

***Dendrocalamus asper* cv. 'Pai Tong Dam'**. 30 m x 30 cm, to -5°C. (Photos 10B, 10C, 21K, 21L, 21M, 21N, 21O)
This cultivar, otherwise similar to *D. asper* above, has slightly larger, darker green culms than the 'green' variety grown in Thailand. (The Thai word for 'black' is *dam*, but it is not black like 'Hitam'.)

Dendrocalamus basihirsuta (McClure). 12 m x 8 cm, to about -5°C or more.
ORIGIN: China. Syn. *Dendrocalamopsis* (or even *Bambusa*) *basihirsuta*. An attractive very erect straight-culmed plant with no branches or leaves for some metres. The young green culms and shoots are white powder covered with a scattering of brown hairs on the culm sheath.

Dendrocalamus bambusoides (Hsueh). A new import.

Dendrocalamus barbatus (Hsueh). (Photo 7E) A new import.

Dendrocalamus barbatus* var. *internodiiradicatusdicatus (Hsueh et Li). A new import.

Dendrocalamus beecheyana (Munro). 12 m x 10 cm, to -9°C.
ORIGIN: Probably China. Syn. *Dendrocalamopsis beecheyana* and *Bambusa beecheyana*. COMMON NAME: beechey bamboo. Culms green with whip-like, pendulous tops, and with no lower culm branches. It often has slightly bulging internodes. Leaves medium but varied in size. Shoots green orange tinted with black hairs reducing from base of culm leaf, which has a very small blade. A highly valued bamboo for its superior edible shoots, sometimes grown in small plantations.

Dendrocalamus bicicatricata (Lin). 10 m x 7 cm, to -5°C or more.
ORIGIN: China. A fine to medium-leafed bamboo with thick-walled culms with slightly convex internodes and a sometimes double node annulus on lower nodes.

■ **7.E** Dendrocalamus barbatus

Edible shoots are green with bronze streaks, lightly covered with black hair and with very small sheath blades.

Dendrocalamus brandisii (Munro). 36 m x 20 cm, to -4°C. (Photos 1L, 11B, 25H)
ORIGIN: India. The tallest bamboo in the world, this vigorous giant produces thick-walled strong green culms covered with a velvet bloom of pale hairs, imparting a slightly milky appearance. It shows strong aerial root growth on the lower nodes. Lower culms branchless for many metres, then masses of very large, light green leaves. Huge delicious edible shoots are dark bronze and hair-covered, with purple blades. Extensively used for house construction, furniture making and paper production, but becoming rare. It is grown in edible shoot plantations in Yunan, China.

Dendrocalamus calostachyus (Kurz). 25 m x 15 cm, to -3°C.
ORIGIN: Burma (Myanmar). This large, tufted bamboo is quite similar to *Bambusa balcooa* and is used for small buildings, water vessels and domestic utensils. It was said to be available in Australia grown from seed sourced from India, but in fact is a clone of *D. strictus*.

Dendrocalamus giganteus (Munro). 30 m x 30 cm, to -2°C. (Photos 1E, 3A, 25C)

COMMON NAME: giant bamboo. Syn. *Bambusa gigantea*. ORIGIN: Burma/Thailand. The world's largest bamboo, it tends to be slower growing and smaller in Australia's cooler climate. (Theoretically *D. asper* is capable of reaching the same size, and is a better performer at Bamboo World.) Its smooth erect culms have a distinctly blue tinge to their dark green, often powdery appearance, with no branches for 12 m or more, and aerial roots on lowest nodes. Medium green leaves. It produces huge dark blue-black hair-covered shoots. Its strong culms are extensively used for construction in the Burma– Thailand–Vietnam area. It has high quality edible shoots.

Dendrocalamus hamiltonii (Nees et Arn). 18 m x 18 cm. A large huge-leafed erect bamboo with no lower leaves for the first 4 m, highly valued for edible shoots, and grown in some plantations.

Dendrocalamus latiflorus (Munro). 24 m x 20 cm, to -4°C. (Photos 6B, 9C, 20B, 21Q, 21R, 21S, 21U)

ORIGIN: Southern China/Taiwan. COMMON NAME: Taiwan giant bamboo. One of the most beautiful of the large bamboos, and the major species grown in huge edible shoot plantation areas in Southern China and Taiwan. Its smooth green, straight, long internoded culms are leaf-free initially, with masses of huge (up to 40 cm x 8 cm) dark green leaves above. Nodes up to 60 cm. The valuable edible shoots are light green with orange to bronze tops, smooth except for a scattering of sparse temporary black hairs revealed as culm leaves telescope upwards.

■ **7.F** Dendrocalamus minor *var.* amoenus

The Chinese cook rice balls in the very large leaves. Highly recommended and commercially valuable. We are tissue culturing the particular clone used in Chinese plantations in plantation quantities to establish the Australian shoot industry.

***Dendrocalamus latiflorus* cv. 'Mei Nung'**. 24 m x 20 cm, to -4°C. (Photos 5C, 10E)

An even more beautiful version of *D. latiflorus*, with lighter lemon-green culms randomly striped with dark green. The very large leaves also have occasional yellow stripes.

Dendrocalamus longispathus (Kurz). A new import.

Dendrocalamus membranaceus (Munro). 20 m x 10 cm, to -4°C. (Photo 6M)

ORIGIN: Burma/Thailand. A beautiful lowlands species noted for its very smooth, straight erect lower branch-free culms followed by fine light green leaves. The green culms are white powder covered when young, imparting a misty blue appearance. Its unusual pale golden shoots are purple leaf tipped, and blue tinged with powder. Its slightly bitter edible shoots are prized, and it produces superior timber. Highly recommended as an erect garden species.

***Dendrocalamus membranaceus* cv. 'Fine Leaf'**. 20 m x 10 cm, to -4°C.

This appears to be a fine-leafed variation of *D.* membranaceus above (not yet confirmed). It has finer clouds of vivid green leaves clustering densely along its branches, but is otherwise similar. A very beautiful plant.

Dendrocalamus minor (McClure). 6 m x 6 cm, to -3°C. A new import. A green version of the next described.

Dendrocalamus minor* var. *amoenus (McClure). 6 m x 6 cm, to -3°C. (Photo 5E, 7F)

A new import. Very erect large-leafed exotic striped bamboo, lime and dark green striped culms. One of the most beautiful bamboos I have ever seen.

Dendrocalamus pendulus (Ridley). 30 m x 30 cm, to -3°C. A pendulous, nodding-topped variety of *D. asper*, otherwise similar.

Dendrocalamus sericeus (Munro). A new import with very beautiful large leaves and erect culms.

Dendrocalamus sikkimensis (Gamble). 20 m x 20 cm, to +2°C. (Photos 1A, 7G)

ORIGIN: India. COMMON NAME: bhalu bans. This magnificent bamboo is very similar to, and has been confused in Australia with, *Gigantochloa levis*. Its dark green culms turn orange-bronze as they mature if exposed to sunlight. Its spectacular edible shoots are coloured by rich dark-red velvet hairs. Much used for structures and 'chungas', a water or milk carrying vessel.

■ **7.G** Dendrocalamus sikkimensis *with its sun-burnished orange culms*

Dendrocalamus sinicus (Chai et Sun). 30 m x 30 cm, to -2°C. (Photos 3F, 7H)
A new import, this is the largest bamboo in China. Its grotesque distorted lower nodes and twisting short internodes make it one of the spectacular bamboos of the world, like huge upside down elephant trunks. Its huge leaves start well above the ground.

Dendrocalamus strictus (Roxb.) Nees. 18 m x 8 cm, to -5°C. (Photo 6G)
ORIGIN: India. COMMON NAME: male bamboo. Syn. *Bambusa stricta*. A drought-resistant bamboo with small light green furry leaves. Its strong, lower erect, grey-green, slightly rough culms form a very tight packed clump. Culms are often without hole for about half their length, and are without lower branches or leaves, displaying the tight vertical culms. The pendulous upper culms and their fine-leafed display are very graceful. An added feature is the visible retained paper-like lower culm leaves. The shoots, light green and lightly powdered, are edible but inferior and bitter. A major paper pulp and structural bamboo of India. Highly recommended.

Dendrocalamus yunnanicus (Hseuh). A new import.

Dinochloa scandens (Blume). 10 m x 1 cm, to -2°C.
ORIGIN: Asian and Pacific rainforest. A climbing bamboo with fascinating rough black culms and large decorative ovate leaves. Suitable as an indoor plant.

■ **7.H** Dendrocalamus sinicus *with its huge twisting culms*

Dinochloa morheadii. 12 m x 2 cm, to +5°C.
Indigenous to north Queensland rainforests. An almost solid-culmed, slightly medium-leafed, climbing, cane-like bamboo with medium ovate leaves, often mistaken for a rattan cane (palm family). The Queensland species may be a misidentified species, unique to Australia.

Drepanostachyum falcatum. 4 m x 3mm, to -9°C.
ORIGIN: Himalayan Mountains, Asia. Syn. *Bambusa gracilis* and *Dendrocalamus gracilis*. A recent small shade-preferring introduction. An exquisite graceful cold-tolerant bamboo with slender cascading culms with thick sprays of fine long light green leaves on multiple branch clusters. Prefers shade or cool climate or indoors, but grows well in a sub-tropical environment.

Drepanostachyum khasianum. 4 m x 3 mm, to -9°C.
ORIGIN: Himalayan Mountains. Similar to *D. falcatum* but with slightly larger leaves.

Fargesia collaris (Yi). Syn. *Himalayacalamus falconeri*.

Fargesia fungosa (Yi). Syn. *Borinda fungosa*. A new introduction.

Fargesia gyirongensis (Yi). Syn. *Himalayacalamus falconeri*.

Fargesia murieliae. 4 m x 1 cm, to -20°C.
Syn. *Thamnocalamus murielae*. COMMON NAME: umbrella bamboo. This very beautiful small bamboo doesn't grow well in a warm climate. It is very popular in Europe and USA where it recently (1995) flowered gregariously and destroyed itself all over the world. It is almost indistinguishable from *Thamnocalamus spathaceus* and very similar to *Drepanostachyum falcatum*, both of which do grow well in a sub-tropical shady spot.

Fargesia nitida (Mitford). 4 m x 2 cm, to -20°C.
ORIGIN: China's high provinces. The identification of this beautiful small bamboo was only clarified in 1995 by Kew Garden's taxonomist Chris Stapleton, made possible by the almost simultaneous flowering of a number of *Fargesia* bamboos, one species for the first time in 110 years! An erect, fine-leafed, delicate species, not unlike *Bambusa multiplex* var. *riviereorum*. Prefers a cold climate.

Fargesia spathacea. 4 m x 1 cm, to -20°C.
ORIGIN: China's Sichuan and Gansu Provinces. COMMON NAME: fountain bamboo. This delightful small bamboo needs shade or a cool climate. As its common name implies, its slender erect culms are pendulous higher up, and covered in fine long leaves on a multiple-branching system; water fountain shape. It is similar in appearance to *F. murieliae*, but a little more erect. There is a cross identification problem here with *Fargesia murieliae* (Stapleton 1995).

Gigantochloa atroviolacea (Widjaja). 16 m x 10 cm, to -2°C.
ORIGIN: Collected by us in Java (1995). COMMON NAMES: Java black bamboo and pring wulung (Java). This magnificent, very erect, sooty, black-culmed bamboo, which retains its black colouring after harvesting, is much valued for furniture and musical instrument making in Java. The culms, sometimes with light coloured stripes, are exposed and leafless for some metres, then capped with dense downward pointing leaves. The dark hair covered shoot is edible.

Gigantochloa sp. 'Timor Black'. See *Bambusa lako*. Recently taxonomically named.

Gigantochloa auriculata (Kurz). A new import.

Gigantochloa albociliata (Munro). 10 m x 6 cm, to 0°C.
ORIGIN: Burma and Thailand. Syn. *Oxytenanthera albociliata*. This beautifully decorative bamboo has densely placed erect, grey/green slightly rough culms with white stripes. It forms a tight leafless clump under the higher, pendulous, vertically hanging, large, slightly rough light green leaves. It has delicious, edible, lightly striped young shoots initially covered in tawny hairs. The almost solid culms are used extensively in light construction and furniture (ideal for heating and bending).

Gigantochloa apus (Schultes). 20 m x 10 cm, to -2°C. (Photo 11A)
ORIGIN: Malaysia. COMMON NAME: string bamboo or pring tali. Dark grey/green slightly rough culms partly obscured by retained lower culm leaves, and very large leaves identify this attractive species. Young shoots are dark green but covered in black hairs. Strong and durable, it is the most used species in Java for roof rafters. The young culms, up to 3 cm wall thickness, are split into thin strong weaving flats for making 'tomplok' carrying baskets, split into grass roof lashing, and made into rope and cord. The bitter young shoots are buried in mud for four days before cooking and eating. Highly recommended.

Gigantochloa atter (Hassk) Kurz. 20 m x 15 cm, to 0°C. (Photo 6C)
ORIGIN: Indonesia. COMMON NAME: pring legi and awi temen (Indonesia). This magnificent, erect, clean green, vigorous, straight-culmed, superior bamboo is a classic amongst the larger species. Its otherwise smooth culms are increasingly sandpaper rough to touch on the upper internodes, and its large light green leaves slightly rough textured. Known as the 'sweet bamboo' for its young edible shoots, which are covered in purple black hairs. It is extensively used for building structures, handicrafts, furniture, weaving, etc. Attractive, Very strong and highly recommended.

Gigantochloa atter cv. 'Pring Legi' (Striped). 25 m x 10 cm, to 0°C.

■ **7.1** Gigantochloa *sp. 'Malay Dwarf Variegated'*

Recently retrieved by us in NE Java as a massive rooted culm, this beautiful cultivar of the preceding bamboo has prominent cream stripes on light green culms, and looks stunning.

Gigantochloa compressa (Parkinson). A new import.

Gigantochloa hasskarliana (Kurz). 10 m x 6 cm, to -2°C. (Photo 4A)
ORIGIN: West Java. Syn. *Schizostachyum hasskarliana*. Planted often to form hedges or to prevent soil erosion, it is also widely used after splitting as a weaving and basket-making bamboo. Its fast growing vigorous very dense clumping structure is attractive with large leaves up to 35 cm x 5 cm, and ideally suited to erosion control or hedgerows. Ours flowered sporadically (which it is known to do regularly) and we managed to find three viable seeds!

Gigantochloa hosseusii (ex Thailand). A new import.

Gigantochloa levis (Blanco). 20 m x 18 cm, to +4°C.
ORIGIN: Philippines and Sabah. Syn. *G. scribneriana* and *D. curranii*. This beautiful superior straight-culmed bamboo develops orange tinted shoots covered in brown hairs. Young culms on mature clumps are branchless for some height and carry an overall cover of brown hairs on the basal internodes, becoming almost hairless and smooth light green up higher. Highly prized for general construction and furniture, and for its sweet edible shoots.

Dendrocalamus sikkimensis was mistakenly sold in Australia for many years as this bamboo, and overseas it is often confused with *G. thoii*, common in Malasia.

Gigantochloa ligulata (Gamble). A new import.

Gigantochloa sp. var. 'Malay Dwarf'. 6 m x 5 cm, to -2°C.
ORIGIN: Malaysia. Its as yet unconfirmed identification is probably *Bambusa hetrostachya*. This attractive erect green ornamental makes a nice smaller statement in the garden, or creates a great controllable hedge. Will grow taller than its specified height with no lower leaves when grown in a canopy.

Gigantochloa sp. var. 'Malay Dwarf Variegated'. 3 m x 2.5 cm, to -2°C. (Photo 7I)
ORIGIN: Malaysia. As with the above 'green' variety, its identity, as yet unconfirmed, is probably *Bambusa hetrostachya* cv. 'Variegated'. Smaller and bushier than its parent, this very attractive bushy variegated green/-cream-leafed ornamental makes a nice smaller statement in the garden, or creates a great controllable hedge. Occasionally it throws a culm that has reverted to the parent 'green' form (described above), easily cut off to retain the distinctive variegated shape and form.

Gigantochloa manggong (Widjaja). 15 m x 7 cm, to 0°C.
ORIGIN: Indonesia, where it is quite rare. Branchless and leafless for about 3 m, the green culms turn yellow with maturity. Dull yellow to brown shoot, smooth except for black haired blade. Edible but bitter. Used in light construction work. A very attractive mid-sized large-leafed species.

Gigantochloa nigrociliata (Buse) Kurz. 20 m x 6 cm, to -3°C.
COMMON NAME: black-hair giantgrass. Erect vivid green culms tinted by dark brown hairs on upper internodes. Lower 2 m or more branchless with large leaves above. The shoots, grey-green and covered with brown appressed hairs, are edible after fermenting.

Gigantochloa pseudoarundinacea (Steudel). 30 m x 13 cm, to -2°C. (Photo 3G)
ORIGIN: SE Asia. Syn. *G. maxima* and *G. verticilliata*. This beautiful, very erect, superior structural giant has cream striped light green, slightly rough culms, with aerial roots

on the lowest nodes, and very large, slightly rough, light green leaves on branches starting about 3 m above the ground. Young shoots are yellow-green with green stripes and orange flushes, initially with a scattering of brown hair. It is cultivated extensively for building materials, water pipes, furniture, household utensils and basketry, and has edible shoots.

It rarely reaches anything like its full height potential, but it is one of the most beautiful large bamboos in the world (there is a stunning example in Guangzhou Botanical Gardens, China).

Gigantochloa ridleyi (Holttum). 18 m x 10 cm, to 0˚C. (Photo 1G) (Identity yet to be confirmed.)

Collected recently in Bali and yet to mature enough for final identification, it is used for roof rafters. A very useful straight culmed large-leafed handsome bamboo, often planted as an ornamental. It tends to retain its culm leaves on the leafless lower culm sections, making it somewhat similar to but greener than *G. apus*. Its origin is not known as it is now only available where cultivated. Having seeded in 1995, our clones came from new seedlings in Bali. This is a different species to *Bambusa ridleyi*.

Gigantochloa ridleyi cv. **'Jajang Stone'**. 18 m x 10 cm, to 0˚C.

This bamboo is identical to the above clone except for an attractive grey/green mottled stone-like appearance covering the culms. As it was flowering at the same time as the 'green' Jajang, we have to wait until both clones are mature to see if the difference is still apparent; however, the local people insist that they are two distinctly different bamboos.

Gigantochloa sp. **'Rachel Carson'** (Muller). 25 m x 10 cm, to 0˚C.

Collected by L. Muller in Jambi Garis Putin, Sumatra, and registered as species 'G.38'. Very attractive cream stripes on a vivid green culm, and large leaves. Cream striped green shoots.

Gigantochloa robusta (Kurz). 20 m x 10 cm, to 0˚C.

ORIGIN: Probably Indonesia. Syn. *G. verticillata*, but this classification includes other bamboos and is not specific. This magnificent superior very erect giant is spectacular, with its yellow/cream striped green leafless lower culms and its verdant large-leafed canopy starting about 3 m above ground. The upper internodes are slightly hairy, and the lowest nodes develop aerial roots. Massive young shoots are brown-green and covered with scattered dark brown hairs. We dug our clone from the back blocks of Java in 1995. Used for heavy construction, handicrafts, musical instruments, and furniture. High quality shoots are edible. There is a magnificent example trying to push the roof out of Kew Gardens, (UK) largest hot house.

Gigantochloa thoii (Wong). 16 m x 12 cm, to 0˚C.

ORIGIN: Malaysia. Often confused with *G. levi* which is more common in the Philippines and Sabah. *Gigantochloa thoii* has whitish waxy culms and a sparse covering of dark hairs on the upper part of the lower culm internodes, different to *G. levi*. This is a strong attractive large-leafed bamboo with superior timber and high quality edible shoots that are pale green covered with dark brown hairs. Culms are leafless for 2 m or more, revealing the attractive lower culm structure. A smaller version, but similar to bamboos such as *Dendrocalamus. asper*, *D. levi*, *D. brandisii*, or *G. atter*.

Gigantochloa wrayi (Gamble). 10 m x 7 cm, to -1˚C. (Photo 6F)

ORIGIN: Malaysia. A smaller very attractive species with long internodes, used for basket making and light structures. When mature it forms a very tight small diameter leafless vertical culm clump that explodes into a medium large leaf cluster about 4 to 5 m above the ground. It is very elegant, and an ideal suburban garden bamboo, taking up less ground and air space than most trees.

Guadua amplexifolia. 18 m x 15 cm, to -2˚C.

ORIGIN: South America. A smaller and less thorny bamboo than *G. angustifolia*, also considered an excellent structural bamboo, but not as straight. It is easily identified by its unique vertically pointing leaves. Medium-small leaves, and single branched lower nodes, the number of node branches tending to increase higher up. Prominent white banded, closely spaced nodes. Green bronze young shoots with dark reddish blade tips.

Guadua angustifolia. 25 m x 20 cm, to -2˚C. (Photos 3H, 21T)

ORIGIN: South America. One of the best and most beautiful structural bamboos in the world, it is also claimed in one reference to be rot and insect-resistant (denied by Columbian architect Oscar Hidalgo), but is probably of similar quality to the most superior bamboos of SE Asia when harvested and treated properly. Plantations in Costa Rica established ten years ago are being used to build thousands of government sponsored earthquake proof bamboo houses. Very straight, thick-walled, well spaced, dark green culms with prominent (25 mm wide) white bands at each of its closely spaced nodes. Culms branchless for 3 to 5 m, with vivid light green, medium-sized leaves (we have two clones, one narrow-leafed and one broad). This is normally a very thorny bamboo, but we do have a less thorny cultivar. See genus descriptions in Chapter 3 for *Guadua's* unique branching system. Dark red to light bronze shoots contrast with the new green internode during early growth. Spectacular when mature. It is a modified unicaespitose sympodial bamboo, which means it has longer rhizome necks that cause the culms to be well spaced, and the clump to take up more ground space than other large genera such as *Gigantochloa* or *Dendrocalamus*.

Guadua chacoensis. 28 m x 20 cm to -2°C.
Commonly called *G. atlantica*, this is a larger species than *G. angustifolia*, a very beautiful, powerful, structural bamboo, similar in quality and strength to the larger *Dendrocalamus. asper* cultivars but very thorny.

Guadua paniculata. 10 m x 6 cm, to -2°C.
A very elegant smaller thin-walled species with showers of fine light green leaves and a beautiful light pendulous form. Small hooked thorns can be a hazard if one is walking by.

Himalayacalamus falconeri. 3 to 5 m x 2 to 3 cm, to -12° or more.
Syn. *Fargesia falconeri*. A new introduction identified as a synonym of *Fargesia gyirongensis* and *Fargesia collaris* (two different species) and *Thamnocalamus falconeri*. Taxonomically confusing. A slender, pendulous, elegant, fine-leafed bamboo from the Himalayas that grows well in our environment.

Melocanna baccifera (Roxb.). 20 m x 7 cm, to -3°C.
ORIGIN: India. Syn. *Melocanna bambusoides*. COMMON NAME: berry bamboo. This unusual bamboo forms a wide spaced open clump (modified unicaespitose rhizomes). Erect straight culms form up to 1 m apart. Its huge leaves (up to 30 cm x 5 cm) and the largest fruit of all bamboos make it individual. The fruit is an edible smooth pear shape up to 12 cm x 6 cm and 180 g, with a fairly small central seed. (Most bamboos have seed not unlike wheat.) This bamboo is widely used for a great variety of activities such as structures, woven objects including mats, hats, baskets, domestic utensils. Shoots are an important food in Chittagong, even sliced and dried for 'off season' use. People also brew an alcoholic wine from the leaves.

It grows well in our nursery, but we have not succeeded in establishing a plant that grows well in the field.

Nastus elatus (Holttum). 20 m x 10 cm, to -1°C. (Photos 1I, 3L, 8B)
ORIGIN: New Guinea. This extremely elegant, fast-growing bamboo has long narrow light green hanging leaves with bright green culms that turn yellowish with age and exposure. Its tall initially erect growth habit ends with gracefully drooping culm tips. Young shoots are spectacular vivid green, white powder tinted and with rose pink culm leaf edges. Some say it is the best eating bamboo in the world, with sweet shoots that can be eaten raw; however, I have tasted *Dendrocalamus. asper* shoots grown covered by a bag that tasted sweet and non-astringent, and better than the *Nastus* shoots I have eaten. It will not tolerate wet feet for even a short time, so don't plant it in a recess. A beautiful garden specimen.

Nechouzeaua mekongensis. 3 m x 1 cm, to +4°C.
ORIGIN: Mekong delta. This small decorative clumper is used as an easily controlled low garden hedge, being

vertical in form and non-spreading. The backs of the leaves are often very glaucous (blue) in colour, and the appearance quite like *Bambusa multiplex* 'Fernleaf' except for its longer sometimes ribbed leaves.

Otatea acuminata acuminata. 5 m x 3 cm, to -9°C.
ORIGIN: Mexico. A close relative of the next described Mexican weeping bamboo. A very graceful ornamental with clouds of fine feathery leaves, its fountain form revealing slender smooth red/black culms initially white powder tinted. Beautiful, young, velvet-like shoots.

Otatea acuminata aztecorum. 6 m x 3 cm, to -9°C.
ORIGIN: Mexico. COMMON NAME: Mexican weeping bamboo. A graceful ornamental with an abundance of long narrow feathery leaves, its fountain form revealing slender smooth very dark red/black culms that are white powder tinted when young. The spectacular young shoots are covered in velvet dark red hair.

Pring Tutul. See *Bambusa maculata* (recently taxonomically identified).

Pseudostachyum polymorphum (Munro). A very thin-walled new introduction, very different to *Bambusa polymorpha*.

Schizostachyum brachycladum (Kurz). 15 m x 5 cm, to +3°C.
ORIGIN: SE Asia. In our opinion, the most beautiful bamboo in the world. Very erect gold/yellow green striped long internoded culms are uninterrupted by branches until mid-height, where it breaks into a crown of huge light green yellow striped slightly rough leaves. Young shoots are bronze red with cup shaped reddish blades that contrast with the clean golden culms as the shoots elongate. The thin-walled culms are used for a multitude of handicraft and light building purposes, including carrying and cooking containers, weaving, 'skin rice' cooking and musical instruments. An outstanding ornamental.

Schizostachyum brachycladum cv. 'Green' (Kurz). 15 m x 7.5 cm, to +3°C. (Photos 3I, 18Q)
Identical to the above bamboo except for having verdant green culms and being slightly more robust, this very vertical bamboo is as beautiful and elegant as its brother. Used for light construction, wall boards and shingles. The thin-walled, straight culms are split and flattened for use in press-moulded furniture and utensils.

Schizostachyum caudatum (Backer). (A provisional identity of a new specimen.)

Schizostachyum dumetorum (Hance). 8 m x 1 cm, to +4°C. (Photo 7J) (Identity yet to be confirmed.)
ORIGIN: SE Asia. An interesting low height bushy bamboo that forms a 1.5 m high scramble of ascending long

pendulous small diameter culms. Given an adjacent tree or structure, the culms climb into the branches. A very attractive low profile, large diameter decorative species if you have the room. Ideal as a weed control bamboo on a dam wall or steep country. Split and pounded culms are often woven into ropes.

Schizostachyum funghomii (McClure). 12 m x 7 cm, to +3˚C. (Photos 5A, 6A, 25A)
ORIGIN: China. One of the most beautiful garden species. Large leaves. Exposed lower dark green culms contrasting with retained culm leaves.

Schizostachyum glaucifolium. 20 m x 5 cm, to +4˚C. (Provisional identification only)
ORIGIN: New Guinea and Pacific Islands. Sold for many years in Australia as *S. lima*. (See explanation under that name.) This beautiful erect tropical has ivory stripes on lime green culms and internodes up to 100 cm long. With its lower culms exposed and the large leaf growth above, it is a very beautiful bamboo (very similar to *S. brachycladum*). Suitable for a sheltered humid seaside location.

Schizostachyum jaculans (Holttum). 8 m x 3 cm, to + 4˚C.
ORIGIN: SE Asia. Forms a verdant almost vertical column of large light green slightly rough leaves. A very attractive smaller garden piece with very long internodes some-times exceeding 1 m. Extensively used for making flutes, and blowpipes for hunting.

Schizostachyum lima (Blanco). The bamboo now known in Australia as *S. glaucifolium* has been sold for many years as *S. lima*; however S. Dransfield (a Kew Gardens taxonomist) recently indicated (1998) that she was now unsure of these species, and would be doing some work to clarify them. At present we have the bamboo listed provisionally as *S. glaucifolium*.

Schizostachyum lumampao (Blanco). 15 m x 7 cm, to +3˚C.
ORIGIN: Philippines. Often confused with *S. brachycladum* 'Green', but it is quite different. (A reflexed, long, thin, pointed culm leaf blade instead of wide and upright.) It has very useful erect straight culms and is a very attractive garden species.

Schizostachyum sp. 'Murray Island'. 5 m x 2.5 cm, to + 3˚C. (Photo 7K)
Recently located on Murray Island in Australia's Torres Straight, this small and attractive very erect, dense, clumped light green bamboo has branchless culms which almost touch until they become pendulous, then break into a mushroom-shaped mass of large, slightly rough-textured leaves hanging to about half its height. It is used for mak-

■ **7.J** *Schizostachyum dumetorum, a vine-like low bamboo capable of climbing trees*

ing the Solomon Island pan flute, and a profusion of other utensils. The thin-walled culms are split by crushing and the strong multiple flats then used for weaving. Internodes grow up to 1 m long. Makes a great hedge or garden piece.

Schizostachyum pergracile. See *Cephalostachyum pergracile.*

Schizostachyum pseudolima (McClure). A very beautiful recent import.

Schizostachyum zollingeri (Steudel). 15 m x 6 cm, to +3˚C. ORIGIN: SE Asia. A very erect densely clumping bamboo with pendulous tops and a leafless branchless lower half. Young green culms are covered just below nodes with pale appressed hairs and a distinct pale waxy zone. Young edible shoots are brown with appressed hairs, and purple cup shaped outstanding blades. Large, light green leaves. A beautiful garden species that is also used for making flutes, spears and split weaving. Edible shoots of moderate quality.

Thamnocalamus spathaceus. See *Fargesia spathacea.*

Thyrsostachys oliveri (Gamble). 12 m x 8 cm, to -4˚C. (Photo 9D)
This truly beautiful, very erect, fine-leafed bamboo is a larger version of the monastery bamboo (next described), and is at least as attractive. Unlike the latter, it discards its culm leaves.

Thyrsostachys siamensis (Gamble). 13 m x 6 cm, to -4˚C. (Photos 1H, 3J, 6J)
ORIGIN: Thailand. COMMON NAME: monastery bamboo. This delightful, delicate, erect bamboo is one of the prettiest ornamentals in existence. With strong, very upright, straight culms that retain their culm leaves and a frothy profusion of very fine leaves starting 2.5 m above ground, it reaches a reasonable height whilst taking up very little ground space. Young edible shoots are light green and hairless (Thailand sells about 400 tonnes of the shoots tinned each year). The thick-walled strong culms are used for light construction, tool handles, basket weaving, etc. Planted around monasteries and on freeways as a windbreak and sound barrier. Highly recommended as a slender central feature in a courtyard.

Cross-bred Species

We also have a number of cross-cloned bamboos, the work of China's brilliant Professor Zhang Guangchu and her assistant Wang Yuxia. Professor Zhang crossed the pollen of one species with the flower of another, an almost impossible task with bamboo because of the difficulty of low viability and ill-matched periods between

■ **7.K** Schizostachyum *sp. 'Murray Island' with culm internodes one metre long*

flowering with sporadic flowering bamboos. With skill, science and patience, she has done it! These bamboos are all attempts to produce a superior species of bamboo, virtually a super bamboo. Examples are as follows:

Dendrocalamus latiflorus x *B. pervariabilis* cross (no 7)
Dendrocalamus latiflorus x *B. textilis* cross (no 11)
Dendrocalamus latiflorus x *G. levis* cross
Bambusa pervariabilis x *Dendrocalamus latiflorus* and
Bambusa textilis cross (no 1)

Bamboo World has its own registered quarantine house, and my wife and I travel overseas every year collecting new species and visiting friends in various research institutes. We have a number of clones of many of the listed species plus quite a number of unidentified species, giving a total of more than 200 different species or clones. With this season's plantings, there are more than 2000 bamboos growing at the property, plus about 10 000 nursery plants and some thousands of tissue culture plantlets in vitro, with some being potted out into the 'real world' on a regular basis.

Australia now has a superb range of useful beautiful species, and as they are distributed throughout the country, we will certainly see changed attitudes because of the great beauty and usefulness of many of these plants.

8 Simple Propagation Techniques

Having read the earlier description of the flowering and seed cycle of bamboo, the reader will readily understand why it is impractical to rely on propagating bamboos from seed, unless you only want to propagate that species every 30 to 120 years! Seed is used for propagation on those rare occasions when the species you need flowers and you are lucky enough to obtain some seed. Unfortunately, bamboo seed is not viable for very long, germination deteriorating to zero mostly within six to eighteen months.

■ **8.A** *In vitro tissue culture plants being potted out from the glass to the 'real world'*

At Bamboo World we have entered the esoteric realms of tissue culture, that is, creating plants that multiply in a test tube (micro-propagation), in order to overcome some problems we experience with vegetative propagation. The process is difficult and expensive, particularly if there is a market for a relatively small number of plants only, but in some instances it will help overcome the problems we have propagating and making available new or difficult-to-propagate species.

As an example, when we find and bring back a rare species from overseas, the planted material creates one or at most two small immature bamboo plants. It is quite difficult to propagate vegetatively from either immature wood or small diameter wood. This means we have to wait, sometimes up to three years, before we can remove enough mature wood from the new plant to start experi-

menting with propagation techniques that suit the new plant. Even if we succeed in propagating that plant first try, it can mean a wait of up to four years before the plant is made available to our anxious collectors.

As an alternative, tissue culture requires only very small chips of wood (called 'ex-plant material'), and such pieces can be removed from a small plant immediately it is released from quarantine. The main problem with tissue culture is the difficulty and cost of establishing even a single piece of plant in the growing media without it being destroyed by either bacterial or fungal contamination or the necessary cleaning and decontamination process. This happens even though it is all carried out in sterile laboratory conditions. Then comes the difficulty of finding a successful individual formula, as each species responds differently and requires modifications to the chemical growing media. It is time-consuming and costly to find the right answer.

We are delighted with our (limited) success and now have some six species established and multiplying, but for other species the solution is elusive. This is not surprising. For 30 years people have been trying to tissue culture bamboo. It is known to be difficult (some monocots are), and so far to our knowledge only four overseas laboratories have had limited success with their efforts. (Now there are five.)

For the above reasons, vegetative propagation is the normal way of propagating bamboo species. The process is often bulky, labour-intensive and expensive (compared to normal nursery propagation), involving cut culm sections with pruned branches, or dug rhizome sections, all from plants that take years to establish that are damaged by the process. Some bamboos are easy to propagate and respond rapidly, whereas others are quite difficult to propagate, and the percentage success rate as low as 10 per cent or even zero for a species in a particular year. Some will propagate from culm cuttings, whereas others will not but will respond with branch cuttings. Some of the branch cutting material necessary takes years to develop on the plant to the point of maturity where it can be used successfully. Others respond to neither, but will give limited success using marcotting or aerial layering.

To include all the propagating variations and species idiosyncrasies in this book would be very lengthy and inappropriate. I have therefore chosen to describe simple propagation systems that will work for most careful people and species, but are not always appropriate for producing large numbers of plants.

It is interesting to note that, except when using seed, there are some fundamental differences in attempting to propagate clumping bamboos as opposed to running bamboos. With skill, it is mostly possible to propagate clumping bamboos from rhizomes, culm sections or branches. It is impossible (again except by tissue culture) to propagate running bamboos from any part of the culm. They can only normally be vegetatively propagated when a segment of rhizome is used, sometimes with and sometimes without a culm portion attached.

The most important thing with propagation is water and time. When the material is removed from the parent plant, it must be processed as quickly as possible, kept damp or even wet during the process, handled out of sunlight and in a high humidity environment. If leaves are involved, remove most of them and spray the remainder with water, and don't let anything dry out. Don't expose roots or rhizomes to sunlight.

Normal nursery propagation techniques involving cleanliness and sterility apply in principle, but in practice they are not necessary unless propagating on the scale of a nursery.

At times we use root hormone on difficult species, but the measurable success is not obvious, and is sometimes negative. This is confirmed by a similar confusion in various scientific papers we have, some advocating its use without actually quantifying its success, and others claiming that their tests indicate no difference in results when root hormone is used.

The following section provides information on various inexpensive practical systems you can try.

Offset Propagation

Bamboo cannot be propagated from new shoots or sections of shoots (except perhaps by tissue culture), because the shoot receives most of its food energy from the mother culm and mature rhizome system. In fact, until a culm has developed leaves and roots to become self-sustaining, it is virtually impossible to dig it up and get it to survive when replanted (very different to banana suckers). One can be almost 100 per cent sure of success by digging up a culm nearly two years old or more complete with its attached rhizome, and replanting in a new location. The piece, when dug out and prepared, is called an 'offset'. If you can find a clump of a species you desire and get permission to remove one culm offset, you will get a successful result.

Offset propagation on large species becomes destructive and impractical if you require a larger number of plants. This is partly because large bamboos don't have enough mature culms to allow large numbers of them to be dug up without damaging the plant, and also because the labour involved in removing large rhizomes is prohibitive. For smaller bamboos that produce masses of close-spaced culms, propagation of larger numbers by the offset method is quite practical, in fact some of the *Bambusa multiplex* cultivars give poor results from alternative methods.

The rhizome should be cut through where it joins its mother culm (Sketch 8.1), and the earth and roots cut through some distance from the rhizome, removing the rhizome and culm from the ground with some roots and earth attached. Cut the culm off three or four nodes above ground level, or above the first branches with leaves on if that species has leaves low to the ground.

Replant the offset, flood water it, mulch it, keep it wet and feed it. New leaf and branch growth will generate from the nodal buds remaining on the culm, and before long it will produce new smaller culm shoots and then begin to regenerate into a new clump.

■ **8.B** Nastus elatus *showing its beautiful emerging shoots and young culms, not suitable as propagation material*

70 BAMBOO WORLD

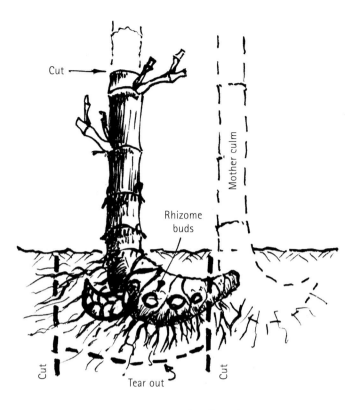

■ SKETCH **8.1** *Propagation by offset. The diagram shows where to cut the rhizome, roots and culm.*

Both from experience and researched data, I have learned that, whilst this method is very successful, after four years of growth it is impossible to see any difference in the size of a clump generated from either a small propagated plant or from an offset. This is even though the first culm shoots produced by the offset are larger than those produced by the young propagated plant.

Culm Cuttings

Because each bamboo responds with varying success and varying techniques to culm cuttings, the best advice I can give to novice enthusiasts is to cut off and bury complete culm sections of a desired species, preferably in early springtime. (Remember that this will not work for running bamboos, which require a rhizome section.)

Choose a mature culm (two or three years old) with branches, and cut it into lengths 1.5 to 2 m long (Sketch 8.2). Cut off all the branches and leaves, leaving one bud undamaged on each branch you cut. You can leave the largest branch at each node longer (no more than one branch per node) if its direction is such that it will project from the ground when buried. Cut that long branch off just above the node closest above the ground after burying it, cutting any secondary branches on these longer primary branches off above their first bud. It is not necessary to leave leaves, in fact it is often detrimental, so don't hesitate to cut them off.

Generally it is only the larger diameter culm sections that have enough energy to generate the necessary roots and shoots, so the small diameter end of the culm is rejected.

Rip or dig a trench and bury the culm section with its top surface about 100 to 150 mm below the ground, with the longer branches left projecting from the ground. Flood the covered trench with water, and do so every day for the first week, twice a week thereafter for about three weeks; then water regularly to keep the soil damp. The projecting branches should start developing buds and new leaves within about four weeks, and with any luck healthy root systems will develop and produce new small rhizomes and shoots that ultimately develop into a new clump. Once you abandon a watering regime that ensures that the buried culm is kept wet, mulch over the length of the culm, and fertilise it. About four to six months later you should be able to carefully dig the culm up complete with roots. Cut the culm off either side of each successfully rooted node, and plant the rooted piece in a nursery bag for further development until it looks strong enough to plant out in the field.

Professional nurseries use culm cutting techniques for those species that normally respond, sometimes one node per cutting, sometimes two nodes per cutting, sometimes with the culm section buried vertically and partly projecting, and sometimes buried horizontally. In all cases the branches are cut back in a similar way to that described above for the 'buried culm' technique. The techniques are so variable for different species, and the success rates for many species so poor without a controlled skilled environment, that it is impractical to go into further detail here.

Branch Cuttings

Some genera, including *Gigantochloa* and *Dendrocalamus*, produce a large central dominant branch on mature nodes, but usually not until that culm is at least twelve months old, and it occurs only on culms of reasonable diameter in clumps old enough to produce such culms. This branch often has a heavily swollen section where it joins the node, which looks very much like a small version of a clumping rhizome. Under a layer of protective leaf, you will find a number of buds. These branches sometimes develop aerial roots, in which case they are excellent for propagation purposes, but even in the absence of roots, one can try.

Select a branch that developed nine to twelve months ago. Usually the clump has to be at least two years old to produce such a culm, and the culm often takes a year to produce this heavy bud, which must have hardened off and matured before it is viable to use. This is consequently a technique not available until about three years or more after planting. Cut the branch carefully from the mature culm, trying (impossibly) not to damage either the culm or the swollen section of branch. Whilst the join is strong, the branch is usually connected by a very slender fibrous section located around the node at the very base of the swollen branch connection. After removal, cut the primary branch off just above the second or third node, and cut off any secondary branches immediately after their first bud. Plant these branches in a propagating mix (salt-free sand with 25 per cent peat moss is ideal), water it in and keep it in a warm, high humidity area. With luck and green fingers (subject to species), you may generate a new plant.

Separation

By growing a young plant on in a pot or bag in a nursery environment, it will produce small new shoots and culms. Once the plant has developed a number of culms, it may be separated into more than one plant if it is done sensitively in the springtime or early summer and before the plant gets into the late summertime shoot-producing period.

To do this, remove the plant you wish to separate carefully from the bag (in a high humidity shady area and only after wetting all the leaves). Shake and/or hose the soil from the roots and rhizomes. Carefully study the rhizome structure and divide the plant into two or more sections (with at least two culms left intact on each division) by breaking or cutting the rhizome neck off where it joins its mother culm, at the same position as that described for cutting offsets (Sketch 8.1).

Then re-pot each separated plant section in friable potting mix, flood watering each, and squelch the sides of the bag or pot when full of water to ensure that the soil floods back into the root and rhizome system. If the plant is carrying too much leaf or wood, cut it back so it has less to feed until it recovers. Place in a shady high humidity warm area and flood water it for two or three days.

Propagation from Seed

Obtaining bamboo seed is like looking for hens' teeth. The flowering cycles are so rare and the locations of the species so remote that it is not practical for most people to even try. The other problem is that bamboo seed is rarely viable for very long. Research is being carried out to try and find long-term storage systems, and cool storage will extend its life a little, but basically if you are lucky enough to get some, plant it and use it quickly.

For the above reason, purchasing bamboo seed is often not successful. Unless it's fresh, it won't generate plants, and some people still sell seed that is losing or has lost its viability. Getting seed that is properly identified is also a problem. I know of a seed supplier who has been selling seed claimed to be *Dendrocalamus giganteus* in one case and *D. calostachyus* in another, the seed being purchased by them from India. In both instances, it was actually a cultivar of *D. strictus*, a far less valuable bamboo that is commonly available. This has caused huge confusion, great disappointment, and financial loss to many people. Thousands were sold through various country town markets. I know of one couple who spent a fortune clearing and planting two hectares of what they thought was the high quality timber and shoot-producing bamboo *D. giganteus*, only to find that the bamboo they had planted produces bitter shoots of low quality and curved timber about one-third the diameter anticipated.

Raising bamboo seedlings requires a high humidity, warm (preferably 30°C temperature-controlled) environment. Sterile seed-raising mixture in planting trays is advisable, and a mist or very fine droplet watering system to keep to soil damp is desirable. The seedlings can be separated and potted individually into good quality loose potting mix when they reach about 75 to 100 mm high. Grow them on in semi-shade in a well-drained damp mix or they will stop growing. When they have produced three or four small culms up to 300 mm high, they can be planted out in the field subject to your weather (see Chapter 5).

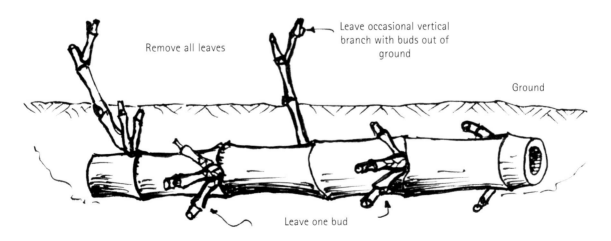

Remove all leaves

Leave occasional vertical branch with buds out of ground

Ground

Leave one bud

■ SKETCH **8.2** *Propagation by burying a culm cutting section*

Obtaining
New Species

Unfortunately the availability and selection of existing mature stands of clumping bamboo is very limited as yet, and it is unlikely that you will find any or many of the ones that you select growing in your area. My advice is to purchase the species you want (our nursery and some few others send plants to all parts of the country), plant them and wait until they are about three years old. Then practice your propagation on your own wood if you wish to multiply your collection.

Make a point of dealing only with reputable specialist bamboo nurseries or you may end up with misidentified plants. There is considerable confusion in the world of bamboo taxonomy (see Chapter 2). Many nurseries are not too fussy about ensuring that the name is correct, and nor do most of them keep up with the nomenclature reclassifications that have occurred for many years (and are still occurring).

■ **8.C** Bambusa vulgaris *cv. 'Wamin', an example of an easy-to-propagate bamboo*

9 Clump Management for Culms

There is a simple clump management system to maximise timber production, as there is for maximising edible shoot production (covered in Chapter 21). The Indonesians have practised an effective system for thousands of years that has been confirmed as scientifically sound in later studies.

Remove all culms that are either three or four years old, but no younger ones. Cut them off just above a node between 100 and 200 mm above ground level to minimise rhizome damage. If there are sufficient healthy culms in the vicinity of the culm that you cut off, the old rhizome retains the ability to produce future culms from its dormant buds. Only harvest timber culms in the dormant season, which is in late winter (see Chapter 11). It is wise to have marked all young culms with the year they appeared (a black felt-tipped marking pen is adequate), so you don't have to try to estimate or guess the culm age by physical signs. If you do have to select by appearance rather than marking, choose culms where the lower branches have older leaves or ones that are losing leaves, or those with a yellowing culm colour instead of bright green. Selection can even be made by plotting the origin of the culm by tracking the rhizomes backwards to count the seasons.

In the shoot season, remove any shoots that are going to create overcrowding, leaving only those of good diameter which have the potential to produce straight, strong poles.

If you repeat this process every year, it should leave you with a mature clump that never contains shabby or dead wood, always looks healthy and attractive, and will always have about the same number of healthy culms in the clump. The number of culms the clump will have depends on the vigour of that species, the quality of, and care available in its growing environment, whether the plant has a good water supply, the maturity of the clump, the number of shoots that are cut off and taken, and the number of culms harvested each year. On a mature clump of a larger structural species being grown for timber rather than edible shoots, there could be anything from eight to twenty culms between two years and four years old.

Chapter 21 will explain that you can manage a clump to maximise timber production each year by removing fewer shoots for eating. Alternatively, you can remove most of the shoots for eating each year to maximise edible shoot production. You do have management choices that will vary from one extreme to the other, or a balance of both if you so choose.

■ **9.A** Dendrocalamopsis stenoaurita, *a beautifully straight species*

■ **9.B** Dendrocalamus asper, *with its large diameter, very strong culms*

The natural growth pattern of clumping bamboos radiates more outwards than inwards, even though there is a distinct limit on the maximum base diameter that a specific species normally reaches, and they will have new shoots within the outer culm circle. Most of the larger good quality species (*Dendrocalamus asper, D. brandisii, D. giganteus, Gigantochloa atter, G. pseudoarundinacea, G. apus* and others) don't get larger than 2 or 3 m diameter across the base, and certainly wouldn't reach that size if managed in the above-described manner.

Vigorous outward-growing performance is limited to very few species, amongst them being species that have modified unicaespitose rhizomes. They have long necks joining the mother culm bud and the rhizome base, which causes the culms to be spaced further apart. Two examples are *Bambusa longispiculata* (Photo 6E) and the *Guadua* genus. *Guadua angustifolia* (Photo 3H), a beautiful and wonderful structural bamboo, has shoots and culms about 1 m apart, and can grow to cover 12 m or more because of that characteristic. The worst offender, however, is *Bambusa balcooa* (Photo 5I), which is just so energetic that it is capable of reaching very large base diameters if left untended for 50 or 60 years. These large clump diameters can be controlled by managing the clump in the manner earlier described, and also by implementing the following procedure. When a *B. balcooa* clump gets to about 3 m diameter, cut out the culms in one location on the outside of the clump to form an access into the middle of the clump. This will allow you to harvest mature culms on the inside of the clump, and to

remove accumulated old or dead wood. It will also give more space for the shoots that generate on the inside of the clump to climb unencumbered. You will in effect have formed a horseshoe-shaped clump. You can also mulch and fertilise the inside of the clump to renew its vigour and, to some degree, create an ingrowing growth pattern.

If you don't want a clump to grow in a particular direction, you can remove all shoots on that side of the clump every year, and it will expand only in the other directions, thereby controlling the shape of the clump.

When actually cutting bamboo from a clump, it should be approached with great caution as many of the culms are under a considerable amount of pressure from their own weight and from the weight of others leaning on them. Never position yourself behind the direction of the applied natural force on that culm because they can split when half cut through and whip backwards at great velocity. A number of people have been very seriously injured. I cut lightly on the compressed side of the bamboo (the direction in which it will tend to fall), remove the saw before it jams, move around and cut on both sides of the culm to an increasing depth, and then finally cut it right through on the tension side of the bamboo. By doing it this way there is less tendency for the culm to split and spring back, and it usually severs itself cleanly without disembowelling you when it gives away. A chainsaw can be used, but I normally use a good quality pruning saw (for example, a Felco 60) unless harvesting a lot of wood. It also pays to have two saws on the site in case one is irretrievably jammed (it happens often).

Because there is so little good quality bamboo growing, most bamboo fans in Australia eventually end up harvesting culms from the fairly common *Bambusa balcooa*. It is an unruly clumper and it should be approached with great caution. First observe which of the desirable well-aged culms can be most easily extracted (in much the same way as one would approach the once popular game of extracting a single stick from a confused pile of small sticks without moving the others). Cut off the lower branches within reach on the culm you want to harvest, and any others you can reach blocking its extraction. When the culm is cut through, often it won't fall. Extract it by pulling it out with a rope and a tractor or four-wheel-drive vehicle. You will sometimes have to cut young culms and rubbish bamboo out of the way before gaining access to the pieces you want. Some people try getting the culms to fall by cutting others off around it, a dangerous practice as you may end up with a ton of cut off culm standing stubbornly upright, then suddenly all falling on top of you! Grow superior species and you will never have those problems, particularly with a little applied management.

Any mature chosen species will produce only culms of roughly the same diameter, that being the size produced by that species in your environment with the care you choose to give it. You don't normally get small diameter culms from a large bamboo. For this reason it is best to plant a number of different species that will give you high quality timber of different diameters to serve your different needs. You can also choose different species to produce either culms suitable for furniture, culms more suitable for structure, or some suiting both needs. As an example, *Bambusa oldhamii* is a good furniture bamboo because of its fairly thin, strong walls, but is not a superior structural bamboo for the same reason. Furniture building often requires one smaller diameter culm to fit snugly into another, which requires the outer culm to have an inside diameter greater than the one entering it. A thick-walled bamboo would be unsuitable because it is too difficult to cut a hole in the side of the heavy-walled larger piece greater in diameter than its inside hole diameter. On the other hand, such solid or almost solid bamboos are very good for structures, and also for making furniture with bent members (the solid wall structure prevents the culm collapsing during the heat bending process).

Following are lists of recommended structural bamboos for different diameters and uses. The lists are by no means complete, but do contain many of the most useful species. The natural tendency for that species to grow straight is depicted by a prefix representing the following:

S1 Normally grows very straight culms.
S2 Normally grows generally straight culms with some curved.
S3 Will grow straight culms if grown in a valley amongst trees.
S4 Culms are normally curved.
S5 Culms are often formed with interesting irregular shapes.

Remember that culms can be straightened when harvested by heating, bending, and cooling whilst held straight. Curved and irregular shapes are often used in building design (or furniture) to enhance the design.

The greater number of asterisks indicates a higher level of structural superiority.

Large Structural Species

(Bamboos generally 125 to 250 mm diameter and larger

S3**   *Bambusa balcooa*
S2***   *Bambusa bambos*
S5***   *Bambusa blumeana*

■ **9.C** *Dendrocalamus latiflorus, just three years old—the three-year-old culms ready to be thinned from the clump*

S2*****   *Dendrocalamus asper*
S2*****   *Dendrocalamus brandisii*
S3***   *Dendrocalamus calostachyus*
S2*****   *Dendrocalamus giganteus*
S1****   *Dendrocalamus latiflorus*
S3****   *Dendrocalamus pendulous*
S2*****   *Dendrocalamus sikkimensis*
S1*****   *Dendrocalamus yunnanicus*
S1*****   *Gigantochloa atter*
S2*****   *Gigantochloa levis*
S1*****   *Gigantochloa pseudoarundinacea*
S1****   *Gigantochloa robusta*
S1*****   *Guadua angustifolia*
S1*****   *Guadua chacoensis*

Medium Structural Species

(Bamboos generally from 50 to 100 mm diameter)

S4**   *Bambusa arnhemica*
S1****   *Bambusa affinis*
S2****   *Bambusa longispiculata*
S1*****   *Bambusa nana*
S1*****   *Bambusa nutans*
S1**   *Bambusa oldhamii*
S3*****   *Bambusa tulda*
S1*****   *Bambusa longispathus*
S1*****   *Cephalostachyum pergracile*
S1*****   *Dendrocalamus bambusoides*
S1*****   *Dendrocalamus barbatus*
S1****   *Dendrocalamus beecheyana*
S1****   *Dendrocalamus membranaceus*
S1*****   *Dendrocalamus sericeus*
S1*****   *Gigantochloa auriculata*
S1*****   *Gigantochloa apus*
S1*****   *Gigantochloa compressa*
S1*****   *Gigantochloa hosseusii*
S1****   *Gigantochloa ridleyi*
S1*****   *Gigantochloa robusta*
S1*****   *Gigantochloa thoii*
S1*****   *Thyrsostachys oliveri*

Light Structure Species

(Bamboos generally from 30 to 50 mm diameter but some larger and thin-walled)

S1**   *Bambusa chungii*
S1***   *Bambusa cerosissima*

■ **9.D** Thyrsostachys oliveri, *a beautifully erect, straight timber bamboo*

S1**   *Bambusa lako*
S2*****   *Bambusa malingensis*
S1*****   *Bambusa nana*
S1***   *Bambusa oldhamii*
S1*****   *Bambusa pervariabilis*
S1**   *Bambusa textilis*
S1*****   *Bambusa tuldoides*
S1*****   *Cephalostachyum pergracile*
S4****   *Dendrocalamus strictus*
S2*****   *Gigantochloa albociliata*
S1***   *Gigantochloa atroviolacea*
S4***   *Gigantochloa manggong*
S2***   *Gigantochloa wrayi*
S1****   *Melocanna baccifera*
S1**   *Schizostachyum brachycladum*
S1*****   *Thyrsostachys siamensis*

For harvesting and curing these bamboos see Chapter 11. Remember that all of the three to five asterisked clumping (sympodial) species listed above are stronger than the same sized running (monopodial) species if properly harvested, so why bother growing the runners unless it is so cold that you can't grow a clumper?

10 Bamboo Shoots for Home Consumption

One of the constant joys of growing bamboo is the multiplicity of uses this beautiful plant fulfills. Most but not all bamboo shoot species are edible, and can make an absolutely delicious contribution to your daily diet. Western people are often not aware of having eaten bamboo shoots, but it is a common ingredient in Thai, Chinese and Japanese food. Unfortunately, most of the shoots eaten in the Western world are tinned shoots, very inferior to fresh.

Fresh shoots from clumping (sympodial) bamboos start appearing during the midsummer season, and subject to rainfall and harvesting precedure, can continue until midwinter. This is quite different to running (monopodial) bamboos which produce their edible shoots during late winter and spring, all within six to eight weeks.

Bamboo shoots vary in flavour and texture depending on a number of factors. These are: (a) the species, (b) how soon the shoot is harvested after first appearing, (c) whether it is harvested early or late in the season, (d) the portion of the shoot being tasted, (e) whether the shoot is grown covered to exclude light after appearing from the ground, and (f) how the shoot is cooked or prepared. Their great virtues are the crunchy texture that survives to some degree even if over-cooked, and their ability to take on flavours from other ingredients. The best eating species require very little preparation, and some few (e.g. *Dendrocalamus asper*, *Nastus elatus* and some others) can often be eaten raw with no preparation if light is excluded after the shoot breaks ground level. Thai people cover the emerging shoot with a planter bag (Photo 21K) full of carbonised rice husk and straw and allow the shoot to grow upwards inside the bag. The 'bag grown' *D. asper* shoots I have eaten taste like a cross between water chestnut and a crisp apple, very fresh, moist and crunchy, in fact ideal for inclusion in a salad.

Most people's concept of bamboo shoots is that they are somewhat akin to asparagus shoots, which is far from the truth! The best commercially grown shoots are huge by comparison. *Dendrocalamus asper* shoots can be up to 10 kg, and most are between 1 kg and 4 kg. Even moso, the famous runner grown for shoots in Japan's cold climate, has shoots that average 1.5 kg, with *Phyllostachys praecox* shoots weighing in at five to eight per kg.

The edible shoot is the young newly appearing growing culm shoot, which is cut off before it has a chance to continue its charge into the sky. The rhizomes of clumping bamboos are quite close to the soil surface (about 100 mm to 200 mm on large clumping bamboos or sometimes

■ **10.A** Dendrocalamus asper *shoots on a two-year-old clump*

■ **10.B** Dendrocalamus asper *shoot (cv. 'Pai Tong Dam'), harvested by the author from a 100-year-old, still-functioning plantation. This six-kilogram shoot was crisp and sweet eaten raw.*

■ **10.C** Dendrocalamus asper *shoot (cv. 'Pai Tong Dam')* *being harvested*

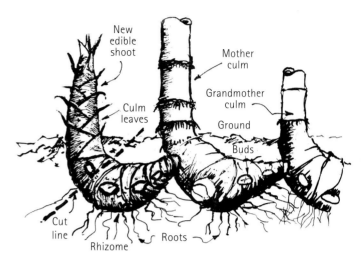

Clumping (sympodial) shoot

■ SKETCH **10.1** *The clumping bamboo edible shoot harvest* *cut-off point (for high quality shoots) is just below ground level.* *Note the developing culm leaves.*

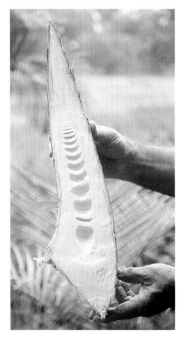

■ **10.D** *A typical shoot cross-* *section showing the developing* *internodes. Bag-grown shoots* *harvested a little earlier are solid* *meat with no internodal cavities.*

This leaves the rhizome just under the surface with its buds undamaged, ready to produce more rhizomes and edible shoots in future years. Rhizomes harvested of their shoot can produce new rhizomes with shoots so long as there are sufficient healthy well-leafed culms available to support the necessary photosynthesis process and its associated starch build-up each year.

The shoots appear from beneath the ground quite suddenly, then seem to pause before gathering energy to climb into the air to become a culm. The time to harvest a good eating shoot is at the beginning of its 'pause' period, which usually occurs between one and two weeks after emerging from the ground. This is sometimes longer for larger bamboos. Shoots left for too long before harvesting become more astringent, and also too coarse and fibrous if harvested when too tall. If you intend eating shoots from more astringent species (e.g. *Bambusa tulda* or *B. vulgaris* 'Vittata', or *Gigantochloa apus*) it is best to harvest the shoot immediately it becomes visible. It will become more astringent the longer it is left after projecting from the ground, particularly if left exposed to light.*

Shoot size varies with the species, with smaller bamboo shoots such as *Thyrsostachys siamensis* being up to 60 mm diameter and weighing less than 150 g, and larger species shoots such as *Dendrocalamus asper* being up to 300 mm diameter, 600 mm tall, and weighing up to 7.2 kg each. Species rather than size also dictates the eating quality of the shoot. The edible portion of a fresh cut shoot is between 30 per cent and 50 per cent depending on species and how early it is harvested, the remaining weight being young culm leaf matter wrapped tightly

even less). The edible portion curves upwards from the rhizome and projects well out of the ground (Sketch 10.1). The projection normally is proportional to the diameter of the shoot (say 500 to 600 mm for *Dendrocalamus asper*, or about 200 to 250 mm for small diameter shoots like *Bambusa malingensis* or *B. ventricosa*).

One can detect the join between the tough fibrous inedible rhizome and the tender crisp shoot by prodding along the rhizome from where it joins the mother culm, using a sharp pointed knife, until the tip penetrates into the crisp flesh; then cut it off at that point (Sketch 10.1).

---

* *Bamboos*, edited by S. Widjaja and S. Dransfield, published by PROSEA, gives some detailed variations on shoot weights and time after emergence for harvesting different sympodial species.

around to protect the fragile shoot. Shoots grown in bags that exclude the light are fatter, have a higher edible portion, and are sweeter, less astringent and crisper than shoots allowed to grow in light. Generally the shoot is harvested before elongating sufficiently to form the beginnings of the culm cavities, when the texture of the white flesh is even and crisp; however, even if a superior species shoot is harvested a little late it is often nice eating after the cavities have just begun to form (see Photo 10D).

The shoots of *Dendrocalamus latiflorus* are harvested about 400 mm long and 150 mm diameter for fresh eating (or tinning), but are allowed to grow up to 1 m high for shredding and drying in China, a tasty way of using the shoots in a stir-fry after soaking the dried shoot in water. Shoots harvested for drying can be up to 30 kg in weight, but produce only about 10 kg of usable product.

Harvesting Edible Shoots from Clumping Bamboos

If you look at the diagram (Sketch 10.1), you will see that the shoot is cut off at an angle across the join line between the uncuttable fibrous rhizome and the crisp, succulent shoot. You can use a heavy kitchen knife, or even an axe positioned on the cut line and tapped with a hammer, but if you are going to be harvesting regularly (if you have a plantation), you should have your local blacksmith make a Thai harvesting blade for you (Sketch 10.2 and Photo 10F). It is a square-ended flat blade beaten from an old car or truck spring until about 4 to 5 mm thick and tapering to sharpened sides and a sharp squared off end. The finished blade size is about 80 mm wide and 290 mm long, with a handle socket cut from 30 mm bore pipe shaped and welded onto the handle end of the blade. Both the square blade end and the sides are sharpened for the full length on a grinding wheel. It can be used as a spear after fitting a 1.5 m wooden or solid bamboo handle, or simply positioned and tapped with a wooden mallet if fitted with a shorter handle.

Simply clear away any mulch or loose dirt (with your hand or the end of the harvesting tool) to reveal the top of the rhizome, then slice the blade in through the culm leaf covering, driving the blade deep into the shoot, swing it back and forth sideways to increase the width of the cut, give it a twist, and the shoot falls off severed. It is a very quick simple operation that can be carried out by any unskilled person following these instructions. Very large shoots may take two or three thrusts but the principle is the same. If you hit the fibrous rhizome, the blade will jar to a sudden stop, indicating that you should strike a little further along towards the projecting shoot (further from the rhizome end of the mass).

Selecting Your Edible Shoot Species

Unless your intention is to plant large areas of bamboo for profit (see Chapter 21), it's advisable to initially select your plant for its beauty, size, ease of maintenance and climate suitability. Then check the eating quality of your selected species, and any other subsidiary needs you might want such as timber quality, etc.

As an example, on a small suburban block, you can certainly grow the very erect, tight clumping bamboo *Thyrsostachys siamensis* (monastery bamboo; Photo 1H). Planted around the temples and along the freeways of Bangkok and Java as a sound-barrier hedge, it can survive -4°C. This stunning, fine-leafed bamboo can produce strong, straight, useful 3 to 6 mm diameter culms from 8 to 13 m high, and reasonable, slightly astringent, edible shoots (Thailand tins and exports more than 400 tonnes/annum). I know of a number of *B. oldhamii* (Photo 1B) clumps (a very vertical tall species) being grown for both decoration, privacy and edible shoots on average-sized suburban blocks in Sydney.

With slightly more room, one could choose the beautiful, vertical large-leafed but frost-sensitive *Gigantochloa atter*, a prolific and valuable timber bamboo (100 to 150 mm diameter and 20 m high) that also produces very sweet shoots. If you grow it for shoots and harvest from it every year, it will take up less air space than most trees (approximately 3 m diameter, and 1.5 m across at the base).

If you live in a heavy frost environment (temperatures down to -9°C), the very erect *Bambusa oldhamii* provides tender tasty shoots, and also lovely straight 60 to 100 mm diameter culms 12 to 18 m high, thick with dark green leaves. It will never normally grow into a clump much more than about 3 m diameter. It is more often 1 m diameter if you harvest the majority of the shoots every year

■ **10.E** Dendrocalamus latiflorus *cv. 'Mei Nung' shoot almost ready to harvest*

and eat them. It can be grown on a suburban block in spite of its height. Very easy to control, it makes a fabulous tall non-spreading hedge or orchard windbreak when planted in a row (see Photo 6H; great for blocking out the new condominium next door!).

The main commercial edible shoot clumping species, *Dendrocalamus asper* and *D. latiflorus*, are grown mainly in large plantations. They are magnificent, vigorous bamboos that would grace any large garden, but you need room as they are capable of reaching 26 to 30 m in height. Certainly they will produce a greater volume of both edible shoot weight and high quality timber than most other bamboos, but they are a little too large for most suburban blocks unless planted in the middle of the yard as a very dominant feature. (See Chapter 21 for plantations.)

The very elegant *Nastus elatus*, a thin-walled, pale green, long-leafed bamboo that can reach 20 m high and 100 mm diameter produces volumes of tender, tasty shoots so lacking in astringency that they can be diced raw and served with your salad (as with *D. asper*). It will survive a light frost, but drown if planted in a depression that floods.

The list is almost endless. Many are superb, some are bitter, and others are edible only if prepared properly because of toxic cyanide. The following clumping (sympodial) species produce high quality, tender eating shoots with low astringency, the more asterisks, the higher the eating quality:

*	*Bambusa arnhemica*
**	*Bambusa bambos*
***	*Bambusa blumeana*
****	*Bambusa burmanica*
*	*Bambusa lako* syn. *Gigantochloa* sp. 'Timor Black'
***	*Bambusa malingensis*
*	*Bambusa multiplex*
***	*Bambusa nutans*
****	*Bambusa oldhamii*
***	*Bambusa pervariabilis*
***	*Bambusa textilis*
***	*Bambusa tuldoides*
**	*Bambusa ventricosa*
****	*Dendrocalamus asper*
****	*Dendrocalamus beecheyana*
***	*Dendrocalamus brandisii*
***	*Dendrocalamus giganteus*
****	*Dendrocalamus hamiltonii*
****	*Dendrocalamus latiflorus*
***	*Dendrocalamus membranaceus*
***	*Gigantochloa albociliata*
****	*Gigantochloa atter*
****	*Gigantochloa levis*
*	*Gigantochloa manggong*
***	*Gigantochloa pseudoarundinacea*
****	*Gigantochloa robusta*
**	*Mellocanna baccifera*
****	*Nastus elatus*
***	*Thyrsostachys siamensis*

■ **10.F** *Shoot harvesting tools. The flat spear-like tool in the middle (see Sketch 10.2) from Thailand is used for harvesting clumping bamboo shoots such as* Dendrocalamus asper. *The large, long-bladed hoe is the tool traditionally used in China for digging up the running bamboo shoots from moso, normally harvested with all or most of the shoot still underground. The small hoe blade is used for harvesting very small, running bamboo shoots.*

Many sympodial bamboos not listed above are edible. Some can be as good or almost as good as the above 'superior' list, but some are an acquired taste. As an example, the shoots of *Bambusa tulda* retain a slightly bitter flavour. The shoots of the *Bambusa vulgaris* family are unpalatably bitter to my taste, but are much valued by the Vietnamese here as an edible shoot.

Harvesting Moso
(a running bamboo)

This book concentrates quite unashamedly on non-invasive sympodial (clumping) bamboos for reasons already mentioned. On average, the tropical and sub-tropical sympodial species are much larger than mono-podial (running) bamboos, and that also applies to the size of their edible shoots. The quality of the shoot is not affected by the size of the shoot, in fact mostly it is the opposite, the clumper *Dendrocalamus asper* and moso, the largest of all the runners, being examples.

It would be unfair not to pay homage to the runner moso (*Phyllostachys heterocycla pubescens*; Photo 21G), the famous monopodial edible bamboo grown in the cold climates of Japan, China and Korea. By far the largest of the running bamboos, this beautiful but invasive species produces high quality shoots averaging 1.5 kg (compared to the sympodial *Dendrocalamus asper* with its 3 to 5 kg shoots). It is not recommended planting for anyone without a concrete retaining box, a water-surrounded island, or the professional skills of a plantation owner to contain it. In its native China, I have seen complete mountain ranges covered as far as the eye can see with natural stands of moso, with rhizomes and culms even growing over cliffs. I have heard it argued that moso is the best

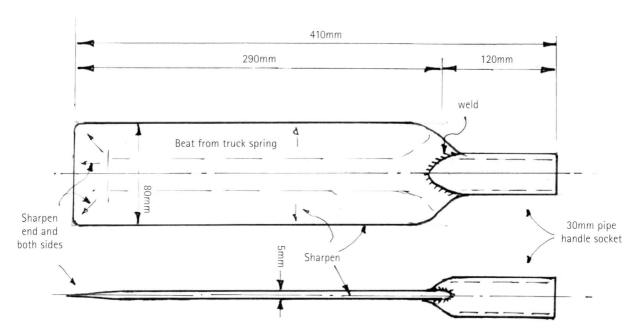

■ SKETCH **10.2** *The Thai shoot harvesting blade, or spear, used for harvesting clumping bamboo's edible shoots*

eating shoot in the world, but people from southern China, Thailand and Taiwan would disagree strongly. In fact, the people of China's Anji province, a major moso growing area near Shanghai, pay only one-third as much for regular moso shoots as they do for *Phyllostachys prae-cox* or *P. prominens* shoots, or for the hard-won uneconomical moso 'winter shoots' dug in the early season from deep underground. Nevertheless moso is undoubtedly an extremely beautiful, productive running bamboo, with high quality edible shoots.

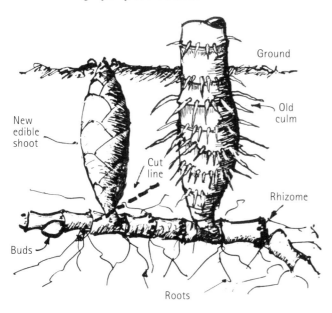

Moso running (monopodial) shoot

■ SKETCH **10.3** *The running bamboo edible shoot harvest cut-off point (for quality moso shoots) must be exposed by digging down to cut them off not far from where they join the rhizome.*

Moso shoots are dug from underground, cut off not far from where the new shoot joins the rhizome, which are usually from 250 to 700 mm below the surface, so it is a more time-consuming effort than harvesting a clumper. The Chinese and Japanese usually use a fairly long-bladed hoe (Photo 10F), quite a bit heavier than the Thai harvesting spear (Sketch 10.2) used to cut clumping shoots off near the surface.

There are many other running (monopodial) bamboos other than moso grown in cold places for their edible shoots, usually very small shoots by sympodial standards, but they are all labour-intensive to dig and harvest. It is far easier to slice a large succulent sympodial shoot off close to ground level. As moso with its 1.5 kg average shoot weigh is the biggest of the running bamboos, smaller runners are easier to harvest, but you need many more shoots to reach the volume of either moso or the larger clumpers.

Choices, Choices!

The clumping species choices are numerous, and there are bound to be species that fit your other selection criteria such as size or beauty. In fact most good sympodial edible species also produce superior timber (unless you live in a very, very cold climate). Chapter 20 gives details of shoot preparation, cooking, food value and recipes, and Chapter 21 will tell you how to establish profitable plantations. The species descriptions in Chapter 7 and 'superior timber' lists in Chapter 9 will give you additional parameters such as size, climate, appearance, etc., so good luck with your choosing.

Finally, if you taste good quality, fresh shoots as a comparison to tinned shoots, you will never want to eat the tinned variety again!

11 Harvesting and Curing Bamboo Culms for Timber

If you want strong, long-lasting bamboo timber (culms), it is absolutely essential that you learn some basic rules to help you harvest and cure your bamboo culms properly, or you will be frustrated and disappointed. Lack of technical knowledge, lack of a reliable supply of superior species properly harvested and treated, coupled with a general suspicion towards the so-called 'invasive' nature of the plant are also significant impediments preventing the wider use of bamboo in the Western world. Bamboo will never be widely accepted as a desirable, versatile

'woody' material until more people understand its limitations, and learn the simple technical skills needed to use this very different wood. Follow the following basic rules and you will eliminate most of the common problems, which apply equally to runners and clumpers.

1. **Mature culms harvested in the dry season are usually resistant to powder beetle attack and will give long life if used inside a building or under cover.** This rule applies more to high quality structural species (e.g. *Dendrocalamus asper*, *Gigantochloa atter*, *Guadua angustifolia*, etc.) than to poor quality starchy species like *Bambusa vulgaris* (see 'Quality' list in Chapter 9).

2. **Any bamboo used in an outdoor environment should be chemically treated for a long structural life.** Bamboo used to build fences or structures in an open air environment exposed to rain, even if properly harvested and properly cured, has a limited *structural* life of perhaps two to four years because of the effects of fungal attack. It may last many years longer (particularly a superior well-cured culm) in an exposed non-structural visual location such as a fence, but not as a load-bearing member.

3. **Immature culms harvested are highly likely to be attacked and destroyed by powder beetle.** This is basically because young wood is high in starch which is the food of the predator.

4. **Immature culms are weak, and likely to shrink, crack and distort.** This is caused by the high moisture and low fibre content of young wood, and applies whether such culms are used inside or outside.

If these simple rules were followed, and a quality supply of properly graded treated and untreated culms were made available through landscape organisations, nurseries and timber yards, there would be an explosion

■ **11.A** Gigantochloa apus, *a very important straight medium diameter structural bamboo*

■ **11.B** Dendrocalamus brandisii *produces high quality timber very similar to* D. asper.

of people wanting to build beautiful outdoor fences, pagodas, chicken sheds, gazebos, split bamboo screens, small buildings, furniture, sculpture, and a proliferation of similar artistic objects. Take heed of those basic rules if you are harvesting and curing your own bamboo.

Eucalyptus timber can take more than 20 years to mature into a hardwood. Individual bamboo culms reach a sufficiently high strength after standing for only three to four years. Recent research indicates that, contrary to earlier belief, each individual culm in a clump then continues to strengthen very slowly until they begin to deteriorate after about seven to ten years, and eventually die after about twelve to maybe even 20 years. The good news is, you can harvest bamboo from your clump every year once it is large enough (no 20-year wait), and you don't need a sawmill.

Bamboo grown on hillsides is known to be stronger than that grown in wet places. This is because sometimes ideal growing conditions produce larger diameter thinner walled wood, and the cellular structure can produce more sappy parenchyma and less fibre content. One report indicates the tensile strength can be up to 50 per cent higher in hilly dryer places (Soeprayito, Tobing and Widjaja, 1988).

Most clumping species can produce maximum diameter culms for their species and their growing environment within four or five years of planting. Harvesting of smaller culms can commence at year four; however, it is best to be patient and wait longer before harvesting full diameter culms.

Avoiding Powder Post Beetle Destruction

Harvest only culms that have been standing preferably for three years or more since appearing as a shoot. Harvest culms only during the dry season. Younger culms

(even the younger mature culms that have stored moisture and starch for the coming shoot season) stand a higher chance of being attacked by powder post beetle larvae after harvesting.

They are attracted by high starch (carbohydrate) levels in bamboo, and also to the sapwood of eucalypt hardwood species. Mature culms on clumping bamboos are most depleted of moisture and starch during late winter (early in the monsoonal dry season). This harvesting time coincides with last season's shoots reaching 90 per cent of their full height, when they are beginning to develop branches and leaves at the top. The right time can vary a little depending on whether it is an early shooting species like *Bambusa malingensis*, or late shooting species like *Gigantochloa atter* or *G. apus*, and it may vary a little because of rainfall patterns in your area. If you wait until the springtime, the culms will begin building up starch and moisture again for the coming shoot season, so it is best to harvest earlier. Running bamboo's season is the opposite, so harvest culms in late summer.

Powder post beetle doesn't attack living culms, but is attracted when a cut culm's moisture content begins to fall after harvesting. They often attack dying parts of living culms where damage has occurred in the clump.

Don't underestimate this menacing little flying microbe. The eggs are deposited by the beetle into the culm tissue, and left to hatch at the appropriate time. Any spot where the culm or branches are cut or even abraded is a valid entry point, the bamboo's outer coating of silica and wax normally being sufficient protection. The destruction process can begin quickly, and the beetle's larvae, also not liking the hard high silica exterior surface or the increasing fibre density towards the outside of the culm, whittle away the inside of the bamboo until often only a paper thin surface is left. The first telltale sign is mostly the small exit hole left by the emerging adult beetle, from which well-chewed fine powder commences to fall. By then the internal damage is well progressed.

If it does happen, you could try drilling holes and spraying the insides of internodes with insecticide, remembering that, whilst it may kill many, sideways penetration of bamboo is difficult and your chances of complete success are not good. Most of the bamboo buildings and much of the bamboo furniture constructed in Australia by well-meaning often talented people have been destroyed by this serious pest.

There are quite a few different types. They are basically all members of the Bostrychid type that actually bores inside to gain entry. It includes the *Lyctus* and *Minthea* species that leave no evidence of their deadly visit. There have also been identified attacks by the long-horned beetle *Chlorophorus annularis*, according to entomologist, John Donaldson. Numerous species of beetle borer exist in every country, so the problem is not unique to Australia, or Asia.

Inefficient
Treatment Systems

Remember that you have two problems that need addressing: powder beetle, and also fungus (when bamboo is used in an exposed location). Many well-meaning people have come to grief by inventing or adopting scientifically unsound treatment methods, such as dipping culms into or injecting hollow internodes full of liquids like diesel oil, sump oil, hydraulic oil, salt water, etc.

Those systems don't work. Research by Professor Walter Liese (Hamburg University) conclusively indicates that both the inside and outside walls of bamboo internodes are highly resistant to penetration by anything, let alone any medium more viscous than water. Bamboo will readily absorb liquid as thin or thinner than water through its natural cellular water carrying system, but in a longitudinal direction only. This longitudinal penetration is only effective whilst it is alive (within 12 hours of cutting). Even then, the conducting tissues will naturally form defensive gelatinous globules to block moisture entry or exit if the foreign liquid is upsetting to the bamboo (we had experience of this with Copper Quat whilst experimenting to find the right treatment system). The bamboo forms these gelatinous blocks shortly after a culm or branch is cut off, thus preventing moisture loss or longitudinal penetration (Liese, 1995).

I know of an only-just-surviving building suffering from these inappropriate treatment systems not far from here. The builder of this very artistic small dwelling has obviously used a variety of treatment systems, including

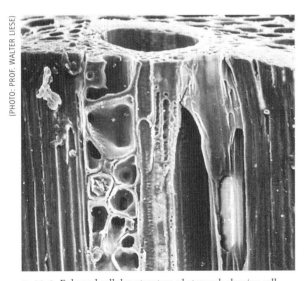

(PHOTO: PROF. WALTER LIESE)

■ **11.C** *Enlarged cellular structure photograph showing cell-like parenchyma divisions, vertical fibre bundles and water-carrying vessels. The capsule-shaped object lodged in the metaxylem vessel is a gelatinous blockage (tyloses) often formed to block water transportation as a reaction to injury or an intrusion unacceptable to the bamboo.*

injecting various mediums (hydraulic oil, sump oil, diesel oil, are some commonly used) into the culms (the holes drilled into the internodes for injection can be clearly seen), and applying heat to a culm, probably over a fire (it leaves a lovely pattern on the bamboo). The beams, species *Bambusa balcooa*, with some up to 150 mm diameter, are riddled with borer holes all discharging little streams of chewed dust as fast as they can go. The building is doomed!

Traditional Indonesian
Treatment System

The Indonesians have long established traditions for harvesting culms, with their calender including a dedicated time called 'the period for harvesting bamboo' (Muller, 1996). They cut off three-year-old culms and leave them standing in the clump, complete with branches and leaves (on a rock to raise the cut surface above the ground). They are left for about four weeks. (Leaving the leaves and branches on makes access by the powder beetle more difficult, and the leaves help reduce the culm's moisture content more quickly by expiration.) They then remove the culm from the clump, remove the branches and leaves, and soak the culm in a pond or stream, weighted underwater, for between ten to 20 days. This soaking process destroys residual starch, giving further protection from powder beetle, and allowing the bamboo to dry faster when removed from the pond. Their bamboo is then air dried in covered racks for (preferably) about two months before use.

Whilst the submerged culm system is widely practised in Asia, modern research indicates that splitting and culm collapse is more severe after soaking (plus unpleasant smells) than without soaking. Thus whilst giving additional protection against powder beetle and some level of extended life against fungus in an exposed location, the soaking does cause a little more physical damage due to drying stresses than allowing it to dry naturally in covered racks (Liese, 1985).

This soaking process, if you decide to use it, causes a negligible reduction in dried culm strength, and a slight increase in its ability to absorb moisture or chemical treatment in the dried state, again mostly in a longitudinal direction. Water soaking is recommended if you are going to try and treat bamboo by submerging it in treatment fluid. Whilst this is also quite widely practised, it has not been verified as effective even if the inside of the culms are filled through holes in the side or holes punched in the internodes. Liese's research and evidence (1995) on bamboo's anatomical structure and its resistance to radial/lateral penetration both internally and externally, does not support the effectiveness of that process.

Salt Treatment

Salt or salt water treatment is useless, in spite of it being recommended in a number of books I have read. Bamboo used in salt water usually lasts no more than 12 months mainly due to marine organisms. There are fungi that are resistant to the effects of salt. Salt is also hygroscopic and causes a significant increase in the moisture level of the wood, which ultimately contributes to its destruction.

The Effect of Fungus

Once any timber or bamboo reaches 20 per cent moisture content, it will be attacked by any number of different forms of fungi (for example brown rot, white rot, soft rot). The deterioration time will depend on the environment, the quality and maturity of the wood, the curing process, and resistance of the species, but the bamboo will rot. Fungus will eventually destroy any bamboo exposed to moisture and which has not been chemically treated (it is the same with softwoods, and inferior hardwoods). Unfortunately, whilst matured, superior species, properly cured bamboo culms are more resistant to fungal rot and powder post beetle, all species of bamboo, both clumping and running, are subject to these problems.

Shrinkage and Cracking

The other very good reason to harvest only matured wood in the dry season is to minimise the shrinkage and cracking that can take place after harvesting. The higher the moisture content, the greater the shrinkage and drying stress (a common problem when seasoning eucalypt hardwood, or any other wood).

Even mature culms can have a moisture content of between 50 per cent and 80 per cent of dry matter ('relative moisture content'), with the lower culm portion having a greater moisture content than the higher culm potion because of its need to provide the upper portion with its moisture supply. The higher culm portions have a higher fibre content (and higher unit strength) than the lower for the same reason. During the drying process, the moisture content of a culm drops to between 12 per cent and 18 per cent, and the internal shrinkage stresses generated can be quite high, sometimes causing splitting and collapse of culms. Younger culms with less developed fibre strength also have an even higher moisture content; therefore the distortion and shrinkage is greater, often causing collapse and heavy splitting. Even matured culms, lower in moisture after year three, shrink anything from 4 to 14 per cent in wall thickness and 3 to 12 per cent in diameter (Liese, 1985). The longitudinal shrinkage, very low due to the long strong fibre length, is less than 0.5 per cent.

Treatment for Furniture Making

In my experience, culms of *superior* bamboo species harvested in the dry season after growing in the clump for at least 3.5 years (preferably longer), and allowed to dry (cure) in a covered drying rack for three months or more, will normally give a very long life when used under a covered structure as either a structural member or furniture. I know of a number of people either selling or making bamboo furniture who would consider that chemical treatment should be used as an additional precaution because they have seen furniture damaged or destroyed that they thought was safe from attack. It is difficult for a furniture manufacturer (even more so a seller) to guarantee that he is being supplied with timber that is at least 3.5 years old. This is partly because Asia's economic reality puts pressure on the harvesters to cut younger immature wood to meet the demand. It is also because it is hard to be sure that the piece you are harvesting is that old (even if you are harvesting it yourself) unless you know and trust that the new culms were marked with their age at 'birth'. My opinion is based on examples of now eighteen-year-old furniture that I have built myself (from culms selected and cut by me) that have never been touched by powder beetle or fungus.

The Indonesian system of pond soaking is an effective additional non-chemical precaution against powder beetle, and it extends the outdoors life of bamboo somewhat, but it will not prevent its ultimate deterioration and destruction from fungus if used in an exposed environment. If you want further protection for your furniture wood, you can either chemically treat the culms, or try heat-treating them, both systems being described later in this chapter.

In a Costa Rican furniture factory I recently saw the people boiling newly harvested *Phyllostachys aurea* culms in long tanks at 100°C for ten to fifteen minutes (about fourteen litres of caustic soda per 100 litres of water), then wiping the hot bamboo off with a sponge. This would have the effect of removing the wax coating so the bamboo can easily be varnished or glued. On such thin-walled bamboo, the heat penetration would probably destroy any powder beetle lavae, and help destroy starch, but they were not harvesting poles younger than five years to avoid that problem anyway. Their simple boiler was made by joining oil drums, and having an access lid at one end. The fire heat supplied from under one end of the drums travelled along a crude brick and concrete duct and out a flue at the other end. One brew of caustic and water lasts for about three to four days.

Miscellaneous Treatment Systems

There are many traditional, non-chemical systems of curing being practised apart from those so far described, the criteria mostly being low cost and minimal equipment. However, 'not much is known about their real effectiveness' (Liese, 1985). The fact that many of the practices seem contrary to the scientific assessment of bamboo's structure and behaviour, creates a considerable doubt about their actual usefulness.

Many other methods such as painting with tar or lime are being practised, but again the results are neither quantified nor scientifically recommended (nor even aesthetically pleasing in some cases). Any impervious coating such as varnish applied to well-cured bamboo will protect it against fungal attack initially, but it will have to be maintained well (as with softwood and inferior hardwoods) or it will be destroyed by fungus when the varnish breaks down.

One bonus is that white ants (termites) tend not to attack bamboo (possibly due to high silica content) but will attack timber in the presence of bamboo; however, the possibility can be avoided by taking the same precautions with foundations normally applied to wooden buildings (see Chapter13).

Heat-treatment— Advantages and Disadvantages

Heat-treatment of small diameter or relatively thin-walled culms in limited quantities can be effective against powder beetle because heat of sufficient temperature destroys the starch that attracts the powder beetle to lay its eggs in the wood. There is, however, no point in trying to cure large quantities of larger diameter, heavy-walled bamboo (for building) by applying heat on the culms. Unless you are using a huge, sophisticated, heat-treating oven, it is impossible to ensure that you are imparting a full-depth, evenly penetrating, high enough temperature to larger culms. Any attempt to apply a direct flame or a crudely controlled heat onto such large or thick-walled culms would burn them to the point of damage before the inner wall temperature was sufficient for effective treatment. In such cases, powder beetle infestations partly survive, or sappy wood pockets remain that later become infected, and the wood is ultimately destroyed.

In Japan, culms are sometimes heated to 120°C–150°C in smokehouses, sometimes with added chemicals. The pleasant colour, together with destruction of some of the starch that attracts powder beetle, are helpful, but there is no strong evidence that it gives long-term resistance to fungus if used outdoors. The extra splitting induced by the heat is destructive and may make it more vulnerable to insect attack later. The deteriorating bamboo house in our locality referred to earlier has 150 mm diameter culms of *Bambusa balcooa* that were obviously treated by heating over a fire or flame to destroy sap content. Unfortunately, when using such a crude system it is impossible to heat evenly all the wood to its full depth to the required temperature (approximately 150°C) and there is no way of measuring internal heat or cold spots. In this building the powder post beetle either survived this treatment or entered the wood after the treatment, as it is rapidly being consumed by beetle as I write.

Heat can, however, be an effective treatment when making musical instruments, or even furniture from relatively thin-walled culms, if you are careful. Concentrate on the single, preferably small culm section that you want to treat, or you will end up half-treating most of what you do.

Try heat-treating short lengths of culm where you are applying heat to a culm wall thickness of only 2 to 6 mm, not the 8 to 25 mm wall thickness you find with 100 mm (or more) diameter structural culms. By applying heat from a soft-flamed blow torch or hand-held burner directly onto the outside of a mature culm, it will further dry off, shrink and harden the wood, and destroy the starch content if it penetrates far enough. This process can leave an attractive, partly scorched patina on the outside of the wood if you are careful. Keep the culm moving and rotating constantly or you will damage the surface or crack the culm. You will see the natural wax on the culm surface melt and turn white, even begin to bubble as it becomes fluid and mixes with the steam and sap rising out of the culm. Keep wiping the resin/wax mixture over and along the culm as you go and it will form a fairly long-lasting, attractive outer coating, that actually seals the burnished surface. You must take it slowly and carefully in order to get the heat to penetrate through the culm wall before the surface wax is all burned away. It is easy to crack, burn or destroy your piece of bamboo (and maybe part of your skin!). With very thin culms, you will have to move more quickly.

This heat technique is recommended to use after and in addition to the normal harvesting and aging techniques for your selected flute wood. However, if you are impatient to make musical instruments or furniture out of uncured bamboo while waiting for your good quality wood to season (or grow), you can try using the heat curing system directly on mature, green-cut wood. You won't get the same quality, and they have a greater chance of cracking or distorting at some point, but it often seems to work. It can accelerate the curing process, particularly on properly harvested, mature wood (normally not prone to powder beetle attack anyway), and it does give a beautiful burnished, sometimes mottled, patina to the bamboo that looks great on musical instruments or furniture. Good luck!

Recommended Chemical Treatment Systems

If you intend to use your bamboo timber in an outdoors environment exposed to high humidity or rain, you must treat it chemically to avoid fungal attack. Such treatment normally also gives complete protection against powder post beetle attack. There are two ways I can recommend for achieving chemical treatment, one simple but slow, and one quick but requiring some basic equipment.

Treatment 1— Sap Replacement by Expiration

You can treat your bamboo by standing the cut culm, leaves still attached, in a bucket of water containing 10 per cent copper sulphate (by weight) for up to two weeks; then remove the branches and dry it in a covered rack for two months minimum. Copper sulphate ($CuSO_4$) is readily available in farm supply shops in economical bulk bags. Copper in its various forms acts as a fungicide but also a relatively mild naturally occurring poison. In the form of copper oxychloride, it is approved by the Australian Organic Growers Association(s) for regular spraying on mangoes and avocadoes. The alternative is using borax (Solubor is one brand name, use 10 per cent by weight). It is less poisonous, more expensive, more difficult to find in a soluble form, and it has a tendency to be less 'fixed' in the wood (more vulnerable to leeching out) if used in a rain-exposed environment. Borax is excellent for use on indoor furniture or structure because it doesn't cause the slight discolouring of the bamboo one gets with copper, and is even more environmentally 'safe'.

Place the base of the culm in the bucket of treatment solution immediately after cutting. The bucket must be kept topped up with solution for the full two weeks. It is easier to get satisfactory penetration with younger culms with their higher moisture content, or shorter culms, than with older, dryer culms. A number of culms can be treated concurrently if the container is big enough to receive them, and it's kept topped up with treatment medium.

There is no easy way of measuring how effective your treatment has been (short of dissection and laboratory testing), but it can work, is much better than no treatment, and will give many years of outdoor service if you get good penetration.

Treatment 2—Boucherie Sap Displacement System

We have built a simple Boucherie treatment plant capable of treating up to six culms in less than one hour (invented by a Monsieur Boucherie and originally to treat timber, not bamboo). By attaching a hose pipe fitted with a rubber clamp to the fresh cut bottom end of a culm, and introducing the treatment liquid under low pressure, we actually pump the sap out of the culm and replace it with the treatment fluid. The plant is simple to build (Sketch 11.1) and can be powered by either a pump, an air compressor, or even by gravity if you can find a way of locating your treatment fluid tank about 9 to 10 m higher than the culm being treated. The operating pressure range is 1 to 1.3 Bar or atmospheres (15 to 20 psi), which is less than the pressure most people get out of their tap.

We suggest that you build the system completely from high quality PVC plastic sewerage piping (Photos 11F and 11G) to avoid electrolysis eroding iron or zinc parts, or depositing a copper build-up that blocks the pipes. The latter is a process that can happen very quickly (electrolysis destroyed two earlier plants we built within one week, the first using a copper drum, and the second a stainless steel beer keg, so don't underrate the advice to use all plastic parts).

We treat 3½-year-old culms up to 6.5 m long and 150 mm diameter in less than one hour, or 4 m long and 75 mm diameter culms in 30 to 45 minutes, using a maximum pressure of 1.3 Bar (20 psi), but 1 Bar (15 psi) is better and more than adequate.

The younger or shorter the culm or higher the moisture content, the faster the treatment. Remember that whilst the system will effectively treat young immature culms against fungus and powder beetle, it doesn't make them any stronger, and it doesn't avoid the higher shrinkage distortion and splitting that young culms with high moisture content manifest. Culms over four or five years old may be more difficult to penetrate, but will yield superior wood.

Our main treatment medium is the 10 per cent solution of copper sulphate specified earlier. A borax

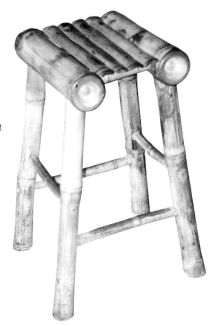

■ **11.E** *A simple stool showing the attractive scorched effect of heat-treatment on the seat, and rather dry-looking stool legs that have not been heat-treated or varnished*

mixture can be injected just as easily if you can get a soluble version of borax economically (Solubor is one brand name), but remember it can leach out over time and reduce the protection. With a six-outlet system such as ours, one person has to work steadily to keep up with putting on and taking off culms to use all six outlets, but a single-outlet machine is too slow if you want to treat enough for a building.

The system works only on fresh cut culms with leaves and branches removed, and they must be processed within 12 hours. If the culm is not connected to the Boucherie immediately after harvesting, both ends should be freshly cut off again immediately before connecting to the machine, or the bamboo will have protected itself by blocking its water carrying vessels with gelatinous secretions. You can expect the culm to discharge about 10 per cent of its wood volume (not including internode hollow) in the form of sap (about 2 L on a medium sized 100 mm *Bambusa balcooa* culm) before seeing the discharge dripping from the culm end change to the blue colour of the copper sulphate solution. Time the duration from applying the pressure to the culm until you first see the blue of the copper sulphate appearing at the other end, then allow the pressure to remain on for a further 50 per cent of that time. It is easy to see the blue colour in the discharge if you allow it to drip against a white plastic bowl or bucket side.

The treatment fluid initially only saturates about 10 per cent of the wood volume to be protected, filling mainly the longitudinal water-carrying vessels in the bamboo's vascular bundle system. After removing the culm from the machine, it then takes about a week for the solution to diffuse into the surrounding fibre sheaths and parenchyma tissue, thus completing the process. It is important to keep the bamboo out of the sun during this time or it may prevent diffusion into the exposed areas of the culm.

The Boucherie sap displacement is the most effective and positive way of treating bamboo because of the plant's unique culm structure. Complete penetration of bamboo can only take place longitudinally because of the lack of a medullary ray type structure to facilitate lateral moisture movement (which trees have). There is also the impervious nature of the culm's inner and outer walls. This is particularly the case with the outer wall which lacks the bark or a cambium layer trees use to protect their inner structure (bamboo has only a very thin layer of wax and silica, but it is virtually waterproof on an undamaged live culm). The Boucherie overcomes these problems by using the plant's own moisture and starch feed system to ensure effective penetration.

Don't be tempted to try using a higher pressure. Too much moisture will be discharged from the cut-off nodes, and you will have leakage and clamp failure problems that will cause a violent discharge of treatment fluid. You can also possibly collapse and block parts of the vascular system you are using for penetrating the culm.

Your Boucherie system clamps must be designed to effectively seal against different culm diameters, some of which are oval instead of round. Use light fibre-reinforced rubber hose (about 7 mm wall thickness for 70 to 90 mm diameter culms) for the clamp section or it will expand with the pressure, sometimes like a football. The rubber sleeve must be long enough to slip well over and past the node closest to the cut-off end before clamping. The clamped section often slips under pressure, and is only prevented from blowing right off by jamming against the larger diameter of the node. It helps to be treating culms of fairly similar diameter because the flexibility of the reinforced rubber hose is limited. You will need a range of different diameter clamps for radically different diameters.

Culms treated with either the bucket immersion or Boucherie system, with copper sulphate, should survive in a rain-exposed environment for many years, in fact longer than untreated pine and many hardwoods. We are conducting tests at Bamboo World, and talking with the New South Wales Forestry Department about possible formal tests to be conducted by them.

Building Your Own Boucherie Plant

Boucherie plants are simple and easily built. There is no reason why you shouldn't build your own plant if you think the amount of bamboo you want to treat justifies the effort. The following listed plant components are numbered on Sketch 11.1.

1. Gravity feed tank (first design alternative). Plastic is adequate.
1A. Compressed air feed tank (second design alternative) Read later construction details.
2. Multiple feed manifold (all standard poly pipe fittings)
3. Main supply valves (Use plastic ball valves — I used ⅜" but ¼" is adequate).
4. Plastic clamp head (I used standard PVC fittings and screw clamps).
5. Bleed/drain valve (a plastic ball valve on a reducing nipple screwed into a tapped hole drilled into the side of item 4).
6. Heavy rubber sleeve and hose clamps (clamped onto the plastic clamp head item 4).
7. Culm clamps. I used heavy duty metal screw clamps.
8. Bamboo culm being treated.
9. Flexible garden hoses with standard bayonet connections.

If you look at Photos 11F and 11G and Sketch 11.1, you will see how we have constructed our simple plant, including the off-the-shelf type PVC and poly pipe, and hose fittings used. This is our third design, and the first that is relatively problem free. Sketch 11.1 gives two alternative plant systems, one a gravity fed, and the other a compressed air fed system. Both are equally effective, but the first (gravity) requires you to position the feed tank 9 m in the air above the level of the culm being treated. One way would be to hoist the tank up a tree, but you have the continuing inconvenience of having to fill it, as each culm requires between 1 and 3 L, depending on size.

For item 1A, I used a 2 m long 150 mm diameter heavy duty PVC sewerage pipe section with standard sewerage fittings glued on with the normal blue coloured PVC plumbing pipe glue. I used a full diameter screw-on rubber ring sealed PVC sewerage fitting on top, drilled for fitting a standard brass compressed-air bayonet fitting with rubber sealing washers to receive the clip-on air hose. The bottom PVC fitting was drilled to receive a standard PVC 1¼" BSP thread outlet screwed and glued into the PVC. All the fittings from there onwards were standard 'poly pipe' fittings and non-metallic plastic ball valves, standard garden hose with plastic fittings, etc. Don't use metal except for the air bayonet inlet.

With the compressed air system, the tank can be placed above or even below the culm being treated. It is far more convenient to operate than the gravity system; however, you do need a compressor with a reliable regulator and pressure gauges. This is to ensure you don't over-pressurise your tank and blow its top off, or put too much pressure into the bamboo (1 Bar or 15 psi is adequate). The PVC sewerage pipe is strong enough to handle the pressure, which is quite low, but it is enough to blow most plastic drums up like a balloon.

This plant can also be carried to the bamboo clump if you have a generator to operate the compressor. By constructing your plant with a number of outlets, as shown, you can treat more than one culm at a time.

Use lightly reinforced rubber hose for the rubber clamps, about 7 mm thick for the larger diameters, and thinner for small diameters to give more flexibility.

The operating procedure is as follows:

a) With valves (3) closed, screw the top off the tank (no more than three-quarters full) with the 10 per cent copper sulphate solution, then replace and seal the screw-top tank lid. Always make sure the air hose is disconnected from the lid (to release any pressure) before removing the tank lid. Then reconnect the air line and apply the air pressure ready for operation after filling the tank, making sure that the pressure is not greater than 1.3 Bar maximum (20 psi).

b) Ensure that the lower end of the culm is recently cut off cleanly, with an intact node remaining close to the cut-off point. Slip the rubber cap and clamp (7) over the culm end past the node and tighten the clamp(s) strongly. With larger diameter culms, I sometimes use two clamps, and will still have occasional leaks, particularly if the bamboo is oval. The pressure

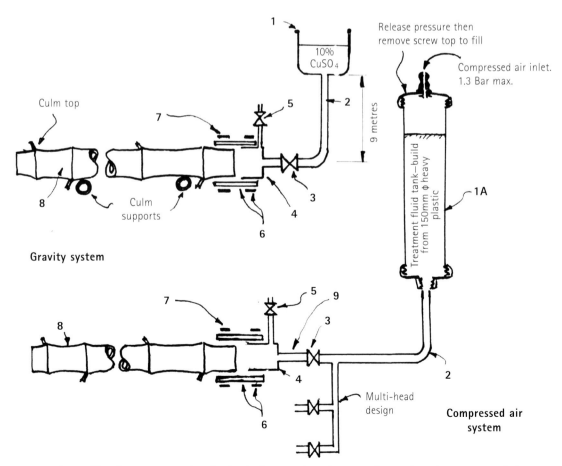

■ SKETCH **11.1** *Two forms of Boucherie treatment plant for chemically preserving culms, one using gravity and one compressed air*

■ **11.G** *A close-up of the Boucherie plant's outlet system. Note the rubber clamps on the culms being treated.*

■ **11.F** *A simple Boucherie plant. Note the compressed air bayonet inlet in the middle of the screw cap on top of the liquid vessel.*

applied by the clamp is shared by a greater circumference if the culm is larger, and leaks become more frequent.

c) Ensure that the bleed valve (5) is closed and in an upright position.

d) Slowly open main supply valve (3) to feed fluid to the culm, whilst observing the degree of swelling of the rubber clamp caused by the pressure of the liquid entering. See that it neither leaks nor expands into a balloon shape. If the rubber 'balloons', close the feed valve (3), release the pressure built up (slowly) by opening the bleed valve (5), wrap the rubber clamp tightly with a wide canvas (blue jeans) bandage. Repeat the process by re-opening the main supply valve (3).

e) Lift the bleed valve (5) vertically upwards and very slowly ease it open to allow the escape of air caught inside the clamp assembly. The air is out when you see the fluid begin to rise from the valve (5), then close it. The object of this is to extract as much air as possible so that only fluid is pressed into the culms vascular system, and not air.

f) Hang a bucket on the end of the culm to catch the sap. Almost immediately you will see the clear-coloured displaced sap begin to drip out of the end of the culm

into the bucket. You can actually track the progress of the treatment solution along the culm by observing the cut-off branch ends at the nodes, which also drip and become blue when the solution has reached that part of the culm. When the treatment fluid reaches the last node, empty the sap from the bucket, and replace it to collect the small amount of treatment fluid that will be discharged when it reaches the end. This small amount of used treatment fluid, even though mixed with a little sap, can later be diluted back into newly mixed treatment fluid so long as there is less than 50 per cent by volume added. Alternatively, you can use the leftover to paint onto your household pathways to prevent build-up of slippery moss or fungus.

When the drip coming out of the end of the culm changes to a blue colour and you have left the culm under pressure for a further 50 per cent of that time, the culm is ready for removal, as follows:

a) Close main supply valve (3).

b) Roll culm over until bleed valve (5) is pointing vertically down. Open valve (5) and discharge the contents inside clamp assembly into a bucket. (This fluid can be returned to the supply tank when you accumulate enough.)

c) Remove the clamp assembly, tip out any residual treatment fluid, then attach a new bamboo culm for treatment, and repeat the process.

Each culm should take between 30 minutes and one hour to treat under pressure, depending on the size and age of culm; thus you can be taking culms off and putting new ones on continuously if you have a multi-headed system.

If you place a sheet of roofing iron under the culm being treated, it will catch any drips coming out of the branches. You should also wear protective clothing, rubber gloves and protective glasses when handling fungicidal liquids, even if they are relatively mild versions.

Final Comment

Remember, you don't have to treat your properly cured culms chemically if they are harvested from superior species and used under conditions where they are not exposed to rainwater, as in under an eave or built into furniture in your house. If you build an exposed fence from uncured bamboo, expect it to eventually rot away, but if it is a well cured superior species not under structural load, it will probably be visually attractive and adequate for many years, but not as a structural member.

12 Building Joints and Techniques (Traditional and Modern)

(PHOTO: PROF. WALTER LIESE).

■ **12.A** *A bamboo bridge at Taiwan Botanical Gardens, Chitou*

The object of this chapter is to give you clear, simple information that will allow you to confidently assemble bamboo culms into soundly engineered structures. First you need some background. Australia now has available very superior, fast-growing structural species. The USA also has many of those bamboos available, but some of the better ones will grow only in the most southern states because of the cold climate. Unfortunately, bamboos have not yet been planted in sufficient abundance here to give a ready supply of *mature* timber, resulting in a lack of straight strong culms. Even we at Bamboo World are short of mature wood in spite of having planted thousands of bamboo plants. This has caused us a lot of frustration and delay while building our own building (still not completed), and we have often had to settle for inferior crooked culm wood.

The alternatives to growing your own clumps and waiting for them to reach maturity are:

■ Find an old clump or forest that has mature culms of the diameter and quality that you need, and get permission to harvest. Don't forget to leave the site clean.

■ Buy cured treated culms ready for use from an experienced person.

■ Delay your building plans, plant your own clumps of superior bamboo now and commence harvesting after five to six years.

These clumping bamboos initially grow much faster than running bamboos, are non-invasive and easy to control. Mature sizes are available in clumping bamboos in four to five years instead of eight to ten years, so unless it's too cold to grow clumpers, don't make the mistake of planting a running bamboo or you may be too old to complete your project!

An effort is being made (Jules Janssen, 1995) to formulate building codes applicable to bamboo. At the present time, Australia's local councils are not authorised to reject the concept of bamboo buildings so long as they comply with all the usual regulations. They can, however, insist that you produce calculations, proof of the material strength of the species you intend using, and proof that your bamboo material is harvested and cured properly to ensure its durability.

In Australia during 1998, there was a rapid increase in new plantations of high quality clumping bamboo. At Bamboo World we have planted seven hectares so far, mainly *Dendrocalamus asper,* and we are currently planting 40 hectares. This will produce high quality wood every year as a by-product to its lovely edible shoots. We have also supplied 35 hectares of plants during the 1997/98 planting season, and expect to supply or plant about 80 hectares during the 1998/99 season. This means that there will be supplies of good quality mature bamboo wood (culms) readily available within about six years.

Mature wood from reasonable quality clumping bamboo is higher in unit longitudinal tensile strength than the best of hardwoods, The best clumping bamboos have an average fibre length (3 to 4 mm) about twice as long as hardwood. This means that on a weight for strength basis, all the superior quality bamboos are much higher in tensile strength than any of the hardwoods, including the strongest of the eucalypts. However, bamboo has a low transverse tensile strength due to its longitudinal fibre structure and the absence of radial fibre (it has no medullary rays as there are in timber). It splits easily, in spite of its very high strength, along the direction of the culm. For this reason it is important to pay special attention to joint construction, which is where most bamboo structures fail.

The other phenomenon engineers need to know is that the tensile strength at the nodes is significantly less than that within the internodes; in other words, if you used bamboo as a 'tug-o-war' rope, it would break at the node rather than between the nodes. This is caused by the change of direction and confusion of the very straight fibres inside the culm as they pass across and through the nodal area and its diaphragm. As an example, the measured physical and mechanical properties for the superior structural bamboo *Dendrocalamus asper* varied in MOE (modulus of elasticity) value from 16780 at the node to 20200 N/mm^2 along the internode, and MOR (modulus of rupture) value from 121 to 142 N/mm^2, tested after drying to about 14 to 15 per cent moisture. When cut green, most bamboo's strength (MOR value) is much less than what it will be after drying. (For derivations of MOE and MOR, see end of this chapter.)

Many species have been measured now, and even though the results vary somewhat, there is a sufficient body of solid information to enable confidence in design of quite complex structures. Engineering design values collated from these tests are given at the end of this chapter.

Joints and Joining Systems

There are basically two systems of structural joints for bamboo now available, 'traditional' and 'modern', both scientifically tested and proven.

Traditional Asian Joining Method

Traditional joints use pins and lashing (Sketch 12.1), or sometimes only lashing with no pins, preferably for non-critical joints (see Sketch 12.2). The pins, usually strong bamboo (or steel) about 8 mm to 12 mm diameter for bamboo 70 mm diameter or larger, are inserted through holes carefully drilled (sometimes even burnt) through the aligned bamboos at the joint. Then the culms are lashed together using either a strong durable cord, or multi-strand galvanised wire. In Hong Kong and Guangzhou they use a very strong nylon type binding about 5.5 x 1 mm (I don't know the composition, but the bundle in Photo 12B was purchased in Hong Kong for almost nothing).

In the huge Hong Kong theatre building shown being constructed in Photo 12C, the culms were all about 50 to 60 mm diameter *Bambusa tuldoides*. This bamboo is a cold-tolerant (to -9°C) straight, thick-walled bamboo extensively used for structures and scaffolding in that area. All the main columns and some main beams were 150 mm pine poles, but the rest was bamboo, including rafters, floor joists, etc. The Chinese artisans lashing the bamboo (Sketch 12.2) were so quick in slipping the lashing around two crossing culms, twisting it into a knot and tucking it into the space in the lashing, that I couldn't even follow their hand movements!

None of the bamboo joins in the building referred to (a huge building) were pinned before lashing, but I still

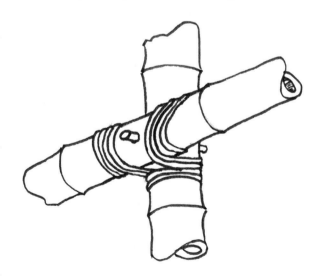

■ SKETCH **12.1** *A simple traditional pinned and lashed Asian structural joint*

recommend that pins be fitted to all major load-carrying joints. The Hong Kong building is a temporary theatre being constructed for a festival, in the same way that all the bamboo scaffolding you see is temporary. If you want your building to last longer, use pins in major joints as a minimum standard.

A stronger joint is obtained if the binding is passed around each individual member as well as passing across from one member to the other. There should be at least two turns in each case (see Sketch 12.1). The turns around each culm resist splitting forces, the pin transmits the load and the cross lashing holds the assembly firmly in position.

Indonesians use a lashing about 3 mm diameter made from sugar palm fibre (called 'ijut'). Multi-strand galvanised soft wire clothes line is a good available substitute, and could be a more permanent solution to either the Hong Kong plastic, or the ijut. In fact, we recently used soft wire about 2 mm diameter very successfully (very neat) — but it must be soft! Apply a minimum of two turns of wire around each individual member on both sides of the joint (see Sketches 12.3, 4 and 5) and two or three turns on each side crossing between the culms being joined. Always wind firmly on in the same direction. Twist the wire ends around a short bamboo dowel to form a twisting handle to pull the lashing tight; then tuck the handle in behind the lashing to prevent unwinding. If necessary, you can use this handle a year later to further tighten the joints.

These lashed joints with multiple turns are stronger yet more flexible than nailed joints used to hold hardwood together. Any flexing of the bamboos under load tends to tighten the wires evenly (like a pulley block) around the individual members. This circular force helps prevent the culms from splitting, and shares the load between strands of binding, and holds the pin firmly to help transmit the load from member to member.

Traditional Asian lashed-joints

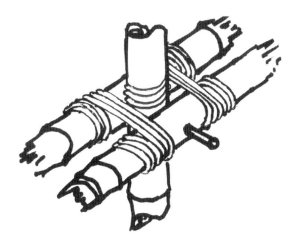

■ SKETCH **12.3** *A simple traditional pinned and lashed 'T' joint*

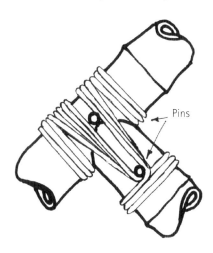

■ SKETCH **12.4** *A simple traditional pinned and lashed double beam Asian structural joint*

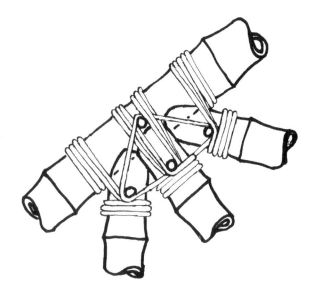

■ SKETCH **12.2** *The simple lashing system with strong synthetic strip used for scaffolding in Asia*

■ SKETCH **12.5** *A simple traditional pinned, lashed and braced Asian structural joint*

Well-matured solid branch sections can be used as pins, but better, straight, round, parallel pins can be made by driving a thick culm internode section through a modified wad punch (with the handle cut off; see Photo 14C). By allowing the bamboo pin to pass right through the wad punch hole, you get a perfectly sized absolutely round pin that will exactly fit a hole drilled to that diameter.

Where a column passes by, rather than stops under, a heavily loaded horizontal beam, it pays to pin and lash a short vertical section to the column under the beam to distribute the load below the intersection (similar to the filled joint on Sketch 12.6). It often pays to locate a beam on both sides of a column (Sketch 12.3) because it eliminates the off-centre twisting moment in the column.

The above joints are designed for strong building construction using good quality bamboo. I have seen many joint variations that may be adequate for temporary light structures such as a chicken house, but many are undesirable even for that.

It makes sense to use a well-designed joint in the first place. Don't pass lashings through holes in the bamboo. The sharp edge of the hole may fatigue the rope or cord, the bamboo may split from the force of the cord trying to part the fibres, and the hole allows unnecessary moisture or insects into the bamboo. Neatly fitting pins in holes are a better solution so long as the bamboo is properly dried and the pin is not driven in too tightly causing the bamboo to split (as it will when it shrinks onto the pin if you use green bamboo).

■ **12.B** *Synthetic lashing now used in China (and Hong Kong) for tying together scaffolding (instead of the traditional split bamboo)*

■ **12.D** Bambusa tuldoides *connected using synthetic lashing to a pine column in the Hong Kong theatre building*

■ **12.C** *The extraordinary theatre building being constructed in Hong Kong, mostly from* Bambusa tuldoides, *with some large diameter columns and main beams from pine*

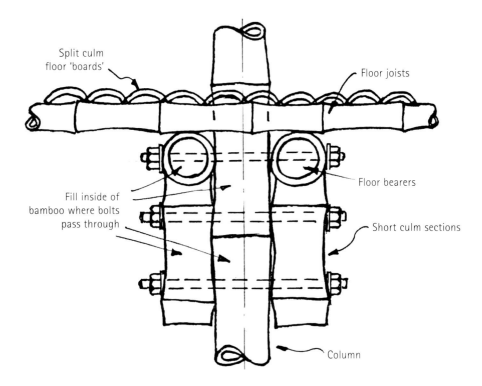

Split culm
floor 'boards'

Floor joists

Fill inside of
bamboo where bolts
pass through

Floor bearers

Short culm sections

Column

■ SKETCH **12.6** *A modern 'filled' structural bolted joint for supporting floor bearers, also showing split flooring, usually covered with woven bamboo (or seagrass) matting*

Modern Joining Method

The often huge, spectacular bamboo designs and constructions by the Columbian architect Simon Velez use bolted joints almost exclusively. Many of his critical joints are 'filled' joints similar to those about to be recommended to you. His obvious success with using filled joints has been further confirmed by Morisco's 1995 research paper quantifying that the following joining system for major structural joints (Sketches 12.6, 7, 8, etc.) is definitely superior in strength and load transmission over the Asian traditional joints. Basically, you construct bolted joints, but fill the inside of the bamboo local to the joint with either a glued wooden plug or a strong solid-setting paste. These filled joints have a greater capacity to resist failure from shear forces, compression, or splitting through the bolt holes.

Various joints of this modern type are illustrated:

Sketch 12.7—How to insert a steel plate into a culm end by punching a hole in the last node, inserting the bolts and then filling. Very good for tension members, or compression if the plate is heavy. The other end of that steel plate can then be either bolted to other plates (similar to Sketch 12.8), or passed into a column.

Sketch 12.8—How to use simple metal brackets (with minimal welding) for a roof beam meeting a column, with added loose-bolted bracing plates. This design is ideal for geodesic dome-type buildings (See Chapter 13

(PHOTO: SIMON VELEZ)

■ **12.F** *An elegant roof interior, designed and constructed by Simon Velez*

for a design). These joints can be used without filling, or made even stronger by filling.

Sketch 12.9—A simple column, beam and bracing joint. It is even stronger if a plate is used on both sides. If a beam needs to meet the joint from the side at that intersection, it can either sit on top, or you can bend a metal flat into a U-shape, bolt the end of the U into the existing central joint bolts and the culm inside the projecting sides of the U.

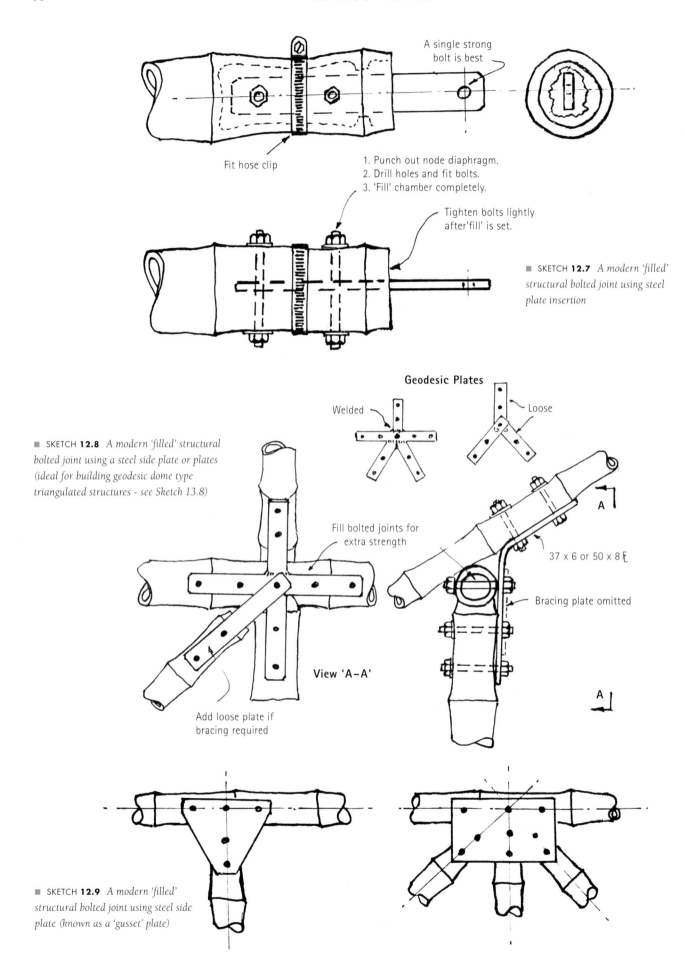

A single strong
bolt is best

Fit hose clip

1. Punch out node diaphragm.
2. Drill holes and fit bolts.
3. 'Fill' chamber completely.

Tighten bolts lightly
after 'fill' is set.

■ SKETCH **12.7** *A modern 'filled'
structural bolted joint using steel
plate insertion*

Geodesic Plates

Welded   Loose

■ SKETCH **12.8** *A modern 'filled' structural
bolted joint using a steel side plate or plates
(ideal for building geodesic dome type
triangulated structures - see Sketch 13.8)*

Fill bolted joints for
extra strength

37 x 6 or 50 x 8 ₣

Bracing plate omitted

View 'A–A'

A

Add loose plate if
bracing required

■ SKETCH **12.9** *A modern 'filled'
structural bolted joint using steel side
plate (known as a 'gusset' plate)*

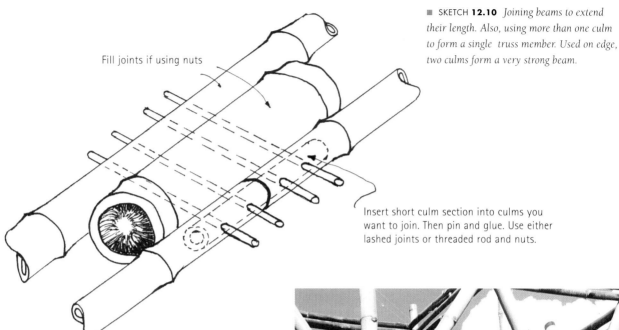

Fill joints if using nuts

Insert short culm section into culms you want to join. Then pin and glue. Use either lashed joints or threaded rod and nuts.

Sketch 12.10—How to join beams when the culm is not long enough for the designed location, and also, using more than one culm to form a deeper or wider member.

The wooden plug is more difficult and restricted in its use, but very strong if a high strength glue is used. The wooden plug must be made specifically to suit the inside diameter of the bamboo to be filled (which varies in diameter and is often oval), and is only useful if the joint is in the end of a bamboo culm instead of a mid-point where the wood can't be inserted, whereas the filling can be injected anywhere along the length of a culm.

The paste can be conveniently injected through a bolthole by partially removing the bolt, or a hole (7 mm) drilled specifically for injecting the paste. If the joint is at the end of a culm, punch a hole in the last node diaphragm to gain access, and pour the paste into the joint. Unless there is a bolthole in the highest spot, always drill a small air release hole (3 mm) at the highest point of the chamber to be filled, or the paste will only partially fill the joint.

A homemade 'cake decorating sock' is an ideal filling device for thicker pastes, or a watering can fitted with a makeshift small diameter nozzle for free flowing pastes, or even a large homemade injecting syringe made from PVC pipe fittings and a rubber washer cut from an old thong (a fisherman's yabbie pump in reverse).

Bolts (gal or zinc-coated) are preferably fitted before filling, but not tightened. If it suits the construction, close clearance bolt holes can be drilled through the bamboo and the solid filler after filling (if the filler is made from a 'drillable' material). Bolts, with nuts and washers, can then be tightened up without crushing the bamboo (don't over tighten). The bond of the filling plug to the bamboo,

■ **12.G** *A somewhat less elegant but massively strong bolted and filled joint building frame under construction at Bamboo World, designed by the author. This two storey Bali-style building is illustrated in Sketch 13.1.*

and to the bolt, strengthens the joint and prevents it from collapsing inwards. On heavily loaded joints, I also like to fit a tight steel hose clip around each culm close to the bolts. These very strong joints then have an even greater resistance to splitting. Research indicates that such joints develop strengths about 60 per cent to 75 per cent of the culm's ultimate tensile strength (Morisco, 1995).

Epoxy is the strongest and most expensive glue for the wooden plug system, but any good quality, water-proofing wood glue will do. The best possible filler taking cost into consideration would be a mixture of epoxy with an added filler such as sand or sawdust, or even both. This cuts back on the cost, but it is still very expensive.

An alternative I favour is a 3:1 bricklayers' sand/cement mix with added Bondcrete (an agent used to increase cement strength), plus some fine sawdust, mixed to a thick slurry consistency. It is good for inserting in large holes but you need a 'greasy' bricklayers' sand to make it 'injectable'. I have heard that cement/sand mixes without additives are unsuitable because the higher shrinkage can result in a loose plug that can 'work' back and forwards like a piston in the joint and eventually punch out nodes and split the bamboo. I find that adding sawdust reduces the shrinkage, while Bondcrete or similar additives increase the bond strength.

An economical answer is to add between 5 per cent and 10 per cent Bondcrete into mixed plaster of Paris. If you are careful, the resulting mix is very fluid for pouring into a 7 mm hole through a funnel. You can adjust the thickness to some degree by adding more plaster so it won't leak out too much around the bolts. It sets very quickly but gives enough time after mixing, if you are

properly prepared, to fill the cavity. Wipe excess plaster off with a damp rag before it sets. Bulk casting plaster can be purchased for about A$12 for a 20 kg bag (Australia, 1997) from a plasterer's supply outlet, but don't buy it from your local hardware store or it will cost! Plaster is not as strong as concrete, but strong enough to resist compression, forms a good bond with seasoned bamboo, and has a very low shrinkage factor.

It is not necessary to fill all your joints, but you would be well-advised to fill all heavily loaded joints. Lashed joints when carried out by skilled people like the Balinese are more attractive than bolted joints, but nowhere near as strong, and not as permanent. If filled, bolted joints will resist splitting or crushing more effectively.

The bolts are best cut from threaded rod, allowing for variation in culm diameters, each fitted with a nut and washer at both ends. By distorting the thread a little near the nut after tightening (use a sharp drill punch) the nuts will stay on.

There is a beautifully built example of a geodesic dome using the joints illustrated in Sketch 12.8 at Byron Bay Backpackers Lodge in NSW Australia, built by an arti-san called Paul Cooper.

Beam Design and Quality Considerations

The above filled joint and plate system for major joints, and the traditional 'pin and lashing' system for less criti-cal joints, have been applied to very large building designs. Many variations of simple filled or lashed joints are possible for either light or heavy structures or culms (see Sketch 12.11). Often the beam and joint design will be influenced by the quality, length and diameter of the

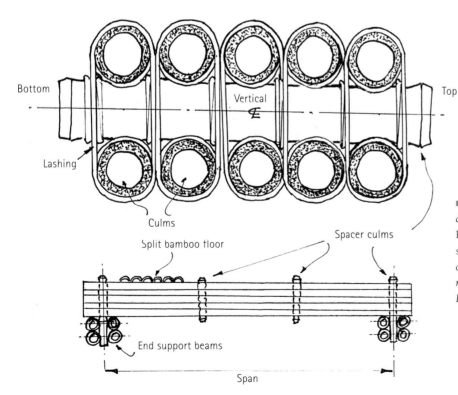

■ SKETCH **12.11** *A deep multiple culm beam. Small diameter culms of the readily available running bamboo* Phyllostachys aurea *can be used to construct very strong beams this way. Lashing must follow a complete circle around each culm and also the short spacer member. Locate each consecutive culm end for end. Larger culms can be pinned as in Sketch 12.10.*

bamboo available. The next chapter will give you simple designs you can build, and advise how to apply simple design principles.

By using a combination of the above joints, a strong joining system that resists collapse can easily be constructed. Aesthetically, bolts are not as appealing as neatly made pinned and lashed joints, but they are superior in strength and will better resist crushing and splitting which are the two main weaknesses of bamboo. You have the option of using bolted joints for your main structural frame, and lashed joints for locations that will not cause the building to collapse if they fail.

At this stage, we at Bamboo World don't have enough *mature* culms of the strong larger species to construct the building currently being erected. (Sketch 13.1 and Photos 13B, 13G, 13H, 13I). We have overcome the problem to some degree by designing the structure to suit the somewhat inferior wood we have been able to harvest locally. The two species available in sufficient quantity in this area are *Bambusa balcooa* and *B. oldhamii*. As described earlier, the old *B. balcooa* clumps are neglected ancient messes full of unsatisfactory twisted wood. We had to visit a number of clumps to get the reasonably straight *B. balcooa* culms of the size and maturity that we needed for the columns. In a few years we will have an abundance of straight strong wood, but not right now.

Bambusa oldhamii is a beautifully straight strong-grained wood, wonderful for furniture and to eat, but it tends to be too thin-walled to define as a superior structural bamboo. We overcame these limitations by using multiple culms rather than a single culm for beam and truss members that were critical to the design, and by joining culms when they weren't long enough (Sketch 12.10).

■ **12.H** *Close-up of the bolted and filled joint truss shown erected in Photo 12G. The side walls were assembled as shown lying on the ground, and then hoisted into the air by pivoting them on their column bases. Note the small diameter multiple beams of* Bambusa oldhamii *used as the bottom cord of the truss.*

Traditional Joints Versus Modern Joints

You now have the problem of choosing which system to use. Certainly some of the traditionally constructed buildings I have seen in Asia are very elegant, and the craftsmanship and beauty of the lashed beams is often inspirational. On the other hand, my background is in engineering design, and I can see the superior strength potential of the modern bolted filled joint systems over the traditional lashed joints, subject to the quality of the bamboo. Where smaller diameter bamboos are being used, particularly if they are thin-walled culms (like most of the runners including *Phyllostachys aurea*), I can see the virtues of using lashed joints on smaller buildings, or with minor members in a large building. This is simply because the small pin or bolt diameter can cause more splitting in those instances than traditional lashed joints. Where both the culms being used and the loads being applied are substantial, I strongly believe that the modern jointing system

is superior both in its load-carrying capacity and its lasting ability. In other words, properly designed lashed joints are fine for small buildings, but go for strength in the bigger buildings, using lashed joints only where the loaded beam is not critical to the stability of the structure.

It is worth noting that the world's most innovative architect for bamboo structures, the Columbian Simon Velez, uses the modern bolted joint system exclusively. He is quoted as 'believing traditional joints are unreliable' (for long-life structures). Architect Darrel De Boer says, 'Organic ropes can't be cinched up in three months when the bamboo shrinks or in two years when the humidity rots the rope.' Velez's often huge, spectacular, elegant, functional designs are built from the very strong South American bamboo *Guadua angustifolia* (see Photo 21T), and have stunned bamboo lovers all over the world.

The following physical and mechanical property summary will be of value to people with engineering design skills. The low value stated would cover combinations of non-superior species and allowance for node fibre weakness, whereas the higher values are relevant to superior structural species and internode tested values, all at 14 to 15 per cent moisture.

■ **12.1** *A Simon Velez construction showing the use of massive beams formed from four* Guadua *culms about 200 mm diameter pinned and bolted together to form single powerful beams*

Static Bending

Modulus of Elasticity (MOE) is the relative deformation caused by a bending stress.

MOE = 16,000 to 20,200 N/mm^2

Modulus of Rupture (MOR) is the maximum bending stress at the point of failure.

MOR = 70 to 150 N/mm^2

Compression

This is the stress or crushing force applied in the direction of the grain required to cause fracture. Various species tested in a range from 35 to 50 N/mm^2, with the low values relevant to the thick sappier wood at the culm base, and high values at the culm top (caused by fibre bundle density increasing as the culm gets higher up).

Tension

Tension values are as low as 80 N/mm^2 in species like *Bambusa vulgaris*, and as high as 300 N/mm^2 for *Dendrocalamus asper*, which drops as low as 138 N/mm^2 at the nodal points.

Shear

The resistance of the fibres to shear off across the axis of the culm. Values vary between 6 N/mm^2 and 12.6 N/mm^2.

For a more detailed analysis, significant studies have been done by Jules Janssen, Surjono Surjokusumo, Subyakto, Dr Ir Morisco, B. Fulford (University of Sydney) and many others (see Reference List for more details).

It's interesting to compare those values with mild steel. The tensile value of mild steel has varied over the years because of improvements in manufacturing techniques, but tensile strength varies generally between 250 to 350 N/mm^2, compared to bamboo's values, varying between 80 and 300 depending on species and culm portion being tested. In effect, some superior bamboos are approaching the tensile strength of mild steel. The startling difference is in flexibility. With steel having an MOE of 200 000 N/mm^2, it is ten times more rigid or inflexible than bamboo, which has an MOE of about 20 000 N/mm^2.

What an extraordinary material is high quality bamboo! Almost as strong as steel, ten times more flexible, and having a weight for strength ratio that far outstrips steel or any of the hardwoods! It's a pity its strength is so directional, which causes its great weakness—its ability to split because of the relatively poor bond between the fibre bundles. Otherwise, it would indeed be a superb material. Now you know how to join culms together, all you need to know is in what order to assemble them in to make a building.

13 Building Design Principles and Some Designs

■ **13.A** *A simple triangulated bamboo bus shelter with a tile roof. The longitudinal triangulation is in the roof section, and the roof acts as a diaphragm to prevent twisting.*

■ SKETCH **13.1** *This is an artist's impression of the building currently under construction at Bamboo World.*

While it's easy to build light useful structures, it is also possible to construct permanent houses that comply with local council standards if you learn some basic skills and procedures.

Good structural design involves simple bracing triangulation and load direction placement of members together with an adequate application and understanding of how to apply the earlier described joining systems. Sketch 13.2 gives two simple truss profiles capable of quite large spans, subject to bamboo quality and good joints. Other good examples are shown on the simple frame building in Sketch 13.9 and the geodesic dome building in Sketch 13.8 (both which you can build easily). Also see the more complex drawings of the building we are now constructing (Sketches 13.5, 6, and 7), which detail an actual column and truss arrangement spanning 4.8 m. It sounds hard but it is actually easy, and the most important thing to keep in mind is the simple principle—triangulation! If you brace it into triangles, it shouldn't fall over (unless the beams or braces are too weak).

If you look at the pattern of the members in the various plans shown herein, each column or truss member forms a triangle which locks the structure rigidly in place in the direction of the horizontal members. The object is to convert the forces and weights applied to a building into tensile and compression instead of bending or

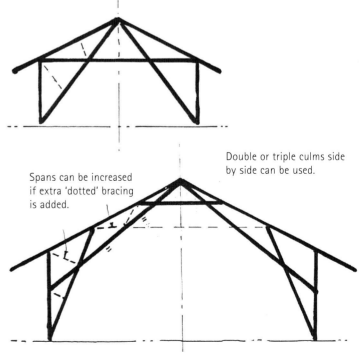

Double or triple culms side by side can be used.

Spans can be increased if extra 'dotted' bracing is added.

■ SKETCH **13.2** *Two strong truss configurations showing bracing triangulation*

■ **13.B** *A two-storey structure with bolted triangulated filled joints. Note the use of smaller diameter multiple beams.*

(PHOTO, SIMON VELEZ)

■ **13.D** *A Simon Velez bolted roof design with a huge eave overhang (Guadua angustifolia). Note the beams constructed from two lots of three culms, side by side.*

twisting forces. This is very important when working with bamboo, which is very strong longitudinally.

Diaphragms such as a sheet floor or a stiff roof construction on a building can also act as (diaphragm) bracing in the horizontal plane if strong enough, preventing the building from twisting around its centre and collapsing. It is often it easier to add a triangulating brace and be done with it. The ground that holds the foundations apart acts as a natural horizontal diaphragm.

Remember that superior bamboo species are much the same tensile strength as steel (per cross sectional area), but ten times as flexible, so your building will flex more than most buildings, in fact much further before it reaches breaking point! This is why bamboo buildings are so well suited to resist cyclones.

You needn't be limited to using single bamboo culms. Massively strong columns, beams and trusses can be constructed using multiple culms arranged side by side, above one another, or both, and then pinned and lashed, or filled and bolted together. Simon Velez is a master at assembling huge beams (Photo 13D), say 600 mm deep and 400 mm wide, from eight culms about 200 mm diameter all bolted together, and trusses giving eave overhangs of 9 m.

Don't cut holes large enough to insert one beam into a larger one similar to a furniture joint, or the 'holed' beam will be weakened.

Incorporate wide eave overhangs in your building design and always use your bamboo in such a way that it is protected from direct rainfall or contact with water, to avoid fungus deterioration (unless it's chemically treated). Preferably, lightly sand and varnish your bamboo structure as an added protection and for aesthetic effect.

To obtain local council approval for larger spans involving trusses or longer beams, it may be necessary to have a qualified engineer prepare simple calculations and drawings, specifications, a definition of the species and

■ SKETCH **13.3** *An artist's impression of a building similar to the one you can make following Sketch 13.9*

■ **13.C** *A beautifully designed and constructed roof interior by Simon Velez, using* Guadua angustifolia. *The fan shape of the roof joists creates triangulation, further strengthened by the roofing material forming a diaphragm.*

maybe even its harvest and curing procedure. It should be a simple obstacle to overcome because design strengths for many species are now available.

The Balinese use blady grass thatched roofing, not suitable for all environments because of possible bush fires. Any commonly used roofing material can be applied to bamboo buildings if care is taken in selecting, positioning and straightening rafters. Bent bamboo culms can be straightened when green by slowly heating them over a fire, applying force and holding when straight until cool (or cooling them with a wet cloth); however, it is better to harvest selectively to avoid this extra (bending) labour. You can use bent ones to create an attractive curved roof, or you can spring the occasional out-of-line rafter into position when fixing it to the purlins or roof tiles. Split shingle roofs look good and are flexible. Curved custom orb iron or very wide Malthoid-covered ply tiles can be used. Velez has used heavy tiles to hold his light structures down, but he is a very skilled designer, so keep it simple with your early attempts and learn to work with your material.

By laying bamboo floor joists carefully and using a planer on projecting nodes, any conventional flooring can be used. Bamboo splits shaped and glued to misaligned joists can be used as packers in some cases, but sand the wax off the joist's culm skin before glueing or it won't stick. Flooring sheets can be strongly wired to the joists at regular intervals. Drill two wire-sized holes either side of the centre of the joist and about 20 mm apart, and join them with a groove to recess the wire just below floor level. The groove can be filled with wood filler after wiring. Pass the two ends of the wire down through the floor either side of the joist and around the joist once, then twist together.

An attractive alternative is to split large diameter

■ **13.E** *An elegant traditional Chinese bamboo building in the gardens at Anji, China. The columns are actually steel pipe encased in a bamboo split culm covering. The roof construction is a masterpiece.*

bamboo culms in half and fit them to the joists curved side up, side by side. This creates a strong, flexible attractive 'bush house' floor.

By using the engineering principles of triangulation together with the strong joining systems illustrated (Chapter 12), you can design any number of interesting combinations to suit your needs. If the only bamboos in your area are the inferior thin-walled running bamboos like *Phyllostachys aurea*, you will have to reduce the building considerably in size and design it by using multiples of small culms strapped and lashed together for your beams and braces (Sketch 12.11). I wouldn't recommend you use *P. aurea* ever for columns (except for a chicken house).

Foundations

■ **13.F** *A more conventional Balinese home using bamboo roof rafters throughout (mostly Gigantochloa apus)*

There are two basic rules that should never be breached:

- **Never bury bamboo in the ground**, even if wrapped in plastic, treated in creosote, etc. Bamboo in the ground is vulnerable to fungus rot and insect attack. Wrapping in any sort of membrane creates a pond which can fill with moisture for the bamboo to sit in. Painting the outside with whatever will not protect the inside from deterioration if moisture seeps into a shrinkage crack.

- **Always tie down columns to foundations** to prevent these very light, strong structures from blowing away. (It happened to me once. I thought I had built a shed but it turned out to be a box kite!)

Foundations are best constructed with a post hole digger, setting a tube or box formwork on the ground above the hole, and filling it all, after adding reinforcement, with concrete (Sketch 13.4). Projecting reinforcing or traditional 'inverted U' steel brackets can then be set into or bolted onto filled bamboo column bases, positioned above ground on top of the concrete.

Our current building has a 300 mm diameter 'post hole digger' hole about a metre deep, reinforced, and with a 12 mm reo bar heated and bent into a loop. The neat reusable formwork we used for the projecting foundation top was a large inverted plastic flower pot with its (bottom) centre cut out where the reo projects. The lower (12 mm) bolt (Sketch 13.4) through the column assembly was also passed through the reo loop, and the inside of the culm 'filled'. The slab floor will be poured last, thereby locking the already more than adequate footings together. It will never fly away.

You can use timber pole columns, lashed multiple-bamboo beams and bamboo bracing, and with some creative flair you could build something very attractive. Meanwhile, plant some decent clumping bamboos for the future.

You may have seen the small Bali-style outhouses built without the angled bracing from the bottom of the columns I have incorporated. They are usually built with heavy timber columns buried deep in the ground, and they often have smaller 'knee braces' fitted, starting up higher instead of at the column base. I don't advise burying bamboo columns in the ground (unless it is CCA-treated, i.e. treated with copper, chrome and arsenic—a treatment about to be banned), and the change in bracing configuration results in a high bending moment being transmitted into the building columns during high wind periods. The object of triangulation (bracing) is to convert the forces and weights applied to a building into tensile and compressive forces instead of bending or twisting forces. This is the ideal situation for bamboo, which is very high in axial or longitudinal strength. Its circular tube shape with its wood located as far as possible from its central axis also makes it an ideal shape for braced columns and truss components, which carry more tension and compression.

■ SKETCH **13.4** *A sound foundation construction with the bamboo kept above ground*

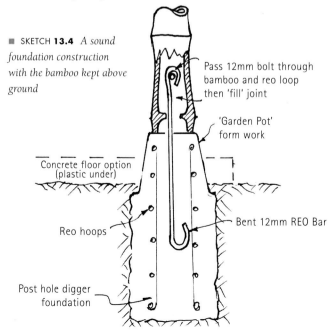

Pass 12mm bolt through bamboo and reo loop then 'fill' joint

'Garden Pot' form work

Concrete floor option (plastic under)

Reo hoops

Bent 12mm REO Bar

Post hole digger foundation

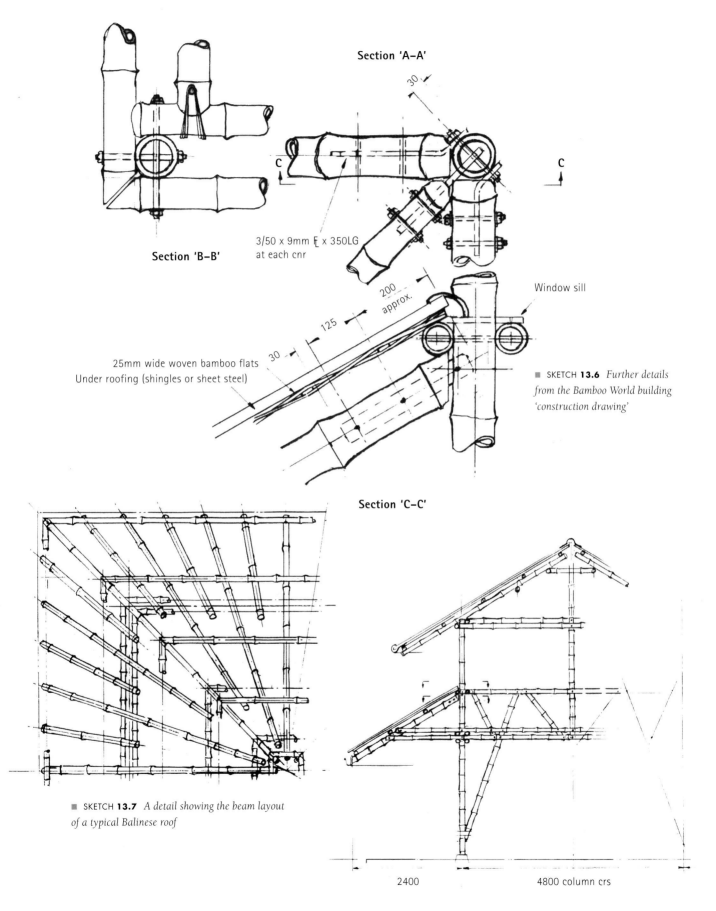

Section 'A–A'

30

C   C

Section 'B–B'

3/50 x 9mm Ⱡ x 350LG
at each cnr

200
approx.

125

30

25mm wide woven bamboo flats
Under roofing (shingles or sheet steel)

Window sill

■ SKETCH **13.6** *Further details
from the Bamboo World building
'construction drawing'*

Section 'C–C'

■ SKETCH **13.7** *A detail showing the beam layout
of a typical Balinese roof*

2400   4800 column crs

■ SKETCH **13.5** *Construction drawings for our 'building under construction'
showing a Bali-style two-storey building profile and truss forms*

Follow the Plan and Build Your Own!

Sketch 13.9 gives details of a basic conventional building similar to that illustrated in Sketch 13.3, very simple to build, and adaptable to enlarging or doubling in length. You can use either modern or traditional joints, a concrete floor or a raised floor either from bamboo joists with split flooring, or an all timber floor. Main members can be anything from 60 mm diameter upward depending on the size of the building and the quality of the bamboo (*Bambusa tuldoides* produces great 60 mm culms).

Sketch 13.8 gives a very simple geodesic dome type building. Using 3 m culm lengths, and Sketch 12.8 joints, it produces a very strong building about 4.3 m across. There is a beautifully constructed version of this quite common form of construction built by Paul Cooper, a real craftsman, at the Arts Factory Lodge, a backpackers resort at Byron Bay, NSW. With a plywood floor and canvas walls, it has roof vents, zippered flyscreen doors, and double bunks for eight people. It would also look great with walls from bamboo splits, a split bamboo floor and a permanent iron roof.

This design also makes a beautiful garden pagoda if you leave the walls out, but don't forget to have a long eaves projection to protect the bamboo from fungal attack.

Design Concept of a Current Construction

As mentioned earlier, we are presently constructing at Bamboo World a reasonably large bamboo building. It is basically an elegant Balinese-style open pagoda with a roof span of 9.6 x 9.6 m and an upstairs room of 4.8 x 4.8 m (Sketch 13.1 is my artist's impression, and Sketches 13.5, 6 and 7 are some of the construction details. Photos 13G, H and I shows it part constructed). It is supported on one central and four outer bamboo columns. Each outer column is actually three culms or columns, one vertical and two climbing at an angle from a common foundation. Thus the building is actually supported by five foundations and on thirteen culms.

The columns and bracing were cut from large diameter thick-walled *Bambusa balcooa* culms measuring between 100 mm and 150 mm diameter and 8 mm to 30 mm wall thickness. The top and bottom cords of the trusses and horizontal beams bolting to the *B. balcooa* are all cut from the smaller *B. oldhamii*, varying from 60 mm to 85 mm diameter and 5 mm to 15 mm wall thickness. Some of the *B. oldhamii* for the top cord was long enough to span the 4.8 m column distance, but none of the lower cord beams were long enough to reach from the outsides of the cantilevered roof sections across both columns. They all had to be joined (Sketch 12.10).

To compensate for the lighter bamboo and the need to join it, we used four culms in parallel instead of one culm

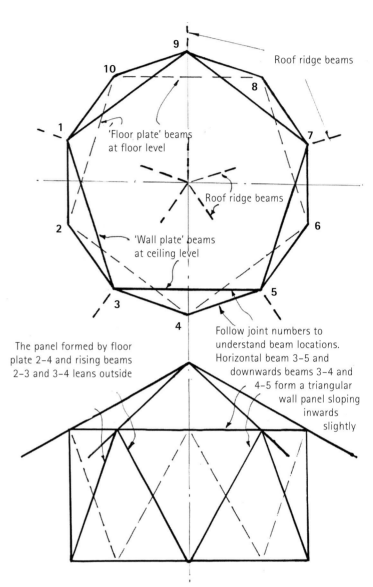

■ SKETCH **13.8** *A geodesic dome type structure, using a series of triangles to construct a very strong five-sided building. Its slightly leaning triangular walls and triangular roof panels are awkward and labour intensive to clad, a small disadvantage when compared to the building design in Sketch 13.9. Using 3 metre culm sections creates a building about 4.3 metres across.*

to form one strong beam. When finished, our building will have a concrete lower floor, and an upper floor of heavy plywood. The access stair is to be bamboo, as are all the floor joists and elegant fan-shaped rafters (all *B. oldhamii*). The roof will be lined with split culms for insulation, and covered with a fireproof (unromantic) long-lasting Colorbond iron.

Overlooking a small lake and island, and surrounded by 150 beautiful different species of clumping bamboos, it will be a significant step forward in our small botanical paradise when we complete it, but the problem is to get enough aged bamboo. It is actually a good example of a project too large for the current available resources,

■ SKETCH **13.9** *Construction details of a simple bamboo building designed to span from two to four metres, depending on the quality and diameter of the bamboo available. As drawn it would suit a three metre span building if using 75 mm diameter bamboo for most beams, and say 120 mm diameter for the columns. You can add more roof rafters and purlins if you increase the size, or subtract some and use smaller diameter culms if you reduce the span. With a three metre span, the length can be increased to 4 metres, or you can make the building twice as long (six metres) by building two joined units (six columns instead of four — see Sketch 13.2 for alternative middle column bracing). The floor can be concrete, dirt or elevated bamboo as in Sketch 13.4. Details of all the joints are as shown earlier, either bolted 'filled' joint or pinned and lashed traditional, with minor joints lashed only. For clarity, lashing, etc. is not shown on the drawing.*

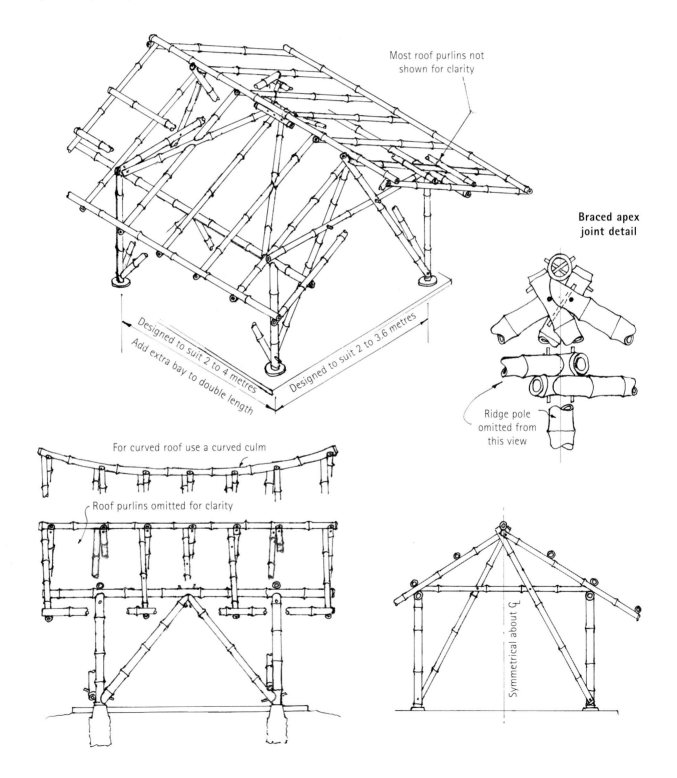

Most roof purlins not
shown for clarity

**Braced apex
joint detail**

Ridge pole
omitted from
this view

Designed to suit 2 to 4 metres

Add extra bay to double length

Designed to suit 2 to 3.6 metres

For curved roof use a curved culm

Roof purlins omitted for clarity

Symmetrical about ℄

■ **13.G, H & I** *Erecting the constructed frame of the two-storey Bali-style building at Bamboo World (see Sketch.13.1). Two frames were constructed on the ground and pivoted into the air where the second frames were constructed between to join them together. Note the 'flower pot' foundation and reinforcing rod projecting, bent to receive a bolt passing through the bamboo columns prior to filling the joint.*

but as the better quality bamboos mature and become available here, we will complete the building, which is also a test example for bamboo chemically treated on our Boucherie plant.

Walls and Ceilings

In Asia they split bamboo into either wide splits or thin flats that are woven into either light sheets, or heavier very strong panels that are used as walls or roof lining. See Chapter 16, Sketch 16.3 and Photo 13J. Strong high quality woven bamboo ply is also available, made in Thailand from *Dendrocalamus asper* culms.

Conventional walls can be constructed by using bamboo culms as conventional studs. The surfaces can either be covered with splits, or half round split culms, or complete culms (Sketch 16.1), or a variety of slat woven combinations (Sketch 16.2).

In the house we are currently constructing to live in, we plan to incorporate elegant hanging panels with a heavy bamboo outer frame and delicate screen panelling, suspended movable walls for picture hanging and room space rearrangement. Very strong bamboo ply made from attractive pressed woven sheets is now available. The options for creativity become increasingly available as more superior bamboo becomes available.

Bamboo-reinforced Concrete

It seems hard to believe but split bamboo is now being widely used for reinforcing steel throughout Asia and South America (Hidalgo, 1995). The theory is that if the concrete mix is correct, and the reinforcing is designed and positioned correctly, bamboo seems to have long-lasting qualities. Remember that if the concrete cracks, the slab will fail whether it is reinforced with bamboo or steel, because the steel will rust or the bamboo will rot, but whilst it is properly protected by the correctly designed cover of concrete, bamboo will not rot or suffer from insect attack. There does need to be further research work done because pectin, the substance that biologically 'sticks' bamboo's cellulose fibres together, is normally destroyed by an alkaline environment, and concrete has a pH of 13 (Janssen, 1995). One encouraging comment came from symposium author D. Krishnamurthy who advised, 'Observations were carried out over a decade and no visible signs of cracking or any damage have been noticed so far.' The Columbian experience over 90 years seems to indicate that long life is probable. It is certainly being used quite extensively in economically disadvantaged countries as a cost-saving device.

It is also important to use well-aged dried bamboo splits or they may shrink and break the bond between the concrete and the bamboo, important for transmitting load to the reinforcing. It is then split into correct sized reinforcing strips and sealed in a shellac varnish (Surjokusumo, 1995) or tar dipped in sand coating

■ **13.J** *A bamboo hut in Bali using woven splits for walls, and bamboo roof tiles. Note that the tiles will need replacing regularly because of fungal rot.*

(Janssen) to protect it from water intake whilst the concrete is curing (Surjokusumo, 1995). The coating should also help isolate the pectin from the effects of the alkaline environment. Use the same method as you would for steel to lay and tie-off the reinforcing splits, and then pour your concrete.

It is certainly an economical medium to use for building your water tanks, footpaths, or even swimming pools. Because its use for this purpose is unknown in the Western world, you may have trouble getting local council approval, if required. Because there are still cautions and unknowns about its use, I would recommend you use it only in non-critical designs.

Bamboo Houses Rendered with Concrete

Many floors in Columbia are built using *Guadua* culms about 150 mm diameter (*Dendrocalamus asper* or very straight *Bambusa balcooa* could be used) spanning up to 3.5 m, laid side by side with a 40 to 50 mm gap between. Steel reinforcing is not added. Formwork is constructed under (against) the culms, and as strong a sand, cement and gravel concrete mix as you would use for a suspended slab poured and spread on top, giving a cover of 35 to 40 mm over the bamboo. The formwork is removed 24 hours later, and the underside is cement rendered to

■ **13.K** *A cement-rendered bamboo building designed for the earthquake-resistant Costa Rican housing project (rendered as yet to sill height only)*

give a smooth ceiling. The top surface is either rendered 20 mm thick to give a smooth concrete surface, or rendered and tiled to the same thickness. This results in a very solid strong floor that will last for a long time. Examples in Columbia are approaching 100 years old. According to Columbian architect Lucy Bastidas, the bamboo sealed in concrete becomes pH stabilised in a condition 'approaching petrification, and deprived of oxygen does not suffer further modification or deterioration'.

Conventional-looking rendered walls are being made by clout nailing or screwing split bamboo laths to the inside and outside of the bamboo studs and columns, with a light wire mesh stretched over the splits and fixed with clouts. Pass the wire occasionally behind instead of outside one of the laths. The inside and outside of the wall surfaces can then be rendered with two coats of strong cement render (first coat 2:1 about 10 mm thick over the laths and pushed deep between the laths, and the second 3:1 as a finish coat between 3 and 5 mm thick), creating a massively strong wall.

Using this technique one can build houses that look like conventional rendered masonry houses, even with 'concrete' floors! They are actually stronger, more flexible, and similar to the more than 3000 modern earthquake-proof houses already built in Columbia and Costa Rica which survive 7.6 Richter scale quakes virtually undamaged. Thousands are now being built using prefabricated factory-produced bamboo trusses, and prefabricated bamboo wall panels erected on site between bamboo columns before cement rendering. The light triangulated trusses are strong, using members made from two long 50 x 20 mm bamboo flats sawn from heavy culm walls. Their inner surfaces are glued and stapled to flat wooden

gusset plates at all bracing intersections. (See Photo 13K showing a Costa Rican building under construction as yet rendered with concrete to sill level only.

Current Use of Bamboo in Buildings

Whilst Australia is located in the middle of Asian countries accustomed to building large structures from bamboo, I know of nothing of significance (except our own small building at Bamboo World, of course!) being constructed in this country. Australia lacks architects, engineers and tradespeople trained to utilise bamboo in buildings, and the resource itself is not available in sufficient volume or quality to make any serious attempt on a significant scale. Nor do I believe that bamboo will ever, or should ever, replace the role of sawn timber in buildings, but the day will come when it will certainly augment it.

There are Australian and American architects in Asian places like Bali incorporating bamboo in their modern resorts, elegant blends of Western and traditional style and technology. In the same way that the best of Australian food now incorporates touches of Asian cuisine, I believe that a touch of Asian, incorporating bamboo, will become fashionable in the architecture of this country, but not before larger quantities of properly cured high grade bamboo are available.

Bamboo does have an important role for those individuals who have the courage to build something artistic, creative and unique from a material which is without cost if you grow your own, or gain access to harvest it. It is impracticable to grow large numbers of trees and wait 25 years to cut your own, saw it into square shapes and then build. But it isn't such a stretch of the imagination to plant bamboos now and build in seven years, with renewable quantities to expand your building every year. You can also harvest smaller early culms and hone your skills by making furniture as you wait!

The Costa Rican government, with help from the United Nations and the Netherlands Government, has applied such foresight on a grand scale. Because of the regular death of people being crushed by stone houses in earthquakes, they actually established (1987-88) 179 hectares of bamboo plantations of a superior South American bamboo not indigenous to their part of their continent (*Guadua angustifolia*). During the pilot stage they built 300 houses, 50 of which survived a devastating earthquake measuring 7.6 on the Richter scale, some with relatively minor damage, and 30 with no damage at all. By 1997, they estimate the plantations will be producing enough wood to construct 3000 architect-designed earth-quake-proof bamboo houses every year (15 per cent of their total annual requirement). (Janssen, 1995). They use bamboo in conventional stud walls, creating rendered walls on split bamboo laths as described earlier (Photo 13K). Conventional windows and doors are fixed and the houses look identical to others. Bamboo studs sealed in the cavity are protected from fungus or insects. They were designed by Columbian architect Oscar Hidalgo Lopez, a man who has contributed much to the world of bamboo.

■ **13.L** *Balinese bamboo roof tiles. The upper tiles protect the lower tiles from moisture and fungus attack, but the upper tiles would need replacing on a regular basis—a superb roof but rather labour-intensive and high in maintenance.*

We at Bamboo World hope eventually to have available a series of building designs covering anything from garden pagodas to small cottages, complete with calculations and any necessary special plate fittings, harvesting and curing instructions, etc. to help the bamboo builder have proposed plans passed by local council. Plant your bamboos now and build your house from free materials in seven years time! Faster than timber and you don't need a sawmill.

(PHOTO, SIMON VELEZ)

■ **13.M** *A Colombian border crossing with an extraordinary Guadua bamboo-trussed roof with huge overhangs, designed by Simon Velez*

14 Furniture Making— Joints, Tools, Techniques and Species

The next chapter gives designs to assist you make beautiful furniture, and a system to help you design your own furniture. However, before discussing design, you will need at least a rudimentary understanding of the materials to select, joints and how to make them and the tools most effective for bamboo work.

I get a great deal of pleasure out of working bamboo. It is a simple, strong material, easy to use if you have some practice and a little knowledge. The tools you need are fairly basic.

Material Selection and Treatment

Heavy, strong structural bamboos such as bambu betung (*Dendrocalamus asper*) are used quite often in some of the modern Balinese furniture, used to project a sense of bulk and strength. Mostly, however, the ideal furniture bamboo is smaller in diameter (from 100 mm down) and with a strong, medium wall thicknesses. Sometimes it is better to choose parts from the top half of a culm, those pieces being thinner walled but very strong nevertheless because of the greater concentration of fibre bundles in the upper culms.

Once mature, each species tends to produce culms close to the full diameter culm possible in its particular environment. This means that you sometimes need a range of bamboos to provide the different diameters and shapes you need. Often it is convenient to obtain smaller diameter pieces from higher up the culm, particularly where you want to cut a hole and insert a smaller culm into a larger one (Sketch 14.1). The top segments of some culms are very heavily branched, however, which tends to disfigure those pieces when compared to lower culm segments of smaller diameter species. (The end of this chapter gives species recommendations.)

It is possible to bend bamboo culms if they are heated whilst green. Heat the area you want bent over fire coals, or even a glowing hotplate, turning the bamboo to get the heat to penetrate slowly enough not to burn it. Then bend it to the desired shape and hold or clamp it in that posi-

tion until it is completely cool (you can use a wet cloth to cool it). A steam box can also be used instead of more direct heat. For bending, you need bamboos that are either very thick-walled, or solid with no hole (see list later this chapter). If you don't have a thick-walled species, sometimes the lowest culm portion is sufficiently thick-walled not to collapse during this process.

Some of the thicker walled or solid bamboos (*Bambusa tulda*, *B. nana*, *B. affinis* and *B. polymorpha*) are virtually solid or have no hole in lower culm sections. They are very good for furniture making except where you need to introduce a culm inside, and of course there is no hole to cut into, making it an impossible joint to construct.

It is best to avoid high starch bamboos with short fibre length structures such as *Bambusa vulgaris*, unless there is no alternative material, in which case choose very old dry wood and cure it well before use.

■ **14.A** *An elegant, simple lounge chair*

Both *Bambusa ventricosa* (Buddha's belly bamboo) and the larger, similar *B. vulgaris* cv. 'Wamin' make wonderful features if used in furniture with their bulging culm internodes. *B. ventricosa* produces superior wood, but the earlier comments on *B. vulgaris* also apply to the cultivar 'Wamin'.

Black-culmed bamboos are the only species that retain their colour after harvesting. All the others change to the traditional bamboo 'straw' colour except *Bambusa maculata* (known until recently as pring tutul) that is covered with a beautiful mottled pattern of dark brown spots after harvesting and curing (the living bamboo has green culms with cream stripes). The black bamboos are highly valued for furniture making, but there are a limited number of black species as follows:

Bambusa lako Syn. *Gigantochloa* sp. 'Timor Black'
    (medium diameter)
Dendrocalamus asper 'Hitam' (large diameter)
Gigantochloa atroviolacea (medium diameter)
Otatea acuminata aztecorum (smaller diameter)
Phyllostachys nigra (a small diameter, thin-walled runner)
Phyllostachys nigra boryana (a small, thin-walled runner
    with black spots)

Of the above bamboos, the first four are strong, heavy to medium-walled clumping bamboos very suitable for furniture making. The last two (*Phyllostachys* genus) are thinner walled and split more easily, generally more suitable for decorative members than for load-supporting members in your furniture, but the lower portions are sometimes thick-walled and large enough. Being running bamboos, the *Phyllostachys* should not be planted unless in a concrete retaining box or pot, or on an island, but it is very commonly available and it may be all you can get.

For making furniture, *Bambusa blumeana* has a special attraction for me (and the Philippinos). It produces culms of especially interesting shapes, with knobs, bends, and sometimes zigzags that are quite wonderful for designing unique pieces. One can virtually create or modify the design to suit the interesting culm shape. It is an immensely strong, quite often thick-walled bamboo that tends to have a bushy bottom portion (with aggressive little hooked thorns). It sometimes has a variety of smaller diameter shapes available in the lower fine-leafed bushy part of the clump. Some Philippino furniture factories have run out of this species due to over-harvesting of both the delicious shoots and the timber, and are now importing *B. blumeana* furniture wood from Vietnam to fill their orders.

All the bamboo that you use to make furniture should be properly harvested and cured. If it is not properly cured, it will almost always split, particularly where you make a nice joint to introduce a smaller piece into a larger piece. Your lovingly carved neat joints will become loose or distorted because of shrinkage. Powder beetle is also the scourge of bamboo furniture, but it can be avoided by good harvesting and curing procedure (see Chapter 11).

Having said that, if you are like me you won't be able to resist the temptation of starting straight away, and the

(PHOTO: CHRIS ELLIS)

■ **14.B** *An unusual sofa designed to fit into a corner, made from* Bambusa blumeana *in the Philippines*

practice is valuable. Pretend I'm not saying this, but go and harvest some suitable older looking bamboo culms, dry it for as long as your patience will allow, and then start practising your joints. If your 'joints' happen to end up furniture shape, some culms will crack, but they will most likely remain strong enough to be usable, and probably won't break. At least you will get the practice you'll need for the 'work of art' you will later construct!

Properly cured bamboo as opposed to green or half-cured bamboo is much easier to work, is less prone to splitting while you work it, and less prone to fibres pulling out and disfiguring the surface. It is also considerably stronger than green bamboo and much less prone to splitting where holes are placed under stress by inserting pins or culms.

Selecting and Designing Joints

There are dozens of ways of joining your bamboo when building furniture. These joints shouldn't be used as structural joints, however, as most of them are based on cutting part of one member away, which diminishes the strength available for carrying heavy structural loads. Before discussing tools and technique, it is best that you understand the form of the joints you have to make.

Type A Joint (Sketch 14.1)

This joint is suitable only for joining bamboos of different diameters. A neat hole is cut in a larger diameter culm of a size allowing a smaller diameter culm to be slipped into the hole. The maximum diameter of the piece to be inserted must be no larger than the inside diameter of the culm hole you want to insert it into, or the hole becomes almost impossible to make. It pays to chamfer the sides of the slip-in piece, or even extend the hole a little into the

■ **14.C** *Making straight, perfectly sized dowels from thick culm sections using a wad punch with the handles cut off*

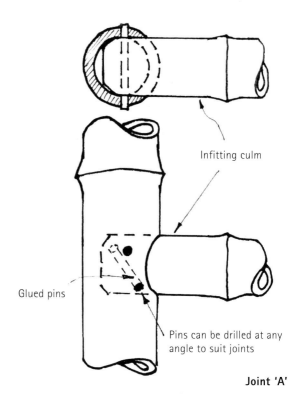

■ SKETCH **14.1** *A simple Type A furniture joint (for housing a smaller culm in a larger one)*

back inside culm section where the bamboo is inserted, to make the culm end seat firmly. Assemble with glue, then drill dowel pin holes at different angles (from one to three pins depending on the size of the bamboo), insert glue in the pin hole and on the pin, and tap the pin home. Cut the pin(s) off flush after assembly.

Sketch 15.1 illustrates a simple low magazine or coffee table that you can construct using Type A joints only. The table design is possible only if each smaller sized bamboo to be inserted into a joint is as close as possible to the inside diameter of the piece into which it fits; otherwise they all get too small too quickly.

Dowel pins can be cut from old well-seasoned bamboo branches, but they are usually tapered to some degree, whereas the drill creates a parallel hole. The best pins can be made by modifying a wad punch (obtainable in any hardware store, and usually used to cut holes in leather). By cutting the handle off the punch, you can arrange the punch cutting edge to point upwards in the vice, then drive well-seasoned lengths of thick split culm internode through the punch to create perfectly round parallel sided pins (Photo 14C).

Dowel pins should be a minimum of 6 mm diameter, and increasing up to 9 mm diameter for very large joints, with more than one pin inserted at different angles for larger joints. You will mostly need series 'W' type dowelling drills to make the holes.

Glues and Gluing Techniques

Use heavy filler type glues, such as Maxibond or NoNails, rather than thinner watery type PVA glues such as Aquadhere. Insert an abundant amount into the socket of joints to support the end of the inserted culm against the back wall of the socket. Make sure you sand off the waxy outer coating on culms where you expect glue to adhere, or it won't stick.

Before you glue, assemble and pin all your joints, work out an assembly procedure that allows the jigsaw puzzle of your designed parts to go together in the correct order; otherwise you may work yourself into a situation where one part, like a lower table leg cross bar, can't be fitted into place.

Type B Joint (Sketch 14.3)

The corners of a bamboo bedhead I constructed eighteeen years ago used a Type B joint. It's an attractive joint that can be used to join bamboos of the same diameter with the aid of a decorative locking pin.

The culm to be butted is marked with a curve of the correct diameter (hold a square cut culm end of the same diameter against the culm), and then carved to a curve for a neat fit against the other member (use a pangot knife). Drill the hole through both walls of the other culm with both members held in place, and through the node diaphragm of the butting member, then insert a pre-prepared locking pin (use an adjustable drill). If you don't have a node diaphragm in the butting member close enough to become part of the support system, you can insert two

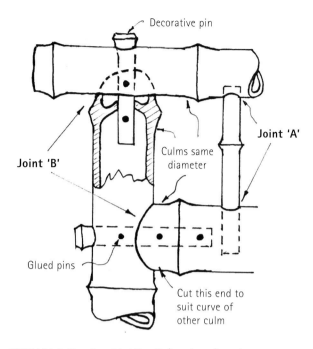

■ SKETCH **14.3** *Furniture joint Type B, for culms of equal diameter (used to make the bed head end shown in Photo.14.D). The sketch also shows the small Type A joints commonly used for decorative 'spokes'.*

reasonably large dowel pins through the locking pin and butting member to hold the pin firmly in place. Cut the locking pin from a thick-walled or solid bamboo, *Bambusa polymorpha, B. tuldoides, B. tulda* or *Gigantochlea albociliata* or *Dendrocalamus strictus* being ideal species or even the lower culm of *Phyllostachys auroa.*

Type C Joint (Sketch 14.2)

Another joint for butting bamboos of the same diameter together, this joint is prepared in the same way as Type B joints, but without the locking pin. Without this pin, the joint should be used to join only lightly loaded thick-walled larger diameter culms to each other, or non load-carrying members if they are thin-walled. For a similar stronger joint, use Type D joints.

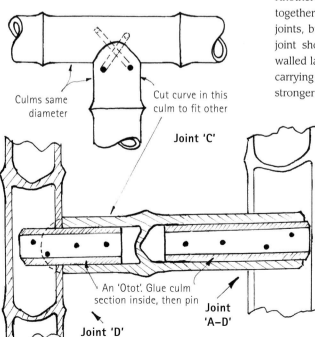

■ SKETCH **14.2** *Furniture Joints 'C' and 'D' for joining culms the same diameter, and Joint 'A–D' for joining different diameter culms*

Type D Joint (Sketch 14.2)

Again for joining bamboos of the same diameter, this is identical but superior to Type C joints, but combines the strength of the Type A joint by inserting a hidden bamboo culm section or softwood plug into the inside diameter of one member, and into a hole cut in the other. The hidden culm section is glued and dowel pinned firmly to both members, making a very strong joint.

Type A-D Joint (Sketch 14.2)

For joining bamboos of different diameter, this joint looks identical to a Type A joint, but is much stronger. It has a hidden bamboo culm section glued inside the culm that is being inserted, giving more support for the pins, etc.

Type E Joint (Sketch 14.4)

Good for joining bamboos of different diameter, and also for making furniture which will be dismantled. The smaller member is passed right through holes cut in the larger culm. Pins are fitted in holes drilled hard against the larger bamboo, passing right through the smaller one. The outer pin should be tapered, or even in the form of a cut wedge (Sketch 14.4), to jam the smaller culm hard into place. By tapping the outer pin out, the joint can be dismantled so long as you have used no glue (except on the inner pin).

Type F Joint (Sketch 14.4)

This is for supporting a culm that crosses above another. The upper culm has a curve cut out to bed it down on the lower, with glue and a pin to hold it in place.

With any of the type A, E, or F joints, if you have any doubts about the wall thickness or strength of the smaller member (to be inserted in the larger), it's easy to insert and glue a smaller culm section or wooden plug into the end of the culm as shown for the Type D or A-D joints, and then add more pins through the reinforced area. It's often wise to use this device where chair legs meet a seat edge, or table legs meet the main table support members, but in many cases it's not necessary, depending on the load on the joint, the quality of the joint you make and the wall thickness of the culms being used (in Indonesia, that inserted sleeve or plug is called an 'otot').

Type G Joint (Sketch 14.5)

This joint is used for joining **bamboo of equal diameter** at a corner in such a way that there is a smooth transitional curve from one bamboo to the other, that is, neither of the bamboos joined project beyond the other. Because such joints look messy if left exposed, they are

■ **14.E** *A corner table joint being constructed with a softwood plug to create a completely round effect. It must be covered in rattan to hide the unattractive joint.*

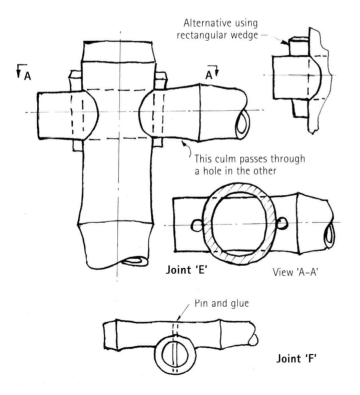

Alternative using rectangular wedge

This culm passes through a hole in the other

Joint 'E'   View 'A-A'

Pin and glue

Joint 'F'

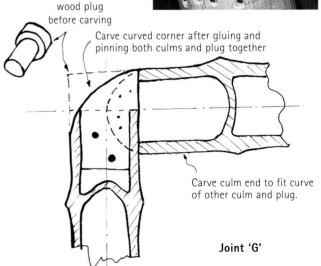

Shape of soft-wood plug before carving

Carve curved corner after gluing and pinning both culms and plug together

Carve culm end to fit curve of other culm and plug.

Joint 'G'

■ SKETCH **14.4** *Furniture joints Type E for joining unequal diameter culms, and Type F for joining a culm resting on, or passing over, another culm*

■ SKETCH **14.5** *Furniture joint Type G, for joining equal culms in a round elbow*

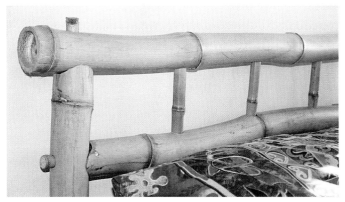

14.D *A bedhead made from* Bambusa balcooa *with* Phyllostachys aurea *pins and vertical bars. Constructed 18 years ago by the author from properly harvested, untreated bamboo, it is as sound today as the day it was made.*

traditionally bound in split rattan strips. The drawing of this joint is shown with the structural parts only without the rattan binding. For the rattan being progressively applied, see Sketch 14.6.

Firstly, the vertical member is cut off square at the centreline height of the other joining (horizontal) culm. A softwood plug is cut to the same diameter as the outside of the members to be joined, and the lower end of it is reduced in diameter to the upright culm's inside diameter so it fits snugly. The plug is then glued and pinned in position. Then carve the culm end of the horizontal culm to fit the curve of the projecting plug. The shaped horizontal culm is then glued (sometimes even nailed if it is *Dendrocalamus asper* or *Guadua*), and pinned to the vertical culm and its upstanding softwood plug. Next, cut the top off the plug square at the exact top, or centreline height, of the joining (horizontal) member. The remainder of the softwood plug end of the vertical member is then carved to give a smooth curved elbow shape.

14.F *Rattan binding covering the softwood plug construction on a Type G joint. Note the panel of cross-lashed splits (see Photo 14Q) held in by a tacked frame, as suggested for the chair sides in Sketch 15.3.*

Binding Joints With Rattan (Sketch 14.6)

To apply the rattan, you need a thin glue that dries transparent (PVA is ideal), a tin of very small flat-headed tacks, and a light hammer. The rattan is applied in such a way that the finished job looks as though it uses some mysterious, endless way of winding the rattan on without joining, but that's not the reality (Photo 14F).

The first layer of rattan travels around the outside of bend in the direction of the grain. Before painting the surface with PVC glue, ensure that the bamboo's wax cover is sanded off. Painting only the area where you are about to apply the rattan with glue, then follow the following steps:

Stage 1. Each piece is tacked at the top end, stretched around the bend and held tight whilst it's tacked at the bottom end and then cut off. The rattan strips are laid side by side in this manner until the whole outer corner is covered, the tacks being located below or past the projected inside corner of the joint.

Stage 2. The purpose of this stage is to cover the tacks put in place at stage 1. Apply more glue; then starting with the piece closest to the point of the elbow, apply rattan by winding one strip at a time around first the horizontal member, then alternately the vertical member, tacking each end of each strip as you go. Each end of each alternate piece is applied in such a way that the tack head is covered by the next alternate piece you attach. The first piece applied in this way is located not far back from the intersecting centre line of the joint. It will be obvious where it has to be located in order not to reveal any of the rather unsightly structural matter underneath.

Stage 3. As you progressively, alternately add these strips, the length of each one will increase as they get further into the inside corner of the joint, and it becomes quite difficult to get the tacks in. At that point, you can actually tack the rattan under the joint and, after applying more glue, wind it round and round until it has covered the first tacks you put in. Use between three and six final loops according to your aesthetic judgment. Then loop the end under itself on the last loop so that it forms a jam

■ SKETCH **14.6** *The sequential application of rattan binding to a Type A joint corner*

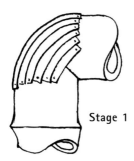

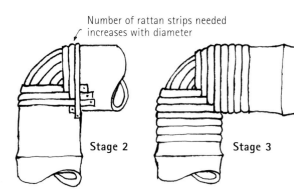

Number of rattan strips needed increases with diameter

Stage 1   Stage 2   Stage 3

hitch that crosses under the culm out of sight, pull it tight and lock it with a tack through the loop's crossover point. Cut the rattan off neatly parallel against the last rattan loop laid and paint the whole rattan assembly with PVA glue. Your joint is now finished.

Type H Joint (Sketch 14.7)

This is a variation of Type G joint where the two **bamboos of equal diameter** are being joined at an angle rather than at right angles. The same wooden plug is prepared, and pinned and glued into one of the members square cut to receive it (in this case the left hand member). The top end of the wooden plug is then cut off level with the top of the horizontal culm, and carved to fit inside the horizontal culm. This carving is quite awkward, but it doesn't need to be too neat or accurate because it is later covered in rattan, and the thick glue can be used as a filler to overcome inaccuracies in your carving. After pinning and gluing the second half of the softwood plug in place, the remainder is then pared away until a smooth transitional curve is achieved. The rattan strips are then applied to the joint in much the same way as described for Type G joint.

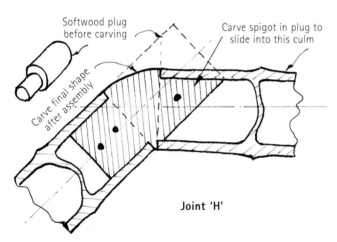

■ SKETCH **14.7** *Furniture joint Type H, for joining equal culms in a smooth-angled elbow*

Type J Joint (Sketch 14.8)

This joint is suitable for thin-walled bamboos like *Phyllostachys aurea*, but you can try it with larger diameters if the part being bent around is large, and you shave the bent section fairly thin. By cutting the major part of the culm out and applying heat to the remaining thin section, you can bend it around another culm and fix it in place with glue or a tack.

Most bamboo furniture and all rattan cane furniture has the joins covered by rattan stripping. I personally prefer the natural look of bamboo joints, and if the piece you are making is skilfully designed, and you are careful with your joints and the positioning of nodes, it will look

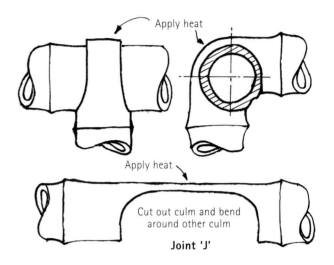

■ SKETCH **14.8** *Furniture joint Type J*

neater in my opinion without rattan binding than it will with. Furniture is also made from rattan cane, but you can't join rattan without binding the joints to give them sufficient strength, because rattan is not as strong as bamboo. Nor does it have convenient holes inside to help with the joining process. A lot of furniture used to be made by combining bamboo and rattan, and I suspect this has led to rattan binding being used with unnecessary frequency on bamboo furniture. If you want round-cornered joints you will have to use a covering medium like rattan because such joints look messy without being bound. Bamboo splits can be used, but rattan is softer, more pliable and easier to apply. Rattan stripping can be purchased from any workshop repairing or working with rattan cane, and also some craft shops. Rattan is a member of the palm family (Palmae), and is not a bamboo, although it is often mistaken for one, with its long climbing jointed canes.

Both fine bamboo splits and rattan splits are also used to lash crossing members together (such as Type F joint) and can be added as a feature on most of the joints described above, but it is unnecessary. It is also used sometimes, again unnecessarily, to create decorative endcaps on square cut bamboo. To achieve this, two strips are positioned crossing at the centre line, each bent around a short distance along the culm at both ends and tacked. Then one by one, additional strips are woven in and out alternately one way and then the other and tacked in place until the whole end is covered with a woven pattern. The circle of cut ends and tacks is then covered by winding the rattan around the culm, starting with a hitch and a tack, and ending with a hitch and a tack once clear of the untidy tacked areas. On smaller culms, the winding is sometimes started by laying a loop along the most unobtrusive part of the length to be covered, then winding on the rattan, and passing the end through the loop, then pulling the other end to jam the rattan end under the binding, like a fishhook knot.

Tool Handling Techniques

There are a number of basic rules that will save you lots of problems when working with bamboo, rules that apply without exception, such as:

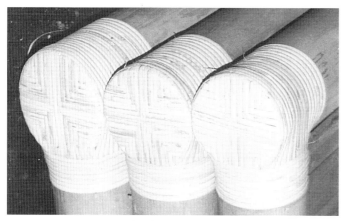

■ **14.G** *Rattan binding covering culm ends cut off square. This is a bed corner, but it could just as easily be adapted for a lounge or table corner with the lower two culms cut short and the upper culms spanning between each corner.*

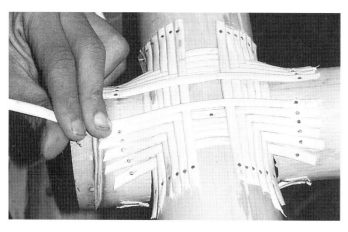

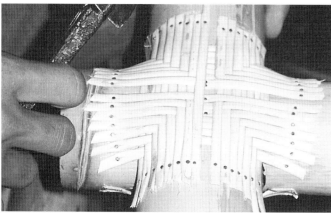

■ **14.H & I** *Rattan binding progressively being positioned, glued and tacked, at the stage before adding the binding around the culms to cover the tacks*

- **Always cut with the grain**, not against it. If you cut against the grain, bamboo's strong fibres and longitudinal structure will always cause it to split, dig in and resist, or lift individual fibres that pull out of the surface and run along disfiguring the wood.

- **Always sharpen your tools on an oilstone** to the point where you can virtually shave yourself with the blade. Bamboo, particularly well seasoned wood, is very sympathetic to work if your tools are sharp. It gives me pleasure to feel the blade sensitively travelling through the wood, sliding across and through the fibres as though it was helping me. The bamboo tells me instantly if the blade is not sharp enough. Bamboo culm surfaces are high in silica (which when melted makes glass), and cutting tools become blunt much faster than if you were working with wood.

- **ALWAYS, *always*, keep both hands behind the blade of the tool**, and preferably both hands on the tool to control it. When the cutting edge is necessarily so sharp, you can do yourself a serious injury by holding the bamboo in one hand, and attempting to cut with the blade. I teach people not to do that but I'm still stupid enough to cut myself occasionally.

- **Find ways of holding your work without having to use your hands**, so that both hands are free to use and guide the tool(s). Sometimes your feet or thighs are sufficient, but watch where you point the blade or you may have difficulty in explaining how you got cut where! (See later description of a bamboo vice.)

- **Always select and work from the largest member(s) first**, and work down in size, or you will tend to lose the sense of proportion necessary to arrive at a sensitive result.

- **Don't force your tools**, but let them cut for you. Remember that as strong as it is longitudinally, bamboo splits very easily. If you push even moderately hard on a slightly blunt drill, you will split the fibres out as it reaches the other side. If you hit a chisel with a mallet too hard and drive it against end grain or between fibres, it will lift the fibres and tend to split along the grain, or even split the whole culm.

Tools

The main process in bamboo furniture making is to learn to make neat holes, large and small, round, oval or square. Most of the rest of it is much like Meccano or Lego set assembly. There are a number of different tools and alternative techniques available. The first four of the following list describes effective hole-making tools. The tool list also includes the most effective saws for harvesting bamboo and describes how to make a vice for working bamboo.

1. Drills

Drills are generally only suitable for small holes (up to 20 mm diameter maximum), and become far too cumbersome and expensive for larger holes. Any sharp object exerting pressure against the side of the culm is exerting a potential splitting force. Normal twist drills are not an ideal shape, but they can be used for smaller holes if they are kept very sharp. Don't press hard and let the drill do the work. For dowel pins you may have to purchase 'long' series drills, or silver solder an extension on your drill. The perfect drill for bamboo is the 'W' series P & K dowelling drill. They are expensive, but worth it because they cut a beautifully clean hole.

You can use high quality woodworking drills with a sharp central 'point' and either one or two outer spikes that rotate around the point as a cutting edge. Many of those drills have a screw thread on the central guiding pin which tends to split the fibres. If you carefully grind the thread off the point to create a flat 'cutter' type point rather than a screw thread, you will find it works well.

2. Adjustable drills

You can buy an adjustable hole drill with a central point and a single rotating cutter on an adjustable slide. The sharp edge of the rotating cutter severs the bamboo fibres cleanly so long as the central part of the bamboo is still in place to guide it (stop before you drill the disc out and cut out the last bit with a knife tip). It works well for holes between about 20 mm and 30 mm diameter. Mine will open to a 45 mm diameter but it becomes increasingly difficult to use above 30 mm, and causes fibre tearing. Don't buy the largest adjustable drill available. It won't work and you will waste your money.

■ **14.J** *Suitable bamboo drills: an adjustable drill (left), a W series P & K dowelling drill (centre), and a wood-working bit with the thread ground off the centre pin (right)*

3. Saw drills

■ **14.K** *Using a hole saw. Note the large number of expensive bits needed for the differently sized holes.*

These are larger diameter drills well suited for working bamboo. A number of brands are available (e.g. Sutton Tools, Sandvic, Sarrett, Gamplex) but they are very expensive, and you need to buy a saw hole cutter for every sized hole you need. The saw drill consists of two parts, a drill mandrel with a centering drill about 6 mm diameter for mounting in your power drill, and a round downward facing saw-toothed cup-shaped 'cutting bit' which screws onto the mandrel. To make oval-shaped culms fit nicely one has to measure the culm with calipers and first drill with the cutter sized to the minimum distance across the oval culm, and then forcefully gouge out the sides of holes to create the oval shape. It does work fairly effectively and I know of professional furniture makers in Australia that find it convenient and quick to make their holes that way. Brian Earley, the talented furniture maker who created Byron Bamboo, and who is helping me construct our bamboo building, swears by the hole saw system. However, be warned. Unless you are making a career of furniture making, it seems impractical to buy a range of cutters from 35 mm up to about 100 mm or more in fairly small increments, and they will cost more than A$1000. Don't be deceived into buying a light duty saw hole, even for one piece of furniture. The blades twist the first time they jam, and once distorted, they are useless. Also, the expensive ones can be resharpened and the others can't. The high silica surface of culms quickly blunts hole saws, and it is very unlikely that your budget model will last for even half of one piece of furniture.

Having learnt by working in villages in Java and Bali, I prefer to make my holes the Indonesian way. For me it's just as quick, does a very neat job, gives me greater satisfaction, and costs next to nothing for the tool!

4. Indonesian furniture knives and chisels (Sketch 14.9 and Photo 14L)

The Indonesians have developed a series of wonderful tools for the various activities you carry out while working bamboo. They need only two simple tools to make any reasonable sized furniture hole. The knife is called a 'pangot', and I find it a superbly simple and effective tool. If you photostat Sketch 14.9 and blow it up until the 160 mm dimension on the pangot measures 160 mm, you will have an exact profile of the knife. It looks deceptively heavy and clumsy, but they haven't spent 2000 years developing that shape for nothing. The blade is beaten (heat forged) from a piece of old spring steel car spring and tapers from about 6 mm thick where it leaves the handle to a very fine sharp curved cutting edge.

The Indonesian or Balinese 'chisel' is a simple piece of beaten spring steel with a slightly cupped end, sharpened to a complete curve, again razor sharp and kept that way on the oil stone (Sketch 14.9). Again deceptively simple, this sophisticated design will never cut the bamboo fibres in such a way as to leave any torn fibres at the edge of the cut, which is what you would get it you use a square ended Western-type chisel. You can buy a standard chisel with a curved blade, but you would need to grind the blade back to create a non-square end, and even then the cup shape would be too severe and not as good as the Indonesian alternative. Their chisel doesn't even have a handle. If you look at their beautiful, often frighteningly complex, wood carvings, you will see what they can do with those chisels!

The secret of the pangot is in the upward curve at the end of the knife, in particular the angle and position of the last 40 mm or so of the cutting edge with respect to the handle. The curve allows the cutting edge to be 'pushed' around the inside of a hole on a culm, to act like a chisel operating inside but square to the culm section being cut. The knife is held blade up, the left hand grasping the back of the blade to guide it, and the right hand grasping the handle, or with the round end in the centre of your palm to push, exerting the cutting force. These knives, if sharpened on a fine oil stone, literally slice through the bamboo. They leave a beautiful clean cut surface so long as you cut around the hole with the grain and not against it. The handle is heavy, smooth and round ended, with a heavy pipe ferrule around the knife tongue end to hold the blade and prevent the handle from splitting.

To make a hole the Indonesian way, you first use the chisel to cut an access hole for the tip of the pangot, and then finish the hole with the pangot. Hold the end of the bamboo to be inserted against the member where you want the hole, and mark the hole diameter with a marking pen, projecting the outside diameter down onto the curve of the culm being marked as accurately as possible. Then take the flat steel chisel (follow Sketch 14.11) and cut into the culm with light mallet taps, with the chisel located on the centre of the culm on the hole edge, leaning towards the centre of the hole and along the grain. Cut carefully into the hole area, working from both hole

■ **14.L** & SKETCH **14.9** *Photo and 'to-scale' drawing of an Indonesian 'pangot', a Balinese furniture knife, a Balinese splitting knife, and an Indonesian/Balinese bamboo chisel (top to bottom). Enlarge on a photostat machine to get a full size profile for making your own from an old truck spring.*

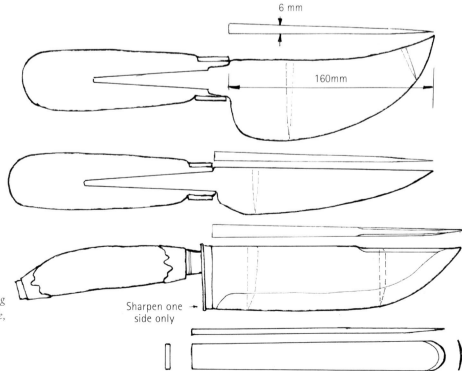

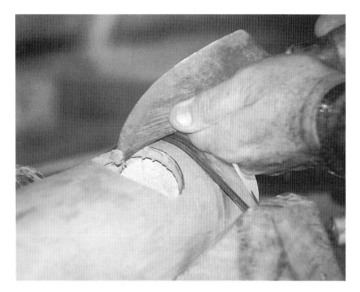

■ **14.M** *Correct way of holding and pushing the pangot (with the grain)*

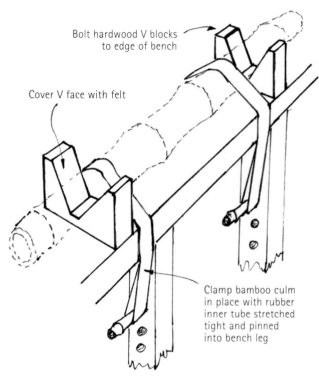

Bolt hardwood V blocks to edge of bench

Cover V face with felt

Clamp bamboo culm in place with rubber inner tube stretched tight and pinned into bench leg

■ SKETCH **14.10** *The bamboo vice, an invaluable tool*

edges back towards the centre, then position the chisel inside the marked hole area (about twice the culm thickness in) and remove chips out of the culm, back towards the hole edge already cut. Repeat the process until you break through the culm centre near both edges of your hole. Carefully reposition and angle your chisel to cut directly along the grain but only between the two holes you have created, starting by removing a shallow V-shaped sliver, and carefully widening it until you have created an irregular reasonable sized long hole down the centre but inside your hole. (If you are too impatient when removing this first V-shaped sliver and the pieces that follow, you will certainly split the culm.)

I have also seen the pangot used instead of the chisel to start the hole (as above), but only with very large diameter holes. In that case, the pangot is laid straight across the grain inside the hole marking at about 50° angle. It is struck on the back of the blade with the mallet, moving it further in and reversing the angle to take out chips until the culm is penetrated. You arrive at the same result as above.

Having cut your access hole, take the pangot and, holding it as described earlier (see Sketch 14.11 and Photo 14M) with its curved cutting tip down in the hollow, slice out the hole, working always with the blade travelling away from the top centre of the hole (where the end grain is exposed) towards and no further than the outside centre of the hole (where the grain becomes tangential with the hole edge). This means you have to change ends frequently, always working back towards the outside middle. Continue to cut, making sure your sides are a projection of the parallel sides of the culm to be inserted, until your hole is very close to the original hole marks. Then take the culm end to be inserted and try it. Hopefully the hole will still be a bit small, so mark it again with the pen mainly on the hole centre line where the culm end is

touching, and commence shaving with the pangot again concentrating on the new central marks. Try it again until it starts to slip in, then mark further around the hole the part now stopping it. Repeat the process until the culm slips snugly into the hole (don't ever force it or you may split the culm).

Then smile, and put bandaids on your various 'first time' cuts, and read the instructions again twice about never cutting towards yourself. You will, nevertheless, be happy!

The pangot is also used to carve a square cut culm end into a curve designed to fit snugly against a round culm. First the culm end is marked with a pen, and the major parts are sawn out without the sawcuts reaching the pen marks. The pangot is then used, working from the middle of the hole towards the protruding edges that taper away to nothing, thus cutting with the grain rather than into it. These joints are particularly awkward to make, but with practice they become quite easy, if you keep your pangot end sharp.

The Indonesians also use a different shaped knife (Sketch 14.9) for smaller sized holes (up to 50 mm) when the curved end of the pangot becomes difficult to fit down into the hole. In fact, the Balinese don't appear to use the curved pangot at all, preferring to use this knife for large and small holes. They mostly hold the knife vertically by the handle and strike the back of the blade with the mallet to drive it around the periphery of the hole with the grain. (I prefer the curved pangot for larger holes. In fact, it is a pleasure to use it.)

This knife (Sketch 14.9 and Photo 14L) is just as heavy and thick, but straighter, and has a long, increasingly fine point which is lowered into the hole and pushed with one hand (or struck on the back with a mallet) while the other holds the handle. Like the pangot, it tapers in cross-section on both sides from its heavy (6 mm) back to a finely honed razor sharp edge. The fine point makes it possible to get into quite small holes to cut, again, with the grain. If you use a (round wooden) mallet, strike on the back of the blade and not on the handle, which is not designed to withstand blows. I rarely find it necessary to use a mallet, partly by keeping my knives extra sharp.

You will find yourself almost standing on your head in an endeavour to get behind either of these knives in order to push them with the grain of the hole away from yourself. You virtually have to swap directions, or almost swap from side to side of the culm to control the cutting stroke, and if you are not ambidextrous (I'm not) you will be constantly tempted to pull the knife towards yourself. DON'T DO IT! Just persevere and it will eventually work for you.

I recommend you either get some knife blades made up by your local blacksmith, or attempt to make them yourself out of old truck springs. They last forever and are certainly more economical than buying a large selection of hole saws and a mandrell! The knife blades have to be heat forged, ground smooth to obtain the transition from the fat tapering back to the fine cutting edge, oil hardened (get your spring works or blacksmith to harden them), and then honed, firstly on a coarse oil stone and then a fine one, to achieve the final well balanced razor sharp shape. The pangot's curved end shape and its relationship to the handle is critical to the efficiency of this beautiful tool. You will need to make both shaped knives unless you decide to make large holes with the straight bladed knife as they do in Bali, or use hole saws.

Burning holes

Burning holes with a red hot rod makes a fairly clean hole but is not always accurate in size and is suitable for fairly insensitive small holes only (flutes fingerholes etc.). It is not very suitable for dowel pin holes.

5. Saws

I mostly use a folding blade 'Felco' type pruning saw, often for both harvesting bamboo and for making furniture. Coarse-bladed rip saws are not suitable as they will tear the fibres and create havoc with your nicely finished surfaces. Fine-toothed saws, even hacksaws, tend to be satisfactory. The Japanese have an expensive range of bamboo working saws used to make their exquisitely made objets d'art (tea whisks, wall hangings, etc.), but they are often hard to get and expensive.

When sawing bamboo, particularly green bamboo, it is necessary to saw with the cutting teeth travelling into the fibres as they enter the culm rather than pulling out of

the fibres, or you will rip individual fibres out of the matrix of the culm wood, causing them to split out from and disfigure the culm surface. Some saws, the Felco included, cut on the back stroke, whilst others, like the hacksaw, cut on the forward stroke, and your technique must be adjusted to suit.

6. The bamboo vice (Sketch 14.10)

The Indonesians work bamboo whilst sitting on the ground, using their feet, hands, backside, underarm, and seemingly every part of their body, in an amazing parody of a contortionist that converts him/herself into a human vice. My stiff old cadaver tries valiantly, but short of doing a crash course on yoga, I recommend you make yourself a simple bamboo vice as I have. It's quick to make, and mounts on a bench top that allows you to stand up and work! It will save you more time on the first object that you make than the very little time it takes to complete it.

It consists of two (or three) vee cut blocks screwed firmly to a heavy bench top, then covered in leather or rubber padding to prevent the bamboo being scratched when it is laid snugly in the vee blocks. Position the blocks so that culm parts you will work on can be positioned free of the blocks. Then make up two (or three) rubber 'hold downs', connected under the bench (or on the back of the bench), which can be pulled over the culm

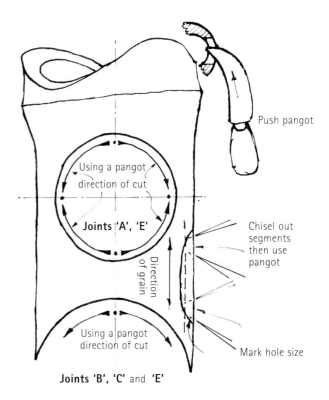

■ 14.11 *Cutting directions when using the chisel and pangot knife to make a hole*

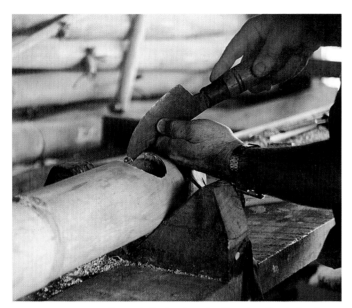

■ **14.N** *One end of a bamboo vice (the other identical end is out of sight on the left hand side)*

you are working on. These are stretched to clip onto a stout peg fitted into one of a series of holes positioned to achieve enough tension to firmly hold the culm whilst you work on it. Pieces of car or truck inner tube tied to strong light rope make ideal clamps. Make the pins and sockets stout or it can fly out and do you a serious damage.

This vice is quick to undo and adjust for different diameters, and convenient for height if your bench is not too high. One has to be 'over' the work to use a pangot comfortably.

Bamboo Splitting and Using Splits in Furniture

Bamboo splits are an incredibly versatile and attractive medium to use, and are very easy to make. Much of the bamboo furniture made incorporates split bamboo, either as the 'flat' table top, or the springy bed platform, or for chair backs or bases, and even fences, screens or floors!

For the sake of clarity, we'll define the three types of split bamboo you will make, or see used, as:

■ **Weaving splits** (see Sketch 16.4) which are much thinner and narrower (mostly used in basket making, or woven roof and wall lining sheets, or sometimes for fine screen making (see Chapter 16 for the Bali screen design). They are fine thin flat sections split from thick-walled culm sections, leaving no trace of either the inside or outside surface of the culm.

■ **Splits** which are split culm segments that still retain

the smooth outer culm surface, with the internode segments and edges cleaned up so that when laid flat and side by side they form an attractive relatively flat surface showing the culm's natural curved finish uppermost. They are used extensively for seat bases and backs, heavier woven panels, fences and screens, etc. Splits are mostly much heavier than weaving splits, but it is possible to make quite fine splits from very thin-walled long internoded bamboos (e.g. *Schizostachyum jaculans* or *S.* sp. 'Murray Island').

■ **Flats** which are thick splits that have had both the inner surface and the outer curved culm surface shaved off to produce a fairly even rectangular flat bamboo section. They can be wide (say 30 mm x 6 to 8 mm thick) for a Balinese screen frame, or fat and almost square (say 12 mm x 10 mm) like the block 'frame' that supports the decorative infill on the chair illustrated in Sketch 15.3.

Bamboo splits easily because of its longitudinal fibre structure. Heavy-walled bamboos are harder to split, so for the purpose of chair bases and backs, etc., it is easier to choose straight, thin-walled strong bamboos such as *Bambusa oldhamii* or *B. textilis*. These will give you straight strong light splits, unlike *B. blumeana* or *B. balcooa*, although the Philippinos do use *B. blumeana* to make very heavy splits about 7 mm to 8 mm thick, spending a lot of effort to artistically shape the heavy individual seat top or table top splits. There are dozens of suitable bamboos that will split easily, but straight-culmed ones are best suited.

For making splits or flats, split your culms with a heavy knife (a machete is ideal), resting the blade centrally across the square cut culm top (of a cut-to-length culm) and striking the blade firstly on top and then beside the culm as it proceeds splitting its way downwards. Each split half culm is then split again and perhaps again until you have pieces the width you need. By laying them flat on a bench with the jagged split node diaphragms upwards, (and the end placed against an immovable block of wood nailed to the bench), you can run the knife vigorously along the split to cut off the node sections and

■ **14.Q** *Splits cross-bound with rattan to form a decorative panel. The bamboo is Bambusa lako or Gigantochloa atroviolacea.*

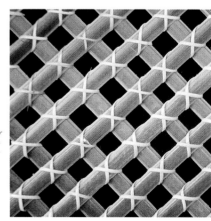

■ **14.O** *A bamboo culm splitter*

■ **14.P** *The author using the bamboo culm splitter*

generally reduce the inside cupped section a little to make it lie flatter when turned face upwards.

At this point you have made a split. If you want flats (splits with the natural outer surface removed), turn the split over and use your splitting knife to split or shave the hard waxy surface off until you have a flat even surface. You will need heavy flats like these to make the beautiful Balinese screen (see Chapter 16, Sketch 16.2).

For this trimming up job, the best knife possible is the Balinese splitting knife (Sketch 14.9), because of its heavy weight and the blade being flat on one side and

chamfered to a razor sharp point on the other. However, a sharp machete will do the job at a pinch.

An even better way to split your culms is to use a bamboo splitter (see Photos 14O and 14P). They are simple and effective, and cut culm lengths very quickly into six or eight longitudinal split sections depending on the number of 'spokes' in the tool. Made from 5 mm thick steel plate, the 150 mm diameter ring is 35 mm high, and the fairly blunt edge-sharpened spokes rise to a point 40 mm above the ring top. Weld on two 25 mm pipe handles 120 mm long. To use it, hold the culm in one hand

■ **14.R** *An unusual bamboo canopy bed and chair made from* Bambusa blumeana *in the Philippines*

with its bottom end on a concrete floor, and the splitter with the other with its point in place on the top of the culm; then carefully lift both and bounce them downwards, striking the concrete. The weight of the splitter drives it into the bamboo; then you can grab the handles and keep bouncing it on the concrete to drive the splitter through the bamboo. When you get close to the bottom, let the splitter go and gather the tops of the almost split-out pieces in both hands and complete the bouncing process, allowing the splitter's weight alone to carry through. You are left with a bundle of splits in your hands. These split sections still require trimming to finish as before.

If splits are to be used side by side, they will fit more perfectly if you keep them in naturally adjacent order. Mark the culm with a spiralling pencil line before splitting and you can work out their original sequence later.

You can quickly trim them all to equal width by carefully forcing them between two sharp blades driven into a bench top with the correct distance between them, passing them first under a piece of wood clamped to the bench to prevent them twisting as you push or tap the splits between the blades. The edges can be chamfered by hand to ensure a neat and even appearance. (I have seen black bamboo (*Gigantochloa atroviolacea* or *Bambusa lako*) with a broader cut lighter coloured edge chamfer to create a dramatic contrast against the black culm surface.)

Heavy wide splits (often used for tabletops or bed mattress support platforms) are sometimes attached by pin and glue only, but it will only work if the splits are very thick. Usually splits are held in place by lashing made of rattan strips, or finely split long sections of pring tali, the string bamboo we know as *Gigantochloa apus*. The splits are rested on light culm supports and cross lashed neatly into place, the lashing passing twice around each piece and then on to the next in one continuous tying operation. For table tops and bed mattress supports, splits from 25 to 35 mm wide cut from large diameter culms give a flatter, stronger, more practical surface.

For chair backs or seat bases under cushions, splits about 10 mm wide and 2.5–3 mm thick laid almost touching and lashed side by side are used. Supports need to be no more than 400 mm apart for that size, but can be increased if the splits are increased in width and thickness.

Decorative effects can be easily obtained by crossing the flats in either a diagonal or square pattern and lashing them with a continuous lashing system at each intersection (see Photo 14Q), although you can do without the lashing if you drill and pin the end of each flat. Decorative panels are usually fixed into chair backs or sides (as in Sketch 15.3) by fixing frames cut from thick-walled culms (use clear glue plus drilled and fitted pins or nails) inside the culm surrounded area you want to fill in. Place the lashed panel into the frame (like a picture in a frame), run a decorative bamboo trim around the outside to cover the untidy ends, and apply lots of clear glue.

It's really very easy to do if you invest the time, and you will find bamboo a wonderfully sympathetic material to work with once you understand the differences between wood and bamboo.

Using Nails, Tacks, Bolts and Screws

Strong, well-cured, aged, heavy-walled bamboo is a dream to work with, and you can get away with 'murder'. When using bamboo like *Dendrocalamus asper*, or *Guadua angustifolia*, people have been observed driving nails into it, screwing screws in, and a multitude of other abuses. You can't get away with this so readily with green or uncured bamboo, which splits easily (you shouldn't be using it anyway), and thin-walled species or ends, and some of the less superior species will readily tend to split if you use screws or nails. Tacks are commonly used in furniture making, and are mostly okay because the shaft of the tack is very small. In places where it is not obvious, you can use nails as pins if you drill a hole very slightly smaller than the nail diameter. The same applies to screws, but the screw thread often needs to be the full length of the screw. It is possible also to use bolts if you fill the culm with the plaster and Bondcrete mixture recommended in the structural section, but bolts are not very elegant. The best way is still well constructed joins glued and with large diameter bamboo pins.

Finishes for your furniture

When using sandpaper or sanding machinery on bamboo, be aware that the natural surface is high in silica, which causes silicosis of the lungs. In Indonesia they use primitive wet sanding systems that are quite effective, sitting with a culm section in sand and water and scrubbing the culm surface with sandpaper, or even Scotchguard kitchen pads onto which they have scooped sand from the pond.

The combined wax and silica surface on bamboo culms is virtually impenetrable, and neither glue, varnish nor oil finish mediums are effective until this is removed. Using water on the bamboo culms does not affect their strength, but if the sanding is done after you cut your different members to size, they will have to be dried thoroughly before applying any further finish.

You can either varnish or oil your bamboo surface when the piece is finally assembled. Varnish is a better protection against moisture and fungus in the longer term, but oil is often more aesthetically appealing. Satin finish Estapol-type finishing mediums are also effective.

There is also heat-treatment to create interesting burnished mottled effects, and rather than removing the bamboos heated natural wax, you can add extra wax to make the finish even better. Food for thought!

Using Inferior Bamboo

One of the difficulties you may have is obtaining the bamboo you need. My first recommendation is to plant a wonderful species like *Gigantochloa atter*, or even *Bambusa oldhamii* as quickly as possible. *B. oldhamii* is an economical, fast-growing, cold-tolerant bamboo that produces culms up to 75–100 mm diameter, can achieve full diameter within four years, is a good bamboo for furniture making, and produces superior edible shoots. By the time you have practised your skills, it will have grown up!

In the meantime, if you can't harvest suitable bamboo from somebody else's clump, you can either buy what you need from a reputable supplier, or you can design furniture that can be made from the inferior, smaller diameter, thin-walled running bamboos that are commonly available throughout this country. Where you can't obtain culms of suitable diameter (say 60–75 mm diameter or more) you can re-design your furniture to create strong aesthetic effects from multiples of smaller diameter culms that are pinned and glued together (see Sketch 15.5).

Species Best Suited for Furniture

Whilst furniture can be made from almost any bamboo, the following somewhat limited list gives some very useful relatively superior furniture bamboos where the species is now readily available (1998). Many superior furniture bamboos have not been included on this list because they are relatively rare and will not provide quantities of wood in the Western world yet for many years.

General purpose, large and straight, 200 mm to 125 mm diameter

Dendrocalamus asper
Bambusa balcooa
Dendrocalamus brandisii
Dendrocalamus giganteus
Dendrocalamus latiflorus
Gigantochloa levis
Gigantochloa robusta
Guadua angustifolia

General purpose, medium and straight, 150 mm to 60 mm diameter

Bambusa oldhamii
Dendrocalamus membranaceus
Bambusa longispiculata
pring tutul

General purpose, medium and straight, 60 mm to 40 mm

Bambusa lako
Bambusa malingensis
Bambusa oliveriana
Bambusa pachinensis
Bambusa pervariabilis
Bambusa textilis
Bambusa tuldoides
Cephalostachyum pergracile
Gigantochloa atroviolacea
Gigantochloa albociliata
Gigantochloa apus
Gigantochloa hasskarliana
Schizostachyum brachycladum

Small diameter bamboos for spokes or in-filling

Thyrsostachys siamensis
Bambusa eutuldoides
Bambusa malingensis
Bambusa multiplex
   (various cultivars will give different diameters)
Bambusa nana
Bambusa ridleyi
Bambusa textilis
Gigantochloa wrayi

Heavy walled or solid species suitable for bending

Bambusa arnhemica
Bambusa bambos
Bambusa burmanica
Bambusa eutuldoides
Bambusa longispiculata (lower portions)
Bambusa multiplex (lower portions)
Bambusa multiplex cv. 'Fernleaf'
Bambusa multiplex cv. 'Alphonse Karr'
Bambusa nana
Bambusa pervariabilis (lower portions)
Bambusa polymorpha
Bambusa tulda
Bambusa tuldoides (lower portions)
Dendrocalamus strictus
Gigantochloa apus (lower portions)
Gigantochloa albociliata
Thyrsostachys siamensis

While you are thinking about how to get your furniture culms, plant some of these lovely species and in no time you will have your own supply!

15 Furniture Designs and Designing Your Own

■ **15.A** *A large lounge (with Bambusa blumeana), as shown in construction Sketch 15.2*

(PHOTO: CHRIS ELLIS)

Bamboo furniture, for me, is evocative of tropical evenings, cool verandahs, the sounds of nature and clinking ice in a steaming glass of G and T! It has an elegance that belies the 'used as is' natural shape of the culm material, and a sense of agelessness, depending on the design. China, which grows more bamboo and has more species than any other country in the world, found hundreds of uses for this sympathetic material, and the artifacts and furniture in their museums confirm that it has been in use for thousands of years.

(PHOTO: KEVIN LANG)

■ **15.B** *An elegant dining suite*

Different Styles and Designs—Filipino, Balinese and Javanese

Each Asian country has developed a style of its own, some very ancient and traditional, and some recent and modern. This chapter gives you sketches and designs you can copy and build, and will show you a very simple system to help you design and build your own. It will also help you understand the different design philosophy behind three popular styles, and help you to develop variations of your own based on the style you prefer.

The Filipino modern designs appear to have been influenced by the ancient, delicate Chinese furniture designs, which had an ethereal sense of weightlessness. Some of the oldest and best-preserved Chinese pottery and artwork artifacts, pieces brought into the Philippines by early migrants and traders centuries ago, still survive, having avoided China's constant warlord battles. One can detect that same sense of lightness in the decorative way the Filipinos use bamboo. Their designs are nevertheless, uniquely their own, neither modern nor ancient, but delicate, elegant and ageless, and with no trace of the heavier Spanish influence apparent in their earlier designs (bamboo, not indigenous to Spain, was not part of Spanish culture). Like the Chinese, the later Filipino designs use

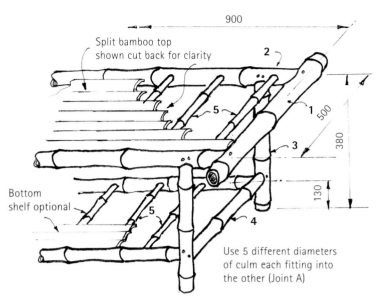

■ SKETCH **15.1** *A simple coffee table using only Type A joints*

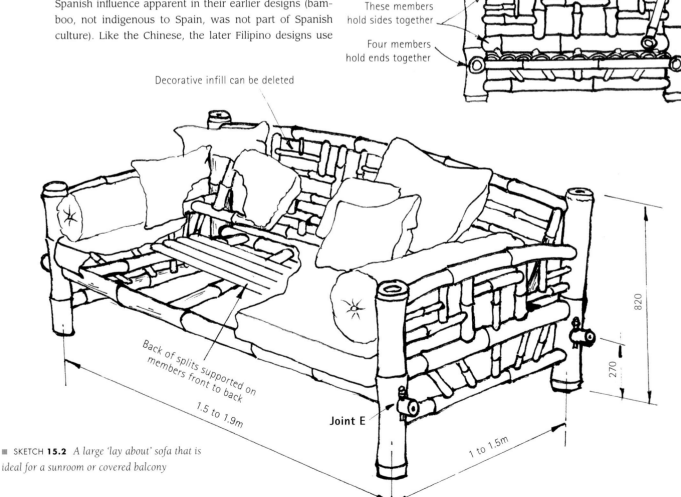

■ SKETCH **15.2** *A large 'lay about' sofa that is ideal for a sunroom or covered balcony*

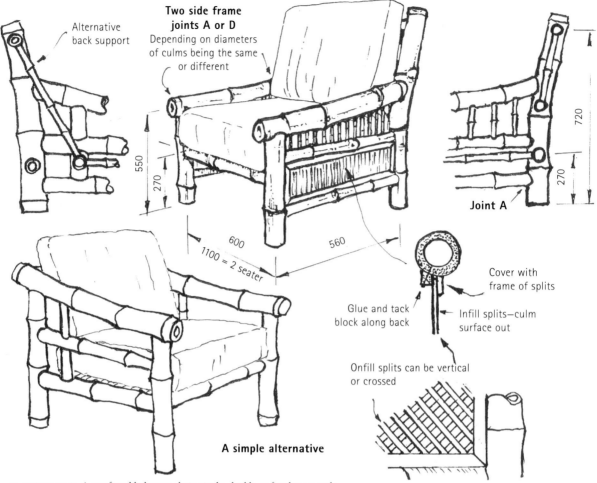

Alternative back support

Two side frame joints A or D
Depending on diameters of culms being the same or different

550
270
720
270

600
1100 = 2 seater
560

Joint A

Cover with frame of splits

Glue and tack block along back

Infill splits—culm surface out

Onfill splits can be vertical or crossed

A simple alternative

■ SKETCH **15.3** *A comfortable lounge chair, single, double or for three people*

curved bamboo to advantage but in a less formal way. Each piece they make becomes a unique piece, because the design and shape is varied to take advantage of the beautiful twists and internode knobs they find such as on *Bambusa blumeana*, the main bamboo used for furniture making in the Philippines. As mentioned earlier, some Filipino factories have been importing supplies from Vietnam because the over-harvesting of *B. blumeana's* delicious shoots and unique timber has jeopardised their regular supply.

Examples of the modern Filipino design approach that you can build for yourself are:

Sketch 15.1. A simple coffee/magazine table. All the joints are Type A. Start with the largest diameter culms working your way down to the smallest, each time choosing a culm diameter as large as possible that still fits into the next size up.

If the top is not flat enough for your cups, use coasters, or cover it with a glass sheet.

Sketch 15.2 and Photo 15A. A large sofa that is ideal for the sun room or covered balcony. This lounge should not be tackled as a first effort, but it is actu-

ally simpler to construct than it appears. Virtually all the joints are Type A (or Type A-D, the stronger version of A if you think your culm material is not strong enough for the joint), except the Type E joint ends of the two lower support beams. Joint types are marked on the drawings. You don't need to make the backs and sides as complicated. Just delete some beams or put in a simple series of vertical culms instead of the typically Filipino pattern. It is a beautiful lounge!

Sketch 15.3. A simple and comfortable lounge chair design. Again, this is constructed with all Type A or A-D joints. The top side fill in is small culms with Type A joints at both ends. The bottom fill in is detailed on the drawing as either diagonal or straight fine splits. The side filling can be left off, but it will reveal the end of the chair splits that support the cushion.

Sketch 15.4. A bed base suitable for a mattress or futon. This simply constructed bed base uses Type D or A-D joints for the leg tops depending on whether they are the same diameter or smaller than the bed side beams. All other joints are Type A or A-D depending on the strength of your culms.

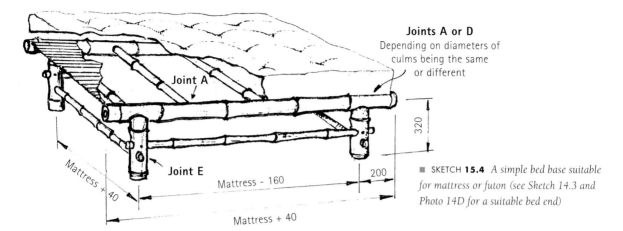

Joints A or D
Depending on diameters of
culms being the same
or different

Joint A

Joint E

Mattress + 40

Mattress - 160

Mattress + 40

320

200

■ SKETCH **15.4** *A simple bed base suitable for mattress or futon (see Sketch 14.3 and Photo 14D for a suitable bed end)*

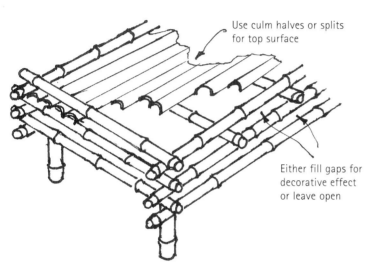

Use culm halves or splits
for top surface

Either fill gaps for
decorative effect
or leave open

■ SKETCH **15.5** *A simple coffee table made from small diameter culms (e.g. Phyllostachys aurea)*

Sketch 15.5. A simple coffee table made from small diameter culms. If all you can get is small diameter running bamboo (say *Phyllostachys aurea*, which grows wildly wild everywhere), build this interesting table, and then adapt the joining ideas to design your own chairs etc. All the joints are Type F, glued and lashed, or even glued and pinned. The legs are pinned to each horizontal member crossing from the end or side, making it a very strong construction in spite of the small diameter culms.

Modern Balinese furniture is a recent innovation to my knowledge based on the original designs of Linda Garland, a well-known Western interior decorator who has dedicated much of her time to living in and helping the Balinese, and promoting bamboo generally. In Bali the people often follow a village industry system, where all the residents are employed to somehow contribute to the specialist product or artifact that becomes the feature of that village. Belega, about 12 km south-east of Ubud, is such a village specialising in furniture making. In fact, it imports most of its bamboo supplies from remote parts of Bali, East Java and Lombok. The village houses a prolifer-

ation of different factories producing furniture that is basically similar in style and design. It was one of those factories my wife and I used as a study base to learn some of the techniques described, the other being near Jogyakarta in Java.

The modern Balinese design is generally based on very large diameter bamboo culms (150 mm to 200 mm diameter) of the species *Dendrocalamus asper* ('bambu betung' in Java and Bali) which is also the great edible shoot producer of Thailand's plantations. The Thais also use a uniquely beautiful black clone of *D. asper* locally known as betung hitam (the local word for 'black'), a bamboo indigenous only to the high volcanic valleys of Java (we have it growing at Bamboo World). A smaller (up to 75 mm diameter) black bamboo, *Gigantochloa atroviolacea* (*Bambusa lako* or *G.* 'Timor Black' is a good substitute), is also used extensively together with the larger *D. asper* 'Hitam' when building beautiful black bamboo furniture. Unlike green, yellow or striped culmed bamboos which all turn cured bamboo 'straw' colour, all black culms retain their colour after harvesting and curing. You will notice that the Balinese styles rarely use bent or curved members.

When the black colour is not required, they use quite a lot of *Gigantochloa atter*, *G. pseudoarundinacea*, *G. robusta*

■ **15.C** *Balinese lounge seats made from black bamboo (Dendrocalamus asper cv. 'Hitam'), similar to construction Sketch 15.6*

■ 15.D *A three-level TV/video stand*

(PHOTO: KEVIN LANG)

corners (Type G joints shown on Sketch 14.5), in some cases using flowing angular bends rather than only right angles (Type H joints shown on Sketch 14.7). The effect is quite modern, as though the furniture was made from bent tubing, but rendered more graceful by the attractive natural look of the bamboo. Because the corners all tend to be smooth curves, there is no opportunity to house one culm inside another (like Type A, A-D or E joints), and all the corner joints must be rattan bound (see Sketch 14.6 and the procedure in Chapter 14), because the exposed surfaces of type G and H joints are unsightly and need to be covered. Examples you can make are:

Sketch 15.6. A large single lounge chair. All the joints are Type G and H (both of which require softwood inserts), except for a few lighter (35 mm to 40 mm diameter) members housed in Type A joint holes into the larger culms. Large culms cut from the usually available *Bambusa balcooa*, or better still, *Dendrocalamus asper*, are ideal. The seat is made from lashed-on splits. You can make this a two- or three-seater by lengthening the whole seat (the horizontal members running along the seat).

and *G. apus*, wonderfully straight, strong bamboos used for both furniture and structures in Bali and Java.

The smooth, flowing lines apparent in modern Balinese designs have been created mostly by using large bamboos of equal diameter joined at smoothly contoured

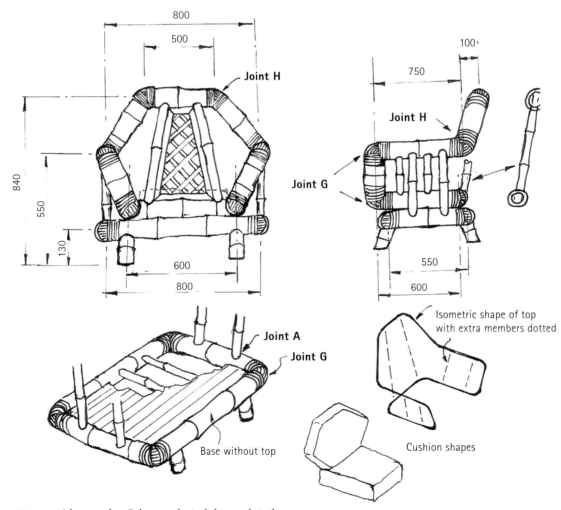

■ SKETCH 15.6 *A large modern Balinese style single lounge chair that can be made wider to become a one- two- or three-seater*

Photo 15D. A simple TV/video stand with three levels. This one has rattan-bound top corners and split bamboo table tops running lengthwise. All the lower joints including the split table top supports are type A joints. The legs attach to the top table side members with type A-D joints, and the top table level corners connect with type G corners, each with an inserted softwood plug that can be left 'square' looking with mitre cuts, or carved round (as in Sketch 14.5). If you don't want to bother with the softwood plugs and rattan binding, increase the diameter and length of the two top end members, and insert the side members into them with Type A joints. If you make a coffee table similar to this (with fewer levels) and you find the top is too uneven, cut a sheet of glass and drop it onto the splits.

Photo 15E. A simple table, a self-explanatory variation on that shown in Sketch 15.1 using only Type A joints. If the leg tops are cut off just above a node, they look quite attractive and there is no need to bind them as shown with rattan.

Photo 15F. A simple plant pot stand. Use Type D joints throughout. For the side fill-in details, use the same method as for the chair on Sketch 15.3, and use splits supported on two cross members Type A jointed into two of the bottom culms.

Javanese traditional furniture is well known and found in virtually every house in Java. There are, however, modern Javanese designers now creating elegant variations, and quite modern departures from their traditional forms. These are often one-off pieces found nearer Jakarta where they have access to the expensive shopping outlets. Unlike Filipino furniture, it is generally made from straight culms. The bamboos used are much the same as those listed above for Bali, in fact Java supplies Bali manufacturers with a reasonable percentage of the culms used for their furniture. One very unusual bamboo used in Javanese furniture (also in Bali, but I've not seen it used in their modern furniture) is *Bambusa maculata,* called locally 'pring tutul'. It is an attractive bamboo with green and cream striped culms that develop a beautiful, permanent, mottled brown culm

■ **15.F** *An elegant pot plant stand*

surface after curing. I have seen traditional furniture made from the spotted pring tutul, from the black pring wulung (*Gigantochloa atroviolacea*) and from various species that cure to a standard 'bamboo colour' such as *G. atter*.

I find the Javanese traditional chairs, the single-seater 'kursi' and the double-seater 'lincak' a little formal for my taste, but for those interested, Len Muller gave a quite poetic and detailed description of how to make the kursi and lincak in the *American Bamboo Society Magazine*, Vol. 16, No 2 (April, 1995).

Photos 15G and 15H show two beautiful and simple children's chairs made by Brian Earley of Byron Bamboo from larger diameter lower culm sections of *Phyllostachys aurea*. All the joints are Type A, and he has heat-treated the green wood to try and avoid powder beetle and give the bamboo that lovely scorched look. You can easily make larger simple chairs of this design for adults by using a clumping bamboo a little larger in diameter.

Japanese furniture appeals with simple elegant statements. The following bed is easy to make.

Sketch 15.7. Use either rattan-bound Type G joints (as shown) or Type D joints with very solid inserts and pinning for the corners, and Type D or A-D for the legs, depending on whether they are the same diameter as the side beams or smaller. All other joints are Type A or A-D. Note that the two outside verticals holding up the upper bed head beam actually pass right through the middle bed head beam, a challenge requiring you to sand back the nodes (or select long internode culms) to pass right through the hole.

(PHOTO: KEVIN LANG)

■ **15.E** *A two-level magazine table, a variation on the construction shown in Sketch 15.1*

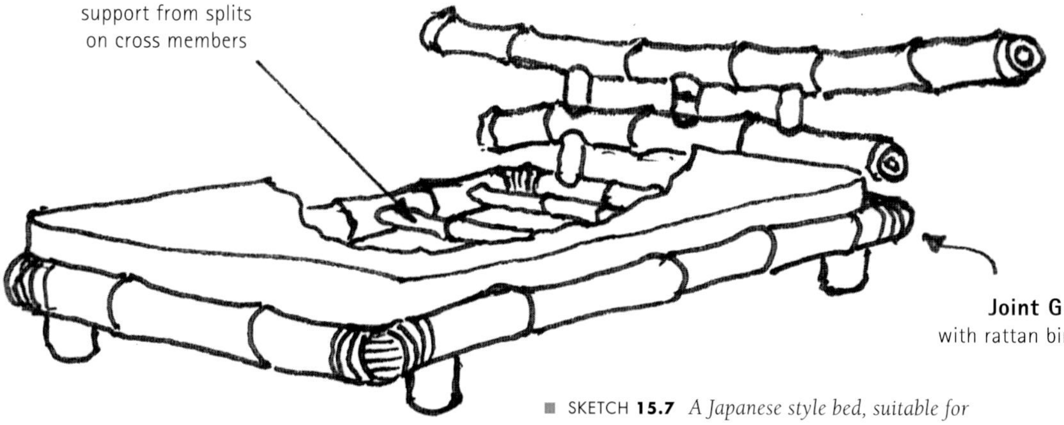

Construct mattress
support from splits
on cross members

Joint G
with rattan binding

■ SKETCH **15.7** *A Japanese style bed, suitable for mattress or futon*

Designing Your Own the Simple Way

There is a very simple way of converting your own ideas (or existing designs) into reality, and it will help you avoid mistakes and plan ahead. This system will give you a clear understanding of how to proceed logically from starting points to finished piece. It will also prevent you from trying to make items that either can't be made, or are too ambitious for your first attempts. It will allow you to foresee and avoid problems before they crop up, and will help you select, cut and assemble members of the correct size.

Buy a roll of very wide cheap paper and draw your design on it in full size, with the paper stretched out on

the floor. Using a dark pencil (2B) that rubs out easily, draw roughly at first, moving the members at your will to achieve the right proportions, drawing each culm in at the full diameter you expect to use. After drawing the side view to a point where you are liking what you see, then draw a view of the front, and then top, preferably each as a projection of the other (if the paper is not wide enough, sticky tape extra sheets on). Then, decide how each joint is going to be made, whether from bamboos of equal size, or of unequal size so they can be cut into each other. Adjust your sketch so each culm is drawn full diameter at each joint to ensure it fits inside the next (if that is what you intend) or needs a Type B, C, or D joint (for joining culms of an equal diameter). If it begins to look good (after much rubbing out and changing) and all fits together, then you can trace over your final profiles with a black felt pen. If you need to change after that, stick more paper over the top and redraw that section.

By all means, practice your major shapes on a smaller scale drawing before you start, but as soon as you are getting anywhere close to making decisions, draw it out full size as described above.

From then on, you don't even need a tape measure. You can:

- Hold your bamboo against the drawing to see if it is the right diameter.

- Try different pieces to get the nodes to coincide with where you want them.

- Cut your bamboo to the correct length by holding it against the drawing and marking it.

- Mark the hole centres by holding the bamboo against the drawing.

- Assemble parts and hold the assembly against the drawing whilst you glue and pin it, and so on.

■ **15.J** *A simple chair you could design yourself using the system recommended in the text*

■ **15.G** *Child's lounge to match the chair in Photo 15H*

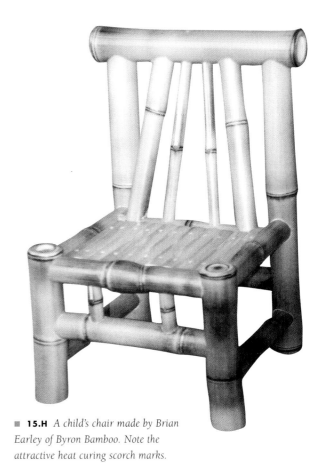

It is hard to make a mistake using that simple system, and all your dimensional problems are solved at the drawing stage before it's too late to change the design. You also get to look at the true proportions of the complete piece, and can make aesthetic decisions like this bit looking too bulky or the proportion being too long for the width. The time you take to draw the piece you want will be more than saved by the confidence you will have in proceeding confidently with its construction.

By applying the above principles and studying the drawings of the furniture pieces included in this text, you

■ **15.H** *A child's chair made by Brian Earley of Byron Bamboo. Note the attractive heat curing scorch marks.*

should be able to either copy any of those pieces, or design furniture to suit your individual needs and taste. It is a most satisfying and creative pastime. Good luck!

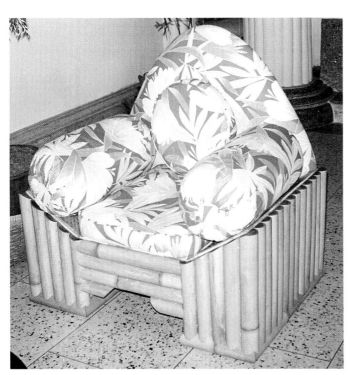

■ **15.I** *An unusual modern chair design from Bali*

(PHOTO: CHRIS ELLIS).

■ **15.K** *An elegant canopy bed with two attached bedside tables*

16 Decorative Screens and Fences

When I began renovating our house at Church Point, Sydney, fourteen years ago, I was faced with an unsightly under-house view from the access pathway, and with the expense of buying timber or sheeting to conceal my pile of stored sculpture moulds. Across the road was a patch of rampant *Phyllostachys aurea*, busy gobbling up the nature strip between a right-of-way and the road. It took me a day to cut and de-branch the bamboo, and create a beautiful bamboo screen of vertical culms, alternately placed one up and one down to compensate for the tapered culms. I finished it with a stout 100 mm diameter end post of *Bambusa balcooa*. The electrician punched a hole in its nodes to carry the cable, and the access light switch was mounted on the culm internode. When people

■ **16.A** *An elegant open screen design using Type A furniture joints*

came to visit, there was always the comment, 'I love your bamboo screen!' It cost me nothing but a day's labour, and, being out of the weather, it remains as sound today as it was when I built it.

I was fortunate to have access to any bamboo in Sydney, but it is unfortunate that I couldn't have used a superior straight larger diameter clumping bamboo (30 to 50 mm diameter) like *Bambusa tuldoides* or *B. textilis*, or a little larger like *Gigantochloa apus* (55 to 70 mm diameter). They are stronger, larger, have longer internodes, just as straight, have longer more parallel culm lengths, and are non-invasive.

Having been to Japan and seen the proliferation of beautiful fences housing meditative gardens, I still wonder why more Australians don't take advantage of this inexpensive and satisfying resource. Instead they spend a fortune on the old paling fence, or the proliferation of even more expensive alternatives that consume valuable timber or tea tree forests.

Before enthusing about fences, it's best to talk about screens, because a beautiful screen design, either simple or elaborate, when fixed between two posts becomes a fence!

Screen Construction and Design

An essential part of the elegant open patio or 'poor boy house' decoration in Bali is the bamboo hanging screen. These exquisitely delicate see-through privacy screens shelter out sufficient sun, wind and curious peeking to be effective, but their open filigree pattern allows reasonable air movement, and creates a wonderful shadow play on the patio floor or the skin of your loved one (Sketch 16.2 and Photo 16B).

They are easy to make once you understand the trick of how to assemble them, and the design variations you can create are infinite. I have never seen them for sale in local craft markets in Australia, but they would no doubt be popular if someone made and marketed them. The components can be precut in hundreds and assembled to bulk produce them.

The design of our house, currently half-completed, calls for open design (no walls) with elegant movable screen panels acting as walls, hanging from the high ceil-

■ **16.B** *The Balinese hanging screen detailed in Sketch 16.2*

ing. The screen panels have large diameter (120 to 150 mm) outer bamboo culm frames, and the fill-in screen sections will be larger variations of the Bali screen detailed below. (They must eventually be installed; our house is almost all glass and no walls. Whoever heard of an artist with nowhere to hang his paintings and etchings?)

We also plan similar screens that fold up under the wide verandah eaves that can be swung down and clipped onto the patio railing to form elegant sun and wind shelters.

These screens are made from split bamboo flats (long rectangles of culm strip with the natural inner and outer surfaces removed), not splits, although you can use fine splits from very thin-walled long internoded species for the 'weaving flat' components in the screen. Chapter 14 gives you detailed instructions on how to make the heavier framing flats, the same process used for making splits or flats for beds and seat bases.

For making delicate thinner flats (the same technique used to make weaving flats) to use for the decorative fill-in designs, use either of the following techniques:

a) This is similar to in the way the Indonesians pre-pare their weaving flats to make their strong baskets from

Gigantochloa apus, (known by the Indonesians as 'pring tali'). These fine flats are split from segments split out of thick-walled culms. The finished splits, called 'iratan' (Muller, 1995) reveal split bamboo on both sides, and no

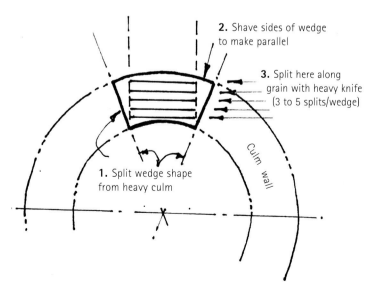

■ SKETCH **16.1** *A splitting diagram showing how to use heavy walled segments to make fine weaving flats*

■ **16.C** *A Balinese craftsman producing splits from a pile of* Gigantochloa apus

sign of the original inner or outer surface. There are dozens of bamboos that are used for this form of splitting, but long fibred strong bamboos are the best. *Phyllostachys aurea*, whilst it can be used and splits easily, is adequate but inferior. Either *Gigantochloa apus* or *Bambusa old-hamii* are excellent, as are most of the better quality structural bamboos. Different countries follow different systems, but the culm surface is usually scraped off. Some split the culm wall into thin slivers cut side by side, but the width of the split produced is then tapered, and limited by the changing wall thickness of the culm. The Indonesians split a thick-walled culm into quadrants of the required split width, then split off the triangular sides to make their sections parallel sided and of the correct width of the flat required (follow Sketch 16.1). They then split the prepared piece the other way, with their heavy splitting knife. (In Sketch 14.9, the blade is flat on one side and chamfered to a razor sharp edge on the other.) First shave off what was the inside surface of the prepared culm piece. Then successively split each flat off, repositioning the knife one 'split' thickness further out towards the culm outer wall.

The technique is easy to master if you cut the nodes off and are only cutting flats less than one internode length, which you can do with, say *B. oldhamii*, when you make short splits for this Bali screen. (Unfortunately it takes a lot of practice to get the long even splits used for basket work. In that case you have to split past and through the confused fibres within each node, requiring much practice and patience, and a delicate pressure with the knife and your other hand to gently lift the split away rather than force the knife blade through the fibres. It is the wedge action, not the sharp blade, that does the work.) Very straight internodes make very straight splits.

Younger culms are often used for splitting weaving flats, but beware of powder post beetle (see Chapter 11).

b) Choose a very thin-walled bamboo with long internodes, like *Schizostachyum jaculans* or *S.* sp. 'Murray Island' (up to 1 m long) or even the upper culm portions of *Nastus elatus* or the *Bambusa textilis* cultivars. Cut the nodes out by sawing them off either side, and split the remaining internode pipe section(s) into splits of the correct width for your design. To make a simple woven uni-directional pattern (similar but lighter than shown on Sketch 16.3), you would need light splits 5 to 7 mm wide from culm material perhaps 2 mm thick for the warp, and pieces slightly thicker and wider for the weft. The panels in the Bali design shown are only a maximum of 350 mm x 250 mm, so the straight light pieces you will get from the two named *Schizostachyum* will be enough to give you a lot of material. You may need to use the top culm sections only for finer pieces if they are larger species, to get the flexibility of the thinner walls. Some of these bamboos can be cracked into weaving splits for baskets, etc. simply by rapping them with your hand whilst resting the culm internode against a hard object. However, if you want to control the width of the cracked pieces, you will have to split them more carefully down the fibre grain with a knife blade. The splits you prepare when using this method will have a slightly curved cross section, with the natural outer and inner culm surfaces still intact and exposed. You should choose to expose either the inner or outer surface to create a rhythm with your infill pattern (either outfacing, or infacing, or alternating patterns of in and outfacing, remembering that Bali screens are often viewed from both sides.

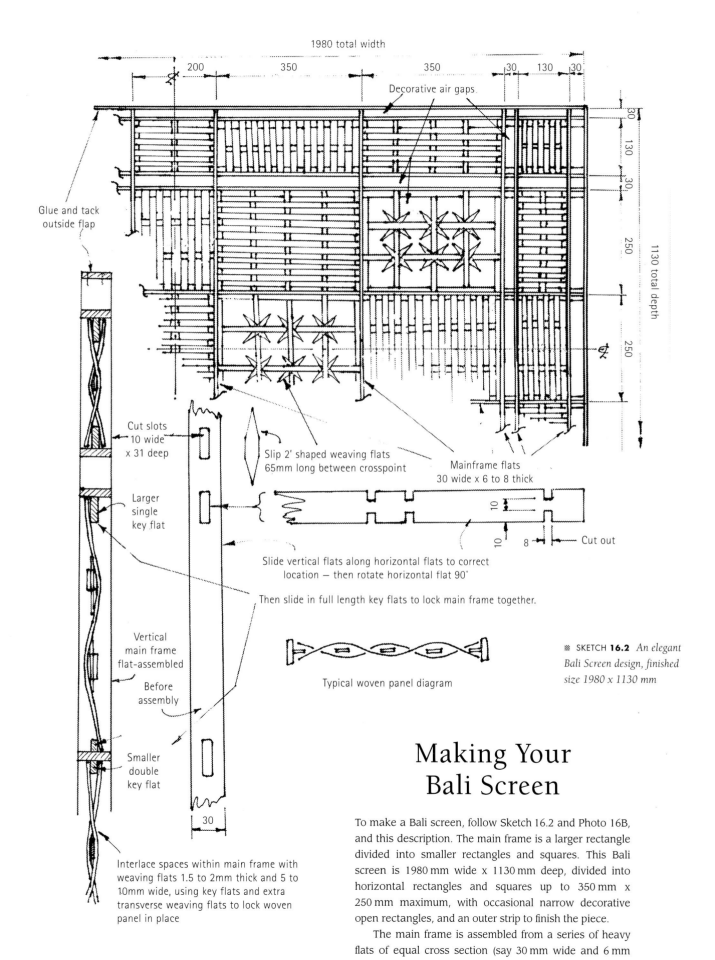

1980 total width

200 | 350 | 350 | 30 | 130 | 30

Decorative air gaps

1130 total depth

30 | 130 | 30 | 250 | 250

Glue and tack outside flap

Cut slots 10 wide x 31 deep

Larger single key flat

Vertical main frame flat-assembled

Before assembly

Smaller double key flat

30

Interlace spaces within main frame with weaving flats 1.5 to 2mm thick and 5 to 10mm wide, using key flats and extra transverse weaving flats to lock woven panel in place

Slip 2' shaped weaving flats 65mm long between crosspoint

Mainframe flats 30 wide x 6 to 8 thick

10 | 10 | 8 — Cut out

Slide vertical flats along horizontal flats to correct location — then rotate horizontal flat 90°

Then slide in full length key flats to lock main frame together.

Typical woven panel diagram

※ SKETCH **16.2** *An elegant Bali Screen design, finished size 1980 x 1130 mm*

Making Your Bali Screen

To make a Bali screen, follow Sketch 16.2 and Photo 16B, and this description. The main frame is a larger rectangle divided into smaller rectangles and squares. This Bali screen is 1980 mm wide x 1130 mm deep, divided into horizontal rectangles and squares up to 350 mm x 250 mm maximum, with occasional narrow decorative open rectangles, and an outer strip to finish the piece.

The main frame is assembled from a series of heavy flats of equal cross section (say 30 mm wide and 6 mm thick). Each flat is assembled by keying the horizontal flats into the vertical flats. At each intersection, the vertical flats have a central slot cut, about one-third of the width of the flat (10 mm) cut out along the grain, just deep enough (30 mm) to slide a horizontal flat through the hole. At those same intersections, the horizontal flats have two cut-outs from the edge towards the middle, each wide enough to accommodate a vertical flat thickness (6 mm+) and cut to one-third of the depth of that horizontal flat (leaving one-third or 10 mm of untouched flat in the centre at each joint).

To assemble your frame, slide a horizontal flat into all of the lined up holes in the row of vertical flats, sliding it through the cut slot in each vertical until the intersection points line up. You should then be able to rotate the horizontal flat through 90 degrees until it is lying flat and no longer upright, in effect keying it in so that it can't slide back and forth.

A 'key flat' (not as wide as the main frame flats but the same thickness) is then inserted into the slot left uncovered in the vertical split, locking it so that it can't be rotated and removed. You will notice that some horizontal frame members have two key flats, one above and one below them, and other have only one, either above or below. Those that have infill panelling on both sides of themselves have two key flats, whereas those with decoration on one side have only one key flat. The total assembled depth of the horizontal frame member and assembled key flat(s) must be no more than the length of slot left in the vertical split.

Continue assembling the frame by inserting each horizontal frame member through the lined up holes in the vertical members, aligning their intersection points and turning them through 90 degrees, and then fixing them in by sliding in the key flats until you have a complete frame assembly. Each rectangular frame section is assembled the same way until your frame, without its fill-in patterns, is complete. On the screen illustrated, an outside finishing flat is added which has no cut outs or key holes, attached with glue and fine pin tacks.

If you wish you can glue the frame after assembly (before inserting your pattern splits) but the Balinese screens are rarely glued, relying only on the reasonably tight (but not forced) key pieces to hold the assembly together. These screens can be completely dissembled into individual parts, and reassembled at will!

The decorative fill-in panels designs are innumerable (Photo 16B). Sketch 16.2 shows details of how to weave the following examples:

- A vertical closed pattern of woven flats, created by using blocks of three or four verticals woven on alternate sides of widely spaced horizontal splits.

- A horizontal closed pattern, as above but turned 90°.

- An open vertical, horizontal, or square pattern of woven flats, by leaving square, or rectangular spaces, either horizontal or vertical, between the flats being used.

- A diagonal pattern, by leaving spaces or holes wider than the flats you are using.

- Star shapes, by creating very widely spaced horizontal, vertical or diagonal woven flats (with large holes in between), and then slipping two double pointed short pieces of flat jammed diagonally between the crossing flats at each woven intersection.

The object is to create a symmetrical but varying open filigree pattern that delights the eye. The possibilities are almost without limit. The completed screen can then be coated with shellac or a good varnish, and hung in place with tie cords.

Robust Panels or Screens

The technique described above for creating small delicate fill-in screens can be applied on a much larger scale by using wider, more robust splits or flats. As an example, splits as large as those used for the frames of the above

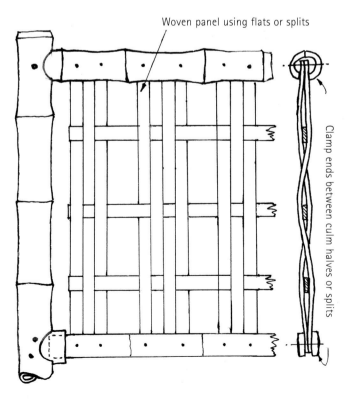

Woven panel using flats or splits

Clamp ends between culm halves or splits

■ SKETCH **16.3** *A simple robust woven screen or fence panel. It can be located with the pattern either vertical or horizontal.*

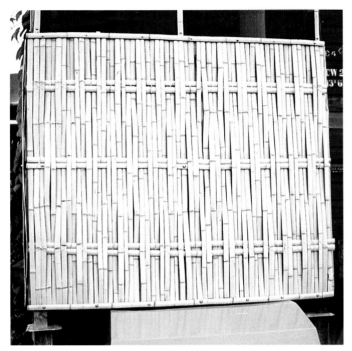

■ **16.D** *A simple, quickly constructed bamboo screen made from splits*

screens (30 mm x 6 mm) can be prepared the same way as the frame supports but without the key holes or cuts. A very attractive woven panel can be prepared by weaving banks of two or three vertical flats alternately in and out of widely spaced single horizontal flats (Sketch 16.3). The stronger your flats or splits become, the further apart your cross supports have to be to take account of the increased stiffness of the material. You must always end these panels with a flat along the top and bottom edge to hold the assembly neatly together. The edges should be lashed, or fixed between two splits, or split culms to contain and strengthen the assembly and stop it springing apart (Sketch 16.3).

Any of the open weave or spaced patterns described above for the delicate screen fill-in designs can be created, as robust large-scale panels for fences or walls of buildings (Photo 13J), or heavy (even burglar proof) partitions. The Japanese often create diagonal or vertical fence tops in this way (Sketch 16.5), leaving heavy sharpened splits protruding from the top of the panel to discourage people from climbing over!

Fences

Remember that bamboo used outside without chemical treatment has a limited life, often only one to three years without deterioration. Its life is mostly much longer if it is harvested older and dry from a superior species, and sometimes up to ten years before actually falling down (see 'harvesting and curing' in Chapter 11). A coat of var-

nish will certainly extend the life. The Asian philosophy is often to rebuild or strengthen the fence as and when it deteriorates.

The following rules will be helpful:

■ Don't bury bamboo fence posts in the ground, certainly not unless they are efficiently chemically treated. If you do, one day your whole fence will snap off at ground level and blow over in a wind.

■ Use good quality hardwood posts, or treated softwood, perhaps round for aesthetic reasons, and use the bamboo in between. (This is what the Japanese do.)

■ If you want the visual effect of bamboo support posts, drive a steel 'star' post deep into the ground with a very heavy sledge hammer (preferably in wet weather so it will penetrate). Punch the internodes out of the bottom of your bamboo fence post, then lower it onto the star post and stand it on a circle of 50 mm high stones. Then cut a slot in the culm near the top of the star post, and fill it with a fairly wet 3:1 sand/cement mix.

The additional designs on Sketches 16.4 and 5 are almost self-explanatory, and you can invent your own variations!

Sketch 16.4. This design is made simply by cross lashing small to medium culm lengths to two or three horizontal support rails that are pinned and lashed to the posts. The top of the fence can be covered by splitting a larger diameter culm in half, knocking the internodes out, and using it cup down over the top of the vertical fence culms, thereby preventing rainwater from getting into the vertical culm cups.

If you want to discourage intruders, I suggest you leave every third culm top longer (leaving a less than foot width space between) and sharpen the top of the culm to leave the two sides of the internode pointing skywards. If you do this, drill a drain hole just above the highest node in both the screen culms (and the fence post if it's bamboo) so that a minimum of water accumulates inside the cup of the culm. Tipping some copper sulphate into the top of upturned culm cups may help extend their life.

Sketch 16.5. This very attractive design can be made by using heavy split half culms assembled back to back diagonally and lashed together. The culms can be well spaced to create a diagonal see-through effect, or placed close together to block out curious viewers. If you create the see-through version, it may be better to use complete culms or very heavy splits with the internodes knocked off and trimmed up in a similar way to that described for making furniture splits (see Chapter 14). Otherwise you see the back view of a split culm complete with internodes. The top of this fence can be finished by lashing a half culm along both sides of the fence, top and bottom,

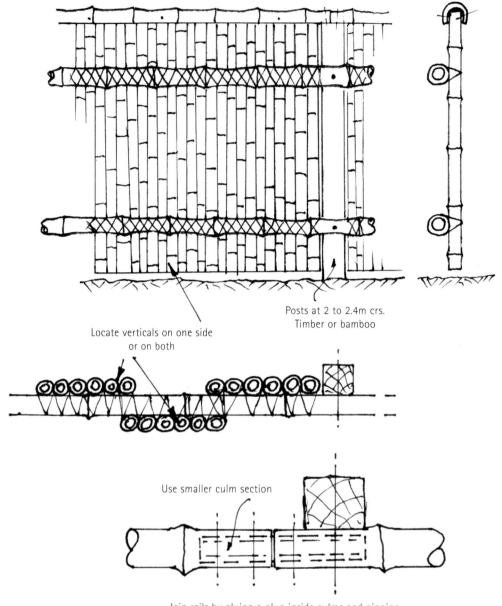

Posts at 2 to 2.4m crs.
Timber or bamboo

Locate verticals on one side
or on both

Use smaller culm section

Join rails by gluing a plug inside culms and pinning

■ SKETCH **16.4** *A simple fence made by cross lashing small to medium diameter culms*

also adding an extra large half culm, or two culms side by side to the very top to create a 'lean-on' fence rail. (You can also leave the diagonal culms projecting and sharpen the tops to discourage intruders as described above.)

Lashing

The Japanese use black dyed cord which contrasts beautifully with the straw colour of the bamboo. If it is to be intruder-proof, you could also use wire, or part wire lashing, and heavier sections can be glued and pinned.

Other Designs

Any of the panel designs described for the Bali screen in-fill sections, but built out of robust flats, can be made in large deep fence panels and fixed between two horizontal culms top and bottom to form very beautiful fences of any height. Or use Type A furniture joints (Sketch 14.1) to house vertical spokes into a top and bottom bamboo rail as shown on the verandah rail of Photo 16E.

■ **16.E** *A simple verandah rail on a Chinese building*

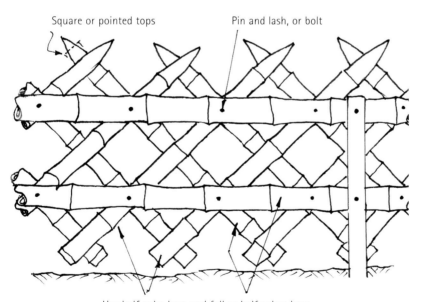

Square or pointed tops

Pin and lash, or bolt

Use half culm here and full or half culms here

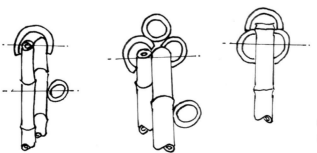

■ SKETCH **16.5** *An attractive design made by using larger culms split in half*

17 Mobile Garden Decorations — Including a Shishi Odoshi

■ **17.A** *A shishi odoshi*

Visitors to Japan will have been unlucky to have missed experiencing the tranquillity and simplicity of their exquisitely designed gardens; space and meditative calm created by the thoughtful placement of water, plants, rocks, sound, and simple functional decorations. What is interesting is that their respect for bamboo is so great that most of the plants, decorations, sounds and fences are either bamboo, made of bamboo, or made by bamboo.

A beautifully simple stone basin welcomes you at the door. Called the 'tsukubai', it must be filled with crystal clear water and graced with a long-handled cup made traditionally from bamboo. The small clear mantra of water falling into the pool of one's consciousness runs through pipes made from bamboo. The occasional hollow woody 'clop' sound that floats through the space, drawing the eye with its beautifully balanced movement, comes from the bamboo 'shishi odoshi', a mobile water toy originally designed to keep deer from wandering into gardens and eating the plants; hence its name of 'deer scare'.

Building an Operating Clock

There are dozens of moving water-driven toys that can be made from bamboo. As an example, in 1996 I was asked by the Chamber of Commerce in a small northern NSW

■ SKETCH **17.1** *The author's design for a bamboo sculpture incorporating an operating water-driven bamboo clock and various water-driven bamboo mobiles and instruments*

town to create a sculpture for them (I have sixteen other large public, mostly bronze, sculptures scattered about the world). As I was in my bamboo period at the time, I designed the sculpture as an environmental rainforest and bamboo garden (Sketch 17.1). It featured water-driven musical instruments that play simple tunes, shishi odoshis, and a magnificent operating, accurate, water-driven bamboo clock (all in chemically treated bamboo that lasts outside for many, many years). Their response was a combination of amazement, fascination and fear of the unknown, but they declared that they wanted it, and asked me to proceed. When I gently suggested that they should have the local government Council approve a suitable site and agree to maintain and insure the instruments, the Mayor was approached. He nervously agreed it could be located in the garden of the new Council

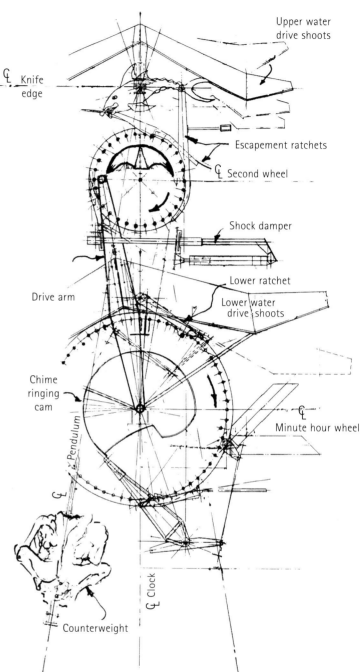

Upper water
drive shoots

C̶L Knife
edge

Escapement ratchets

C̶L Second wheel

Shock damper

Lower ratchet

Drive arm

Lower water
drive shoots

Chime
ringing
cam

Pendulum

C̶L

Minute hour wheel

C̶L Clock

Counterweight

■ **17.B** *The author's bronze and glass water sculpture 'Man,*
Time and the Environment', which contains many moving water
devices and is just as easily built from bamboo

■ SKETCH **17.4** *The water-driven pendulum clock mechanism*
diagram from the author's sculpture 'Man, Time and the
Environment', which was to be incorporated in the bamboo
sculpture shown on Sketch 17.1

Chambers then being constructed, subject to the architect and landscape designer/contractor approving. The architect was ecstatic, and instantly instructed that lighting and a water supply be installed for it. The landscape contractor, who saw his complete concept being dominated by my concept, declared that it wouldn't fit and was not in keeping with his theme, whereupon the Council (famous for its politics, indecision and confused chaos) decided that another site should be found and I was asked to visit the town for an inspection! At this stage I suggested it

would be best if I offered my services after Council and the Chamber had located a suitable site, and had a clear agreement that the sculpture would be maintained, and I would then be happy to build it for them. Everyone got tired and it was never built.

That bamboo clock in Sketch 17.1 is a smaller version of the huge water-driven Hornsby pendulum clock that forms part of my bronze and glass sculpture 'Man, Time and the Environment' (see *Public Sculpture in Australia* by Michael Hedges, pages 17 and 22). Larger than Big Ben, that clock keeps time within 90 seconds every two months (see Photo 17B). The devices that drive that huge clock can just as easily be made in a smaller version from bamboo (I used toughened glass for the water chutes and dials on the original). A detailed explanation of the pendulum clock's workings is contained in the December 1993 issue of the *British Horological Journal*. The workings also include three different forms of clock, a carillon that the large pendulum clock rings on the hour, and a ratchet system that rotated the complete 20-tonne sculpture twice every 24 hours to tell the time with water spouts in the outer pond. However, rather than starting with a complicated project integrating more than one moving component, try building a simple elegant shishi odoshi (Photo 17A) to build your confidence.

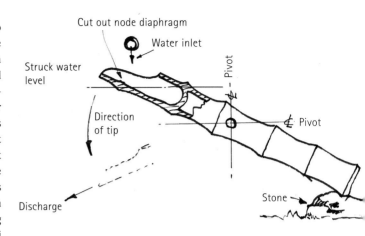

■ SKETCH **17.2** *A Japanese shishi odoshi*

Building a Shishi Odoshi (*Sketch 17.2*)

This device is a pivoted bamboo culm (Photo 17A) with a receiving cup end carved out of the top culm internode, and the top node diaphragm removed altogether. Water is dribbled into the 'cup' (from a bamboo 'pipe' made from a culm with the nodes knocked out). The slowly accumulating weight of water in the cup causes the shishi odoshi to overbalance, which pivots on its shaft as it tips. The base end of the culm, normally resting on a rock, lifts into the air until the water being tipped out of the cup changes the balance again, when the culm base drops back onto the rock making a 'clop' noise. The frequency of the movement and its accompanying noise can be adjusted by changing the flow rate of the water dribbling into the cup.

A shishi odoshi requires some simple trial and error adjustment as you build it. The balance point depends on the best angle that maximises the amount of water that the cup can hold. It must be balanced so it sits firmly on its back end without water, but tips forward readily when the cup's water weight is added (to an almost filled condition). The diameter of the culm has a bearing on the water weight, which influences the length behind the pivot.

The bearing can be very simple. This one utilises a small diameter bamboo culm section as a shaft that passes right through the shishi odoshi (glued in place with silicon rubber to seal the culm) and rests in bearing holes cut in bamboo supports. Two short bamboo culm tube sections acts as spacers to position the shishi odoshi between the supports, and stop it moving sideways against the supports.

Start by selecting a reasonable diameter straight culm section (75 to 100 mm diameter) and cut it off square just after an internode at the base end, and half way between two internodes at the filling end. Carve the top out at the filling end for two half-internode lengths, which means carving halfway along the first still sealed internode after

your cut off, and includes removing that last node diaphragm to form the water cup. Carve it into the shape on Sketch 17.2, leaving the sides as high as reasonably possible to retain the water.

After finishing your carving exercise, balance the culm in your hand (or across a sharp edge) to find the point of balance. Mark that point, then measure and mark a point about 5 per cent of the total length further towards the filling end. That point will be your tentative pivot point, the theoretical centre line of your support shaft. To check that, balance the culm in a tipped back static filling position with the back on the ground and the pivot point supported on a piece of soft clay to keep it upright. Then proceed to fill the cup which should begin to tip forward just before the cup is full. If it moves too soon or doesn't move, or is too sluggish, move the tentative pivot point a little and try again. When you are happy, drill your shaft hole, slide in and silicon the shaft in place, and you have a shishi odoshi!

My largest one is 130 mm diameter and 1730 mm long, and my smallest is 60 mm diameter and 1000 mm long, so the proportion of length to diameter can vary considerably. The supports you can invent yourself, but they can be as simple as split half culms driven into the ground with holes for the shaft. If you use old cured bamboo and varnish it occasionally, it will last for a long time even in a wet environment. The one in Photo 17A has an unnecessarily elaborate bearing support system.

Building a Tipping Clepsydra

The clepsydra was the first clock invented by man, going back beyond Egyptian civilisation. It is a simple calibrated bowl filled from a meniscus filled tank to ensure a steady flow. A more advanced Greek version with vertical sides can be seen in Athens's 'Tower of the Winds'. For 'Man,

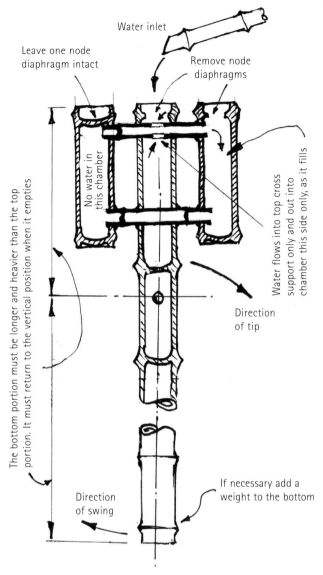

Water inlet

Leave one node
diaphragm intact

Remove node
diaphragms

No water in
this chamber

Water flows into top cross
support only and out into
chamber this side only, as it fills

Direction
of tip

The bottom portion must be longer and heavier than the top
portion. It must return to the vertical position when it empties

Direction
of swing

If necessary add a
weight to the bottom

■ SKETCH **17.3** *A tipping clepsydra, designed
by the author as part of a sculpture*

them to slide through the fixing holes). Drill a good-sized hole into the top fixing pin only, in such a position that the main feed water filling the central chamber can flow from the central chamber into one of the side chambers only (the one with the open top). The water thereby causes an imbalance that will tip the clepsydra sideways. It is important that the two side chambers are equal in weight when empty so the device hangs vertically without water, and also that only one side chamber can be filled with water, which is discharged when the clepsydra tips. The device will operate more effectively if the two top chambers are fixed so that they are not hard against the central chamber, but held some distance out from that chamber to increase the 'out-of-balance' effect.

The clepsydra will rotate in a complete circle on occasions; in fact I had to put paddles on the bottom that struck the pool water on the bronze version to slow it down. A very small hole (3 to 4 mm) in the bottom of the central water chamber will ensure it always empties enough to return to the vertical position so it can receive water.

Bamboo Water Pipes

To make your bamboo pipe, grind a flat on the end of a steel rod, say 12 to 15 mm diameter (reo is good), and punch the nodes out (the longer the pipe culm, the longer and larger diameter the rod). If you can seal the inside by pouring varnish inside and swilling it around, it will last a lot longer.

Time and the Environment', I decided to mount the clepsydra on bearings that would allow it to tip its own water out when it was full. (In fact I incorporated two side by side with the balance tanks sculpted as bronze hermaphrodite faces symbolic of humankind's confusion, and sculpted bronze rams' heads as counterweights.)

Sketch 17.3 and Photo 17C show a simple bamboo version of the self emptying clepsydra clock, which, if filled with a steady water flow and fitted with anti-friction bearings, would operate as a crude clock or self setting 'egg timer' clock. The simple device, with crude bamboo bearings, sits vertically because the weight below the pivot must be greater than that above the pivot. Knock out the node diaphragm near the top, but leave the node diaphragm above the pivot intact, and all the ones below the pivot. Fix on the two side chambers using hollow culm sections (with strategically placed node diaphragms) as pins, and with the nodal projection ground back to allow

■ **17.C** *A bamboo tipping clepsydra*

18 Musical Instrument Making

■ **18.A** *The incredible bamboo 'brass' band performing at the IV International Bamboo Congress in Ubud, Bali, 1995*

The most extraordinary musical sight I ever encountered was the bamboo 'brass' band I heard and saw performing at the Fourth International Bamboo Congress at Ubud, Bali, in 1995. It was about 50-strong, and every instrument was made of bamboo! The traditional bamboo instruments were expected, but imagine a tuba made completely of bamboo! They had saxophones, clarinets, trumpets, French horns, drums of all sizes, trombones with culm 'slides', piccolos and flutes, bright red uniforms and hats, and, of course a conductor's baton of bamboo. The sound was superb, far softer than a true brass band, but the quality of the sound with its slightly woody trumpet and tuba tones seemed to add something quite unique to the music. The craftsmanship and imagination applied to make these instruments was extraordinary. Where the bends or changes in diameter were obviously not available 'as harvested', the culm sections had been carefully split and cut into tapered wedge pieces. These sections had been glued together in hundreds to create the increasing diameter or bend, and then carefully sanded

inside until the required shape was achieved. They looked and were incredibly light. The huge tuba also looked very fragile, but I suspect that it was made from a superior bamboo like *Dendrocalamus asper*, and was a lot tougher than it looked.

I made my first flutes, and a crude pan flute, when I was 12 years old. I happened to be the captain of the Manly Primary School Flute Band, a terribly significant and important position for me at that time, and I took my flute playing and drum beating very seriously. The bamboo I used was the terrible old *Phyllostachys aurea* cut with a coarse bladed hacksaw, and I ended up with fibre emasculated lips from blowing it, and burnt fingers from using a red-hot poker to burn the finger and mouth holes through the culm wall of the flute. But they worked, and I thought the sound they made was superb, because I had created it. I still enjoy playing my bamboo flutes, and over the years I have collected many from various places around the world.

Few people will realise that the Australian Aborigines

made their first didgeridoos from the attractive native Northern Territory bamboo, *Bambusa arnhemica*, a thick-walled species producing culms up to about 100 mm diameter that we now have growing here at Bamboo World. Roger Spencer's article 'Aboriginal Associations with Native Bamboos' from ABN, 1986 and 1989, states 'Although didgeridoos are now used by Aborigines from many parts of Australia, their use was once confined to Arnhem Land. Here the naturally occurring *B. arnhemica* was the only species available.' Apparently the didgeridoo was sometimes called a 'bambu' by the Arnhem Land natives. It is interesting that one of the words for bamboo in nearby Indonesia is 'bambu'. The internationally known didgeridoo player, Alan Dargin, played a number of his different bamboo didgeridoos at the Fourth International Bamboo Congress, and ended up in a 'jam' session with the famous shakuhachi master, John 'Kaizan' Neptune, both playing bamboo instruments. Alan also played a bamboo didgeridoo with a symphony orchestra at the official opening of my Hornsby sculpture in 1993.

The bamboo instrument list is endless, and new instruments incorporating bamboo are being invented all the time. A number of very effective marimba-type instruments use large diameter bamboo tubes to resonate the sound struck on metal xylophone plates suspended immediately above the open culm top. There are also Chinese and Indonesian xylophones with the note producing plates made from thick, hard bamboo segments cut from culms. A Filipino Christian church I visited has a very famous and quite large European pipe organ that they built of bamboo many years ago that is still going strong (they may have replaced some of the bamboo 'pipes', but it is in tune and makes a wonderful sound). The pan flute bands of the Solomon Islands have a base rhythm instrument made of large diameter bamboo culms like a cross between a pan flute and a percussion drum, struck with the flat surface of a rubber 'thong'.

Brass bands aside, one would need to write an encyclopaedia to describe all the traditional and modern instruments made from bamboo. A few of the better known ones are listed below. And now is your chance! This chapter gives you a simple step-by-step

■ **18.B** *A very elegant Chinese bamboo xylophone*

guide on how to make the first seven of these most popular instruments!

Didgeridoo (Aboriginal drone tube)
Pan flute (a series of tubes of different length and diameter)
Flute (cross-blown version)
Indonesian flute (end-blown flute with a bamboo ring mouthpiece)
Whistle flute (an end-blown flute with a whistle-like mouthpiece)
Shakuhachi flute (Japanese end-blown flute)
Jegog (the Balinese bamboo xylophone)
Click sticks (solid bamboo makes a clear, sharp, resonating sound)
Angklung (an Indonesian instrument one could compare to a bamboo handbell)
Reed flute (an end-blown instrument with a reed like a clarinet)
Bamboo skin drum (made from the largest diameter culms possible)

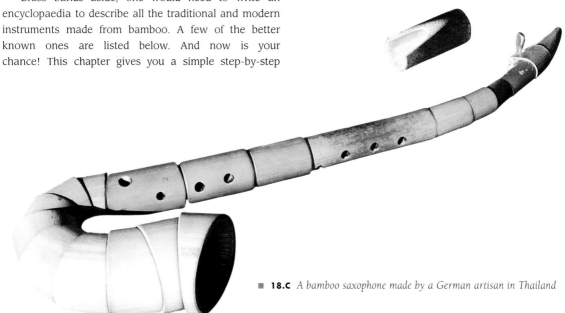

■ **18.C** *A bamboo saxophone made by a German artisan in Thailand*

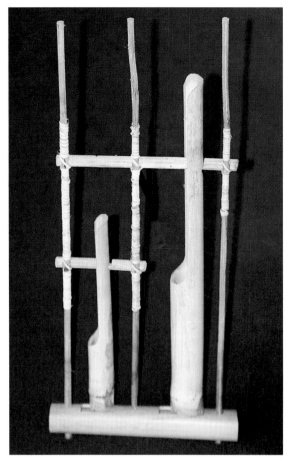

General Principles

Thin to medium-walled hard bamboo will resonate more clearly than thicker walled sappy bamboo. For this reason, try and use high strength species and avoid the very bottom parts of a culm if possible (unless you are making a shakuhachi flute, which needs the thickness) because it is less dense than the higher parts of culm. (There is a higher percentage of parenchyma cell matter and water-carrying vessels in the lower culm walls, and a higher fibre content as you get higher up.)

Instruments made from unseasoned, unhardened, or young culm parts tend to crack or distort easily as they get older and dry out. The other problem is water absorption from the air, or from moisture introduced into the instrument whilst blowing or playing it. I have an 'antique' Indonesian blow pipe (a hunting weapon rather than a 'blowing' instrument), obviously made from two very long internodes of *Schizostachyum jaculans* that was neither old enough when it was recently harvested, nor properly cured. It has cracked and distorted; however, every time it rains the blow pipe returns to original shape, and every

time we strike a dry period it bends and distorts again. The best way to avoid movement from moisture is to ensure that your bamboo is mature when harvested, well-seasoned before you use it and sealed with varnish after making it. It is better to harvest a very old culm, even beyond its structural prime, because the dryer, older wood will be more stable.

Generalised Technique, Curing and Species

Making musical instruments often involves using smaller diameter medium to thin-walled bamboos like *Bambusa textilis*, *B. malingensis*, *B. oliveriana*, *B. ridleyi*, *B. tuldoides*, *Cephalostachyum pergracile*, *Gigantochloa wrayi*, *Schizostachyum zolingerii*, and often very thin-walled bamboos like *Schizostachyum jaculans*, or *S.* sp. 'Murray Island'. If you have nothing better, the running bamboo *Phyllostachys aurea* can be used, but properly round sections occur mostly on that species in the larger diameters of the lower culm sections that are sometimes too thick, with the remaining culm length being mostly heavily grooved and thin-walled.

In Chapter 11 you were advised for good reason not to bother trying to cure or treat bamboo for powder beetle by using heat on thick-walled large diameter culms. However, heat curing can be an effective treatment when making musical instruments. Here you can sensitively concentrate on the single relatively small piece you are treating, particularly where you are applying heat to only 2 to 6 mm of wall thickness instead of to 8 to 25 mm of 100 mm+ diameter culms. Applying a broad-flamed blow torch directly to the outside of a mature culm will further dry the wood by destroying the starch content, and it leaves an attractive partly scorched look on the wood. Keep the culm moving and rotating constantly or you will damage the surface or crack the culm. You will see the wax melt and bubble on the surface as it becomes fluid and mixes with the steam and sap rising out of the culm. Before heating, knock a hole in any nodes you don't need to remain intact to let any steam pressure and moisture out. Keep wiping the resin/wax mixture over and along the culm as you go and it will form a long-lasting attractive outer coating, sealing the surface effectively. However, be careful or you will crack, burn or destroy your piece of bamboo (and maybe part of your skin). With very thin culms, you will have to move faster.

This heat technique is recommended to use after, and in addition to, the normal harvesting and aging techniques you would use for any bamboo. However, if you are impatient to practise or make musical instruments out of uncured bamboo whilst waiting for your good quality wood to season (or grow!) you can use the above heat curing system directly on mature green cut wood. You won't get the same quality, and it has a greater chance of cracking, shrinking or distorting on you at some point but it seems to work. (I feel a sense of guilt in telling you that you can bypass the culm aging process, at your own risk, but if you accept that it is an expedient rather than the best practice, I will survive. Don't blame me if your instruments are not around in 1000 years time!)

Marek Fluteman, the very talented flute maker of the New Brighton/Byron area in New South Wales, cures green cut mature culm pieces within days of harvesting, imparting the beautiful sealed 'scorched' look that has become a trademark with his flutes. I remember being amazed at seeing a row of recently heat-treated culm sections on his studio work bench that looked completely dry and finished, but they had bright green new recently cut ends untouched by the heat (obviously where he held them) sticking out beyond the finished wood. Marek, who recently released a new tape of him playing one of his shakuhachi flutes, invests extremes of time and patience when aging, curing and making one of his master quality instruments. However his more economical range are heat-cured only days after harvesting, and he tells me they rarely crack or suffer with age!

If you knock out the internode before you cure the wood, it should dry more quickly with less stress, partly because the reduced node diaphragm will reduce shrinkage stress, and also because it allows air flow through the culm to remove moisture and dry the inside at the same time as the outside to some degree. In my experience it results in less cracking, but I haven't conducted a properly monitored test to prove my observation. Bamboo used for reinforcing or composite beam construction is certainly split to allow it to dry more quickly and evenly, and removing the diaphragm should help. Marek Fluteman knocks the nodes roughly out of his chosen culm sections before heat-treating them green, and early after harvesting, well before heat-treating, if he is aging a culm section for a superior flute.

The thinner walled bamboos need to be cut very carefully to prevent them from splitting. You can use a sharp fine-toothed blade in a hacksaw, or you can buy a heavy fretsaw with a fine-toothed blade sized between a hacksaw and a fretsaw. Rotate thin-walled culms slowly towards the direction the teeth cut as you saw, to ensure you are cutting into and across the fibres on the surface. If you continue to saw until you are halfway through, a thin wall may crack if the saw blade jams whilst under pressure. This technique also avoids the teeth pulling the fibres out of the culm surface and tearing them along, which weakens thin-walled structures and spoils the look of the wood.

If you need to reduce the end of a flute by a small amount, say for fine tuning adjustment, you can grind the end back carefully on a sanding disc if it's not too coarse and you don't use too much pressure, but don't forget that

bamboo's sanding dust is high in silica and should not be breathed (wear a face mask). The ideal tool for finishing the mouthpiece of a whistle flute or a shakuhachi flute is a sanding disc or drum or even a fine grinding wheel.

Drilling or creating the small holes such as finger and mouth holes in bamboo instruments, must be done precisely and without fibre-frayed edges. You can achieve this by using 'W' series 'P and K' dowelling drills, which have two downward pointing cutting tips rotating around the centre guide.

An invaluable inexpensive tool is the sandpaper mandrel. Take a straight steel rod, say 8 mm diameter and 600 mm long, and cut a slot about 25 mm to 30 mm long straight down its centre at one end. By slipping a strip of sandpaper of the same width into the slot and winding it anti-clockwise around the rod (when looking down the rod towards the slot) you have created a drum-shaped sanding auger that can be inserted, in your drill, down the

■ **18.E** Bambusa textilis *var.* gracilis *and the other various long-internoded cultivars are ideal for flute making.*

bore of a flute to smooth the interior. By winding more paper on, or off, you increase or decrease the diameter of the auger. By making them with shorter, or longer, or smaller diameter rods, you have a range of adjustable augers at your disposal, even very small short ones for enlarging fingerholes, but remember to wear a mask and don't breath the high silica dust.

Diaphragms can either be punched out with a round steel rod ground to a square end and then sanded with the sandpaper mandrel, or drilled with a reduced-shank drill welded or silver soldered to a piece of steel rod to extend its length. Long drills can be purchased but they are very expensive for the few applications where they will be used. Sometimes you can buy a wood burr and weld it to an extension rod to use for cutting back rough projecting areas of internal node diaphragms when necessary, but the sandpaper mandrel does a great job.

A simple vee-block support (like a small version of the furniture culm vice—see Sketch 14.10) is handy when drilling or working your flute. Sandpaper wrapped around a small rod and pushed gently across the flute when positioned on a finger or mouth hole is ideal to remove the sharp edge.

Bamboo instruments benefit from a coating of very thin sealing medium inside to minimise the effects of weather and playing moisture, but don't apply it unless the bamboo is properly cured and dried. The resonance of an instrument will change a little if its moisture content changes, so superior bamboo flutes should be sealed, sometimes with more than one coat. An Estapol-type varnish (they tend to be thin) is suitable, but thin it down with the recommended thinner if it looks at all thick. There are also very thin high quality epoxy wood sealers such as Everdure.

To treat the inside, seal all the holes, except at one end, with plastic sticky tape. Pour about 75 mm flute depth of your chosen sealing medium into the open end, cap it with your hand (protected with rubber or plastic), and shake and roll the instrument vigorously to ensure the liquid gets into all nooks and crannies. Tip the residue back into the tin via a disposable cloth strainer (unless it's a two-pot mix), pull all the sticky tape off the holes whilst still wet, and suspend the instrument from an external noose on a long piece of string, end hole down. If you give it a twist to set it in motion, it will quite happily keep moving in a breeze, drying evenly and minimising varnish 'pooling' as it dries.

If you don't seal the outside of your instrument with the heat-treatment method described above, or if the seal you achieve with heat-treatment doesn't look adequate, it will need to be either waxed, or very lightly sanded and painted with the same sealer you used for the inside.

Don't use glue or wood sealers (varnish) on the outside surface of a culm without removing the natural silicone/wax coating or it won't stick. Varnish does appear to adhere to the culm skin after using the heat curing process, but I wouldn't try gluing it without first sanding the surface. Use only waterproof glues, or they may melt as you play!

When you've finished your flute, it pays to bind the cut-off exit end, and sometimes even above the top hole, with fine cord, and lacquer the cord neatly in place. Bamboo's strong tensile strength is not much help with thin-walled species when it comes to cracking. Interestingly, whilst bamboo's tensile strength drops at the nodes, it is actually higher there in its resistance to cracking because of the confusion of fibres being less linear and sometimes climbing in and out towards the node diaphragm. This means that if you end your flute just after the diaphragm, even though it is fully drilled out for the flute exit, it will resist cracking more than if it is cut off anywhere along the internode. Unless you are lucky enough that the end falls exactly on the node after adjusting the length for the correct pitch, it is unlikely that you will end up just after a node. You can drill a hole (8 mm minimum) in the bottom of the flute to adjust pitch instead of cutting it off.

Making a Didgeridoo

The traditional bamboo used years ago by the Arnhem Land Aborigines, *Bambusa arnhemica*, is a thick-walled bamboo, which belies the 'thinner the wall the better the resonance' theory. It is, and was, the only indigenous Australian bamboo large enough for their purpose. I am currently conducting curing and shrinkage tests on *B. arnhemica* because the structure and texture of the culms are unlike any other bamboo I know. When cut with a saw, it is almost sappy and soft, and yet it seems quite strong. Its natural environment is four months of torrential rain and flooding, followed by eight months of relative drought, the northern Australian monsoonal climate. I suspect that its structure is designed to store more moisture than most bamboos, which would account for its very thick-walled open celled structure.

The best bamboo to make didgeridoos from would be straight, strong, thin to medium-walled, and well seasoned bamboos like *Gigantochloa atroviolacea*, *Bambusa lako*, *B. oldhamii*, perhaps the lower culm section of *Nastus elatus*, and the upper culm sections of *G. atter*, *Schizostachyum brachycladum* and others. Be warned though that if the wall is too thin for the diameter, or not hard enough or still high in moisture, the resonance is destabilised and dull. The pitch will depend on your chosen length, but the diameter plays an important part in the tonal quality, with smaller diameters producing better higher tones in shorter instruments, and larger diameters best for deeper longer 'didges'. Alan Dargin, the famous Aboriginal master, has a range of different diameter and length 'didges' to achieve various effects.

Cut your well-aged, preferably very old culm from the clump during the first half of the dry season. Select the

■ **18.F** Bambusa lako *is sufficiently thin-walled to successfully heat-cure.*

various pieces you want to convert to a didgeridoo, and cut them from the culm leaving at least one complete node and internode length longer at both ends than you need. A good standard size would be a culm section with a 40 mm to 50 mm bore about 1.2 to 1.4 m long, which means the piece of bamboo you will be seasoning needs to be about 2 m long to allow for cut-offs.

The earlier comments on ageing bamboo—in a covered dry rack, preferably for at least six months—apply, but you can try the heat-treatment shortcut if you are impatient to get going, and it will give the didgeridoo a beautiful burnished finish. Either way you will probably have to discard some cracked or unsound pieces after drying, so prepare a number of pieces.

To make the instrument after curing, cut both ends off the culm to discard the end-dried pieces that are often cracked, still leaving both ends long for later adjustment. Then remove the internodes (or the remainder of the internodes if they were punched out after harvesting) by punching them out using a flat-ended steel rod between 12 mm and 18 mm diameter. Position the rod down inside

against the culm wall against the nodal diaphragm and then tap the rod with a hammer to punch out disc shaped segments. By walking the end of the rod around the inside diameter of the culm, you can punch the complete node out. It sometimes helps to grind a slight angle (maybe 20 degrees off flat) and use it like a blunt chisel on persistent node parts. Then use a large diameter sandpaper mandrel a little smaller than the didge bore to clean out the remaining node diaphragms. (You can make a large diameter mandrel from a round piece of wood with a sandpaper slot cut in it similar to the smaller steel mandrels described. Jam the round block onto a 9 mm steel rod, and use it with the slow speed control on your hand drill.)

The mouthpiece is usually formed by sculpting it from warmed, softened bees' wax, or a similar wax with a high melting point. There is nothing particular about the (culm-shaped) mouthpiece other than to reduce the diameter to something that is more comfortable for and not abrasive to your mouth. Trim the exit end off just after a node and test the tone, without the mouthpiece if possible. To make the pitch higher, cut more off the mouthpiece end to reduce the length. When you are happy, varnish seal the completed didge, warm your beeswax and construct the round holed mouthpiece to suit your lips. As a final precaution against cracking, you could bind the mouthpiece end of the culm (or both ends, but if the node is near the end it should be okay) with a half a dozen turns of light strong cord, and glue them in place with more varnish. It is best to test the resonance before and after adding the end binding, as too much lashing around the end could reduce, or change the resonance.

Then start practising your circular breathing!

I used to decorate some of my bamboo flutes by drawing designs on them, and burning them into wood, sitting patiently in the sun with a magnifying glass. I have neither the time nor the patience now, but it does give such an instrument an interesting finish.

I'm sure the Aborigines didn't have Estapol-type varnishes, but applying a coat will help stabilise the bamboo.

Making a Pan Flute
(Sketch 18.1)

The pan flute, one of my favourite instruments, has that hollow haunting sound so well known from the fabulous playing of George Zamfir. It's interesting though, that it is not exclusively a European instrument. One could argue that the South American pan flute may have come with the Spanish, but I suspect it was there long before the Spanish arrived. The same applies to the Melanesian and Micronesian islanders from the Solomon and Cook Islands across through the Torres Strait Islands and Papua New Guinea, who were making pan flutes from bamboo long before European influence.

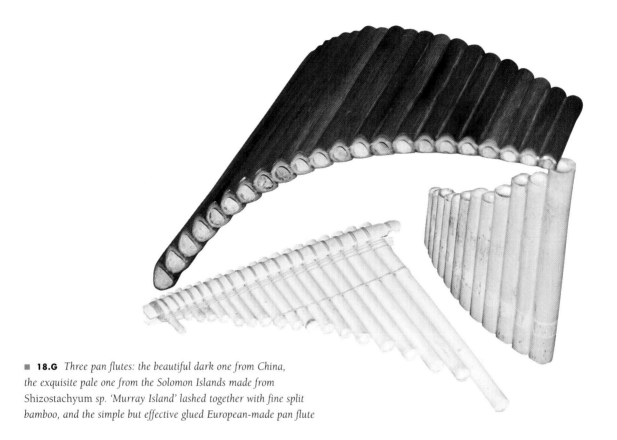

■ **18.G** *Three pan flutes: the beautiful dark one from China,
the exquisite pale one from the Solomon Islands made from*
Shizostachyum *sp. 'Murray Island' lashed together with fine split
bamboo, and the simple but effective glued European-made pan flute*

The bamboos used for pan flutes are usually the light
and thin-walled smaller bore bamboos. Possible species
are *Gigantochloa wrayi*, *Bambusa textilis*, *Cephalostachyum
pergracile*, *Schizostachyum jaculans* or *S.* sp. 'Murray
Island' (the latter is the bamboo used by the Pacific
Islanders, and is indigenous to Australia's northern
islands), or the smaller diameter culms of *S.
brachycladum*. As stated earlier, I have also made pan
flutes from the thin-walled running bamboo, *Phyllostachys
aurea*, commonly available throughout Australia.

Pan flutes are very easy to make. The pitch of the note
is set by the length of the hollow chamber, measured from
the top of the hole (where you cut off the culm), to the bottom of the hole inside formed by the node that you leave
intact (Sketch 18.1). The diameter does affect the tone and
your ability to blow the note sensitively, but not so much
the pitch of the note. Whilst the pitch is set by length, the
hollow soft resonant sound of the note, so attractive with
pan flutes, has more depth as the diameter of the chamber
increases and more sharpness as it decreases. Larger
diameters, however, require more breath and lungpower
to blow, and there comes a point when a diameter too big
for the length destabilises the note.

As an example, the resonant length for the note F
above middle C is approximately 245 mm. I have one pan
flute with that note being 10 mm diameter and another
with that note being 24 mm diameter. I prefer the tone of
the larger one, but can't play it for very long before I'm
exhausted. The notes on my favourite small 12-note pan
flute range in diameter from a maximum of 15 mm down

to a minimum of 10.5 mm, decreasing in diameter in even
steps as the culm sections get shorter and the notes get
higher. I have a beautifully made 20-note Solomon Islands
pan flute (made from *S.* sp. 'Murray Island') ranging in
diameter from a maximum of 10 mm to a minimum of
5 mm. Whilst it takes a little less air to play than my
favourite 10 mm to 15 mm flute, the Solomon Islands
flute's notes are sharper and less haunting to my ear.
My most magnificent pan flutes have 22 notes ranging
from 18 mm to 10 mm diameter, and the hardest notes
to play are the smallest ones, even though they take
less lung power.

If you follow the drawing, each note is a chamber
made by cutting off a culm section of the right diameter
just below the node so that the nodal diaphragm is intact.
Then cut off the top, before a node, to suit the chamber
length required to give the sound wave length and resonance you require. Select larger diameter culms for the
deeper notes graduating progressively down in diameter as
the notes get higher, with the highest always the smallest
diameter. This provides a balanced sound throughout the
flute's range (otherwise either the top or bottom range of
your instrument will be softer or sharper than the other).

The Solomon Islands instrument is arranged with all
the notes in a straight line, and they are beautifully bound
(with their tops all even) between two bamboo flats using
very fine split bamboo as string. It is one of the nicest
pieces of bamboo craftsmanship that I have seen; however, it is not as comfortable to play as the slightly larger
instrument, which has its notes arranged in a curve so

that the middle note is approximately 2 cm back from a line projected across the tops of the highest and lowest notes. The curved instrument is more comfortable and a little faster when moving your mouth from note to note when playing the instrument. The larger diameter also gives it a mellower sound and makes it easier to play.

The tops of all notes should always be level to facilitate your lips sliding along the flute top. Great care should be taken to smooth off, and even slightly round off, the blowing edge of the tubes; otherwise you wear a hole in your lip from sliding back and forth rapidly. After completely finishing your instrument, it pays to gently fine-sandpaper and wax the blowing edge to give a rounder, smoother transition when playing. The large Chinese master instruments I have are not even flat-topped, but sanded to an almost semi-circular curve from front to back with the centreline through all the tubes (where they touch) being the highest point. It is very easy on the lips.

The tubes can be glued together or simply bound together between bamboo splits, preferably (but not necessarily) hot bent to give the curve. Use very thin lashing (bamboo splits less than 1 mm thick can be used if from a good 'string' species), or the lashing passing between notes will separate the tubes too far apart and add to your playing difficulties.

If you glue your tubes to each other, it's best to reinforce both sides by glueing light split culm sections, or even a thick cloth ribbon, along both sides of the flute's outer tube surface about 25 mm below the blowing edge. Before you glue, don't forget to sand off the wax surface or it won't stick. If your bamboo is fairly thick-walled, say close to 3 mm or more, you should plane or carve off the surface slightly between where the notes contact each other to form a flat bearing area to make the glued joint stronger. Remember that each surface you cut will have to be angled slightly from the other if you want a curve in your assembled flute.

The octave between middle C and upper C requires resonance lengths starting from approximately 158 mm and ending with approximately 75 mm. To make your instrument, I would start by choosing a (well-cured or heat-cured) culm 15 mm bore, cut a section of the right diameter out below two nodes, then cut it off about 162 mm above where you think the inside node surface is located. You can locate the node position by inserting a rod down the culm and marking how deep it went on the outside. Borrow a piano (or a pitch pipe), strike middle C and then blow a sound on your new cut 'note'. It should sound a little deeper than your piano note. Then carefully reduce the length of the chamber (on a sanding disc), testing its note against the piano's middle C as you reduce it until your ear tells you they are exactly the same pitch.

Next choose a culm section 10 mm bore and repeat the above process, tuning it to the C above middle C, cutting it to approximately 78 mm initially rather than its approximate finished size of 75 mm. Work it down in length to raise the note up to the piano's C pitch. This will give you the top and bottom note of a complete octave. If you want a simple single octave pan flute with no half notes, all you need to do is to choose six more pieces of culm that gradually reduce in diameter from 15 mm to 10 mm, and tune each to the next note on the piano in reducing lengths from middle C to the next C up. Sometimes you can get this graduation of diameters from a single culm. Then assemble your instrument (gluing or lashing). Always work from longer, lower notes to shorter notes, because if you accidentally reduce a note by too much, you may be able to use it for the next note up.

If you are ambitious and want half notes, or a greater range than one octave, simply extend the same process to produce the extra notes or half notes you need, and assemble your notes, in order, in the same way; however don't go above 20 mm in diameter or you run out of air and it gets too hard to blow. There is an alternative assembly where the half notes can be arranged, almost as a separate pan flute, attached behind and above the full notes. You would need to experiment to get the position right to suit a comfortable lip position (and one's protruding chin) but I have seen 'double decker' pan flutes that seem to work effectively.

I get great satisfaction from sitting on my hill playing invented haunting melodies. I hope making this simple instrument will bring you the same joy.

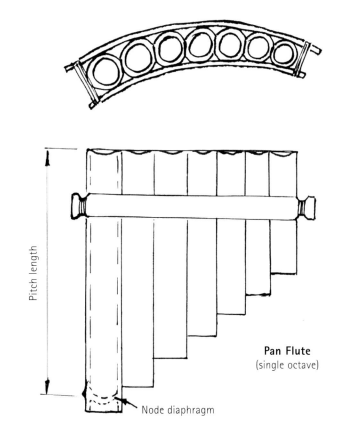

Pan Flute
(single octave)

Pitch length

Node diaphragm

■ SKETCH **18.1** *The pan flute*

Principles Applying to Most Flutes

With the exception of the traditionally made Japanese shakuhachi flute with its drilled bore tapered from both ends, most Asian bamboo flutes utilise the natural hole size of the bamboo selected, rather than bore or drill a specific hole size in a culm that had a smaller hole. As before with the pan flute, the most resonating flute sounds come from medium/thin-walled material, but you can get some nice woody sounds from culms a little thicker, particularly if the wood is hard and well seasoned, or heat-treated. The harder the material in your culm, the longer and clearer the sound wave is sustained. (I created Australia's only bell foundry for casting and tuning carillon bells as an offshoot of my art foundry, and the same acoustical technology still applies, even to bronze bells where harder metal sustains the ringing sound for longer.)

As with the pan flute, the longer the tube, the lower the note. By drilling adequately sized holes along its length and covering all of them with your fingers, you get the same note that you would if that flute had no holes at all. By taking your fingers off the holes one at a time from the bottom upwards, you are, in effect, artificially shortening the length of the tube by letting the air and vibration escape earlier, which causes the note to climb higher in pitch. The trick is to know where to drill the holes, and how big to make them! Rather than cutting the end of his flutes off in between internodes, Marek Fluteman sometimes leaves the flute longer to retain the last node, and he adjusts the flute's pitch by drilling a hole at the correct 'length' position for that pitch.

The pitch or lowest note is set by the length from the sound hole (or blowing hole) to the air exit end. The higher the pitch of the flute, the shorter the distance must be from the blowing hole to the air exit end. As your flute design becomes higher in pitch and shorter, the sound quality and ease of blowing improves if the diameter is reduced, like the piccolo. As it becomes lower in pitch and longer, the sound quality, balance and ease of blowing improves when the diameter is increased a little, until it will start to take more air to blow, and be more difficult to control as it gets too big in diameter for its pitch. The optimum diameter for a bamboo flute is actually a compromise between the larger diameter that sounds so wonderful for the deep notes, and the smaller diameter best suited for the higher notes. This compromise is ideally illustrated if you look at the classical concert flute, superbly thin, hard metal with a bore large enough to sustain the vibration of the lower notes beautifully, but small and stable enough for the very high notes, a performance beyond a wooden or bamboo flute; however, the sounds available from the lesser range of a wooden or bamboo flute can be very beautiful, and two octaves is readily achievable.

Thinner walls give clearer, bolder sounds in the lower register, but the vibrations tend to destabilise the (non metal) tube as the notes become higher unless you have a way of reducing the diameter of the tube as the note gets higher. This is what happens with the pan flute design and its reducing diameters for higher notes. This just can't be done with a single culm bamboo flute, so the chosen bore diameter and wall thickness is always a compromise between the needs of the higher and lower registers.

Making a Flute (cross-blown European style)

For the above reasons, together with the tangential entry of the blown wind, the diameter, straightness, wood hardness, wall thickness and finish in the bore are more important with a cross-blown flute than with most other flutes. They are harder to blow, and to control note quality, and more difficult to achieve a two-octave range if you don't get the balance right.

The best way to make a simple cross-blown flute is to copy the dimensions of another. Find a flute that you like, that plays easily and is pleasing to the ear, and use it as a pattern (hereafter called the 'master'). It doesn't have to be a bamboo flute. It can be wood or metal.

Find a dry, firm, straight piece of culm with an internal diameter close to the same diameter as the master. (If the master flute has keys on it, ignore them for the time being.) If you are going to heat-treat your culm, do so before you cut holes in it or it will crack along the holes as you treat it. Cut it off cleanly just beyond the node that will represent the sealed (blowing) end, then lay it beside the master and cut it off about 20 mm longer than the master.

If you are using bamboos like *Schizostachyum jaculans*, *S.* sp. 'Murray Island', *Gigantochloa wrayi*, or some others, depending on the length of your flute, the bamboo's internodes are so long that there is no need to remove a node from the middle 'playing' section of the flute; however, if it has a node diaphragm that needs removing, now is the time to do it. In this case the diaphragm is best removed with a long series drill of the same diameter as the bamboo's bore, but if you don't have one, don't buy it as they are too expensive. Find a flat-ended steel rod of the right diameter and punch it out. Ream out the bore to give a smooth interior with the earlier described sandpaper mandrel.

Mark the mouth hole position (only) on your culm to be exactly the same distance as the master's mouth hole is from the diaphragm blocking off the blowing end of that flute. You can establish the end diaphragm's position accurately by sliding a rod firstly into the master until it rests against the end wall and marking the mouth hole on

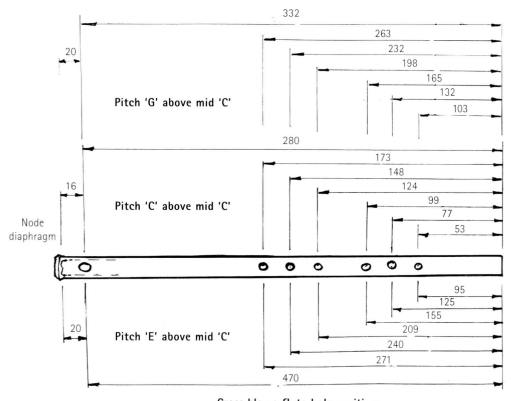

Cross blown flute hole positions

■ SKETCH **18.2** *The cross-blown flute and some details of ones you can make*

the rod; then pull the rod out and slide it into your culm until it touches the node, and then mark the cut off end of your culm on the rod. If you pull the rod out and lay it beside your culm with that end mark lined up with its open cut of end, you can then mark the position for your mouth hole adjacent to the mouth hole mark you earlier made from the master.

Study the shape of the mouth hole on the master carefully, and then drill your mouth hole (using W series dowelling drill). Sometimes they are slightly oval; if so create the same shape and size by choosing a drill to suit the smallest hole dimension and using a short sandpaper mandrel to elongate the hole along the flute. The clean edge of the hole, which 'splits' the wind, is important.

You have now created a single note flute, its pitch being the lowest note on its possible scale. Blow a sound on your flute, and you will find that its pitch is a little lower than the bottom note of the master. By carefully and progressively reducing the length of your culm (by cutting off or sanding back its open end), you can raise the pitch until it is exactly the same as the master (or the equivalent piano note).

Next lay your flute beside the master with the exit ends together, and mark the exact position of the last fingerhole (closest to the air exit). Drill a hole in that position, but make the hole half the size of the one in the master, or full size if you don't need perfect pitch. This should produce a note, when blown with the hole

uncovered, slightly flatter or lower than the same master note. The principle applied here is that you can adjust the pitch from being flat (lower) to correct for that position very slightly by varying the size of the hole between being smaller and fully open. You can simulate this by half covering the hole with your finger when playing a flute note, or by raising and lowering the note between that hole's pitch and the next one down by rolling your finger slowly 'open' and 'closed' over the hole as you blow.

Having established that your flute note is a little flat, increase the size of the fingerhole a little at a time by using a very small sandpaper mandrel to enlarge the fingerhole, cutting away on the mouthpiece side of the fingerhole only, until the pitch of the master and your flute are exactly the same. In effect, you are then not only enlarging the hole, but shortening the distance to the mouthpiece.

Repeat this procedure with each of the six note holes until your instrument is complete. Make sure your flute's inside is clear and smooth, lacking in feathery, hanging fibres left from drilling fingerholes, if necessary by reaming with a sandpaper mandrel close to the bore diameter. Use fine sandpaper held on a small round section to take the sharp edge off the fingerholes, pushing the sandpaper across the flute with the curved sandpaper surface resting in the fingerhole depression.

If you can't find a master flute to your liking to copy, use the dimensions shown on Sketch 18.2, which gives you three different-sized (pitched) flutes to make. Use a culm with a bore about 15 to 17 mm diameter and a 2 to 3 mm wall thickness for the longer ones, and about 13 to 14 mm for the smaller one. Be cautious about blandly measuring out hole positions and drilling without following the above tuning procedures if you want a tuned chromatic scale flute. Also, fingerhole positions are often in a straight line, but can be located in a slightly rotated position to suit the different lengths of your fingers without affecting the pitch or tone.

Play it, dry it thoroughly and seal it (see earlier notes), and you have completed your instrument. If you haven't been happy with the bamboo you had available, plant the best species NOW!

All the six-hole flutes have a simple fingering system. To get the lower octave from the bottom note upwards, start with all holes covered and remove the lowest finger for each progressive note, replacing them all except for the top one for the note one octave above the bottom. By firming the lips and changing the airstream, you can replace the top finger, lift the bottom, and progress upwards through the top octave in the same way, the main difference between getting top or bottom octave notes being lip shape and blowing technique. It sometimes helps to cover only the second and third hole from the top when blowing the top note, two octaves above the lowest note. A skilled flute player, depending on flute quality, can sometimes get more than two octaves.

Making an Indonesian Flute (end-blown)
(Sketch 18.3)

To blow a clear note from a cross-blown flute or the shakuhachi flute requires more practice than to blow the Indonesian end-blown flute. If you blow into this mouthpiece it makes an acceptable noise. With a little practice you can introduce vibrato and improved tonal values (it's all to do with breath control and lungs). An unskilled person can quickly learn to play an acceptable tune on this attractive, forgiving instrument.

The principles laid down above for your cross-blown flute apply exactly to this flute, including the note hole positions, the diameter and length for pitch, and the method of making one, except for the mouthpiece, which is quite different. Whilst the distance (from the hole that makes the sound to the fingerholes) is the same in both flutes, the overall length of the end-blown flute of the same pitch will be shorter. This is because the blowing point is at the end of the flute, instead of some distance beyond the blowing hole.

My favourite instrument, pitched E below middle C, is 482 mm overall length, 18 mm bore, and made, I think, from a small *Schizostachyum brachycladum* culm with a 3 mm wall thickness (see Sketch 18.3). The downstream sound hole edge is 470 mm from the exit end (exactly as shown on Sketch 18.2 for the cross-blown flute, including the fingerhole positions). The blind cut-off end of the flute is 12 mm from the downstream end of the sound hole (as shown in Sketch 18.3 and described in the following mouthpiece making procedure). The six holes give you a range of two octaves, and a bit more if you are highly skilled. Use the given dimensions and make it using the technique described for the above cross-blown flute, tuning it to a piano instead of a master flute.

You can also make the smaller cross-blown flute shown on Sketch 18.2 with an Indonesian end-blown mouthpiece, using the same mouthpiece and fingerhole dimensions.

You can also use your favourite cross-blown flute as your master. If you select your piece of bamboo with the same bore size as the master, and make it with the dimension from the down-wind edge of the end-blown flute's sound hole to the exit end of the flute the same as from the centre of the cross-blown sound hole to the end of the master, it will be fine. The mouthpiece will be the same as Sketch 18.3.

Indonesian flutes are often made from thin to very thin-walled bamboos such as *Schizostachyum brachycladum* or *S. jaculans*, but there are many bamboos that will be excellent for this purpose (e.g. *Bambusa textilis*). The main selection criterion is to get a culm piece that is straight, has the correct bore, and has no nodes or only one node to remove to make your open tube.

Always follow the sequence of cutting your culm piece a little longer, then making the mouthpiece, then tuning the flute to pitch by cutting back the length, then forming each fingerhole starting from the bottom upwards, all the same procedure described for the cross-blown flute.

The Indonesian flute's mouthpiece (Photo 18I) is made by cutting off the culm carefully at a node to leave the diaphragm blocking off the culm hole (Sketch 18.3.E). It must be cut so close to the diaphragm that it slices through the edge of the diaphragm, so that it forms a square ended exterior wall with no sign of a culm hollow left at the blowing end of the flute. It may pay to cut off a few sacrificial nodes until you are confident you can do it on your selected piece of culm. Follow Sketch 18.3 as you study this mouthpiece, remembering that it is drawn larger than life to help you see the detail.

Carefully shave the flat sloping section on the spot where you choose to blow, starting from nothing about 15 mm in from the end. Cut deeper into the culm until you have cut about 2.5 to 3 mm off the culm diameter, creating a flat about 10 mm wide by the time it gets to the end of the flute with its square cut diaphragm (Sketch 18.3.C and E). Then cut a square hole, about 6 or 7 mm square, straight down into the middle of the flat area of your wedge-shaped shaved off area, starting about 6 or 7 mm in from the end of the flute so that you miss the internal diaphragm. You will need a 6–7 mm wide, very sharp square-edged, wood-carving chisel to make that hole. It is easier if you drill a 6 mm round hole first and square it up afterwards with a sharp fine pointed knife. Then remove the inside square edge of that hole furthest from the diaphragm, back at an angle sloping down into the flute until it forms a sharp knife edge on its top outer surface. The shape should slope down into the flute, inside it at an angle of about 35° to 40° from the culm's flat cut surface (as on Sketch 18.3.E). It is a difficult piece to cut out because you are cutting against the grain and inside through the square hole. It will be easier to abrade the bamboo off using a 50 mm x 6 mm strip of emery cloth glued to a 7 mm wide thin flat steel strip (or a thin 7 mm wide bamboo flat). It will require patience, and you may need to renew the emery cloth, but using it inside the sound hole as a rasp will work.

Now you need to make the bamboo mouthpiece ring that slips onto the end of the flute (Sketch 18.3.D) and the recessed diameter on the end to receive it. When this ring is fitted, it leaves a narrow slot between the bamboo ring, and the flat wedge area you cut from the top of the culm (with the sound hole located further in). This becomes the blowing point, and the slot forms a wind channel that directs the air over the sound hole when you blow.

First shave off the very end of the culm above the diaphragm to reduce the diameter slightly for the first 5 mm of the culm length (Sketch 18.3.D), forming a small step about 1 mm high that will stop the mouthpiece ring from sliding down the flute (roll the culm end around whilst supported on a semi hard surface, pushing down with a sharp knife, to form the edge of the small step, then split or shave the small shelf off the outer end).

The ring itself (Sketch 18.3.D), is formed by splitting a section of flexible young, green bamboo (*B. multiplex* or *G. apus*) about 5 mm wide and 3 mm thick and about five times the flute's diameter in length, from inside a thick culm wall after discarding the waxy surface layer. Then heat or steam it, and bend it around a hot bar (not red-hot), very slightly smaller than the prepared culm surface it is going to fit onto, clamped into position by pinching

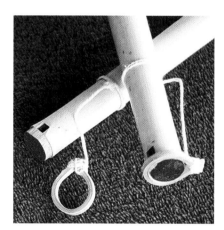

■ **18.1** *The mouthpiece end of two Indonesian end-blown flutes, one with the mouthpiece ring detached for clarity. Note the tapered sound slot and the rebated end of the flute to hold the mouthpiece ring.*

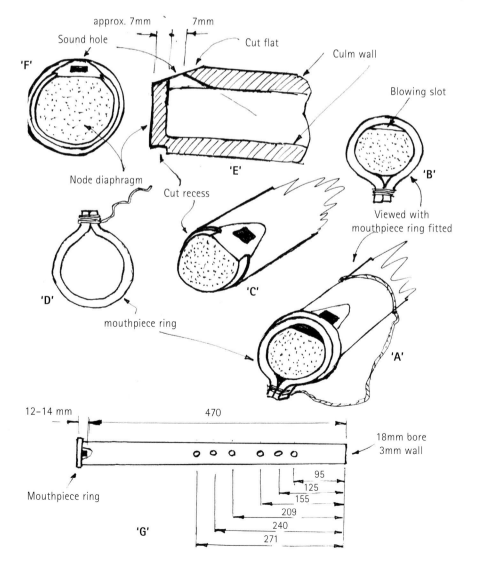

■ SKETCH **18.3** *The Indonesian end-blown flute and its mouthpiece details*

the two ends in a clamp. Then leave it to cool in that position. When it is absolutely cold, it will stay close to the bent shape (a small pair of multigrips makes a good clamp). Then unclamp the ends, lash them together with fine cord, cut the unwanted long bamboo ends off, and slip your mouthpiece ring onto the prepared flute mouthpiece end, with the lashed ends located opposite the blowing side. The ring should be tight enough on the flute to hold itself in place without falling off, but attached loosely by its lashing cord (left deliberately long) to the flute so it will not be lost if it does fall off.

The rest of the flute is then, as stated before, made in the same way as the cross-blown flute, by blowing the note and cutting the exit end off to adjust the pitch to what you want. Drill and adjust each hole from the bottom to achieve the octave (Sketch 18.3.G).

The virtue of this flute type is the ease of creating a clear note. If you blow into the mouthpiece it immediately produces a pleasant sound, whereas you may take some time to learn the necessary skill of blowing a cross-blown flute or a shakuhachi flute. Good luck!

Making a Bamboo Whistle Flute

This is an end-blown flute with a whistle-like mouthpiece. Usually made from the same thin-walled material as the Indonesian end-blown flute, it is quite similar. Follow Sketch 18.4 when reading the mouthpiece description. Like the Indonesian flute (which I prefer), the whistle flute is very easy to blow, and some people may find it easier to make than the other.

In this case the culm is cut to remove the node completely on the blowing end. A bamboo plug made from a

Whistle flute mouthpiece

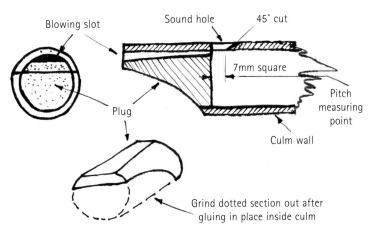

■ SKETCH **18.4** *The whistle flute and its mouthpiece details*

thick-walled culm segment (or from wood) is cut to the same diameter as the inside diameter of the flute, made about 10 per cent longer than the outside diameter of the flute's culm. To form the blowing slot, a tapered flat area is shaved along the plug until you have reduced the top of its curved surface by about 2 mm at the blowing end, and 1 mm at the down wind end. Then glue the plug into the cut-off culm end without getting glue in the blowing slot.

The next operation is best done slowly on a grinding wheel, making sure the wheel is cutting into the culm surface rather than out of it, to prevent splitting out the fibres. Opposite the blowing slot, grind the culm and the glued-in block away in a negative curve until there is only about a 2 mm flat end surface of block left showing below the blowing slot when you view it from the end of the flute.

Next you cut the sounding hole, which is 7 mm square. The back end of this hole is located flush with the flat internal end of the glued-in block, and the other end 7 mm further down the flute (the same size as the Indonesian flute, but with a different angle on the downstream slope). You can dowel drill the hole first and then make it square with a very sharp chisel. If the wall is thin it's best to cut into the side of the hole and not from above which may split the culm.

Then abrade the downstream edge of the sound hole at an angle of about 45 degrees sloping out of and upwards from the bottom inside edge of the hole. Your mouthpiece is now ready to blow.

From this point follow the same procedure including length and hole positions described for the cross-blown flute or the Indonesian flute, all measurements being taken from the down wind (sharpened) edge of the sound hole. Good luck and enjoy your playing!

Making a Shakuhachi Flute

I have never made a shakuhachi flute, and wouldn't presume to tell you how to do so. This ancient Japanese art goes back to the seventh century, and I am sure that surviving Japanese master flute makers guard their secrets well. (There were only fifteen masters left in Japan in 1970.) However, I have done the next best thing and persuaded Marek Fluteman, the master flute maker of Byron/Brighton Beach NSW in Australia (he has made hundreds) to describe his technique for you.

The shakuhachi was named after its most popular form, because that flute was one 'shaku' and eight 'hachi', old Japanese units of measure, long (545 mm). It is a five-holed pentatonic scale instrument, with the thumb (upper) hole on the back of the instrument. It is completely open at both ends, and when blowing, the area immediately below your lower lip becomes, in effect,

■ **18.K** *The author reclining on a bamboo lounge attempting to play his shakuhachi*

part of the mouthpiece, covering almost all of the lower part of the blowing hole. Your lip shape blowing air across the sharp edge of the mouthpiece creates the sound vibration.

The Japanese have almost ritualised the making of the shakuhachi flute from *Phyllostachys bambusoides* (madake), marking, nurturing and monitoring individual culms for years in the bamboo forest. They then carefully cut and cured them for three months outdoors, and then up to three years indoors in a dark dry place before making them into a flute. The selected culm section is then straightened using heat, and the heating becomes part of the curing process before they make the flute. Interestingly, the shakuhachi flute is the exception to the thin-walled resonance theory. It's made from thick-walled basal culm pieces, and the hole inside is ideally not parallel but taper bored from both ends to an ancient established proportion. Madake is used traditionally because it is about the strongest and hardest of the running bamboos, and because it can produce thick-walled culms near the base capable of being bored out. It also has interesting distortions where the culm base swells to join the rhizome, used to create an end decoration on the flute. (In ancient days this swelling was designed to use as club in times of war.)

Because Marek can't always find good quality thick madake in Australia (or any other commonly available species of that diameter, for that matter), he uses the basal sections of well matured *Phyllostachys aurea* culms. Some of these also have the same knobby 'club' base that is used for decorating the shakuhachi's wind exit. He has had no access to superior clumping bamboos, nor any experience in making shakuhachi from them, but agrees

■ **18.J** Bambusa nana, *grown in plantation in Thailand, is an ideal bamboo for making shakuhachi flutes because the solid bore can be drilled out and shaped as required.*

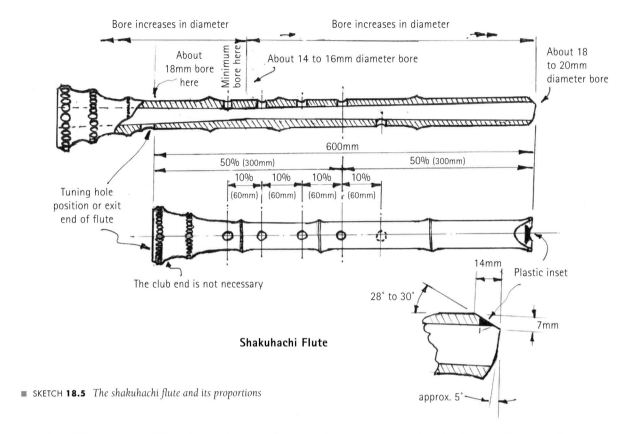

Bore increases in diameter   Bore increases in diameter

About 18mm bore here

Minimum bore here

About 14 to 16mm diameter bore

About 18 to 20mm diameter bore

600mm

50% (300mm)   50% (300mm)

10%   10%   10%   10%
(60mm)   (60mm)   (60mm)   (60mm)

Tuning hole position or exit end of flute

The club end is not necessary

Shakuhachi Flute

14mm

Plastic inset

28° to 30°

7mm

approx. 5°

■ SKETCH **18.5** *The shakuhachi flute and its proportions*

that the solid or almost solid species would make them ideal (though lacking in the club end).

I recently had a Japanese flute maker visit us looking for some madake to make shakuhachi flutes. His disappointment, when I told him we were not interested in growing invasive running bamboos, turned to joy when I showed him beautiful straight pieces of thick-walled solid bamboos like *Bambusa tulda*, *B. polymorpha*, *B. nutans*, *B. nana* (Photo 18J), *Gigantochloa albociliata* and a number of others. He felt that, because of their superior strength and wall thickness, he could make very good shakuhachi flutes from those clumping bamboos, species not available in Japan

A Step by Step Shakuhachi
(Sketch 18.5)

Harvest a carefully selected live mature culm of the desired diameter, preferably one with the traditional 'club' culm base shape intact to where it joins the rhizome. This attractive culm base section (visually and traditionally desirable, but not absolutely necessary) must be dug out of the ground with delicacy and care because it is quite fine and strong where it joins the rhizome at a point quite some distance underground. If forced it will twist the fine strong join and crack the culm base, ruining the culm. You can use a sharp chisel and mallet to chop away the earth

and roots to expose where it joins the rhizome, and even cut it off finally with a pruning saw or a chainsaw. It is best to look for a culm at least 28 to 30 mm diameter about 700 mm above ground, with preferably very thick-walled wood increasing in diameter at the base, but it is not easy to find the perfect shape. My 'club ended' flute is 33 mm diameter bored to 20 mm at the mouth node, and 40 mm bored to a 17 mm exit hole at the club end, so it obviously has a very heavy wall thickness. (My 'clubless' shakuhachi is actually about 2 mm larger at the mouthpiece end than at the close ended downhill end, but that is not desirable.)

Marek decides on the flute he wants to make and then selects the appropriate culm piece from his harvested stock, intuitively considering factors such as the distance between the nodes, culm wall thickness diameter, fibre density (to do with age and growing conditions), overall shape, etc.

Photo 18H shows two of Marek's flutes (both owned by me). One is made of madake (*Phyllostachys bambusoides*, the species traditionally used in Japan), and has the club end (Photos 18L and 18M) and a beautifully inset perspex blowing edge (the Japanese use water buffalo horn) set into the mouthpiece. The other is a simple straight piece of *Phyllostachys aurea* (the economy version) with no club, no inset mouthpiece edge, and no taper in the bore. Whilst I obviously prefer the better made one (much more expensive), they both sound quite beautiful to my ear.

I am recommending that you make a flute with a pitch length of 600 mm, as in my Marek-made flutes. Cut the

■ **18.L** *The traditional club end on the shakuhachi utilising the close internodes on the base of the culm, left protruding for decoration*

■ **18.H** *Four different forms of flute: (from left to right) 1. A shakuhachi flute with a shaped bore, a traditional club end, and an inset mouthpiece, made from* Phyllostachys bambusoides; *2. A simple shakuhachi flute using the natural unshaped bore of* Phyllostachys aurea *made with a bamboo mouthpiece without an inlay; 3. A beautifully made bamboo Chinese cross-blown flute; 4. A simply made Chinese end-blown flute; 5. An Indonesian end-blown flute made from a single internode length*

■ **18.M** *The mouthpiece of a shakuhachi showing the inset*

blowing end of your culm off about 150 mm longer than your chosen finished length, the 'extra' long enough to hold in a gloved hand during the heat curing process.

Then cut off the very end of the retained culm base section (the club end) longer than you need (just after it bends towards the rhizome join) and trim the projecting roots (hard on the tools because of the dirt!). Trimming the roots is not easy because of locked-in dirt, and must be done by progressively cutting roots and digging out the dirt.

Now you must decide whether to cure your culm for years as the masters do before heat-treating it, or simply heat-treat it now and make it. Either way the following is relevant. During the heat-curing process (described earlier) the culm scorching with the blowtorch has a number of beneficial effects, steaming out moisture and various other compounds from the culm, and melting and blend-

ing resins and compounds on the surface. You will see the resin turn pale with heat as it melts before becoming hard and beautifully glossy as you wipe it, with the heat burnished finish showing through underneath.

When a section of culm is still hot the bamboo becomes slightly flexible so that, at this stage, you can straighten any bends in the culm by putting heat and pressure on the bent portion levered between two immovable objects, and holding it in position whilst it cools to its then hard, durable condition. Bending has to be the last activity of your heat-treatment. Marek says flutes cured this way virtually never split even after years of use in very different climates.

Now, cut off the unwanted knobby culm base section just after a root joining circle, just before the curve where it bends towards the rhizome, to form the club end. Cut it carefully so as not to split the culm (Marek uses a fine hacksaw). Then shape the club base carefully (Photo 18L), retaining the stubs of the club end roots as a decoration (preferably use a powerful bench sander).

Shakuhachi flute culms always have nodal diaphragms, and usually a solid club end that need to be drilled out even before you begin to shape the bore. First very carefully drill out the club end to a size 5 or 6 mm smaller than your final contemplated exit size (this club end is normally completely solid for some 50 to 100 mm), and then tackle the other end, drilling out the nodes. Marek uses various tools for this, many of them similar to the extended drills and sandpaper mandrels described earlier, starting with different long shaft augers or drills, and he works from both ends after drilling the club end hole.

At this stage he is not looking for a perfect inside finish. When you can see daylight throughout put the piece aside for a couple of weeks (patience please!). Airflows through the piece will help remove remaining moisture.

Achieving the final ideal bore shape is quite time-consuming and requires perfect wood and skill. Most shakuhachi flutes are made as a compromise acknowledging the individual culm shape, diameter and wall thickness, and bore size, with the instrument maker developing individual characteristics as the instrument is made. Many of them are not even straight. Because of this, Marek shapes each bore to the best possible form for that individual culm. Varying bore sizes are possible for flutes of the same key, the bore affecting the tone more than the pitch.

For ultimate performance, the bore is reshaped to a form which tapers from both ends inwards. In the modern forms of this traditional instrument (now used with classical orchestras), the bore ideally reduces from a mouthpiece diameter of about 18 to 20 mm, to a diameter of about 14 to 16 mm. This is at a point roughly 75 per cent along the length from the mouthpiece. It then increases in diameter for the remaining 25 per cent until reaching the exit end diameter of about 18 mm. (The more ancient handmade shakuhachis were much larger in bore diameter, starting with a mouthpiece hole 26 to 28 mm and reaching a minimum bore of about 20 mm—so there is a reasonable bore variation possible.) Whilst only skill and sensitivity in instrument can achieve the optimum dimensions of the bore, don't despair because many shakuhachi instruments that are beautifully played by professional musicians are made from parallel sided plastic pipe! Whilst your instrument may not be the in the tradition of world's best, it may sound very beautiful and individual to you and others.

A rough mouthpiece shape is first cut on the blowing end (Sketch 18.5), located just outside the nodal scars of a node conveniently located to give you a length of 600 mm or more to the exit end. If your mouthpiece position is not exactly 600 mm from the exit end, it should be far enough back that you can drill a 'tuning' hole in the underside of the exit end of the flute.

The length of the flute from the blowing edge to either the end of the flute (if it has no tuning hole) or to the upwind end of the tuning hole determines the pitch, or lowest note. If you wish to raise the pitch higher, this can be done by drilling a large hole, 12 to 16 mm diameter, in the bottom of the flute in from the end. If you locate your mouthpiece more than 600 mm from the blowing hole, you must now drill a tuning hole with its edge 600 mm from the mouthpiece. (My 'clubbed' flute is 690 mm long

with a 16 mm hole edge 600 mm from the blowing edge.)

This first roughcut mouthpiece shape must be sufficient to enable you to blow a sound (quite a challenge if you can't play a shakuhachi flute in the first place). Then refine the bore with various augers and sandpaper mandrels, and keep blowing a note to see how it sounds. The sound of the flute determines how much further the bore needs to be shaped, the blowing and shaving inside process being repeated until you are happy with the sound.

Next finish the mouthpiece (Sketch 18.5 and Photo 18M). If you choose to fit the hard blowing edge normally fitted to high quality shakuhachis, you need to carefully cut a dovetail shaped piece out of the blowing edge and slip in a piece of carefully shaped black perspex (or hard bone), using a thin strong epoxy glue, or similar, and carefully sand the mouthpiece to shape when dry. This finished edge will produce a much finer tone. The approximate angles for the two fundamental faces of the blowing hole are shown on the drawing, but the smaller top face is fundamentally flat like a saw cut, and the larger lower face is flat across the flute, but curves slightly as it gets further from the sharp blowing edge.

Next mark your hole positions. For Marek, this is based on intuition and judging what he can get from each individual piece of wood. There is a rule of thumb, however, that you can use, which was the original basis of the traditional shakuhachi.

The traditional lengths and fingerhole positions were originally placed to a very simple formula that could be varied by master craftsmen to suit their own intuition and experience. If you take a flute with a 600 mm long pitch length, the first fingerhole will be centred 120 mm from the bottom, and each of the four successive holes centred 60 mm apart, that last one being under the flute, and located 240 mm from the mouthpiece. In other words, the first hole on top from the mouthpiece is 50 per cent down, the hole under the flute is 40 per cent down, and the second, third and fourth (top holes) are each 10 per cent further down than the first, thus placing the last hole 20 per cent from the end of the flute or to the edge of its tuning (adjusted pitch) hole.

The finished fingerhole sizes on my two Marek shakuhachis are 9 and 10 mm respectively; however, drill the holes smaller than needed, starting with the bottom hole and adjusting the pitch a little by increasing the hole either up or down the flute (using a sandpaper mandrel). Essentially use the same drilling and tuning process described for normal flutes earlier in this chapter. Repeat the process, marking and drilling a hole, playing the notes and adjusting the pitch by increasing the hole diameter in one direction (upwards to raise the note). Marek intuitively knows from the sound where to place the next hole, but I suggest you stick to the standard placement until you feel you know better. The bore usually needs further fine work during this process, smoothing out any fibres displaced by the drill.

When the flute performs to your satisfaction, the bore and blowing edge are fine sanded, the club end and shaft polished up, and the bore coated with a few layers of lacquer as described earlier.

I suggest you then enter a state of meditation before playing, so that the frustration of perfecting the blowing and control of this beautiful but difficult instrument doesn't send you stark raving mad! Good luck!

Making a Jegog, a Balinese Bamboo Xylophone

One of the great musical experiences of my lifetime was hearing Bali's huge Jegog (pronounced 'chegok') Orchestra play for the first time (Photos 18N and 18O). There are ten players in that orchestra and nine separate sets of xylophone tubes, with one set so huge that it takes two people sitting on top of the instrument to play it! This largest tube set, made from bamboo culms about 200 mm diameter more than 2 m long, has two squatting players wielding four massive hammers simultaneously, each made from layers of laminated car tyre on bamboo handles. Their furious pounding on the great tubes produces a wonderful sound akin to thunder that changes pitch at the conductor's command! You can feel the vibration literally pounding into your body. It was a most strange and exhilarating

experience; in fact quite a number of people found it too frightening to approach too close, not because of the noise volume, but because of the immense depth of vibration, the strange jungle wildness of the sound produced by those large bamboo tube sets. The music of the orchestra literally soars into the air with great sweeping thunderous leaps, hammered chords changing, growling and singing in turn as it evokes the Balinese spirit people writhing and dancing within their grotesquely beautiful masks. It is truly a memorable experience.

Back on earth, I suggest you start by making a modest sized jegog, and you can experience the meditative evening indulgence enjoyed every day by so many Balinese. If you take an evening walk in the hill villages outside Ubud, the air is softly fragmented by the delightful liquid sounds of the jegog, like a meditative perpetual motion of moving water. I find the instrument a complete delight, and it is so easy to make and play.

A single jegog (Photo 18P and Sketch 18.6) consists of eleven shaped bamboo tubes suspended on a frame. It is

■ **18.N & O** *The extraordinary Balinese jegog band performing at the IV International Bamboo Congress in Ubud, Bali, 1995*

■ **18.P** *A simple jegog identical to the one described in the text*

hand or two in each hand, to create a three- or four-note chord effect. The smaller jegogs are not loud instruments, but they strike with a clear attractive Oriental woody sound, very pleasing to the ear. Whilst mostly played as a solo instrument, or together with a flautist, they are often very effectively played with two or more instruments together, or, of course, by Bali's famous jegog band described earlier.

If you follow Sketch 18.7 and the attached table of note sizes, you will see that each tube is a simple form that can be easily made with a pangot or bamboo knife (or even an electrical jigsaw if you shape it more sensitively later). Each tube (see table) has a total length 'L', an enclosed length 'L1', an open length 'L2', and is cut from a culm diameter 'D'. The following tube sizes give you two different sized jegogs. The instruments are (traditionally) arranged in a six-note Asian octave rather than an eight-note Western octave. Each jegog has a two-octave range from the eleven tubes available, the octave notes being F, G#, A#, C#, D# and F. The smaller of the two jegogs shown ranges from the F below middle C upwards for two

played by sitting on the ground, legs crossed, and striking the various tubes simultaneously with two hammers. One hammer is in each hand, or if you are skilled, sometimes even three or four hammers can be held, two in the left

■ SKETCH **18.6** *The jegog (an Indonesian xylophone) and its frame*

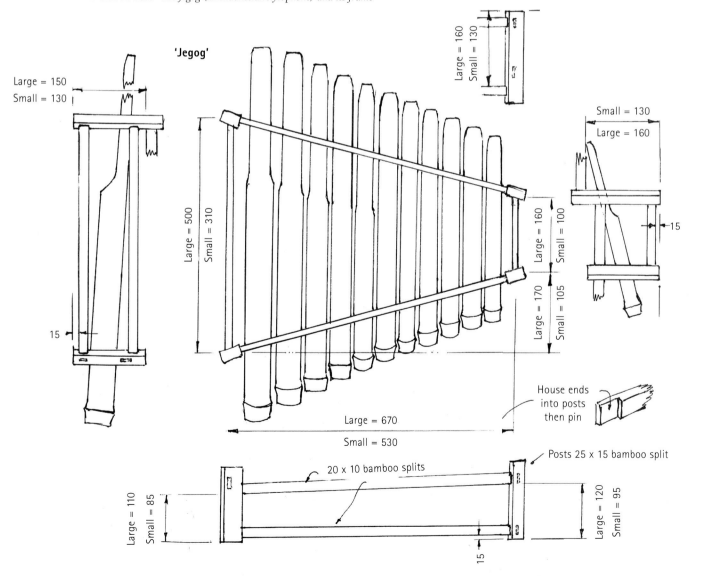

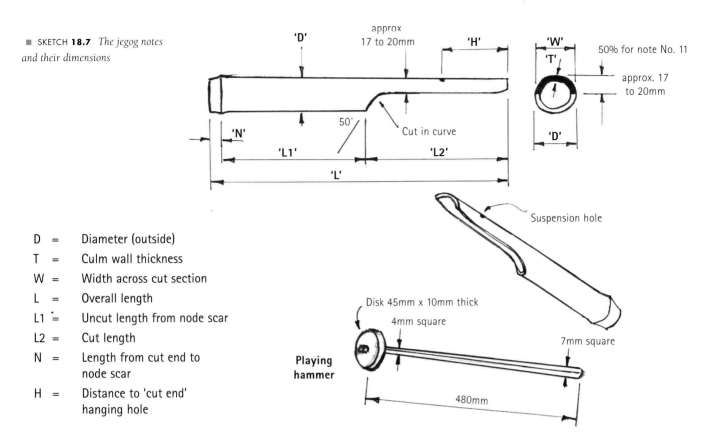

■ SKETCH **18.7** *The jegog notes and their dimensions*

D = Diameter (outside)
T = Culm wall thickness
W = Width across cut section
L = Overall length
L1 = Uncut length from node scar
L2 = Cut length
N = Length from cut end to node scar
H = Distance to 'cut end' hanging hole

TABLE OF NOTE SIZES

	Note		D	T	W	L	L1	L2	N	H
octave	F	1	58	5mm	50mm	828	455	343	30	206
	G#	2	53			753	400	323	30	179
	A#	3	50			700	340	330	30	166
	C#	4	48			640	293	317	30	162
	D#	5	47			585	252	303	30	147
octave	F	6	45	4.5mm		512	224	258	30	125
	G#	7	44			474	199	245	30	110
	A#	8	43			435	180	240	30	97
	C#	9	42			405	138	237	30	92
	D#	10	41			375	117	228	30	80
octave	F	11	40	4mm	50%	345	100	215	30	72
	G#	12	38			312	79	203	30	70
	A#	13	35			290	66	194	30	66
	C#	14	34			259	54	175	30	58
	D#	15	31			238	42	166	30	57
	F4	16	27	3 mm	25 mm	215	33	152	30	55

(T column: graduating from 5mm to 3mm. W column: graduating, more than 50% of culm cut away, to less than 50%.)

Larger jegog (notes 1–10), Smaller jegog (notes 6–16)

The notes must be tuned as described in the text, as considerable variation will occur in the tuned length of the note compared to the above charted lengths, mostly due to the varying position of the internal node diaphragm. Note 11 has an L = 355 and L2 = 240, compared to L = 345 and L = 215 on the two different instruments, but the note has the same pitch! Similarly, note 6 is L = 552 and L2 = 307 compared to L = 512 and L = 258.

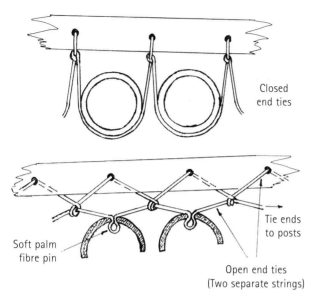

Closed
end ties

Tie ends
to posts

Soft palm
fibre pin

Open end ties
(Two separate strings)

■ SKETCH **18.8** *The jegog note suspension*

octaves, and the larger one from the second F below middle C to the F above middle C. This means that the top octave and the bamboo notes of the larger jegog are exactly the same as the bottom octave of the small one.

You will notice that the closed end (L1) of the smaller higher pitched notes is much shorter than the open end (L2), but the ratio changes by the time you get to the larger lower pitched notes where the closed end (L1) has become longer than the open end (L2). As with a flute, it is the length of the closed chamber (L1) that primarily sets the pitch.

The two (or even three) hammers used concurrently (see Sketch 18.7) to play these instruments are made from single discs of fairly flat car tyre (complete with fibre ply and tread almost worn down). They are cut 45 mm diameter and about 8 mm to 10 mm thick (variable), with the centre skewered by a flexible bamboo handle 490 mm long tapering from roughly 8 mm diameter (only roughly round) to between 3 mm and 4 mm diameter.

The bamboo tube wall thickness graduates from 3 mm for the smallest tube on the smaller instrument, up to 5 mm for the largest tube on the large instrument, which is fairly thin-walled for the diameter of the culm. Instruments of this smaller size are usually made from what they call pring wulung (*Gigantochloa atroviolacea*), or its close relative *Bambusa lako* (syn. *Gigantochloa* sp. 'Timor Black'), or *Schizostachyum brachycladum* (Photo 18Q), all straight, fairly thin-walled, long internoded, strong wooded bamboos. Other suitable bamboos would be *Cephalostachyum pergracile*, *Schizostachyum zollingeri* and *Bambusa oldhamii* in this size range. As the instruments increase in diameter the species used becomes larger and thicker walled, or even very large like *Gigantochloa atter* and others in the 100 mm to 150 mm range, and then bambu betung (*Dendrocalamus asper*) for huge 160 to 250 mm notes. I once made a larger tube note

from a 60 mm diameter culm that was too thin-walled (4 mm) for its length and diameter, and it was too 'tinny' to resonate with the correct sound.

On the two instruments that I have, only the four lowest notes have a node located along the note's culm length, because the note was longer than the internode length. The other notes were made from single internode lengths, with a node left at the closed end only. The two noded notes always have the extra node located in the 'open' (L2) section of the tube, carved out (somewhat roughly and not flush) on the inside, and completely flush and smooth on the outside. Most of the culm sections show the scar where the branch cluster was cut from the node, which indicates that those particular instruments were made from upper node sections that had developed branches, rather than lower node sections that are branchless on most of the species mentioned above. That may have been because the lower culm walls are too thick, or more likely, that the higher fibre density of the upper culm portions yields denser harder wood that resonates more clearly. The branch scar near the closed end is located out of view on the underside on the smaller notes (without the extra node along their length), and on top clearly visible on the closed end node on the four largest notes, the branch scar at the node in the open section (L2) cut out and discarded.

The support frame is simple and light in both cases (although the frames on instruments used for public performance are more elaborate and often carved with designs that may well have religious significance). The closed node end (N) of the tubes is suspended about 80 mm above the floor, but the angle of suspension of each note is slightly different, the top of the longest notes' open-end (L2) being about 125 mm and 140 mm respectively above the floor for each instrument, and the shortest notes' open-end being higher at 140 mm and 180 mm respectively. The frame sections on both instruments are made from 20 mm x 9 mm split culm section housed into heavier vertical corner sections also cut from thick culm wall, with pinned and glued joints, however the frame material can be and often is made of wood.

The note suspension system (Sketch 18.8) is simple, being very light cord (about 1.8 mm diameter braided nylon would be fine). The open end is suspended by passing a loop through a single hole drilled in the top of the culm. That loop is passed one turn around a soft palm husk plug (a round pin shape about 20 mm long and 7 mm diameter), and the note is pressed squarely downwards to locate it whilst hanging in its position between the note either side of it. The pressure exerted crushes the palm husk pin a little and bends its ends down from the culm, which prevents it from slipping out of the cord loop and minimises its damping effect. At the closed end, the note is suspended by passing a simple loop under each note and back up to the frame. The cord tying systems at both ends of the note tubes pass through holes drilled in the frame between each note position, and the knots and

■ **18.Q** Schizostachyum brachycladum, *a long-internoded bamboo quite often used to make various musical instruments*

suspension system is designed to minimise sideways movement, as the notes are quite close to each other (10 to 12 mm gap between each).

To make each note, the closed end of the culm is cut off about 30 mm past the node culm leaf scar (N), the distance always being such that the saw doesn't cut or touch the node diaphragm. The notes are cut so that the closed end is always the lower culm section. The drawing should now be self explanatory if used with the above description.

To tune the note, make the culm shape with the closed (L1) and open (L2) ends a little longer than specified, say 10 mm to 15 mm longer depending on note size on the closed end, and proportionally longer on the open end. Then suspend it in a temporary cord hanging rig. Strike it with the rubber hammer and compare the note with the piano note it represents. It should be a little flat or lower. Carve small amounts off both the open and closed ends, striking it as you go, until it produces the same note as the piano. When you are satisfied with the result, seal your notes to minimise environmental effects.

If your bamboo is too thin, too young, not properly cured or not hard bamboo, it is unlikely to vibrate with a clear note, let alone the note you expect. If it is too thick it will give a dull note. It may well be advantageous to heat cure the culm section before you cut the notes, but don't attempt to do that after cutting the note shape from the culm or it will crack. It is possible that you can make a jegog from the commonly available *Bambusa balcooa*, if you select old wood and cure it by aging and/or heat until it is hard.

The results you can achieve should be very satisfying. Send me a record!

19 Paper Making

For the Chinese, the finest and most expensive art paper they use is made from young bamboo culms cut three months after emerging as a shoot. They use culms that are in the stage where they still have no leaves or branches but have developed just enough fibre to have discarded their culm leaves. On the other end of the spectrum are the thousands of tonnes of harvested bamboo culms one encounters piled precariously high on three-wheeled trucks clogging the roads in parts of China, chugging their way to the paper mills. In Anji Province they use runners, and in Guangdong province they use culms cut from *Dendrocalamus latiflorus* shoot plantations, and many other species. I have no idea of the amount of bamboo used for papermaking in China (perhaps the statistic doesn't exist, as it doesn't for the hectares of planted *D. latiflorus*) but it must be huge.

India used to make 70 per cent of its paper from bamboo. The tonnage they make from bamboo is still the same, but they have been unable to increase the plantings sufficiently to keep pace with the destruction of their bamboo stands, so they are now cutting down timber forests to get enough paper. The same tonnage of culms now represents only 30 per cent of their requirements.

The beauty of using bamboo for making paper is that you do not kill the source of your raw material. Each year it will produce new culms, a constantly self-renewing resource. There is (early) research being done that seems to indicate that by adding 30 per cent bamboo to woodchip, the paper produced is actually improved without having to change the machinery required to make it. Bamboo pulp normally requires a different digester process than that used by wood pulp, but the fibre, about 3 mm long, is twice as long and twice as strong as most hardwood fibres.

Making Your Own Paper

This simple system was taught to me by the very talented Jo Quinn, a local artisan who has taught many people in this area. By following these instructions you can make an attractive paper, fine or textured, from bamboo leaves and branches, or bamboo culms. This is not the fine art paper of China, but paper with a character of its own that is ideal on which to draw beautiful brushwork design for use as your personal stationery. The small amount of equipment you need, simple to obtain or make, is as follows:

- A simple two-part frame to make A4 sized paper. If you want other sized sheets, make different sized frames, or even different shaped frames. The two parts of the screen are called the 'decal' and the 'screen frame', sometimes called the 'mould' (Sketch 19.1). The inside dimension of the decal is the same as A4 paper, with the screen frame sized to slip comfortably inside the decal's rebate when assembled. The frame is covered with either stainless steel or copper mosquito mesh stretched firmly across the frame, stapled into place and glued with a strong waterproof glue. The decal must sit flat and firmly against the mosquito net when assembled to the frame.
- A clean unused paint roller.
- A boiler or large boiling pot.
- A tub (we use a plastic 44-gallon drum cut in half lengthways).
- The use of a garden mulcher or food processor.
- A mortar and pestle, or a sharp paint stirrer in a hand drill.
- 15 to 40 felts, pieces of old calico a bit heavier than a bed sheet, about 500 x 400 mm. These felts give texture to the paper, silk giving a fine finish, fine wool or cotton for reasonably smooth, Chux Superwipes or hessian giving a coarse finish. You need one felt for each sheet of paper plus about six extras.
- Rubber gloves to prevent your hands being burned by the caustic solution.

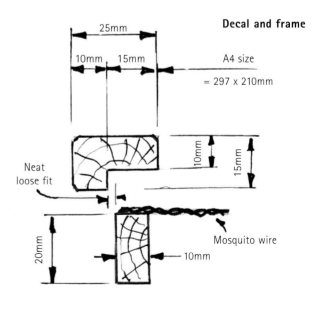

SKETCH 19.1 *The simple decal and screen frame you need to make paper*

- A paper press made from two heavy (18 to 25 mm thick) ply pieces 350 x 250 mm, plus four G-clamps. The press is called the 'post'.
- An old holeless nylon stocking and a coarse sieve (a colander will do).

You will also need at least 500 g of caustic soda, which can be bought bulk from an agricultural store. Follow these steps:

1. Collect about 1 kg of bamboo leaves together with small branches, about half a garbage bag full, or alternatively some young culms, complete with branches, of the same weight. If you want very fine high quality paper, use culms that are only 3 months old that still have no leaves or branches.

2. Shred the plant material as finely as possible in a garden mulching machine and/or a food processor (Photo 19A). Any system that works is acceptable—sharp knives and pounding, etc.

3. Place 500 g of caustic soda in a boiler with 1 kg of shredded material in the boiling pot, just covered with water, and boil for about five hours, topping the water up from time to time to prevent it boiling dry. Test the fibre material by feeling it (with rubber gloves on). It is ready when it feels slippery or slimy (Photo 19B).

4. Discard very large pieces by passing through a coarse sieve (a colander), pouring the liquid and fibre into a nylon stocking (wear the gloves or the caustic will damage your hands). Wash the fibre in clean fresh water (as close to pH7 or neutral as possible, rain water being ideal), squeezing the bulge in the stocking under the running water until you are sure it is clean.

5. Beat the fibre (removed from the stocking) until it is pulpy. A kitchen blender generally works, or a paint stirrer in a hand drill, or even a large mortar and pestle. You will need to add water as what you want is a very wet paste. Photo 19C shows the paste with the water wrung out in a stocking so you can see the consistency, and also liquid as it should be, in the jar.

6. Place the paste into your tub, and add a lot of water, at least 10 (maybe 20) litres. You will know when there is enough water when you scoop your frame through the mix. If the mixture doesn't have enough water in it, the paper will be too thick, in fact you adjust the water to suit the thickness of the paper you want. (Photos 19D and E.)

7. Lay about three layers of 'felt' material on one of the plywood post pads (hanging over the edges) and leave it sitting ready to receive your sheets of paper.

■ **19.A** *Bamboo leaves (*Bambusa multiplex *in this case), and the leaves after pulverising*

■ **19.B** *The caustic boiled 'slimy' pulp ready to pass through a coarse sieve*

■ **19.C** *The same caustic boiled pulp after sieving and washing in fresh water in a stocking. On the left, the pulp wrung out, and on the right the pulp in suspension in water*

■ **19.D & E** *Lifting the decal and frame out of the tub after scooping a layer of slurry onto the frame*

8. Stir the slurry thoroughly (with your hands). Then, holding the frame at both ends, assembled with the decal on top, and the screen mesh pressing against the decal, scoop it down into the slurry side on and lift it in such a way as to cause the slurry to run through the mesh. Quickly tip the frame in all directions to distribute the still moving slurry evenly, then slant towards one corner and allow the free water to drain off (Photos 19D and E).

9. Carefully remove the decal, leaving a layer of pulp exactly A4 size still on the mesh. Turn the frame upside down and position it in the middle of the felts lying on the post pad. The water in the pulp sheet will begin to soak into the felts. Press the sides of the frame down firmly, working the pressure around the frame edges until you have circled the frame with your pressure, then lift the frame starting at one corner. The frame will lift cleanly off, leaving the

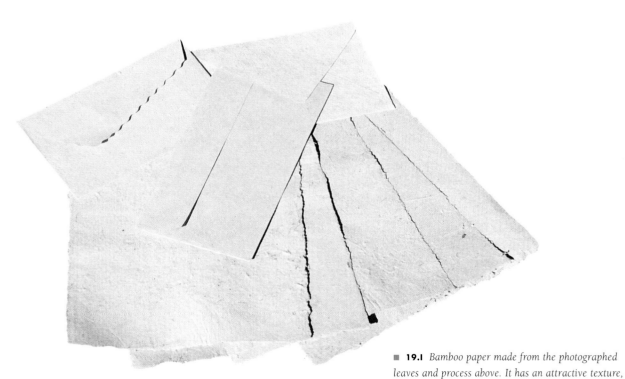

■ **19.I** *Bamboo paper made from the photographed leaves and process above. It has an attractive texture, and a delicate green colour.*

■ **19.F** *Laying progressive layers of paper onto the felts, each with a felt between each layer*

■ **19.G** *A newly laid paper sheet, with the decal and frame shown separated. Remove the decal from the frame before pressing the paper sheet against the felt.*

paper lying on the felts (Photo 19F). Then lay a felt over the newly deposited pulp sheet (this process is called 'couching', to couch the sheets).

10. Repeat the process until you have as many sheets as you want, up to about 30, lying on the press pad, each with its felt between the sheets. (Sometimes for reasons unknown some of the pulp sticks to the mesh for the first couple of sheets, but it usually settles down after a while and comes off the mesh cleanly.) (Photo 19G)

11. Lay three extra felts on top, then position the other post pad on top, and clamp the four G-clamps on each corner of the post pads, tightening them evenly to squeeze the water out. The paper is pressed in the post for 24 hours, with the clamps being tightened occasionally to take up slack as it dries (Photo19H).

12. Remove the clamps from the post, and remove the top sheets to reveal the first layer of paper. Lift each paper on its felt in turn and lay it against a window pane, rolling it flat with the paint roller so that it is stuck to the window with the felt outwards. Leave it to dry.

13. When completely dry, the paper sheet will readily peel of the felt. The sheets are then normally given another pressing in the post (sheet to bare sheet), or ironed, for their final flat finish.

Sometimes when using mainly bamboo leaf, the fibre is not easy to handle, and will benefit from the addition of some very long fibred component like flax or papyrus

■ **19.H** *Assembling the press (the 'post') with a load of paper sheets and felts inside*

stalk. Don't forget to coat (and occasionally recoat) your decal and frame with good quality marine varnish, or it will deteriorate quickly.

You can add size, gelatine or laundry starch to the tub before lifting your sheets if you want a stronger paper, but some insects like to eat such products. The finished sheets can be sprayed with an ironing spray such as liquid starch or Fabulon before ironing if you choose.

I decided it would take too long for me to make enough bamboo paper for my long-suffering publisher to print this book on, but it was a lovely thought! It is great for brush renditions of bamboo though. Good luck with your paper making. Send me a bamboo letter!

20 Recipes for Edible Shoots

I spend a considerable amount of time experimenting with new ways of cooking this simple food during the shoot season, and the rest of the year salivating lustily whenever I think of the wonderful dishes we enjoyed. I'm also very fond of stir-fries, and nothing adds that crunchy texture like fresh, or freshly prepared, bamboo shoots. If, like most Western people, you are used to eating tinned bamboo shoots, and you get the chance to taste good quality fresh shoots, you will never want to eat a canned shoot again. Simply throw some prepared cubed or slivered shoots into a pan with a little oil and oyster sauce, or just tamari and garlic. Consume with white wine and you will be transported to heaven!

Before diving ecstatically into your recipe book, however, there are shoots, and shoots, and the quality of the shoot will dictate how and how much preparation is required.

Properly grown high quality edible shoots do not need to be pre-boiled before adding to your recipe. In fact many of them, such as *Dendrocalamus asper* and *Nastus elatus*, can be chopped up raw and added to your salad for an extra crunchy effect. Those shoots, and some others, taste like a cross between a water chestnut and a very crisp, slightly sweet apple, if they have been grown with the light excluded from when the shoot first appears at ground level until it is harvested. (Commercial *D. asper* growers mostly cover their emerging shoots with a 600 mm high black planter bag stuffed with straw, and harvest the huge shoot when it starts to lift the bag off the ground.)

I am often asked what fresh shoots taste like, and my main answer is, mild and very crunchy. Each shoot species has a flavour of its own, some nutty, some sweet and non-astringent, some with various nuances that I have heard compared to anything from lobster to macadamia nut. The main virtue of bamboo shoot is its wonderful crunchy texture, which varies with the species and the preparation, and its ability to take on flavours from other ingredients in the recipe.

Most shoots have a naturally bitter flavour varying from very slight (e.g. *Dendrocalamus latiflorus*) to extremely bitter (e.g. *Bambusa vulgaris* cv. 'Vittata'). Some people, as

■ **20.A** *A delicious feast prepared for us in China that included six different ways of preparing bamboo shoots*

■ **20.B** Dendrocalamus latiflorus *shoots split down the middle ready to peel away the outer culm leaf covering*

the Vietnamese, even prefer bitter shoots, but most Western and Asian races prefer non-astringent shoots.

Whilst overcooking and pre-preparation does change the texture, even overcooked shoots tend to retain some of their crunchy flavour (great if you can't cook). I enjoy them most of all fresh and lightly cooked, with their wonderful crunch preserved, simply superb in a stir-fry or as a feature dish.

Generally speaking, most bitter shoots must be pre-prepared before being added to the recipe. This is mostly a simple procedure, and has a valuable secondary function. Like most vegetables, fresh cut shoots have a shelf life of only about five to ten days if kept cool. However, if prepared soon after harvesting, they can be kept in the fridge in a plastic bag for two months or more and used at your convenience.

To pre-cook your shoot for reducing bitterness or extending shelf life, split your harvested shoots down the middle (Photo 20B) , then peel back and discard the protective culm leaf coating around the white flesh. Sometimes the tender inner leaves on the inside top can be eaten, and taste more like French artichoke than bamboo shoot. Small shoots up to 25 mm diameter can be cooked whole if the culm leaves are peeled off, but larger shoots are best cut into segments no more than 20 mm square before boiling, particularly if from an astringent species, to give water access to leach out any bitterness.

For most shoots it is sufficient to boil them in an abundant pot of fresh salted water (1 tspn salt/2.5 L water) for between two and fifteen minutes. If the species produces bitter shoots, or if it is unpleasantly astringent to your taste after the first boiling, drain the shoots and boil again in fresh salted water for the same period. Throwing a small handful of rice (or boiling the shoots in leftover rice water) into the water also helps leach out bitterness.

Depending on the recipe, I prefer a slightly astringent shoot flavour with savoury dishes, and a non-astringent shoot for sweeter or more delicate flavours. With the hundreds of different species available in our garden, we can choose the shoot for the dish, but with two or three species planted, you can do the same.

There are limits to what my taste buds consider pleasantly astringent. *Bambusa vulgaris* and its two cultivars (cv. 'Vittata' and cv. 'Wamin') produce tender creamy shoots that sometimes turn pink when boiled, and remain bitter and peppery to my palate to the 'bitter' end; however they are much enjoyed by the Vietnamese! (The left-over water is used to treat hepatitis.)

The shoots of *Bambusa balcooa*, the large green clumping bamboo commonly seen growing up the east coast of Australia, *B. vulgaris* cv. 'Vittata' and some other very bitter species produce an acceptable eating shoot. However they contain up to 1600 ppm of cyanide and must be properly prepared. This is achieved by dicing into 20 mm pieces and boiling three consecutive times for at least ten minutes in abundant fresh water replaced each time. Cyanide (not uncommon in a number of popular vegetables) is present in some but not in all astringent bamboo species, and is easily removed and destroyed by the boiling process.

Preparation techniques vary greatly within different ethnic areas and for different species. Some species are fermented prior to eating whilst others are valued for pickling (e.g. *Bambusa tulda*). Others are eaten fresh in season as well as sliced and preserved by drying (e.g. *Melocanna baccifera* and *D. latiflorus*). The shoots of *Gigantochloa* apus, a bitter species known as 'pring tali' in Java, are buried in mud for three to four days to remove the astringency before cooking and eating. This technique will help with some other bitter eating species (if you have nothing better).

To prepare dried shoots, scrape the edible 'meat' with a coarse grater to produce flat strips, maybe 6 to 7 mm wide and 3 mm thick, then lay them in the sun until thoroughly dry. In China they leave *D. latiflorus* shoots to grow until they are about 1 m high before harvesting them for drying. Dried shoots may be stored in a dry sealed container almost indefinitely, then taken out and soaked for about 12 hours, and used in cooking in much the same way that Thai or Chinese noodles are used. They are very popular in China, and the unusual texture makes them an interesting worthwhile substitute for spaghetti.

Wait at least two years after planting before harvesting shoots, and sometimes even three, depending on the vigour of the species and the plant. Each culm that

■ **20.C** Bambusa vulgaris *cv. 'Vittata' shoots, bitter, peppery and high in cyanide, but eaten by the Vietnamese*

which makes them an excellent food for the diet-conscious. A typical shoot analysis based on 100g weight is as follows:

Carbohydrate: 4.2 to 6.1 per cent
Protein: 2.6 to 4 per cent
Fat: 0.3 to 0.5 per cent
Ash (silica): 0.8 to 1.3 per cent
Fibre: 0.5 to 0.9 per cent
Glucose: 1.8 to 4.1 per cent
Water: 89 to 93 per cent
Calories (Joules): 118-197

and containing:

Thiamin and Niacin (Vitamin B1, B2 complex):
    0.7 to 0.14 per cent
Calcium: 81 to 86 mg
Phosphorus: 42 to 59 mg
Iron: 0.5 to 1.7 mmg
Magnesium: 32 mmg
Sodium: 91 mg
Chlorine: 76 mg
Copper: 0.19 mg
Thiamin: 0.08 mg
Riboflavin: 0.19 mg
Niacin: 0.2 mmg
Vitamin C5: 3.2 to 5.7 mg
Choline: 8 mg
Oxalic acid: 2 mg
Water: 89 to 93 per cent

reaches maturity acts as the 'mother culm' to supply starch and buds for one or more shoots the following year, and often for some years to come.

Most of the superior species eating bamboos are capable of producing maximum diameter culms for that particular environment within four to five years. If, however, you take shoots too early in the life of the plant, it damages its ability to produce both the number of future shoots and larger diameter shoots the following year. Once it is two or three years old, it is better to take any obviously smaller than average shoots, and even remove small older culms to encourage the plant to produce only larger diameter shoots and culms. The small shoots removed during culling can be eaten. The mature culms provide the starch source for the production of future shoots and culms.

The food value and composition of bamboo shoots is complex and interesting. Bamboo shoots are very high in trace elements and vitamins, including Vitamin B complex, etc. They represent a significant contribution towards necessary body building components; however, they are extremely low in carbohydrates, fat and protein,

What is also interesting is that the leaves are extremely high in crude protein (about 20 per cent), and anti-oxidants, the cell renewal anti-cancer ingredient now considered very important in diet, so we not only eat our bamboo shoots, but also dried powdered leaves each morning. I try not to 'moo' at my wife!

Having prepared your shoots as indicated earlier, you can then immediately incorporate them into your cooking, or store them in the fridge in a plastic bag for two months or more, removing the required portion as required. You will notice that, whilst high quality properly grown shoots like *D. asper* are more consistent, each shoot varies in texture within itself, the top being most tender, and the bottom where it was cut from the rhizome being the most fibrous. You can select different portions according to your recipe, with tender non-fibrous sections for salads or dishes featuring the shoots, and the more fibrous sections for stir-fries. Slice tender portions into bite sized pieces or attractive slivers, with fibrous sections cut finer (don't, whatever you do, cut them into the fine fettuccine like ribbons you commonly see in tins).

To titillate your taste buds whilst waiting for your bamboos to grow large enough to harvest shoots, we suggest you think about the following recipes.

1. GINGER GARLIC SHOOTS
(my favourite of all recipes)

500 gm fresh bamboo shoots
3 tbspn chopped garlic
butter or margarine
3 tbspn chopped ginger
1 glass white wine
Ground pepper and salt

Select (preferably) sweet, non-astringent shoot flesh and slice into attractive longer triangular slivers about 1 to 1.5 mm across. Lightly pan fry some chopped ginger and garlic in butter or margarine, then add the shoots, ground pepper and salt and fry only until the shoots are hot throughout. Pour a little white wine in and cook until the alcohol has evaporated off, and the sauce has thickened a little. You can add a little fresh chilli if it suits your taste, but try it without first time. Serve as a feature dish or entree with the remainder of the wine, and you are transported to heaven!

2. BEEF CURRY
WITH BAMBOO SHOOTS

2 tbspns oil
1.2 kg rump steak, thinly sliced
400g fresh chopped bamboo shoots.
2 small fresh red chillies, chopped
2 small fresh green chillies, chopped
2 tbspns fish sauce
1 dried kaffir lime leaf
1 tspn brown sugar
2 tbspn chopped fresh basil

CURRY PASTE

5 dried red chillies
1 tbspn chopped dried galangal
1 tbspn chopped dried kaffir lime peel
1 cup water
2 green shallots, chopped
2 cloves garlic, crushed
2 tspn grated lemon rind
1 tbspn finely chopped fresh lemon grass
1 tspn finely chopped fresh ginger

CURRY PASTE: combine chillies, galangal and peel in bowl, cover with water; cover, stand several hours. Drain peel mixture, reserve ½ cup liquid. Blend or process peel mixture, reserved liquid, shallots, garlic, rind, lemon grass and ginger until smooth.

Heat oil in large wok, add steak, stir-fry until browned all over. Add ¼ cup curry paste, stir for 2 mins. Add bamboo shoots, chillies, sauce, lime leaf and sugar, stir-fry unti steak is tender; stir in basil. (Serves 8.)

3. LAMB WITH BASIL,
BAMBOO SHOOT AND VEGETABLES

2 cloves garlic
2 large fresh red chillies
1 carrot
1 onion
1 tbspn oil
1 tbspn oil, extra
1½ tbspn tandoori curry paste
500 g lamb fillet, thinly sliced
230 g fresh sliced bamboo shoots.
4 green shallots, chopped
⅓ cup shredded fresh basil
1 tbspn fish sauce

Cut garlic, chillies and carrot into thin strips. Cut onion into wedges. Heat oil in wok, add garlic and chillies, stir-fry until lightly browned; remove from wok. Reheat wok, add onion, stir-fry until soft, remove from wok. Return lamb and onion to wok with remaining ingredients, stir-fry until heated through. Serve lamb mixture topped with garlic and chilli. (Serves 4.)

4. MINI SPRING ROLLS
WITH BAMBOO SHOOTS

200 g fresh fine sliced bamboo shoots
2 sticks celery
2 medium carrots
1 tbspn oil
1 clove garlic, crushed
1 small fresh red chilli, finely chopped
½ tspn sambal oelek
50 small spring roll wrappers
1 egg white, lightly beaten
Oil for deep-frying

DIPPING SAUCE

1 tspn sambal oelek
1 tspn grated fresh ginger
1 clove garlic, crushed
1 tbspn chopped fresh basil
2 tspn chopped fresh coriander
2 tbspn cider vinegar
1 tbspn brown sugar

Cut bamboo shoots, celery and carrots into thin strips about 5 cm long. Heat oil in medium frying pan, add garlic, chilli and vegetables, stir over medium heat for about 3 mins or until vegetables are soft. Stir in sambal oelek, cool to room temperature.

Place a heaped tbspn of vegetable mixture on one side of a spring roll wrapper, brush edges with egg white, fold sides in, brush ends lightly with egg white, roll up firmly. Repeat with remaining mixture, wrappers and egg white. Deep-fry rolls in hot oil until golden brown; drain on absorbent paper. Serve with dipping sauce. (Makes 50.)

5. HAM BALLS WITH BAMBOO SHOOTS

2 large chicken breasts
250 g leg ham
200 g fresh bamboo shoots
250 g can water chestnuts
30 g dried mushrooms
2 tbspn dry sherry
3 tspn soy sauce
1/2 tspn sesame oil
1 tbspn cornflour
3 tbspn oil
1/4 tspn salt
Extra cornflour
Oil for deep-frying

BATTER

1/2 cup cornflour
1/2 cup plain flour
1/2 tspn salt
1 tspn baking powder
3/4 cup cold water
1 egg white

BATTER: sift dry ingredients into bowl, gradually add water, mixing to a smooth batter. Just before using batter, beat egg white until soft peaks form. Fold into batter.

Cover dried mushrooms with cold water, cover bowl, stand overnight. Remove skin and bones from chicken meat. Drain water chestnuts. Very finely chop chicken, ham, bamboo shoots, water chestnuts and drained mushrooms. It is important that the ingredients are very finely chopped, or the mixture will be hard to form into balls.

Heat oil in wok or frying pan, add finely chopped ingredients, toss over high heat for three minutes. Add combined sherry and soy sauce, sesame oil, cornflour and salt, toss for a further 2 mins. Remove pan from heat, allow mixture to cool.

Take tbspns of mixture, press into balls with hands; do this gently; mixture will crumble slightly if rolled too firmly. Coat balls lightly with cornflour.

Place a few balls into prepared batter; with spoon gently lift balls, one at a time from batter, draining slightly on sides of bowl. Place into deep hot oil, fry until golden brown; drain on absorbent paper; keep warm. Repeat with remaining balls. (Makes approximately 45.)

6. GOW GEES

250 g wonton wrappers
250 g minced pork
125 g green prawns
60 g dried mushrooms
115 g fresh bamboo shoots
6 shallots
1 tspn grated green ginger
1 clove garlic
2 tspn sesame oil
1 tbspn soy sauce
1 tbspn dry sherry
Oil for deep frying

SWEET SOUR SAUCE

1/2 cup sugar
1/2 cup white vinegar
3/4 cup water
2 tbspn tomato paste
1 tbspn tomato sauce
1 tbspn cornflour
1/4 cup water, extra

SAUCE: Put sugar, water, vinegar, tomato paste and tomato sauce in saucepan, stir over medium heat until sugar dissolves. Mix cornflour to smooth paste with extra water, add to saucepan. Stir over medium heat until sauce boils and thickens, reduce heat, simmer 1 min.

Using an 8 cm cutter, cut wonton wrappers into circles; stack a few wrappers on top of each other and cut all at the same time.

Cover mushrooms with boiling water, stand 30 mins, drain, chop mushrooms finely. Combine mushrooms with pork, shelled and finely chopped prawns, finely chopped bamboo shoots, finely chopped shallots, ginger, crushed garlic, sesame oil, soy sauce and sherry. Mix well.

Place small amounts of mixture into centre of each circle. Brush edges of wrappers with water, fold in half, pinch edges together firmly. Drop gow gees into deep hot oil, fry until golden brown, remove, drain on absorbent paper. Don't have oil over-hot or gow gees will brown before filling is cooked. Serve with sauce for dipping.

7. PORK, BAMBOO SHOOTS AND LETTUCE ROLLS

250 g minced pork
155 g can crab
60 g dried mushrooms
6 shallots
½ x 155 g can water chestnuts
125 g fresh bamboo shoots
1 tbspn oil
2 tspn sesame oil
1 tbspn soy sauce
2 tspn oyster sauce
2 tbspn dry sherry
Lettuce leaves

Cover mushrooms with boiling water, stand 30 mins, drain, remove stems, and chop mushrooms finely. Chop water chestnuts and bamboo shoots finely. Drain and flake crab. Chop shallots finely.

Heat oil in pan or wok, add pork, toss until dark golden brown. Add mushrooms, water chestnuts, bamboo shoots, crab and shallots, toss well, cook 1 min. Combine sesame oil, soy sauce, oyster sauce and sherry, add to pan, toss until well combined, remove from heat.

Put heaped tbsps of pork mixture (this may very according to the size of the lettuce cup) into the centre of each lettuce leaf.

Fold in the ends and sides of lettuce leaves and roll up to form a neat parcel. Generally the meat filling and lettuce leaves are served separately; guests fill and roll their own lettuce leaves. (Makes about 8 rolls.)

8. SEAFOOD COMBINATION WITH BAMBOO SHOOTS

250 g scallops
250 g squid
250 g green king prawns
2 large fish fillets
285 g fresh bamboo shoots
265 g can water chestnuts
8 shallots
3 sticks celery
1 tspn cornflour
½ cup water
1 chicken stock cube
2 tspn dry sherry
1 tspn sesame oil
2 tspn soy sauce
4 tbspn oil

Clean scallops, clean and prepare squid, shell and de-vein prawns, skin fish, cut into large pieces.

Slice celery diagonally; slice shallots diagonally; drain water chestnuts, cut in half; thinly slice bamboo shoots.

Heat 2 tbspn oil in pan or wok, add the prepared vegetables, sauté 2 mins, remove from pan. Add remaining oil to pan, heat. Add scallops, squid, prawns and fish, saute 2 mins. Mix cornflour with a little of the water until smooth, add remaining water, crumbled stock cube, sherry, sesame oil and soy sauce. Add sauce to wok, stir until boiling, add vegetables to wok, toss until heated through. (Serves 4.)

9. BAMBOO PRAWNS

500 g green king prawns
3 tbspn oil
1 tspn grated green ginger
500 g fresh bamboo shoots
1 stick celery
4 shallots
3 slices ham
½ cup water
1 chicken stock cube
1 tspn cornflour
2 tspn dry sherry

Shell prawns, make shallow cut along back of prawn and remove back vein.

Cut bamboo shoot into 1 cm slices, then cut each slice into 5 mm strips. Cut celery, shallots and ham into strips approximately the same size.

Cut a 1 cm slit right through prawns, along the line of the vein. Push a strip of bamboo shoot, celery, shallot and ham through slit in prawn.

Heat oil in wok or large frying pan, sauté ginger 1 min, add prawns, saute until light pink. Combine water, crumbled stock cube, cornflour and sherry, add to pan, stir until sauce boils and thickens, reduce heat, simmer 1 min. (Serves 4 as an entree.)

10. BRAISED PRAWNS
WITH BAMBOO SHOOTS

500 g green king prawns
250 g fresh bamboo shoots
250g broccoli
470g can straw mushrooms
1 tbspn oil
1/2 cup chicken stock
1 tspn cornflour
1 tspn oyster sauce
Salt, pepper
Pinch sugar
1/2 tspn grated green ginger

Note: If straw mushrooms are not available, replace them with canned champignons (small whole mushrooms).

Shell prawns, using sharp knife, cut down back, remove back vein.

Cut broccoli into thick pieces. Drain mushrooms and cut into thin slices. Cut bamboo shoots into thin slices.

Heat oil in pan or wok, add prawns, sauté quickly until tender and light pink in colour, approx. 3 mins.

Add to pan the bamboo shoots, broccoli and mushrooms, toss well. Blend cornflour with chicken stock, oyster sauce, salt, pepper, sugar and ginger. Bring to boil. Stir continuously and cook 1 min. (Serves 4.)

11. MARINATED CHICKEN WINGS
WITH BAMBOO SHOOTS

750 g chicken wings
6 shallots
2 cloves garlic
2 tbspn soy sauce
2 tbspn dry sherry
1 tspn grated green ginger
1 1/2 tbspn brown sugar
Salt
3 tbspn oil
345g fresh bamboo shoots
1 tbspn cornflour
3/4 cup water
1 chicken stock cube

Cut shallots diagonally; put into bowl with crushed garlic, soy sauce, sherry, green ginger, brown sugar, salt and chicken wings. Mix well.

Let stand 1 hour. Drain, reserve marinade.

Heat oil in wok, add sliced bamboo shoots, fry 2 mins.

Remove from pan.

Add chicken wings and shallots to pan, cook over high heat until golden brown on both sides. Reduce heat, cook further 10 to 15 mins, or until chicken is tender.

Blend cornflour with a little water, add remaining water, crumbled stock cube and reserved marinade. Add to wok, stir over high heat until sauce boils, add sliced bamboo shoots, reduce heat, simmer further 2 mins. Put chicken wings on serving dish, spoon sauce over. (Serves 4.)

12. BRAISED DUCK
WITH BAMBOO SHOOT

1.75 kg to 2 kg duck
Cornflour
2 cloves garlic
Oil for deep frying
3 tspn soy sauce
1 1/2 tbspn dry sherry
1 tspn grated green ginger
2 cups water
2 chicken stock cubes
6 dried mushrooms
230g chopped fresh bamboo shoot
225g can water chestnuts
Cornflour, extra
3/4 cup water, extra
1/2 tspn sugar
Salt, pepper
1 tspn soy sauce, extra
1/2 tspn sesame oil

Wash duck, cut into serving-sized pieces. Drain water chestnuts. Thickly slice water chestnuts and bamboo shoots. Soak mushrooms in hot water for 20 mins. Drain, squeeze dry. Remove stalks, slice mushrooms thinly.

Coat duck pieces lightly in cornflour. Heat oil in pan or wok. Add crushed garlic and half the duck pieces, cook until well browned. Remove from pan, repeat with remaining pieces.

Drain oil from pan, add duck and combined soy sauce, sherry and ginger, cook 2 mins. Stir occasionally. Add water and crumbled stock cubes, bring to boil. Put duck and liquid into saucepan, cover and simmer gently 2 1/4 hrs or until duck is tender. 30 mins before cooking is completed, add mushrooms, sliced water chestnuts and bamboo shoots. When duck is tender skim off any fat, stir in combined extra cornflour, sugar, salt, pepper, extra soy sauce, extra water and sesame oil. Stir until sauce boils and thickens. Top with sliced shallots. (Serves 6.)

13. CHICKEN, BAMBOO SHOOT AND ALMONDS

4 chicken breasts
1 tspn salt
1 tbspn cornflour
1 egg white
1¹/₂ tbspn dry sherry
Oil for deep-frying
6 shallots
125 g mushrooms
1 large carrot
230 g fresh bamboo shoots
3 sticks celery
1 tspn grated green ginger
2 tbspn oil, extra
60 g blanched almonds

SAUCE
1 tbspn cornflour
1¹/₂ cups water
1 tbspn soy sauce
1 chicken stock cube
1 tbspn dry sherry

SAUCE: Blend cornflour with water, soy sauce, sherry and crumbled stock cube. Stir over medium heat until sauce boils and thickens.

Slice mushrooms roughly. Slice celery diagonally. Cut shallots into 2.5 cm pieces. Slice bamboo shoots thinly, cut into 1 cm strips. Peel and dice carrot. Bone chicken breasts, remove skin; cut meat into 2.5 cm pieces, combine with salt, cornflour, lightly beaten egg white and sherry. Mix well.

Deep-fry chicken pieces in hot oil until just changing colour, drain well.

Heat extra oil in pan, add almonds, fry until golden brown. Remove from pan, drain on absorbent paper.

Add grated ginger and diced carrots to pan, fry gently 1 min, add remaining vegetables, sauté until tender but still crisp, stirring occasionally, add chicken, heat through. Add sauce, mix through, stir in almonds. (Serves 4–6.)

14. COMBINATION CHOP SUEY

2 chicken breasts
¹/₂ Chinese cabbage
125 g beans
3 sticks celery
2 onions
1 large carrot
250 g green prawns
2 tbspn oil
250 g minced pork
1 cup water
2 tspn cornflour
1 chicken stock cube
1 tbspn soy sauce
240 g fresh bamboo shoots

Steam or boil chicken until tender, cool; remove meat from bones, cut into cubes. Shred cabbage, slice beans and celery diagonally, peel and chop onions; peel carrot, cut into cubes. Shell prawns, remove back vein.

Heat oil in pan or wok, add minced pork, cook until well browned, about 5 mins. Add cabbage, beans, carrot, onions and celery to pan, toss until all ingredients are well combined. Cook further 3 mins.

Add combined water, cornflour, crumbled chicken stock cube and soy sauce to pan, stir until sauce boils and thickens. Add chicken, prawns and bamboo shoots, cook further 3 mins, or until prawns are cooked. (Serves 4–6.)

15. BEEF WITH BAMBOO SHOOTS IN BLACK BEAN SAUCE

750 g rump steak
1 egg white
1 tbspn dry sherry
2 tbspn soy sauce
1 tspn cornflour
¹/₃ cup oil
4 shallots
1 red pepper
¹/₂ cup fresh bamboo shoots
1 tspn curry powder
1 tbspn canned black beans
Pinch sugar
¹/₃ cup water
2 tspn cornflour, extra

Trim away any fat from steak. Cut steak into 5 cm x 5 mm strips. Combine in bowl with egg white, sherry, soy sauce and cornflour, mix well. Stand 30 mins.

Put beans in bowl, cover with water, stand 15 mins, drain and rinse under cold running water. Put on to plate, add sugar and 1 tspn water, mash well. Chop shallots into 2.5 cm pieces, cut pepper in half, remove seeds, cut each half into thin strips.

Add 2 tbspn oil to pan or wok, add shallots, red pepper, bamboo shoots and curry powder, sauté 2 mins, remove from wok. Heat remaining oil in wok, add meat and marinade, cook until browned.

21 Plantations—Edible Shoots and Timber

Most people will be staggered to hear that the world is consuming at least one million tonnes, probably more, of bamboo shoots every year. I find it amazing that a country like Australia is currently said by one researcher (Midmore, 1997) to be consuming more than 8000 tonnes of bamboo shoots every year (imported in tins). However, when one realises that we have more than one million citizens of ethnic Asian origin, as well as Caucasian Australians consuming tinned bamboo shoot almost every time they eat Chinese or Thai food, and with imported tinned shoots on the shelves of every supermarket in the country, it becomes believable. The situation is much the same in the USA where they consume more than 30 000 tonnes per year. I know that Canada with its large ethnic Chinese population, and Europe, are also major importers of tinned bamboo shoots.

People's lack of knowledge and accompanying lack of curiosity in bamboo as a plant extends also to edible shoots. Disguised as those vaguely white unidentifiable sliced things that are slightly crunchy (tinned shoots don't have the texture of fresh ones), they are acknowledged and remembered by some who eat them; generally however, most people deny having ever eaten bamboo shoots.

It fascinates me that most people will wax lyrical over beautiful coffee table books showing Japanese gardens with elegant simple bamboo fences that form secluded meditative niches maximising the feeling of space. But look out the average suburban window in Australia and you will see mostly timber paling fences, or at best, a tea-tree brush fence harvested from forests currently under threat as part of our environmental destruction process.

Obviously, Australia is quite capable of growing enough bamboo to supply enough edible shoots and bamboo timber for its own needs, and yet it remains unaware of the very need. In spite of there being no promotion for bamboo timber (for fences, screens, pagodas, furniture, etc.) there is a steady demand for bamboo timber. It is almost unavailable because the resource is just not grown in the quantity or quality of species necessary to meet the need. With a little education and promotion, bamboo, in fact can and will become fashionable, but not before the resource is available. That will only happen when sufficient plantations are established to guarantee a reliable supply, and people are educated to know more about the wood and how use it.

■ **21.C** Dendrocalamus asper (Indonesian cultivar) with its huge new shoots, growing at Taree, NSW

Overview and Potential Australian Production

I believe there is a good opportunity to grow bamboo as a commercial crop in plantation quantities both for its edible shoots and timber culms (you get two saleable crops each year after maturity). We are busy establishing our own plantations at Bamboo World. The opportunity is particularly relevant for southern hemisphere countries

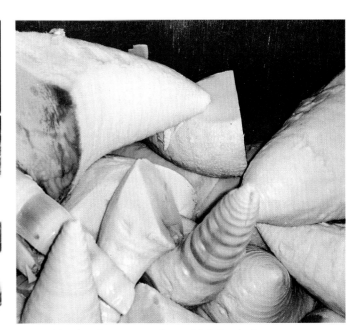

■ **21.B** Dendrocalamus asper *(pai tong keo) shoots recently harvested*

■ **21.A** Dendrocalamus asper *shoots with their culm leaves removed ready to enter the cannery*

like Australia that can take advantage of pockets of opportunity to supply the off-season fresh shoot export market in northern hemisphere Asia, and also the USA, Europe and Canada. Italy and Germany are trying to establish plantations for fresh shoots, and the USA is just beginning to think about it, all with cold-tolerant species that are slow to develop and have short shoot supply seasons.

The best of these species are capable of producing more than 10 000 kg of edible bamboo shoots every year when grown in the right area, and statistically those are conservative figures. There are two saleable crops every year in a mature plantation. Between 400 and 800 saleable timber poles (culms) can also be harvested and sold (at a different time of the year to the shoots) as a consequence of the plantation management system used to maximise shoot production. The mathematics of the crop yield and price per kg plus timber sales, even at the most conservative of estimates, makes it potentially the most viable (legal) agricultural crop currently available in Australia ($10 000 plus per hectare for each $1/kg plus timber, with recent high quality shoots returning between $4 and $8/kg to the grower).

Whilst many species of bamboo produce high quality eating shoots, reliable production statistics exist for four major species that will become the main focus of this chapter. Tens of thousands of hectares of these particular bamboos are already established and well researched, and have been in full production for many years in northern hemisphere plantations. There are other possibly suitable bamboo species grown in smaller plantation areas in China and Taiwan (*Bambusa edulus*, *Dendrocalamopsis beechyana*, *Dendrocalamus brandisii* and *Dendrocalamus hamiltonii*), but those are not well researched. There are also many smaller running bamboos grown in China that are too labour-intensive to seriously consider for our labour costs, which leaves us with four species most suitable for various Australian conditions: two suitable for almost frost-free, monsoonal rainfall sites, one less productive species suited for cooler monsoonal rainfall sites, and one for winter rainfall.

Australia's fresh shoot market has not yet been developed or promoted in spite of recent small tonnages reaching markets, but a commercial association, the Australian Commercial Bamboo Corporation (ACBC) has just been formed to do that job. A fresh edible shoot sales potential definitely exists for providing about half of the approximately 8000 tonnes of edible shoots currently being consumed on our domestic market (say 400 hectares). In addition, after learning to handle this new crop, we can export fresh shoots for the vast northern hemisphere Asian market where fresh shoots are not available during some months of the year. There are also possibilities in Europe and north America, Japan, China, Taiwan, Korea, Vietnam and Thailand which are large consumers of both fresh shoots, dried shoots and tinned shoots, with a preference for 'fresh' varieties when available. There is no other southern hemisphere country currently growing bamboo shoots in plantation quantities, although Indonesia, Africa, Papua New Guinea and South America have that potential.

The current planted area in Australia is about 150 hectares (January 1999), an increase of about 130 hectares in the last twelve months mostly from *Dendrocalamus asper* and *D. latiflorus* plants supplied by us at Bamboo World (we now tissue culture the correct clones). The oldest plantations in Australia are all moso, a large slow-developing running bamboo (about 10 hectares altogether, some eight years old), none of it yet mature enough to be fully productive.

With reasonable marketing and education, the already high (8000 tonnes/year) imported tinned consumption should yield up a significant share of its market to the fresh shoot market, and the demand will continue to grow even more quickly. According to a New South Wales Department of Agriculture source, Australia with its growing ethnic Asian population (more than one million), 'is consuming more than A$50 million per year of Asian vegetables'. This is something that has happened very quickly indeed, because a few years ago they were not available in supermarkets.

Fresh shoots are infinitely superior to tinned shoots, and superior species taste much better than inferior ones, even to the point that the best species can be used raw in salads to add a unique crispness. It seems reasonable to assume that, with reasonable promotion and product presentation, the fresh shoot price should be higher than the tinned shoot price. Because fresh shoots have not been available or marketed for very long in the Western world, and then only in negligible quantities, it is not possible to reliably predict the ultimate fresh wholesale selling price in Australia, or in any other non-producing country.

I believe in the potential of this new industry. Bamboo World with a partner has planted 50 hectares of a 110 hectare planting in northern NSW, and are now establishing a 1000 hectare export plantation in north Queensland.

It takes about five to six years for a clumping bamboo to reach maturity, and between eight and ten years for a running bamboo plantation to reach maturity, that is, full edible shoot production, depending on the climate, management and growing conditions. A smaller, early income from some earlier shoots is available after the third year for clumpers, and the fifth year for runners. Full timber harvest of properly aged wood commences in the seventh year for clumpers and in the tenth year or so for the runner (moso) with some smaller culms normally available earlier. This early harvesting of both shoots and wood becomes mandatory because of the necessary thinning procedures during the developmental stage of a plantation.

World Consumption and Overseas Production

Consumption statistics available out of Asia are confusing and conflicting. For this reason, I have deliberately stated 'low-end' conservative data, and can take no responsibility for any inaccuracies.

World consumption of bamboo shoots is obviously an estimate, but with more than 70 000 hectares planted in Japan, 90 000 hectares in Taiwan, 60 000 hectares in Thailand, and 10 000 hectares in China, together with more than 2.8 million hectares of moso growing (mostly wild mountain stands, with some efficiently run plantations), the world consumption figure with China included is said to be in excess of two million tonnes/year. The actual figure probably exceeds that considerably. China alone eats 1.2 million tonnes annually (Fu Maoyi, 1997).

One Thai paper (Thammincha, 1995) stated there were 55 000 hectares of *Dendrocalamus asper* planted in Thailand in 1994, much not yet mature. One province alone was processing 68 000 tonnes of shoots/year and exporting 40 000 tonnes/year of steamed shoots, and that didn't include figures on local consumption. Dr Thammincha wrote recently saying that between six and seven million young *D. asper* plants (30 to 35 000 hectares) were sold to farmers in 1998 for planting out.

One statistic says Japanese growers send about 90 000 tonnes of domestically grown moso shoots to market (only a portion of the shoots locally grown, sold and consumed), and also imports more than 100 000 tonnes of shoots from Thailand, Taiwan and China. Another states the small municipal area of Tokyo (population unknown) consumes 8000 tonnes of fresh shoots plus 6200 tonnes of boiled shoots every year (plus large quantities of off-season tinned and dried shoots). Taiwan, said to consume about the same tonnage of shoots as Japan, also exported about 40 000 tonnes of *D. latiflorus* shoots to Japan (PROSEA, 1995). China is said to export about 140 000 tonnes/year of that same species, plus large volumes of moso shoots. I couldn't even begin to guess the local consumption of fresh shoots within Korea, Thailand and Vietnam. Singapore and Hong Kong are available as fresh shoot markets also. The available figures I have studied are incomplete and to some extent confusing, but they point to the fact that massive amounts of this vegetable are consumed throughout Asia, and the unquantified demand and consumption in Australia must be growing and will grow more with education and availablility.

Each country prefers to eat the shoot it generally grows, Japan and north China favouring both moso winter shoots and shoots from runners like *Phyllostachys praecox*. South China and Taiwan favour *D. latiflorus* and Thailand favours *D. asper*; however, all producers seem to export and import and eat each others' shoots, either fresh, steamed, tinned, pickled or dried. According to one large Australian importer, most local restaurants here prefer the Thai tinned shoots from *Dendrocalamus asper*, but there are as yet virtually no fresh shoots available. *D. asper* is certainly a sweet non-astringent shoot if properly grown. An increasing number of Asians will want to purchase 'off-season' fresh shoots as the economies of these countries strengthen, and I suspect that Australians will ultimately have to compete with Asia for a share of the Australian grown shoots.

Market Value of Shoots and Timber

As there is no long-established market for fresh shoots in Australia, estimating an ultimately reliable selling price is a pure guess. Fresh high quality shoots have been available only in negligible quantities since 1996. During that time, most high quality shoots sold on the Melbourne and Sydney markets have returned between A\$4 and A\$8/kg (about five tonnes in 1998), with a definite preference for larger shoots. Some smaller ones were harder to sell so the grower split them open, packed them in cryogenic bags in foam boxes, and sold them for A\$8/kg, the equivalent of just under A\$4/kg if sold as a complete as harvested shoot.

As they're the only fresh shoots available, the price is not a long-term indicator. If one assumes a theoretical shoot harvest of 10 000 kilograms/hectare/year from a well-run plantation, the prognosis for profit is very good whatever price per kg you adopt for your feasibility study, but it would be irresponsible to predict an ongoing gross annual income of A\$60 000/hectare from shoot sales! I have my own idea on what the price will settle down to, but it's best that each person be his or her own judge.

In 1998 some tonnes of inferior shoots from the Northern Territory indigenous stands of *Bambusa arnhemica* (stolen from Government land) appeared on the market, together with a few shoots from scattered stands. These inferior, bitter, scruffy-looking small shoots were being sold in Woolworths for A\$5.99/kg as harvested and A\$3.50/kg wholesale. A gourmet food supplier in Brisbane markets was reported as selling edible shoots for A\$13/kg. I don't believe any of those prices are necessarily indicative of what price will be paid for high quality shoots once a reasonable education and marketing program has been implemented. I have been told that Northern Territory Parks and Wildlife have since banned people from raiding the National Parks for shoots and timber.

I think that some restaurants will continue to buy tinned shoots, partly from convenience and partly because they are inexpensive, but a limited number of up-market Sydney restaurants have been paying A\$16 to A\$18.00/kg in the 1995, 1996 and 1997 seasons for a limited supply of fresh moso shoots, an unrealistic early stage price (the price includes air freight, couriers at both ends, etc.). Some restaurants will obviously pay reasonable prices for quality fresh shoots rather than settle for inferior, more convenient tinned shoots, and my local surveys of Thai, Vietnamese, Chinese and even high quality Australian restaurants has confirmed a strong interest.

The following is a summary of some tinned shoot and their cost, recently available in Australia (1997):

a) Tinned *Thyrsostachys siamensis* shoots (1.2 kg net weight with water) yielding 732 g drained weight, retail for \$4.09/kg in a bulk Chinese specialty grocer.

b) The same tinned brand wholesale from the importer is A\$28 per carton equating to A\$3.18/kg drained weight.

c) Tinned *Dendrocalamus asper* shoots ex Thailand from the same Chinese retail outlet are A\$5.40/kg drained weight.

d) The same tinned shoots are supplied directly to restaurants in six-tin cartons at A\$2.33/kg drained weight from the same wholesale importer at A\$25.20 per carton.

e) Tinned shoots purchased through normal major retail outlets sell for between A\$6.00/kg and A\$10.00/kg drained weight, obviously a very high price.

One large importer commented that 'in restaurants in Australia, both Chinese and Thai prefer the Thai shoots (*D. asper*) rather than the Chinese winter shoots (moso)' and that 'the Thai shoots were of better eating quality'. I don't doubt the quality of fresh moso shoots, or fresh *D. asper* shoots, but I must agree that our experimental tasting of tinned moso and tinned *D. asper* confirms the importer's opinion. The Chinese in Anji province also pay A\$3/kg for moso winter shoots and *P. praecox* shoots, but only A\$1/kg for normal peak season moso shoots, and I have heard that the Japanese have the same quality preference.

I believe the above factors are likely to result in higher prices for quite a few years until supply begins to meet demand, and that's without considering the export potential. It is quite possible that obtainable export prices will cause a higher local price to be paid (as with prawns, etc.), something that is happening right now in China. The export of fresh shoots to Japan has resulted in the local Chinese near Shanghai and inland having to pay A\$3/kg to purchase their own high quality shoots (and about A\$8/kg during their spring festival when it is traditionally important to eat bamboo shoots.

Hence tinned shoots are being purchased for between \$2.30 and \$10 per kg drained weight. It seems logical to me that people will pay at least as much per kg for the fresh shoot on a 'usable weight' basis as they will pay per kg on a usable weight basis for tinned shoots. Harvested edible shoots are between 50 per cent and 60 per cent waste matter, mostly culm leaf, whereas with tinned shoots you also pay for the water. Education and eating quality of individual 'branded' species will definitely influence the price being paid, much the same as it does for fruit quality (as it does in China for different shoot species).

■ **21.D** *Moso shoots being processed in a Chinese cannery*

Remember that the usable flesh on a shoot harvested is usually somewhere between 40 and 50 per cent of its gross harvested weight, the waste parts being culm leaf, and some tough or damaged parts near where it is severed from the rhizome. Fresh shoots are sold generally unprocessed and complete as cut. Similarly, tinned shoots are nearly 50 per cent water, which is why the drained weight, sometimes not mentioned on the can, has been quoted above.

Moso shoots, in spite of having a higher labour cost, should also be very saleable and profitable because the income will still be high in proportion to the labour. I believe that Japanese and northern Chinese ethnic restaurants may pay higher prices for fresh moso shoots, but Thai, Taiwanese and Southern Chinese ethnic restaurants may pay more for *D. asper* and *D. latiflorus* shoots. Western people seem to prefer a sweet non-astringent shoot, and will probably prefer *D. asper*, and the Vietnamese the slightly more astringent *D. latiflorus*. The largest growth potential is with Western (Caucasian) people, and I believe it will be rapid with education, as many are already beginning to cook with tinned shoots, and Thai/Vietnamese food is now increasingly popular and influencing Australian food.

The Japanese (1995) paid up to A$10/kg for off-season shoots available. A New South Wales Agricultural Department Asian vegetables adviser told me that he gets enquiries for bamboo shoots from Japan, and that the fresh vegetable air freight cost 'to anywhere in Asia' is about A$2.30/kg (1997). Jetro, the Japanese government's external trade organisation, wrote that they could see 'no real reason for you not to export fresh shoots to Japan. There are no evident quarantine restrictions, however there is a tariff of 7.5 per cent imposed on bamboo shoot

imports'. This export market potential has not yet been properly explored yet, but is part of the current ACBC/UNIQLD research and marketing development.

Timber Sales and Market

Remember, shoots are only part of the annual crop, the other half being timber culms. A conservative estimate for a mature *Dendrocalamus asper* plantation would be 600 culms/year/hectare (say 10 tonnes dried) with, say, a minimum of 6 m of usable, saleable wood per culm, between 80 and 125 mm diameter. The current wholesale price being obtained by the few people harvesting and selling bamboo poles is about A$1/m x diameter divided by 25 mm (A$4/m for 100 mm culms) which calculates at a theoretical gross annual income from timber of A$18 000/hectare! I stress that all this is speculation in a country where the demand for, and the supply of, the products hasn't been developed to the point where a reliable price record or market exists. However, I do know of one supplier importing container loads of culms from China and selling them, and two other groups harvesting and selling local culms. We at Bamboo World are however, busy establishing plantations, and we expect that the gross sales from harvested culms will more than cover the operating costs of our plantation, whatever it is.

When considering bamboo timber sales, all *immature* culms sold will be vulnerable to powder beetle attack, shrinkage and cracking from high moisture, or be structurally low in strength. This practice will damage (and is damaging) the developing potential of the bamboo culm market. Further, if people are not advised that bamboo cannot be used outdoors and give long life without chemical treatment, it will damage the potential further. We are recommending that all growers implement the following policy:

- Harvest only mature bamboo for sale (three years for clumpers and five years for moso).

- Sell two grades of bamboo culm, 'treated' or 'untreated', branded as such and accompanied by an advice leaflet giving details on how it can be used and in what environment.

Obviously, buyers of culms should check that what they purchase originally came from a reputable grower who is following these practices.

Edible Shoot 'Shelf-Life' and Market Presentation

The shelf life of a fresh bamboo shoot is between seven and fourteen days, but for market presentation it is best to think seven days maximum. Shelf life is improved by cool room storage, handling, etc. I was told by the Chinese that their *Phyllostachys praecox* shoots harvested early morning now arrive for sale on the Japanese market that same afternoon. If China can do it, so can we (at the relevant time of the year).

Shoots are normally cut early morning, dropped unwashed into foam boxes and sent promptly in refrigerated vans to market, or to airport outlets. Washing the shoot causes deterioration, but they are sometimes brushed to remove loose dirt or dust. There may be regulations in various states or countries with specific treatment requirements, but the NSW Department of Agriculture doesn't believe there are problems in that Australia is already selling large volumes of various fresh vegetables on the Asian markets.

Shoots are marketed and eaten in Asia in many forms, such as tinned, pickled, dried, salted and steamed. I do not think that Australia should or will compete with the Asian tinned, pickled or dried product, but our off-season location for export coupled with the quality advantage of fresh shoots versus tinned shoots does create a unique export niche market. There could also be an Australian market (and possibly an export market) for fresh peeled shoots in salt water, and the possibility exists for cryogenic bag packing for extended life. The growers' association (ACBC) and the Federal Government's RIRDC are already researching extended fresh shelf life, packing, etc.

and a sophisticated marketing system with the University of Queensland.

Recommended Species— 'The Big Three'

The three species most successfully grown in large northern hemisphere plantations are as follows:

1. *Phyllostachys heterocycla pubescens* (common name: moso)—a large running bamboo;

2. *Dendrocalamus asper*—a clumping bamboo, larger than moso; and

3. *Dendrocalamus latiflorus*—a clumping bamboo, also larger than moso.

(PHOTO: DR SONGKRAM THAMMINCHA)

■ **21.E** *A fairly young* Dendrocalamus asper *plantation in Thailand*

Species Comparison—Which One to Plant?

If you are contemplating establishing a commercial plantation, it is very important to study the differences in these three bamboos carefully before deciding which species is right for you, your environment and your property. If you are going to grow for your home kitchen, by all means plant all three and some other delicious species as well, but don't plant moso without first working out a management system to control its spreading habit. One other less productive bamboo that has some limited advantages (*Bambusa oldhamii*) will be analysed later.

The first criterion of selection is the lowest temperature experienced on your site each year. The large non-invasive clumping bamboos *Dendrocalamus asper* and *D. latiflorus* have a low tolerance point of -5°C and -4°C respectively, whereas the invasive runner moso tolerates -15°C.

The second criterion is the amount of available rainfall water, say 1.4 m/year at least for all three species. If you either don't get that much rain or can't irrigate to supplement it to that magnitude, then grow it for fun, but not in plantations. If you are lucky enough to have an even higher rainfall or even more irrigation water available, you have a good chance of possibly increasing your yield by 50 per cent or more.

The third criterion is at what time of the year the water is available. The clumpers *D. asper* and *D. latiflorus* are more comfortable in monsoonal type late summer and autumn rainfall patterns because their shoot season starts and finishes with this rainfall. In the southern hemisphere, monsoonal rainfall patterns occur mainly from January or earlier until June or later. Running bamboos have their much shorter shoot season in late winter–early spring (August and September in the southern hemisphere), and therefore require large amounts of winter and early spring rainfall, again about 1.4 m or more. It follows that the natural environment in northern NSW and Queensland with very little rain during late winter and springtime, and with many low-frost areas, is suitable for plantations of clumping bamboos. Southern NSW, South Australia, Victoria and Tasmania, with their high winter rainfall, low summer rainfall and heavier frost conditions are environments more suitable for plantations of running bamboo like moso which must have abundant rain from July to at least November, and preferably later for the development of new rhizomes.

Unless you can deliver large amounts of water during the six-month shoot season for *D. asper* and *D. latiflorus* (clumpers) or prior to and during the six- to eight-week shorter shoot season for moso, it will be difficult to establish your plantation quickly, or to ultimately reach the high yields possible. It is, in fact, almost impossible to rely

on only catchment dams to provide the seasonal volume of water required unless your plantation is small or you receive your major rainfall at the right time of the year. As an example, to collect and have available 1 m of water to apply in the 'dry' season requires a dam averaging 2 m deep and 0.5 hectare in area for each one hectare of plantation, plus extra for evaporation. Don't try it unless you have access to a very substantial creek or river, complete with the appropriate pumping rights.

The yield statistics for all three species indicate that given reasonable conditions and management, one should expect 10 000 kg of high quality edible shoots per hectare. The published statistics I have on all three species indicate that crops of 15 tonnes/hectare/year, even up to 20 tonnes/hectare, may be achieved given ideal conditions and management. It is, however, best to use a very achievable figure like 10 tonnes/hectare/year for your projected expectation and viability studies, and you may well be pleased.

The cost of harvesting, management and establishment for moso is higher than with the clumpers because of various factors. These include slower establishment time, smaller shoot size harvested from deeper underground, no tractor accessibility, etc. Moso is however still a very worthwhile viable crop for those in the ideal growing environment.

The second two bamboos, *D. asper* and *D. latiflorus* are both large, non-invasive clumping (sympodial) bamboos, larger than moso, but also more frost-fragile (-5°C and -4°C respectively). Clumpers are much faster growing than runners and they reach full production more quickly. Their operating costs are also less because you use simpler, quicker harvesting techniques, very large shoots meaning less to harvest, and tractor access being possible in the plantation.

All three species have advantages and disadvantages when compared to each other, although the differences between the two clumping bamboos are minimal. Each species is described in detail later, but the following comparative comments will help you decide what is right for your needs and environment.

1. The smaller moso shoots (1.5 kg average) mean one must harvest twice as many shoots than with the clumping bamboos (between 1 and 5 kg each depending on species and cultivar) for a given tonnage, which increases labour costs when growing moso.

2. Having to dig underground to the running rhizome (averaging 300 mm to 700 mm underground) to harvest moso shoots as compared to cutting a lesser number of clumping shoots off close to ground level also increases labour costs when growing moso. There is a noticeable difference between the heavy hoe-like digging tool normally used by the Chinese to dig down and cut of the moso shoots, as opposed to

the light, almost delicate, slicing spear used to cut off the clumping shoots just below ground level (see Chapter 10, Sketch 10.2 and Photo 10F).

3. Being unable to utilise vehicles in a moso forest to harvest shoots or timber, or to carry in mulch and fertiliser, increases labour costs when growing moso.

4. Moso is the main edible shoot bamboo grown domestically by the Japanese (because of their cold climate) and may attract higher prices in Japan during its short shoot season.

5. By planting both moso (running) and the clumping species, the harvesting season is spread to cover five weeks of spring and all of late summer through to midwinter (24 weeks). This thereby extends the harvest season and reduces the need for outside hired labour for harvesting larger plantation areas of running or clumping only bamboos (Taiwan has some moso planted for this reason, mostly grown in their very high mountains). One needs, however, to have abundant water available to suit their different requirements.

6. Both moso and the clumping bamboos produce desirable timber poles (culms) which can be sold. The clumping bamboos produce large diameter culms with superior strength wood, therefore better structural timber to moso, but often not as straight as moso. All species produce saleable wood (all of which should be chemically treated if intended for outside use).

7. *D. asper* (-5°C) and *D. latiflorus* (-4°C) have temperature limitations and should not be grown where regular heavy frost is experienced. In the tropics, *D. asper* is known to grow up to 1500 m above sea level, but thrives best at about 400 to 500 m. *D. latiflorus* is recorded as growing naturally at elevations of 1000 m in Taiwan (PROSEA) which is probably a lower average ambient temperature condition than the higher elevation for *D. asper*, but still not below –4°C.

8. Moso has a distinct advantage in very cold climates, in that it can and is being grown in plantations exposed to –15°C and snow (in China and Korea).

9. *D. asper* and *D. latiflorus* are clumping bamboos and are totally non-invasive, whereas moso is a very vigorous running bamboo that will need yearly control measures or designed barriers to contain it within the plantation area (see Chapter 1).

10. Moso, being a running bamboo and investing so much energy in its rhizome system, takes three to five years longer to reach maturity, depending on growing

conditions. *D. asper* and *D. latiflorus*, given reasonable conditions and late summer rain, grow much faster than moso when young and produce much larger and more numerous shoots and culms earlier.

11. The crop statistics available seem to claim much the same achievable yields for all three species when mature, with perhaps *D. latiflorus* claims being a little higher. The differences may be more to do with management techniques and growing conditions in different countries rather than species differences.

12. During moso's (longer) establishment period, it is difficult and labour intensive to control weed growth until a canopy is achieved. Clumping bamboo plantations can be slashed to control weeds until the canopy is established, because their rhizomes and new shoots are contained within a clearly defined clump circle (all you need is a little caution on approaching too closely during the shoot season). With moso, it is not advisable to use machinery within the plantation area whether it is young or mature. This is because the extensive and constantly developing rhizome system is fragile, susceptible to damage, and covers the whole area, and hidden new shoots are likely to pop up anywhere within the plantation. Since it is a grass, controlling moso weed growth by spraying may damage or retard the bamboo. We have found this to be a major problem on our site. Running and clumping bamboos both tend to eliminate weed growth once the plantations have reached maturity, although the Chinese experts told me they have to hand chip a mature moso plantation every two years (not so a clumping plantation).

13. All three species are statistically capable of comfortably producing 10 tonnes/hectare/year based on the fact that statistics available vary from a low of 6 to 8 tonnes/hectare/year to a high of 20 tonnes/ hectare/year, and sometimes even higher. Productivity will obviously depend on the specific conditions at the plantation site in a southern hemisphere environment where they have not been grown to maturity in plantation form; however, a visiting Thai expert recently confirmed they are growing here as well as or faster than in Thailand.

14. If the clump spacing of the sympodial species is correct for the soil and site, overseas experience indicates their longer root system feeds from the whole plantation area just as efficiently as the shorter roots and long rhizome network of moso. Statistically there is much the same shoot productivity for all three species, once they reach maturity.

15. Clumping bamboo culms are normally harvested on a three-year harvest cycle, whereas moso culms, being

■ **21.F** *A moso shoot being dug from underground near Fuyang in China. Note the long-bladed hoe traditionally used for harvesting.*

■ **21.H** *A moso shoot projecting from the ground. Whilst harvested when projecting like this, it will bring a lesser price in both Japan and China because the shoot has been allowed to be exposed to light before harvesting.*

Individual Plant Descriptions

Moso
(Phyllostachys heterocycla pubescens)

Moso is the main bamboo shoot eaten in Japan, Korea and central to northern China. Japan is said to have well in excess of 50 000 hectares growing (Farrelly, 1984), and China more than 2 800 000 hectares (Zhang Guangchu, 1997), but much of the latter is wild indigenous mountainous forest certainly not operated under plantation conditions. Moso is the largest, most vigorous, most aggressive of the running bamboos. This essentially cold-climate bamboo is slow and difficult to establish. Most of the early energy of the plant is invested in establishing the underground rhizome system and constantly trying to extend its territory without much visible above ground indication (see Chapter 1 and Photos 21G and 1N).

Shoots average 1.5 kg each (Oshima Jinsaburo, 1937), so you harvest about 6600 shoots to achieve a 10 000 kg harvest, which happens over about eight weeks, but mostly within a five-week peak period. Moso shoots must be dug substantially from underground, severed not far from where they join the rhizomes which are mostly between 300 and 700 mm below the surface of the ground on mature plantations (Fu Maoyi, 1997). With moso, vehicle access for harvesting and fertilising is not advisable because of potential damage to developing shoots and rhizomes. Moso (as with all running bamboos) produces shoots during late winter and spring as opposed to clumping bamboos, which have their shoots in the summer time.

Once a moso forest reaches maturity (which takes eight to ten years) and has covered the plantation area, it can change from its slow-to-develop state to become quite prolific below ground. It is capable of invading large areas of land if not controlled. Moso will not travel under waterways, even if they are dry for part of the year; nor sealed roads or heavily used dirt access roads; however, it is well to remember that some effort may be required to contain moso within the intended plantation area. Rhizomes are capable of reaching 1.2 m below ground level, up to 60 mm diameter and many metres long (Oshima Jinsaburo, 1937). Each rhizome has dozens of buds that develop into either shoots or new rhizomes. An individual moso rhizome normally produces no shoots in the year it develops, nor the following year when it fattens itself up and produces more rhizomes for the future. During the third and fourth year of its life, it will produce most of its large healthy shoots and culms. By the fifth year, its ability to produce culms diminishes, and it becomes a starch repository and feed system for the younger rhizomes it has produced in its second year.

more brittle and prone to cracking, are harvested older, on a five-year cycle in timber plantations or even a seven-year cycle in moso shoot plantations, so you wait longer to harvest your timber.

16. Moso (and some other running bamboos) will grow in a warmer climate, but it is generally only grown in quantity in the cool temperate areas of China, Korea and Japan, except in Taiwan (usually above 3000 m) where it is grown for its off-season edible shoots.

It is *critically* important when establishing any bamboo plantation to study the flowering cycle of the bamboo you intend planting to protect yourself from the massive destruction bamboo plantations suffer when these rare flowerings occur (by planting either the right clone or species). This applies to these three bamboos also, and is clarified later in this section (also see Chapter 4).

■ **21.G** Phyllostachys heterocycla pubescens *(moso) forest managed for timber in Anji province, China*

This accounts for the slower development of a moso plantation (and runners generally).

The effect of the plant having to constantly produce large, long rhizomes over the whole growing area eventually causes the ground to become clogged with rhizomes no longer capable of producing many shoots. Because of this, moso plantations are deep-ripped to a depth of 700 mm in 6 m strips on a 20-year cycle and the ripped ground subjected to heavy nutrient and compost replacement. It takes about three years for each successive ripped area to recover full production.

There is substantial evidence that a well-run moso plantation can produce more than 10 tonnes of shoots/hectare/year (an extrapolation of most common overseas yield figures of 8 to 15 tonnes/hectare, with some claims that 20 tonnes/hectare/year is possible. All the shoots are harvested within eight weeks, the great majority within a peak period of about five weeks only (a much shorter harvest than the clumpers). Moso is, however, an alternatively high yield/low yield bearer each alternative year (Wu Liangru, Xiao Jinghua, 1997), and average productivity over many years must take into account its long establishment time and the 20-year reduction caused by yearly progressive ripping to maintain the forest's full productivity.

The shoots produced are generally between 75 mm and 125 mm diameter and weigh 1.5 kg average each, (6600 shoots per 10 tonnes), but apparently the Japanese prefer smaller earlier harvested moso shoots that weigh between 0.5 and 1 kg each. Early dug 'winter shoots' or shoots harvested from an immature plantation (leaving the larger ones to develop the plot) will be considerably smaller. Winter shoots, highly valued but small and expensive to harvest, are dug from well below ground level before they can be seen, and require very sensitive removal. These very early shoots have only recently begun to swell and are covered in a hard casing of yellow culm leaf, but have very tender meat and a special flavour (Fu Maoyi, 1997). The harvester judges that an early shoot is developing by observing that a adjacent culm is showing foliage stress, digs down beside it to locate the rhizome and digs along until reaching the shoot (the Chinese system described by Lou Yiping, 1997). Alternatively, the harvester looks for cracks in the ground after removing mulch, probes the crack with a 300 mm steel or bamboo spatula, and then digs up the shoot (the Japanese system described by Oshima Jinsaburo). If the rhizome is damaged, it causes the shoot crop to be reduced for up to three years into the future because of the reduced feed system available to younger rhizomes already produced by the damaged one. Because 70 per cent of moso rhizomes are between 300 and 700 mm beneath the surface (Fu Maoyi, 1997), I can't see harvesting winter shoots being viable in Australia because of the cost of harvesting them, but 'normal' moso shoots are certainly very viable.

When growing out of the ground and exposed to air, moso shoots become increasingly bitter which is why they are generally cut off underground not far from where they join the rhizome, mostly at a depth between 150 mm to 600 mm deep. They are dug out the minute the tip of the shoot becomes visible at ground level. Oshima Jinsaburo reports 'shoots that rise above the ground soon become dark and fibrous; the base becomes too tough to eat and the shoot loses its fresh fragrance'. The same reference indicates that moso rhizomes can be as deep as 1.2 m underground, but deep rhizomes produce inferior quality shoots, and fewer shoots than shallow rhizomes, therefore not worth harvesting.

Japanese moso farmers sometimes use straw mulch to keep the shoot from the light for a longer period, sometimes heaping soil on top, or even covering them with a box to increase the size of the shoot before harvesting. I am aware that sometimes shoots that project from the ground a little are harvested, but they are considered inferior in quality and bring a lesser price in both China and Japan. The very early winter shoots are from the rhizomes closest to the surface, and the last shoots of the season are often deeper and become unpalatable because of increasing seasonal bitterness.

A mature plantation of moso is a beautiful and awe-inspiring sight. The culms are between 80 mm and 160 mm diameter (usually 100 mm to 125 mm), up to 26 m in height and are without branches and leaves for the bottom 6 to 12 m. One can walk comfortably through the forest, as the culm spacing is maintained by selectively harvesting older culms to encourage vigorous shoot production.

In an efficient moso plantation run for edible shoots, the aging five- to seven-year-old, less vigorous culms are cut out at the rate of 250 to 350 culms/year to leave a fairly constant number of mature healthy culms (between 1600 to 2500 culms/hectare), giving a space of 2 to 2.5 m between each culm. The spacing depends on soil quality and growing conditions, the spacing being decreased to say 1.5 m x 1.5 m (4440 culms/hectare) in poor soil to produce more of the smaller diameter shoots.

In the efficient moso plantation run for timber rather than edible shoots (by the Research Institute at Fuyang, China), the culms are spaced at about 1.3 m x 1.3 m (5917 culms/hectare) and once mature, will yield between 900 and 1275 culms/year (about 37 tonnes of dried wood/year). In this scenario, the edible shoot yield is reduced to only 1.5 tonnes/year instead of 10 tonnes or more per year (Fu Maoyi, 1997). Timber is harvested from May to August (southern hemisphere). The tapered culms are very straight and decorative, with short furry velvet-like internodes, and without branch scars for a significant part of their lower larger diameter length, good saleable timber in spite of being structurally inferior to *Dendrocalamus asper* wood. Whilst being a relatively inferior structural bamboo mostly used for paper pulp and craft, moso culms are very straight, attractive and extremely useful. It is much valued in northern Asia for manufacturing hundreds of smaller objects from tea whisks to chopsticks, and it is used for structural work, particularly if harvested as old as seven years. One statistic gives average yields of about 7 tonnes/hectare/year for natural moso forests (about two-thirds of China's moso) and 20 to 30 tonnes/hectare/year for intensively run timber plantations (Shai Quantai, Yaorong and

Yongxi, 1985). The latter is about 75 per cent of the figure achieved in the Research Institute's own well-managed forest.

Professor Fu Maoyi of the Chinese Research Institute told me that moso is a gregariously flowering bamboo with a cycle of about 70 to 75 years. He said that moso seed is almost always available in small quantities from somewhere in China because there are many different genetic mutations or families amongst China's vast natural forests of moso (2.8 million hectares according to Yulong Ding's 1996 paper and 2.6 million according to Fu Maoyi). This means that it is flowering gregariously most of the time somewhere in China, each clone flowering in an area for about two years, and then usually dying. (See Chapter 4.) The earliest moso plants in Australia were grown from seed, mostly introduced in the 1980s; hence they will most likely flower some time near the year 2050, causing the destruction of the earlier (Australian) moso plantations.

Research into growing moso is being conducted by Central Queensland University (Rockhampton). Whilst some people claim that moso should be grown and will only grow in cool climates, it is growing successfully in some parts of Queensland, but only where there is plenty of non-rainy season winter irrigation available. As moso requires large amounts of water during late winter, it is much more suitable for growing in Australia's southern states. Moso, according to one Japanese authority (Oshima, 1937), 'is best grown in warm climates', but, as stated before, it is grown in plantation conditions where temperatures fall to -15°C in snow, etc. By local choice, the major plantation plantings in Taiwan and Southern China are clumping bamboos, like *Dendrocalamus latiflorus*, but moso is also grown domestically in the mountains of Taiwan to extend their fresh shoot season.

Dendrocalamus asper

Dendrocalamus asper is a magnificent, large-leafed, vertical giant bamboo with some cultivars capable of growing 30 m high and 30 cm diameter (but is not normally so large in a plantation). It is the major large structural bamboo of South-East Asia, a mature clump being a truly awesome sight with its large relatively straight lower culms climbing into dense large-leafed upper growth. It is one of the strongest and most researched bamboos in the world, much sought after in Asia for furniture making, large structures, plywood manufacture and even as reinforcing splits substituted for the steel in concrete.

It is best grown in warm or almost frost-free areas where the temperature never drops below -5°C, and where the natural rainfall is 1500 mm/year or more falling predominantly from December/January to May/June, which is the normal monsoonal pattern experienced in Queensland and the northern half of NSW. Unless a grower has huge amounts of irrigation water available to supplement what nature doesn't deliver, it is best not to

■ **21.J** Dendrocalamus asper *shoots on a two-year-old clump*

grow it in plantation quantities. Grow it for fun instead!

Whilst there are no mature plantations of *D. asper* in Australia yet (1999), three- and four-year-old examples of this species are performing in excess of our expectation on our property. Six-year-old examples in Taree and Bundaberg Department of Primary Industry indicate by their shoot production that they are capable of exceeding 10 tonnes/hectare/year in the right conditions and with the right management. At Bundaberg DPI in 1998, their six-year-old specimen had fifteen shoots in the first three months, without being encouraged to produce more by cutting shoots off, and with apparently little irrigation because of drought conditions and water shortage (15 shoots @ average 3 kg x 200 clumps/hectare equalling

9 000 kg/hectare/year without any increase from management practices).

Overseas-published productivity figures on all three bamboos tend to be confusing and need analysis before accepting them. PROSEA states: 'In Thailand, a properly managed plantation [of *D. asper*] may produce 10 tonnes to 11 tonnes of young shoots/hectare/year, and 'according to farmers in Indonesia, a good clump bearing about ten culms produces 60 young shoots annually. A well-managed plantation with 400 clumps/hectare may produce 20 tonnes of young shoots/hectare/year'. The same book also states that one Thai province yielded 37 975 tonnes of shoots from 446 hectares, averaging 8.7 tonnes/hectare over a planting which included some young and some badly run plantations. This makes it reasonable to assume that a properly run Thai plantation of *D. asper* can conservatively produce more than 10 tonnes of edible shoots/hectare/year (as with moso) plus at least 400 saleable culms that must be harvested each year to maintain the vigour of the plantation. That same Thai province had (1994) 28 factories processing 68 000 tonnes of fresh shoots each year which are exported, mainly to Japan, but all over the world including Australia. The recent final report of a three-year study by Kasetsart University, Bangkok, has one major study area producing 18.7 tonnes/hectare of shoots plus 23 tonnes of timber culms (dry weight) per hectare every year.

Thai scientists and growers have left me in no doubt that it is not difficult to exceed yields of 10 tonnes and considerably more (even 20 tonnes/hectare), however, it would be irresponsible at this stage to base cash flow studies on more than 10 000 kg/hectare/year.

I believe that the correct planting density for *D. asper* is no more than 200 plants/hectare (planted on a square

■ **21.I** *A young* Dendrocalamus asper *plantation in Thailand*

grid of about 7 m x 7 m). Any closer than that would make vehicle access difficult, and increase labour. Managed *D. asper* clumps can grow to about 3 m diameter across the base, or even a little more, which leaves 3 to 4 m tractor access. Seven by seven metres or eight by six metres is also the recommended spacing by Kasetsart University for their new plantings after recent studies of various spacings and yield figures. Remember that, whilst the rhizomes remain within the defined clumping circle, rarely more than two metres diameter, the roots radiate out great distances, and will easily meet competing roots from clumps seven metres away.

Thailand had 55 000 hectares of this species planted in 1994, specifically for shoot production; in 1998 the country was planting 35 000 hectares. Most of their production is tinned or eaten locally, but some is exported as fresh, fresh frozen, or steamed to Japan.

Dendrocalamus asper is a very fast-growing bamboo given reasonable conditions, good water, and some care. Within eighteen months of planting a young cutting we had propagated (it had a single culm less than 3 mm diameter), it produced three large shoots in its second shoot season, the largest being more than 120 mm diameter at ground level! We have both two- and three-year-olds on this property that have produced a number of shoots close to 300 mm diameter at the base. PROSEA advises, 'A clump becomes mature in three to four years', which seems to be in the process of being confirmed by the growth rates we get at Bamboo World and elsewhere. That does not mean, however, that maximum productivity harvesting can begin. The shoots and culms produced in the shoot season four years after planting out will normally reach the maximum diameter achievable on that particular site commensurate with the care you have given the plants. At three years old, you would be harvesting the smaller shoots and leaving the larger ones to ensure that you maximise the future multiplication of large shoots within the clump. This means you will get your first small crop when the plants are three years old. You should certainly get a reasonable but still not maximum crop during the fifth shoot season, and should be approaching or achieving about 10 000 kg/hectare/year from five-year-old plants, with maximum possible productivity from seven-year-olds.

These predicted yield projections for *D. asper* are at least three years, and up to five years faster than you can achieve from moso, based on the growth rates achieved for those particular species here at Bamboo World, and elsewhere in Australia and overseas.

Different *D. asper* cultivars in Thailand and Indonesia have distinctly different characteristics and shoots sizes, flavours, culm diameters and productivity, as the table below indicates.

It is absolutely critical that you plant the correct cultivar of this bamboo, or your plantation may be destroyed by a gregarious flowering cycle in the not-too-distant future (see notes later this chapter). The only cultivar that has gregariously flowered is pai tong keo (see above) which is unlikely to flower for 100 years or more. It also has some advantages over the other cultivars:

a) It produces shoots about one month earlier than the others.

b) It is considered the most productive for shoots.

c) It produces a range of smaller different size shoots between 1 and 4 kg. This may help marketing (large ones to restaurants and smaller, less expensive ones for the cautious housewife experimenting).

d) The timber is a little smaller in diameter, and it is capable of having a higher number and tonnage of timber culms than the other cultivars. The very large diameter timber produced by some cultivars may not be as useful as the 50 to 120 mm diameter culms produced by pai tong keo.

Pai tong dam has larger shoot and culms, and has a slightly better quality eating shoot, but the difference is small. All bag-grown D. *asper* shoots are of superior quality and can be eaten raw in a salad, or introduced into a

Species	Pai tong mo	Pai tong dam	Pai tong keo	Pai tong nu	Indonesian
Shoot weight	5 to 10 kg	3 to 6 kg	1 to 4 kg	1 to 3 kg	3 to 7 kg
Shoot colour	dark brown to purple	dark brown and shiny	black	dark brown and shiny	dark brown
Shoot flesh	white, sweet and coarse	white, sweet, fine and crisp	cream with minor fibre	white, sweet, fine and crisp	cream with minor fibre
Culm diameter	12 to 16 cm	9 to 12 cm	5 to 12 cm	3 to 6 cm	9 to 16 cm

recipe without pre-cooking. Pai tong keo was the most popular shoot species established in Thailand before the flowering death in 1994 (40 000 out of 54 000 hectares), and is certainly the cultivar being currently planted there now, with 35 000 hectares being planted this year alone. Because all the plants originate from seed (1994 to 1996), the 'sexual' reproduction will result in a variation in form and growth that may later need to be rationalised by selective interplanting to maximise productivity.

Dendrocalamus asper (bambu betung) normally grows in Indonesia at altitudes between 400 and 1500 m above sea level where it is quite a temperate climate. Lettuce and cool climate vegetables are grown in both the areas in Java and Bali where I saw bambu betung growing. It is well suited to clay soil, but also thrives in acid sandy loam in the tropical lowlands in Thai plantations (pai tong). As with moso, mature plantations produce two saleable crops each year, shoots and timber, both at different times. The maximum production in one large area of Thailand was achieved from pai tong keo, measured at 18.7 tonnes/hectare/year of edible shoots, and 23 tonnes of 12 per cent dried timber. A 10 tonnes/hectare/year shoot production, and a little more in timber each year, should certainly be achievable with reasonable management.

As with edible shoots of all species, only about half or sometimes even less of a shoot is edible. PROSEA says an average of about 38 per cent of a shoot is the edible portion, but this varies with both the cultivar and the way it is grown.

In Thai plantations, growers of high quality shoots cover them as they emerge from the ground with a black plastic planter bag stuffed with straw or rice husk (see Photo 21K). The shoot, isolated from light, grows longer, fatter and fuller, with a higher percentage of edible meat, a whiter colour, has a better, less fibrous texture, and is less astringent, if harvested at the right time.

When the shoot is tall enough to reach the top of the bag (and subject to the bag being the right height), it begins to lift the bag off the ground, indicating that the shoot is ready to harvest. The bag is removed (Photo 21L) and placed over another emerging shoot, which causes the plant to both transfer its energy towards fattening and growing the next emerging shoot, and towards producing a replacement shoot.

Shoots grown in a bag can be harvested in a pristine, clean condition (a little like the Tasmanian apples grown in paper bags). Post harvest only requires the slightly soiled end to be cut off cleanly in the packing shed for market presentation. In Thailand, some unscrupulous practices such as bleaching shoots not grown in bags to get higher prices occur, but the bleaches used are certainly unhealthy and would not be allowed by Western health authorities. Cooling harvested shoots to +2°C maximises fresh shelf life.

There are two other systems sometimes practised by Thai farmers to maximise shoot quality:

a) They sometimes use a tin of the correct height, with the top cut out. A tin is placed over the emerging shoot and is filled up with black carbonised rice husk. When the shoot begins to project from the filled tin, it is ready to harvest. I prefer the bag system because of its simplicity.

b) Some farmers cover the rhizome area with mulch about 500 mm deep so that the shoots have to grow through the mulch before they are ready to harvest. This is very similar to the system used by the Chinese for *D. latiflorus* and *B. oldhamii*, but it has its drawbacks. It causes the clump to climb out of the ground more quickly because all the rhizome necks reach upward, and it is hard to see the shoot size and position properly when choosing healthy appropriately located shoots to grow on into culms. Thai experts recommend that the mulching system should be used sparingly, certainly not more than each second year. (In Taiwan they also cover that mulch with black plastic to increase heat and humidity.) This extra layer of 500 mm deep mulch must be removed at the end of the shoot season or the next season's rhizomes will tend to climb upwards more quickly.

The above shoot cover mulch is quite separate to the mulching of rhizomes and surrounding root area that is part of the annual fertilising process described later.

The shoots are harvested by severing just below but very close to ground level (see Sketch 10.1 and Photo 10F), at a point beyond the bud line on rhizomes located either on or just below the ground's surface. The huge base diameter of *D. asper* shoots accounts for their great weight and size, sometimes up to 300 mm diameter for some cultivars. Shoots are harvested from each clump on about a three- to four-day cycle during warm weather, and a four- to six-day cycle during cooler weather, with more shoots being harvested during 'peak' harvest periods, which can vary with rainfall irregularities.

The tool used is the very light Thai harvesting spear shown in Sketch 10.2 and described in Chapter 10. The male version with the longer handle shown is just thrust into the shoot, whereas the female version has a shorter handle with an end knob that can be tapped by a wooden mallet.

The harvesting period for *D. asper* shoots is spread over six months or more (December to June in Australia) if the shoots are regularly harvested, and subject to there being enough rain or irrigation. Thailand's main shoot growing area has somewhat less than 2000 mm/year of monsoonal rain during a five-month period, commencing at the beginning of the shoot season (much longer than the short six- to eight-week shoot harvest of moso or other runners). If a *D. asper* plantation was being run to maximise timber production rather than edible shoots, the shooting season would be more akin to the natural cycle of the plant, which is, say, late December/January until early April (southern hemisphere), but not if the majority of shoots are removed. These bamboos gather energy to produce huge culms that are driven by the plant's internal reserves to within 90 per cent of full height within three months. The 3 to 5 kg shoot cut off only uses 10 per cent of the energy the plant expected to expend on driving that culm into the air. It will naturally replace the shoot with another to achieve its ambition, then another, etc. until it runs out of energy or is allowed to fulfill its ambition to have complete culms, not just shoots. In other words, harvesting shoots both extends the shoot season and increases the yield, and one shouldn't leave too many early shoots to grow on.

Researchers and growers separately advised me that, with off-season irrigation, it is possible to get a clumping bamboo to produce shoots all year around, obviously at a considerably reduced rate in the off-season, and only if the shoots are harvested. It is likely that these off-season

clumping shoots would be quite bitter, and not grow into mature culms if allowed to develop. Some of our clumping bamboos do develop shoots during winter despite low winter rainfall, but they don't grow on into culms.

I saw little evidence of irrigation, but was told (as I was by the Chinese about *D. latiflorus*) that it is possible to achieve much higher yields with irrigation, even as much as double. Some of the flat areas had a shallow central trench or depression (50 to 75 mm deep) between each second row of clumps, with side trenches running towards each bamboo (rather like a fish backbone) that could be flooded from a hose.

Most timber harvested in pai tong keo plantations is between 50 and 130 mm with some a little larger, giving an unusually large range. It is necessary to harvest timber (culms) each year, partly as good plantation management, and partly to sell as a second crop. To train your *D. asper* clump, follow the following procedure: .

■ **21.K** *A bagged* Dendrocalamus asper *shoot, obviously ready for harvesting because it is lifting the bag off the ground. This plantation of pai tong dam was planted more than 100 years ago and is still productive.*

(PHOTO: DR SONGKRAM THAMMINCHA)

■ **21.L** *Young shoots projecting from a rhizome. This plant should be mulched to a level close to the tops of the projecting shoots, and the shoots bagged as they emerge, but management is not always so conscientious.*

■ **21.M** *The shoot shown in Photo 21K with the bag removed*

■ **21.N** *The author holding that same shoot now harvested*

■ **21.O** *Harvested shoots and the tool used for harvesting*

(PHOTO: DR SONGKRAM THAMMINCHA)

■ **21.P** *The 100-year-old pai tong dam* D. asper *plantation*

- One year old—leave all culms.
- Two years old—cut off any very small culms.
- Three years old—You should have about ten to twelve culms of various sizes by now. Remove all inner shoots that appear. Leave large shoots at even intervals spaced around the outside of the clump, and harvest all other shoots, all small ones, and any that dry up. Keep about five to ten culms depending on the clump. Late winter to early spring of that year, cut off all the three-year-old culms above a node close above ground level.
- Four years old and each year thereafter—repeat the year three procedure, but building up to having eight to twelve culms in each clump depending on its vigour. You should have about the same number of one-year-old, two-year-old and three-year-old culms in each clump.

Using that system, all timber harvested should be at least three years old to avoid powder beetle. Earlier harvested wood should be treated with suspicion; however when the bamboo is seven years old, it should be possible to reliably harvest between two and four culms per year per clump (400 to 800 culms/hectare/year at a density of 200 clumps/hectare). In very old plantations that have grown out to about 3 m diameter (see Photos 21K, 21L, 21M, 21N, 21O, 21P of the 100-year-old Thai pai tong dam plantation), growers often leave more culms because an active culm is needed within a reasonable distance of emerging shoots to help feed them. This shoot management system appears to stress the plant, as plantation *D. aspers* tend to produce a percentage of slightly less vertical culms of reduced height and diameter than isolated clumps in a similarly shaded rainforest.

A *D. asper* culm, if allowed to grow on, draws substance from its abnormally large diameter shoot, actually shrinking the shoot as it grows, causing it to shrink back

■ **21.Q** Dendrocalamus latiflorus, *just four years old. In a plantation, this bamboo would have had all the smaller culms removed, and one would be harvesting edible shoots by now.*

from its culm leaves. This is quite different to *D. latiflorus*, moso and most other species where the shoot is the same diameter as the culm it produces.

Vehicle access between the clumps is possible during both harvesting periods, and for fertilising and mulching, and the plantation can be tractor slashed to control weeds during its development stage. The canopy and leafy mulch dropped by *asper* in a mature plantation tends to eliminate weeds, which are ploughed in once each year.

Dendrocalamus latiflorus

Dendrocalamus latiflorus is also a magnificent vertical giant bamboo, normally a little smaller than most cultivars of *D. asper*, capable of growing 25 m high with 20 cm diameter culms. It is also a major paper-making bamboo in China and Taiwan, and is used for building structures. A mature clump with its huge leaves forms one of the most beautiful plants one could see. The huge dark green leaves, up to 450 mm by 75 mm wide, are used to wrap and cook rice balls in Asia.

Taiwan has at least 90 000 hectares of this bamboo, and exports about 40 000 tonnes of bamboo shoots per year over and above their own very large consumption. PROSEA reports of *D. latiflorus* shoots: 'With 200–400 mature clumps per hectare, total annual yield averages 20–40 tonnes/hectare. In southern China young shoot yields per year average 12 tonnes/hectare but can be as high as 30 tonnes/hectare. Young shoots weighing 3 to 5 kg are harvested seven to 25 days after emergence, when they are 35–60 cm tall. Harvesting may start in the second year of growth of a clump.' Whilst not doubting the integrity of the authors who are no doubt putting forward information given to them, for me the above statistics seem unrealistically high and should be treated with caution. I think that a conservative summary of available data makes it reasonably safe to predict 10 tonnes/hectare/year, and anything higher in a country where we do not yet have established plantations is speculation. In ideal conditions it should reach 15 tonnes/hectare/year, like *D. asper*.

Having said that, the growth we are achieving on the *D. latiflorus* we have planted is nothing short of spectacular, with 7 m of growth and 50 mm diameter culms being produced only eighteen months after planting and 100 mm diameter culms appearing after three years (again like *D. asper*). Our plants appear to be growing as fast as those on trial in Darwin, Northern Territory, and Bundaberg, Queensland. The species is growing comfortably in New Zealand, and I am told it achieves spectacular growth and size planted close to the seaside in the most southerly part of Western Australia.

It has been difficult making a decision which species, *D. asper* or *D. latiflorus*, one should plant in our area, because both are well proven performers. Also on our property. *D. latiflorus* timber is marginally straighter than *asper*, but a little thinner walled and not quite as good as a structural bamboo. *D. latiflorus* produces a slightly more bitter shoot, but still high quality, and some people prefer bitter shoots (as the Vietnamese). Perhaps *latiflorus* statistics claim a slightly larger yield than *asper*, but I suspect that rainfall, growing conditions and management will influence yield more than species, but we will have to wait and see. We have planted 75 per cent *asper* and 25 per cent *latiflorus*, influenced partly by the cost per hectare of *D. latiflorus* plants being higher than *D. asper* because the recommended 6 m x 6 m *latiflorus* planting requires

■ **21.R** *An edible shoot from a mature* Dendrocalamus latiflorus *in China*

277 plants/hectare as against the recommended 7 m x 7 m *asper* planting requiring only 205 plants/hectare.

Dendrocalamus latiflorus shoots average 4 kg each (PROSEA), are about 120 to 200 mm diameter, and are basically the same diameter as the culms they produce. This is very different to *asper*, which produces larger shoots and smaller diameter culms when grown in plantation conditions.

Shoots are harvested on about a three- to five-day cycle from each clump during warm weather, and a five- to seven-day cycle during cooler weather, with more shoots being harvested during peak harvest periods, which vary with rainfall.

As with *D. asper*, vehicle access is possible between the clumps for slashing young plantations, and maintaining and working mature plantations.

When mature, *D. latiflorus* shoot plantations should provide about 500 culms/hectare/year, possibly even 800 (two or maybe up to four culms/clump/year x 270 clumps/hectare). They are strong, fairly straight, saleable quality timber culms, but not as thick-walled as *D. asper*. Mature young Chinese plantations I saw had between three and six culms per clump, depending on the vigour of that clump. This means that they would be harvesting only one or two culms per clump (280 to 560 culms/hectare/year), leaving the same number of shoots to grow on each year, and harvesting all other shoots. However, other written data from the Chinese forestry authorities indicates they leave about seven to eight culms in each mature culm, which makes more sense.

PROSEA has published spectacular timber (culm) productivity figures for *D. latiflorus* that should also be treated with the same caution I advised for shoots. PROSEA states: 'In the Philippines, a mature clump can produce 80 to 160 culms annually under ideal circumstances, but usually average production is 20 to 30 culms or 10 000 culms per hectare.' Such a figure seems extraordinarily high, and if possible would certainly only apply to a plantation being managed solely for timber and not for shoots. This bamboo is definitely a fast performer in the ground in our environment, and also in trials being conducted at Darwin. Nevertheless, to harvest 30 three-year-old culms in one year would mean that there were 30 two-year-old culms and 30 one-year-old culms also present in the clump, plus 30 extra young culms newly out of the ground for part of the year—that is, a total of 120 culms in a single clump! They describe culms as being 70 mm diameter and 15 m high as opposed to its maximum size of 200 mm diameter and 25 m high, which means they are pushing the plant to produce a large number of smaller diameter culms rather than harvesting edible shoots and a smaller number of larger culms (see later culm management comments). These spectacular claims would also involve intensive cultivation, with closer spacing making it impossible to use a tractor in the plantation. Most young plantings I saw were 6 m x 6 m, with some older ones at 5 m x 5 m spacing.

Dendrocalamus latiflorus is also best grown in warm or almost frost free areas where the temperature never drops below -4°C, with a rainfall or irrigation water availability of 1500 mm or more mostly available in late summer through to winter. In China it is grown mainly in the provinces of Guangdong, Fujian and Guangxi. I was told that they have 'more than 310 days each year without frost', which sounds pretty cool to me, and that 'frost causes minor damage but it is not important'. With a mean temperature of 12°C in January (northern hemisphere), the areas where I have seen *D. latiflorus* plantations grown would have a lower average winter ambient temperature than the *D. asper* plantations in Thailand. That, however, may not be important as they are certainly both performing well here (*D. asper* also grows up to 1500 meres above sea level in some places).

Rainfall in the Chinese planting areas is between 1700 and 2200 mm per year, with the major rain falling from March to October and coinciding with their northern hemisphere harvest season from late May to late October (with the harvest peaking July/August). I was told that they don't normally irrigate but that 'it would double the harvest if you did!' Note that the rainfall requirements are high and almost monsoonal in pattern. Unless massive irrigation is available, it would be difficult to get high yield crops in areas where winter rainfall prevailed.

One Chinese text I have says '*Latiflorus* needs rich and loose soil to grow in and should be planted at the lower part of the hill slope or beside a village'. One plantation I saw growing well was halfway up a hill, in rather poor-looking, sandy loam, but doing well (and not near a village).

No doubt it will do better in a damp, cool environment, found more often near the bottom of valleys that up the top, but check the frost level.

The Chinese cover their emerging shoots with mulch to exclude light and cut the shoot off where it changes into fibrous rhizome (See Sketch 10.1). They prefer this cut point to be about 150 to 200 mm below ground level. As the shoots are usually about 600 mm high, they are projecting about 450 mm. Most of this the Chinese prefer to keep mulch covered. Their mulch covering technique is quite different to the Thai system of covering the emerging shoot with a straw filled plastic bag to achieve the same effect. I prefer the Thai system, and we will be experimenting with trying to apply it to *D. latiflorus*. The Thais also don't dig up and rebury an offset deeper in the ground as the Chinese do (see later details) but content themselves with a little mulching to keep roots and rhizomes cool and damp, and use the bag instead of heaped mulch to totally exclude light from the growing shoot. Shoots used to produce dried product are allowed to grow 1 m tall and weigh up to 30 kg after harvesting (only 10 kg reclaimable), so I don't think they keep them totally buried in mulch. They clear the loose mulch and dirt from around the shoot and cut the shoot just beyond the rhizome with a short cutting knife.

The Chinese have developed more elaborate systems than the Thais for controlling the tendency of bamboos to climb out of the ground as they grow older. This phenomenon occurs because the shoot buds are all located in the side of each rhizome, causing each new rhizome and shoot to be higher than its 'mother'. One

■ **21.5** *A four-year-old* Dendrocalamus latiflorus *plantation in China during the dormant period*

knowledgeable researcher explained that they dig out about 25 per cent of the rhizomes in a clump in one quarter when the clump is ten to twelve years old, and replant an offset deeper in the ground. This has the effect of re-establishing a portion of the clump deeper, with its shoots starting deeper in the ground than the older plant section, which by that age has its rhizomes close to or projecting from the ground, and its shoots exposed to light earlier than when it was younger.

I also have a text on *latiflorus* explaining that in the sixth year after planting, three to four new shoots are grown on as mother culms. In the seventh, eighth, and ninth year 'only shoots are harvested' implying that all shoots are harvested, and none are allowed to grow on into culms. In the tenth year, three or four new mother culms are allowed to grow on, and all other shoots are harvested. Later that year, timber is harvested that is still in the clump from before the sixth year; the rhizomes as well as the culms are dug and removed.

At this stage you are left with seven or eight mother culms, which will be replaced by allowing four shoots to grow on every four years, and harvesting and digging out the culms and rhizomes produced four years earlier (harvested later than the shoots, that year). In effect this process is saying that you would only harvest culms for sale every four years, and all other shoots produced would be harvested, and each time you harvest a culm (four every fourth year) you would also dig out that rhizome! It is certainly an elaborate system by comparison to the very laid-back Thai procedure. I have not seen it in practice, but as it is described in a document produced by a Chinese provincial authority. I intend experimenting on some individual mature clumps to compare the result with a more conventional system.

Dendrocalamus latiflorus is considered to be a sporadically flowering bamboo, and it does require a specific handling technique to handle this flowering phenomenon, described later this chapter.

Other Species

Bambusa edulus (not to be confused with Taiwan's plantings of *Phyllostachys edulus*, moso) is grown in smaller plantations in Taiwan, and *Dendrocalamopsis beecheyana*, *Dendrocalamus hamiltonii* and *D. brandisii* in smaller plantations in southern China, but no production figures are available. Those species are currently unobtainable in plantation quantities in Australia. The first two we have growing and under observation. *D. brandisii* is a much slower performer in our environment.

Bambusa oldhamii is grown in plantations in Fujian Province in China (Lin Qingyi, undated paper), where there are about five million established plants (at 4 m x 4 m planting, this equates to about 8000 hectares, a very small area compared to the 'big three'). It produces high

■ **21.1** Guadua angustifolia, *a South American bamboo, with much potential as a timber plantation species*

quality eating shoots (confirmed by the shoots we eat every year from our twelve-year-old clump), but unfortunately they only weigh between 0.25 and 0.5 kg each, and will only produce maybe 6 tonnes/hectare/year, about half the shoot yield of either moso, *D. asper* or *D. latiflorus*.

B. oldhamii has an advantage for growers in colder climates because it will tolerate temperatures down to –9°C, and, being a clumping bamboo, will mature much more quickly than moso (four to five years to a full crop). It has none of the disadvantages of moso (or runners) and most of the advantages of the clumpers. The timber is straight, saleable, and suitable for furniture, but is not a good structural bamboo because of its thinner light walls. Remember that it still requires its main water volume late summer and early winter (similar to monsoonal areas).

The latest Chinese taxonomical publication, *A Compendium of Chinese Bamboo,* appears to have reclassified *Bambusa oldhamii* as a *Dendrocalamopsis* genus. I'm not surprised, as I think the bamboo looks more like a *Dendrocalamus* genus than a *Bambusa*.

Lin Qingyi's undated but fairly recent paper states: 'Annual shoot yielding could reach 5 to 6 tonnes/hectare, even surpass 8 tonnes/hectare if cultured and managed very well. The increments of *Dendrocalamopsis oldhamii* and its shoots increase along with temperature, relative humidity and precipitation.'

His references to yield become confusing because in another part of the paper he says 'bamboo shoot yielding reached 12–15/hectare, the highest one was more than 100 kg per clump (600 clumps/hectare)'. My estimate of 6 tonnes/hectare/year is based on observations of the species growing here, plus the fact that, whereas *D. asper* only has to produce 2000 to 4000 shoots, or 10 to 20 shoots/clump averaging between 2.5 to 5 kg to reach 10 tonnes/hectare/year, *B. oldhamii* would need to produce 20 000 to 40 000 shoots, or 32 to 64 shoots/clump at 0.25 to 0.5 kg each to yield the same crop. Unlikely!

The NTDPIF Research Station is removing its *B. oldhamii* because of lack of performance. Mulch is heaped over the emerging shoot, to protect it from sunlight causing bitterness. Being a small (0.3 kg) shoot, its harvesting labour would also be higher than *D. asper* or *D. latiflorus*. With so many small shoots, the Thai bag-growing system would not be possible. Plant spacing recommended is 4 m x 4 m, or 625 plants/hectare, which makes it more expensive to plant than *D. asper* (only 200 plants). Vehicle access for small tractors may be possible at that spacing. Our twelve-year-old *B. oldhamii* has a 3 m clump diameter, but management techniques should restrict it to about 2 m diameter, leaving 3 m access, a bit close for my liking.

Bambusa oldhamii is a beautiful, vigorous bamboo, and I am not discouraging the idea of establishing plantations in Australia, particularly as it is so cold-tolerant; however, if you invest in a *B. oldhamii* plantation, you should be aware of its probable productivity limitations. Research has been conducted into an existing *B. oldhamii* plantation by Central Queensland University, Rockhampton, but the yields they recorded are not impressive.

Clump Management— Edible Shoot versus Timber

Some species are very suitable for high quality timber production but less suitable for edible shoot production, either because the shoots are too bitter for popular consumption (*Bambusa tuldoides* and *Gigantochloa apus*), or because their smaller but delicious shoots make that species less productive than the three main shoot production species ⸱(*Thyrsostachys siamensis, Bambusa nana,* oand *Gigantochloa albociliata*). In such cases the clumps may be more economically viable and valuable to you if managed for timber production, with few shoots being harvested, and more culms left standing until they are harvested when aged three. *Guadua angustifolia* and the even larger *G. chacoensis* are examples of plantation bamboos grown only for their wonderful timber.

Harvested culms are normally cut off just above

■ **21.U** *A young* Dendrocalamus latiflorus *shoot being allowed to grow on*

ground level just above a node, to minimise the moisture pocket and the possible damage to the remaining rhizome (which can still produce shoots). Cut them early in the dry season after the new young culms have reached close to full height and are starting to develop top leaf and branch growth.

To encourage large diameter, the smaller culms should always be removed, leaving the largest, which in turn tend to produce the larger sized shoots. Nevertheless, the practice of leaving more culms for timber harvesting may tend to reduce the average diameter of the culms. Remember that just before harvesting, your clump will be carrying four generations of culms; the newly arrived three- to four-month-old youngsters, followed by the one- and two-year-old maturing culms, and the about-to-be harvested three-year-old culms. Each new culm should be marked (with a marking pen) with the year it appeared, for aging.

Within reason, the more smaller shoots you take, the fewer new culms the clump will have to feed, and the larger will be the average diameter of the future culms. If you want larger diameter timber, reduce (sacrifice) the number of culms you will have available to sell in order to increase their diameter, removing the smaller shoots or those likely to cause overcrowding or congestion.

The three major shoot producers, moso, *Dendrocalamus asper* and *D. latiflorus,* can all be managed to maximise either edible shoot production or timber production, but it's not possible to achieve both goals at once. By taking more shoots and leaving only a reasonable geographic distribution of large healthy shoots each year to grow into large culms that will feed and photosynthesise for the clump, there will be fewer culms available each year for harvest. There will be a greater number of larger diameter shoots appearing available for harvest each year. The clump will try to redress the imbalance.

The principle of the harvest system described earlier for *D. asper* should be applied with minor adjustments to all species, even to running bamboos like moso, where the active culms are mostly not harvested until they are about seven years old in a shoot plantation or five years old in a timber plantation. Clumping bamboo culms are usually harvested when they are three years old, but one text on *D. latiflorus* harvests only every four years. A defined number of culms per hectare is maintained to maximise shoot production. The number of culms is varied to suit the quality of the soil and the level of care being practised. The better the soil, the fewer number of culms, all of the larger diameter being retained, and the greater the number and diameter of the shoots produced. With clumping bamboos the clump spacing chosen also becomes part of that management formula. A well managed shoot plantation will produce a little more dried weight (12 per cent water) timber tonnage each year than it does shoots. Reduce the shoot harvest to 10 per cent and you will more than double the timber harvest.

Soil and Growing Conditions

It is important to know that, while most clumping bamboos will grow satisfactorily in quite low rainfall areas, for plantations you need to be in an area where major rainfall comes from midsummer to midwinter (monsoonal) for clumpers, and midwinter to midsummer for runners like moso. This will achieve fast growth and high production. In fact it also helps to have some rain at other times, particularly for moso as the rhizome system is still growing after midsummer for a short time until it reaches its dormant period (beginning about mid-March here). For clumpers, if your rainfall is normally very low before and during the shoot harvesting period (such as in Perth, Western Australia or in Victoria or South Australia) don't attempt to grow them in plantation quantities unless you have river sourced irrigation available because the size of the dam you need is impractically large during the period.

China's moso is often grown in poor soil, usually considered worthless for other crops, mostly clay loam and sometimes sandy loam, but avoid gravel patches as the shoots will be hard to dig up. Clumping bamboos generally prefer heavier clay soil, but bamboo will thrive in a variety of soils if properly mulched and fertilised. In Thailand, *Dendrocalamus asper* plantations are often in fairly acid, sandy soil over a base of clay. Bamboo will not grow successfully in a swamp but most species, including the above, will thrive where there is a good supply of water. This includes situations where there is a water table not far below the surface. Being a very tough plant, it will generally survive even in poor soil with occasional droughts, but the effect is to 'bonsai' the plant and reduce productivity.

Shoot plantations will need irrigation, or a ground water supply under dry conditions, plus fertiliser and mulch to reach the production levels indicated possible.

With moso, for ease of plantation handling, the Japanese say 'a slope of 15 degrees or less is preferred' (Oshima Jinsaburo, 1937). In China it grows naturally on steep mountainsides. With clumping bamboos where vehicle access is possible, the slope would be limited primarily by the ability of the vehicle to service the sloping plantation. There may be some 'cliff effect' from downhill rhizomes climbing out of the ground, offset by uphill rhizomes happily climbing into the ground, which may cause a slight reduction in productivity.

If your climate is warm (a minimum yearly temperature of 10°C) clumping bamboos can be planted at any time of the year subject to them being watered throughout any dry periods. Though our winter temperatures get down to 1°C, we find that by planting clumping bamboos even in midwinter, strong young plants accelerate their growth when planted out if they are strong enough to establish rapid feeder root systems to support leaf growth. They are then capable of even more vigour in the summer shoot season. If you are planting in a frost prone area, wait until the last frost has gone before planting because the plant will grow faster in the nursery subject to the pot being big enough. Clumping bamboos are much faster growing during the establishment period than running bamboos (see earlier comments).

Established plantations tend to suppress weed growth to a great degree, but in the establishment stages some weed control is necessary. Slashing is easy with clumping bamboos because the location of the shoots and rhizomes is predictable; however, slashing in a moso plantation damages underground rhizomes, young buds and shoots. We keep weeds down in the developing moso plantation with a brush cutter and heavy mower, but it is expensive, and it takes years to develop a canopy. Spraying before planting to get rid of weeds and planting a legume cover will help. Spraying with herbicides after planting is not advisable because of potential damage to the bamboo, which is a relative of the grass you are trying to eradicate.

Fertiliser and Techniques

Whilst it is better to feed your decorative bamboos smaller frequent applications of fertiliser rather than annual applications, this is not so with edible shoot plantation bamboos. Fertiliser application during the shoot season causes soft-textured darker coloured shoots lacking the crisp texture so valued, and such shoots discolour and bruise easily. It also causes large inferior shoots to develop with excessive culm leaf content and reduced edible flesh.

In terms of total fertiliser requirements, the different

species grown in different countries all have about the same amount applied. Total nitrogen applied is about 450 to 500 kilograms/hectare/year, with one comment that it can be as high as 600 kilograms/hectare/year applied on some intensively cultivated moso plantations in China.

The Thais apply their 450 to 500 kg of total nitrogen in the following manner and form. (*D. asper*)

a) In October (two to three months before the shoot season) they rip 200 mm deep down and across both sides of each row, isolating each clump inside a ripped square about 1 to 1.5 metres outside the rhizome circle. They then distribute between 6 and 9 tonnes of manure or compost (3 per cent nitrogen) per hectare, *plus* between 420 and 840 kg of 15:15:15 NPK fertiliser partly into the trench thoroughly mixed with mulch, and the remainder is scattered completely over the ground area surrounding the clumps (not inside the ripped square). They then disc plow the complete area outside that ripped square to a depth of about 150 mm, thereby plowing in the fertiliser and the heavy leaf deposit that would have recently dropped during the dormant period, and destroying and mulching the surface roots.

b) About four weeks later, in November (one month before shoots are about to appear), they distribute between 1 and 2 kg per clump (200 to 400 kilograms/hectare) of urea (40:0:0) or 16:20:0 NPK fertiliser inside the ripped area, throwing part of it onto the old cut off rhizome area in the centre of the clump. This has the effect of causing shoots to appear up to four weeks earlier than they otherwise would. In the case of pai tong keo, they appear one month earlier than other cultivars, and can be persuaded to shoot just as far into winter as other cultivars, thus giving them a slightly longer shoot season.

The above information came from two booklets compiled by the Thai government as recommendations to growers, translated into English by Dr Songkram Thammincha, Thailand's foremost researcher and expert on *D. asper* plantations. One of those booklets also advocated the additional cautious progressive application of one kg per clump of both 13:13:21 NPK and 46:0:0 urea divided into small increments over the whole shoot season.

The Chinese and Thai systems are different because the Chinese use the deep mulch system described for *D. latiflorus*. I prefer the Thai bagging system because it does not encourage the new rhizomes to climb out of the ground so quickly. The above fertiliser application system is relevant to that Thai practice. The mulch inside the ripped area is built up to a level close to, but not above the tops of, the rhizomes; to a level above the rhizome buds where the new shoots will appear, but not deeper.

In highly acid soils, lime will increase productivity, although they grow happily in our 5.2 pH soil, and I know of bamboos thriving in soil with a pH of 4.5.

PROSEA has various fertiliser recommendations, usually containing potash, nitrogen and phosphorus; but the recommendations are much lower than that used in practice in Thailand. A very low application of silica is said to be helpful, particularly in timber plantations, but it can cause fibrous shoots to develop in edible shoot plantations. Bamboos are essentially shallow-rooted surface feeders and heavy applications of urea can damage or kill the plant.

Over-fertilising is a waste of money and an environmental hazard unless the water is available to enable the plant can use it. I favour the Thai's partly or substantially organic feed system, which will depend on your philosophy and what organic fertiliser is economically available in your area. I suspect that constant exclusive use of chemical fertiliser will damage the plant and soil.

There is some concern about contamination of vegetables grown with organic fertilisers such as manure, but by applying it only well outside the rhizome system as the Thais do, it may be possible to avoid that problem.

Plant Cycle and Flowering Death

Understanding this phenomenon is *very* important if you are planting bamboo in plantation quantities! You should first read Chapter 4, and then read how this affects the particular plantation species.

Dendrocalamus asper is a gregariously flowering bamboo. In 1994 one of the cultivars of *D. asper* flowered in Thailand, absolutely devastating their massive shoot plantation system (in fact a Laos cultivar did the same thing two years earlier).

The death of 40 000 hectares of plantation bamboos and the decline in shoot production is estimated to have cost Thailand an US$80 million loss in the first year with a continuing reducing loss each year as their production is re-established. The Thai government invested US$40 million in rescue, research and re-establishment to ensure that this does not happen again (Thammincha, 1995).

Prior to this 1994 flowering *D. asper* was considered to be a sporadically flowering species not at risk from death by flowering. Quoting a Thai university paper by S. Thammincha, 1995: 'It is beyond expectation that the flowering behaviour of *D. asper* is of gregarious type, since only few of this individual species have been in flower sporadically during the late 1980s. *D. asper* was brought to Thailand without genetic descriptions. For nearly a century, people have enjoyed the wealth of this species.'

It is absolutely critical that anyone contemplating commercial plantings of *D. asper* ensures that the stock they plant comes from those Thai *D. asper* clones that recently flowered (called pai tong keo, or *D. asper* 'Green' by the Thais. That precaution should ensure a plantation life without flowering damage for perhaps 100 years or more.

There is definitely more than one cultivar of *D. asper* as listed earlier. It is on record that only 70 per cent of the Thai plantation *D. asper* flowered (S. Thammincha, 1995). The remaining 30 per cent were from the other three or four Thai cultivars, together with two Indonesian clones that definitely did not flower. Those remaining clones, known as pai tong dam, pai tong lai, pai tong nu, pai tong mo from Thailand, plus bambu betung and betung hitam from Indonesia, are all likely to flower at any time in the not-too-distant future. Some of the clones that have not flowered are available in Australia, and it is not possible to confidently identify the difference, so be careful. Even vegetative cuttings from those plants will not avoid the gregarious flowering when it arrives.

Available records indicate that *D. latiflorus* is a sporadically flowering bamboo, with records going back more than 100 years. It is not expected to create a disaster by flowering and dying gregariously in an Australian plantation, however dealing with its flowering habit requires a management system you should know. In Chinese plantations, about six to eight per cent of *D. latiflorus* clumps produce flowers on one or more culms dedicated to flowering on about a four- to six-year cycle. Those clumps will not produce saleable shoots that year, causing about a six to eight per cent reduction in yield in those years that the flowering occurs. Those few dedicated culms are cut off to help the bamboo to produce a normal shoot crop the fol-

lowing year. Being a sporadic flowerer, most of the seeds produced are non-viable, but a small percentage are viable if you leave the culm for long enough to develop viable seeds and you look hard enough.

Moso is a gregariously flowering bamboo with a 70 to 75 year cycle, but with many mutant clones, and it is often flowering in different parts of China with consequential damage to plantations or forests. The moso available in Australia has all been developed from seed, the first being introduced in the 1980s, and since then from later seedlings. The plant is therefore unlikely to gregariously flower in Australia before about year 2050.

Establishment Costs, Operating Cost and Potential Income Comments

Our plantations of all three species are too young yet to allow us to calculate accurate harvesting man-hours. We have, however, been harvesting shoots and timber from individual mature bamboo clumps for some years. Statistics for man-hours for Australian conditions (or even for Asian countries for that matter) are not available, but we believe that labour costs per kilo will be low compared to most crops. This is the case particularly for the clumping bamboos with their readily accessible larger shoots, and tractor access for fertilising and harvesting of both shoots and culms. Even if you assume one could only cut

■ **21.V** *Young* Dendrocalamus asper *plants in the on-site nursery of a 40-hectare plantation being established in northern NSW, Australia*

off one shoot every two minutes (which seems excessive for the clumping bamboos), a 10 tonne crop of average 4 kg *D. latiflorus* shoots, that is 2500 shoots, could be harvested in about two weeks by one person. As the shoots are produced over a period of five to six months, one person should be able to harvest about 4 hectares without hired help without having to harvest every day.

The cost of harvesting moso shoots will obviously be somewhat more than *D. asper* or *D. latiflorus* because moso shoots are dug from underground, and within a peak five-week harvest period involving three times the number of shoots (1.5 kg versus 4 kg). However, I am confident that the costs should still be moderate compared with the income. (That applies to any of the three main species.) The author has no reliable moso harvest times available. If one accepts the disadvantages of moso and also plants that species (we have a small moso forest), you will be able to harvest a spring time moso harvest, and the summertime *D. asper/D. latiflorus* harvest. A single person could then handle more hectares again without hired labour.

In Australia (1998), the first year's costs for establishing one hectare of *D. asper* including plants @ A$6000/hectare, drip irrigation parts, bulldozer or tractor hire, mulch and fertiliser are approximately A$6900, not including labour, which should be between 150 and 200 hours/hectare, and not including land cost. The yearly expenditure (fertiliser, mulch, tractor fuel) will vary between $600/year/hectare for the second year climbing to about $1300/year/hectare from about the fifth year onwards and about 270 to 300 man-hours/hectare/year, with a one-off capital cost extra of about $2200 plus 40 hours labour to install a larger irrigation system. Labour estimates include fertilising, mulching, timber harvest,

■ **21.X** *A young* Dendrocalamus asper *being inspected by Dr Songkram Thammincha and the author in Thailand. This is typical of the growth experienced during the second twelve months after planting, the new tall culms projecting through the shorter bushy growth of the first twelve months.*

shoot harvest, weeding, general inspection and slashing when younger. The harvest times are estimates only, based on our own experiences with our display bamboos, as our plantations are not yet mature (1998), but the major establishment costs are reasonably accurate, being the costs per hectare we are paying to establish our own plantations (1997/8) and the actual plant costs.

The first year establishment cost of species other than *D. asper* for the plants only in 1988 is: A$8200 for *D. latiflorus* planted 6 m x 6 m, A$9375 for moso planted 4 m x 4 m or A$16 666 planted 3 m x 3 m, and $9375 for the less productive *Bambusa oldhamii*. The differences are caused by both the cost per plant and the increased number of plants/hectare required. One should also allow extra for the lower expected survival rate and replacement cost of the bare rooted *B. oldhamii* plants or newly dug moso rhizome cuttings and the extra man-hours for planting and maintaining the individual plants. Rooted potted plants like *D. asper* and *D. latiflorus* have a more than 98 per cent survival rate, whereas the best ever survival rate we had with our three dug moso rhizome offsets was 70 per cent. I would estimate bare rooted *B. oldhamii* plants' survival rate to be between 80 and 90 per cent depending on plant size and handling; otherwise *B. oldhamii* rooted plants can be obtained for about $25 x 625 = $15 625, very costly per hectare.

■ **21.W** *The first tissue-cultured bamboo produced in Australia* (Dendrocalamus asper). *Note the tight clumping form with many small culms and a height of 700 to 900 mm, which is the typical growth experienced during the first 12 months after planting.*

Judging by the growth of these species in our environment, and overseas data, my feeling is that a *D. asper* or *D. latiflorus* plantation three, four, five, six, and seven years old will have a crop volume of 2.4, 5.4, 9, and 10+ tonnes/hectare respectively. These are conservatively credible figures on information available for a well-run plantation. The first small timber income would contribute during the sixth year, with a full timber crop or more than ten tonnes per hectare from the seventh or eighth year. If, and this is pure speculation, one received $4.00/kg for fresh shoots, the first small income available when three years old would grow each year to approximately $40 000 gross plus timber sales in the sixth year, growing to approximately $50 000 or more gross/hectare/year from the seventh year onwards. One can only speculate and try to be conservative with the data available, but if it is only half as good, it is still extremely profitable. A *B. oldhamii* plantation will develop its first crop just as quickly and in similar volume as the latter two, but its year by year increase will be less until it reaches a peak of about 6 tonnes/hectare/year. Moso will be much slower to produce crops and increases, its yield increase spread out from a first small crop from four- or five-year-olds to a full crop in year eight to ten depending on site conditions and management.

If land is not a factor, the major cost is the one-off establishment costs for plants, preparation and labour, which we believe would be more than covered by the return from the first mature crop, or even the return from the earlier young crops. In a mature plantation, it is more than likely that the sale price of the timber culms alone will more than pay for the running costs of the plantation.

Availability of Planting Stock

Because bamboo normally has to be vegetatively propagated, we realised some years ago that it would take many years to propagate sufficient plant numbers to establish our own plantations, let alone enough to establish a small industry. As a result, we invested in a large quarantine house and heavy costs to import *Dendrocalamus asper* and *D. latiflorus* in sufficient numbers to establish our plantations and some others (we lost more than 8000 plants in 1997/98 because of the fumigation process they are subjected to on arrival in Australia). We also invested some years of energy in learning and establishing tissue culture techniques, including the acquisition of a laboratory of our own. Bamboo World has the correct clones of these plants available now in plantation quantities. The imported plants, fortunately, we no longer need to bring into the country because our tissue-cultured plants are taking over from imported stock.

It is possible for a grower to start small by planting a few of the right species, and propagating from those plants beginning when they are about three years old onwards. You can generate new plants at the rate of ten plants or more from each three-year-old clump, without slowing the growth of those already planted. Bamboo World teaches people the specific techniques for propagating those species, and are also consulting, establishing and managing plantations for others.

Moso plantations are usually established by rhizome cuttings with an attached culm, unless seedlings are available. We have tried both advanced seedlings and rhizome cuttings and both appear to be equally slow in their initial establishment times. Rhizome cuttings are available for about A$1500/100 plants and more for seedlings. Our success rates varied between 40 per cent and 70 per cent respectively with rhizome cuttings planted in the autumn or spring. One researcher advised that he favoured young rhizomes with small culms attached, dug in winter before the shoot season, because those rhizomes, whilst having fragile shoots, are more likely to produce culms that year, and new rhizomes within six months, than offsets dug after the shoot season late spring. Japanese literature seems to favour autumn plantings but our late spring plantings were more successful. Advanced seedlings look smaller and are more expensive, but they gave us a 100 per cent success rate.

Bambusa oldhamii plants are readily available, and fairly easy, if somewhat bulky, to propagate once you have established a few two- or three-year-old clumps.

Concluding Comments

If you are growing *Dendrocalamus asper* or *D. latiflorus* in this country, there appears to be nothing that will require chemical spraying in Australia. There are pests and diseases overseas that require spraying, but they are considered a minor problem in those countries (see Chapter 22 for pests and diseases).

By March 1999 there will be only 150 hectares of *D. asper* and *D. latiflorus* planted in Australia, a long way short of enough to satisfy the potential Australian market, and a 'drop in the bucket' when compared to the export potential of any of the major producers northern season plantings.

The above data on current tinned and fresh selling prices, existing plantation sizes, locations, productivity and species has been assembled with the view to allowing potential growers to make their own educated evaluations and predictions with respect to profitability, costs and labour. Meanwhile, we are busy planting.

Good luck and good thinking!

22 Pests, Diseases, Problems

As a general statement, living sympodial bamboos appear to be free of significant disease here in Australia and normally do not require a spraying program. I have certainly not seen or heard of any sign of a problem on either *D. asper* or *D. latiflorus.*

I have seen heavy infestations of leaf scale on running bamboos, and they are also prone to leaf mite, but those pests don't seem to be attracted to many of the adjacent clumping bamboos except the genus *Fargesia*, and *Bambusa tuldoides,* which always seems to carry the pest without it seeming to affect performance during the growth season. These wax scales may become a problem for moso, but at this stage there is no evidence of this happening on the more mature healthy plants.

I have occasionally seen an insignificant waxy leaf scale on *B. tuldoides* and on some of the smaller cold climate bamboos (*Fargesia* and *Thamnocalamus* genera). Another wax scale insect is almost always present on the culms of some species—mainly *Bambusa balcooa* and *B. oldhamii* (but not on *Dendrocalamus asper* or *D. latiflorus*)—and even then seems to have no effect on the plant.

North of Rockhampton I have seen leaf roller fairly active on clumping bamboos grown in a more or less monoculture situation (in the Cairns area), but I don't know at this point whether this would affect plantation production, and it doesn't appear to be a problem further south. Early experiments on about fifteen different bamboo species in Darwin indicate that leaf roller may be a problem, but less so with large-leafed species because the insect finds the leaves too big to roll as a refuge. It is too soon to know whether this may develop into a problem in northern Australia, but in China the growers do spray for leaf roller on the smaller leafed *Bambusa oldhamii* (not on *D. latiflorus*).

In Darwin they also have both soft scale and clear scale on leaf and culms on some species, particularly *B. oldhamii*, but again not such a problem on *D. latiflorus* or *D. asper*. The experimental plots at Darwin are too young to assess whether these pests will have any detrimental effect on future plantations in that area, or whether control spraying will be necessary.

Bamboo mealybug is present in Australia. It forms an ugly black sooty scale in symbiotic existence with a white wax insect and small black ants attracted by the sugar. It attacks a very few decorative species of small-leafed *Bambusa* genus, mainly *O. multiplex* (also *B. longispiculata*, *B. malingensis* and sometimes *B. textilis*—mostly cold-tolerant Chinese species). The control for this persistent pest needs to be repeated to kill successive generations. Use Rogor two weeks apart and then a high pressure hose to remove dead fungus.

Bamboo mosaic disease, a viral infection apparently spread by leaf contact, exists in Australia, and has for many years according to quarantine authorities. Some bamboo species in Australia (and the same species overseas) are known to have the problem (*Gigantochloa ridleyi*, *Dendrocalamus beecheyana*, and *D. latiflorus* cv. 'Mei Nung', a decorative cultivar of the plantation bamboo). These bamboos normally show no signs of having the disease, and seem to grow quite happily in various parts of Australia. PROSEA comments: 'Mosaic virus (BoMV) is another important disease attacking leaves, shoots and culms. It causes shoots to harden, resulting in poor quality for consumption and canning.' In the absence of more comprehensive information, growers would be well-advised to minimise contact between their plants and outside material, but there is no sign that the virus is present in any of the 'big three' species, or *B. oldhamii*.

There are a limited number of insect and fungal problems existing in various Asian countries that can cause damage to living plants, but they are not presently active in Australia. Hopefully quarantine regulations will manage to keep them at bay.

Most bamboos don't suffer from this problem, but some large untended bamboos, particularly *Bambusa balcooa*, build up dead wood and trapped leaf mulch, and become a fire hazard. If the dead wood is removed annually, or better still, if the aging culms are harvested before they die and the shoots are thinned, bamboo doesn't become a fire hazard. The high moisture content of younger live culms causes them to produce enough steam to dampen a fire's enthusiasm. We have had major fires sweep past or through three of our bamboos, leaving most of the culms and the rhizome system undamaged. If the leaves are dense, they are moisture laden. If conditions are dry, many would have fallen off and are not readily available to fire except as leaf litter (bamboo tends to be deciduous when moisture-stressed). The explosion and the noise of expanding steam blowing open wet culms can be quite dramatic. In Asia, fire is considered a hazard because of the damage it can do to a healthy clump, but in our experience from three fires on this property, it recovers quickly. Bamboo is not explosively combustible compared with eucalypts.

The greatest problem we have with the sympodial species is convincing people that there is such a thing as a non-invasive bamboo! One can draw diagrams of rhizome species, explain the difference between a root and a rhizome, and assure them that sympodial bamboos cannot be propagated by man or nature from the root system, but most people remain sceptical and still convinced that they will break out and run like the monopodial species. Ultimately, when sufficient of these beautiful plants find their way into our gardens, the sceptics will be convinced.

23 Medical Uses

An extraordinary amount of Chinese and Indian medicine is derived from bamboo. Stem oil, sap, rhizomes, roots, leaves and mineral accumulations of hundreds of different bamboos are used for specialised cures or enhancing qualities as diverse as asthma, consumption, gonorrhea, fever, coughs, diarrhoea, kidney problems, liver problems, jaundice, eye problems, worms, ulcers, abortion, fertility and virility. One common example is a loose solid deposit, known as 'tabashir', found as a loose rock deposit that accumulates inside the culms of many species (including *Bambusa vulgaris* and *Dendrocalamus asper*). It consists of almost pure salicylic acid, which is known as aspirin to the Western world, and is basically the same ingredient absorbed by the British for centuries by chewing willow bark. (The same ingredient was also used as a deoxidising agent in ancient bell foundries, where molten bronze was stirred with willow branches to release bubbles of gas that would otherwise flaw the castings.)

This book can't begin to list (or be responsible for the validity of) the hundreds of different medical or health uses bamboo is said to be good for, but a few examples are as follows:

Bambusa bambos (syn. *Bambusa arundinacea*): Used in Ayurvedic medicine (mainly leaf infusions) for eye wash, inflammation, leucoderma, blood purification, bronchitis, gonorrhoea and fever. The de-alcoholised leaf extract is said to have an anti-bacterial effect (Tewari, 1981).

Bambusa vulgaris: The leaves are a sudorific and febrifuge agent used in combination with other drugs for jaundice and dropsy. Raw shoot sap treats dropsy, fever, anorexia, foetal disturbances, haematuria, coughs and phlegm congestion. Culm leaves are emmenagogue and antihemorrhagic, are said to relieve hiccups, vomiting, and help prevent miscarriage (Tewari, 1981).

Dendrocalamus strictus: Has an abortifacient effect (Tewari,1981) and is also used to treat kidney problems and gonorrhoea (Othman, 1995).

Bambusa tuldoides and *B. pervariabilis*: Culm shavings are used as chuk yu in Chinese medicine for febrile diseases, haematuria, epistaxis, and infantile epilepsy (*Hong Kong Bamboos*, 1985).

The list is formidable, and can't be covered in this book. I found one recent scientific discovery—announced at the International Bamboo Workshop we attended in Anji China (Sept. 1997)—very exciting. Zhang Ying, a food science researcher, has been researching the fact that 'bamboo leaves contain a class of functional component

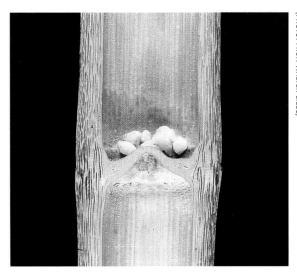

(PHOTO: PROF. WALTER LIESE)

■ **23.A** *A cross section of a culm showing a rare deposit of tabashir inside, highly valued for its medicinal qualities*

which has a bio-antioxidative action'. To quote some parts of this long, very well researched technical paper, 'Limpid peroxidation is strongly associated with aging and carcinogenesis' (aging of cells and cancer). 'Bamboo leaf has dietary antioxidants that include flavonoids that are effective in protecting cells from peroxidative damage, especially to aged and /or injured cells' (in other words a youth drug)! 'Bamboo leaves contain valuable flavonoid and phenolic acid compounds, which have strong scavenging capacity on active oxygen radicals... functional factors in bamboo leaf are capable of inducing the activity of endo-antioxidases of aged mice.' Bamboo leaf had an inhibiting effect on lipid peroxidation (LPO) which is measured in concentrations of LPO in plasma and LF in liver tissue, measures associated with cell aging in human beings. After a 35-day bamboo leaf extract feeding program, 'the concentration of LPO in plasma and LF in liver tissue of experimental mice fell significantly. Results show that functional factors in bamboo leaf are of strong inhibiting capacity on limpid peroxidation and scavenging ability to peroxidative products'. (Peroxidative products are carcinoma-inducing and cell aging agents.)

Since hearing and studying their very well researched exciting paper, I have chopped up bamboo leaves with my breakfast toast every morning! This is probably why the Japanese have been wrapping their fish in bamboo leaf for thousands of years to keep it fresh and without smell!

(Maybe I should sleep in a fresh bamboo leaf blanket each night?)

For those interested, there are dozens of references to the use of bamboos in Asian medicine in *Hong Kong Bamboos* and Professor Tewari's book (see reference list).

■ **23.B** *The shoots of* Bambusa vulgaris *cv. 'Wamin'*

What I find strange is the fact that Western medical science doesn't appear to have shown much interest in investigating the complex medical uses and compounds of bamboo in spite of, or perhaps because of, its wide use and acceptance by Asian cultures for medical use. As a result of my making the earlier mentioned paper on bio-antioxidases available to Southern Cross University, they also are researching this aspect using clumping bamboo leaves from this property. But this is the only Western research I know of. Perhaps that will also change if we can popularise the plant in Western society. Two thousand million Chinese and Indians can't have got it all wrong, and there has to be a valuable basis for many of their traditional cures, one that deserves attention from modern medical research.

Unfortunately, without such research, I can neither recommend the treatment nor confirm that the results of trying it will be positive, or even harmless.

24 Cultural and Traditional Aspects of Bamboo

Why is bamboo such a significant, often sacred, factor in the lives of Asian people, whilst barely touching the conscious lives of Western civilisation? The answer becomes obvious when you study the countries where bamboo is indigenous and available in any quantity. More than 1500 different species of bamboo grow naturally throughout most Asian countries plus South and Central America, and its continuing importance in the lives of those peoples is directly proportional to the number of useful species commonly available. None of the Western countries have had any significant useful bamboo species growing in their populated areas, many none at all. Bamboo is not indigenous to Europe or the Middle East, and the one relatively inferior indigenous running species in the USA (southern states) had little impact.

Of Australia's four or five species (not yet all properly established taxonomically) the 110 mm *Bambusa arnhemica* indigenous to sparsely populated northern Australia (near Darwin), and the long internoded *Schizostachyum* sp. 'Murray Island' growing in Australia's Torres Strait Islands, have both been significantly useful to the original populations of those areas. However, with the exception of those Aborigines, most Australians are still unaware of their existence, and the rest generally think they are introduced plants. Because of the Aboriginal Australians' nomadic life style, their utilisation of this bamboo didn't include building permanent houses or furniture, but museum collections include portable bamboo items such as smoking pipes, water containers, spear shafts, castanets and drone tubes of various types (didgeridoo).

Various Aboriginal legends confirm bamboo's significance to the northern Aboriginal population. A legend of the Kunwinku people relates how a fight between Ngarrbek (the spiny anteater) and Naluna (the tortoise) caused them to be changed from humans into their present animal form, and given separate living habitats. Naluna, who showered Ngarrbek with bamboo spears that became quills, was subsequently flattened with a heavy rock in retaliation.

Whilst playing little part in Western social customs, the range of traditions and customs involving bamboo in Asia is formidable. Long before paper was invented, the Chinese recorded their history on thin slivers of bamboo. Both Japanese and Chinese have raised the painting of bamboo to a spiritual art form, and all formally trained artists are taught first to paint bamboo in many forms. Both Japanese Haiku poetry, Chinese poetry and Indonesian poetry abounds in simple philosophical statements idolising bamboo. The shakuhachi flute along with a huge proliferation of other traditional bamboo musical instruments converts this meditative adulation of the plant into exotic sounds. The Japanese tea ceremony, central to their historical philosophy and culture, cannot be conducted without the 'chasen', a delicately made bamboo tea whisk, and a bamboo ladle of a form that requires specialised craftsmen sometimes cut up to 100 poles to make one superior ladle. In some areas, the tea itself is made from the leaves of the bamboo *Sasa vetchii*, said to give energy because of the high content of vitamins (in particular vitamin K) which are said to be effective as a preservative and deodoriser.

Most fresh Japanese seafood is sold wrapped in bamboo leaf to extend its fresh life and minimise odour and many dishes are cooked wrapped in the leaves as a flavouring and preserving agent. To a lesser extent but still traditionally important, the Vietnamese use bamboo

■ **24.A** *A beautiful Indonesian basket made from* Gigantochloa apus

■ **24.B** *A delicate lidded decorative container made from lacquered split bamboo in China*

leaves for the same purpose. Sake, the Japanese rice wine that was originally called 'sasa' after the bamboo of that name, makes use of the white powder on the young bamboo culms as a preservative and flavouring agent. One Japanese text I have says manufacturers in recent years have tried to find an artificial substitute, but their results were inferior and produced headache and sickness (*Take to Sasa—large and small bamboo*, Muroi Okamura, 1971).

The Chinese also make a wine from young bamboo culms, and the Tanzanians of Africa do much the same from *Oxytenanthera braunii,* harvesting from sap flowing from specially cut young culms from plantations established to make that wine, so highly prized that they also tin it to make it available all the year round. For centuries, drink and water vendors throughout Asia have used the natural insulating qualities of larger culms with some internodes removed to transport their wares.

Japanese, Chinese and Indonesian legends abound in stories symbolising bamboo as energy, sexuality and fertility, prosperity and longevity. Many festivals in these countries cut poles to create quite elaborate decorations such as the Japanese new year festival that used bamboo cuttings to symbolise mysterious life powers. The people of Kobe buy fresh bamboo leaves on January 10th each year to ensure good luck and prosperity in their business dealings for the remaining year. Bamboo joss sticks, incense sticks and fortune-telling sticks are in use in every Chinese temple in Asia. Almost every Asian has had their umbilical cord severed, or their circumcision performed, with a ceremonial bamboo knife.

It is an invaluable medium in their screens, walls, fences, and hundreds of regularly used symbolical and functional objects, weapons, art forms and jewellery. The Ethiopian bamboo house has been built in a traditional 'beehive' form for more than 3000 years.

Often even the particular species is important to the ceremony, as with *Schizostachyum brachycladum* with its yellow colour sacred to Asian Hinduism and highly valued for the beautifully decorated Balinese ceremonial poles; also the bamboo they call 'tying papah', used in ceremonies connected with sanctified water (Muller, *American Bamboo Society*, vol.15, no 5) and said to have been first brought to Java, and then later Bali, by the revered Brahman priest, Nirartha, in the 15th century.

The prayer bells of many Asian Muslim people are made from large bamboos, and the Indian death stretchers, traditionally constructed from bamboo, make them wary of using bamboo to construct cots for their children.

For many applications, bamboo is more suitable than other plants. As an example, the Asians use the bamboo carrying pole's ability to flex without breaking to reduce shock load and bruising on the shoulders. Indonesia's war of independence from Dutch colonial rule is known as the Bamboo Revolution, because the people armed themselves with bamboo weapons because they lacked Western firearms. The proliferation of bamboo weapons for war and hunting, bows and arrows, cross bows, blow

24.C *Traditional Chinese punting rafts*

pipes, spears, clubs, traps and lures is endless.

The massive bamboo cable ropes traditionally used to tow barges upstream on the Yangtze River are reported to be up to 400 m in length, 100 mm diameter, with as many as 300 men pulling them. Made from the outer split-off portion of the culm wall with its high fibre density and hard, more abrasive resistant skin woven to the outside, they are claimed to have a working stress of 1800 kg/sq.cm or 140 tonnes per cable (Farrelly, 1984). Such cables have traditionally been used all over Asia to support suspension bridges spanning more than 200 m, some of which carry trucks!

An extraordinary amount of Chinese and Indian medicine is derived from bamboo as recorded in chapter 23. For as long as Asian history has been recorded, those peoples have made building, ropes, string, boats, eating utensils, bridges, a multitude of art objects, as well as the plant being a significant food resource. Even the first Chinese cannons were made from heavy bound bamboo culms! Is it any wonder that the plant commands such respect in Asian societies?

All of this history and tradition is lacking from Western civilisation because of the absence of the plant over the hundreds of years it takes to develop and refine these uses. My appeal to Western people is that we upgrade our knowledge of this magnificent annually renewable plant, to become more aware of the fundamental differences between species, in particular running versus clumping bamboos, and to reallocate bamboo to a more appropriate level of respect in our society. Its incredible ability to grow so quickly in often difficult conditions may make it an important factor in restoring the photosynthesis balance of a world we have been damaging for centuries. This can only be of benefit to us, and will also enhance our lives, and our understanding of some of our Asian neighbours. Culture and tradition don't happen overnight. If we ignore bamboo's potential, it will never become a useful everyday part of our lives.

25 The Future of Bamboo in Western and Eastern Society

■ **25.A** *A tranquil scene at Guangzhou Botanical Gardens. The right hand species is* Schizostachyum funghomii.

If you have reached this point in the book, you must be amazed, as I am, at the almost total lack of practical knowledge that Western people have about bamboo generally, but particularly about clumping bamboos. With Australia located in the midst of islands and lands that abound in beautiful sympodial species, and the USA located just above the fabulous *Guadua* forests of Central and South America, both areas with ancient bamboo cultures that create fabulous modern and traditional buildings, we have obviously nurtured a blurred, somewhat romantic blind spot. Western concepts of bamboo have also been damaged by the irresponsible planting of runners. People innocently plant without having a management system to control the spreading habit of monopodial bamboos, or even the knowledge that they do spread and invade. This will all change, and this book is an attempt to change it.

Bamboo provides a greater diversity of mankind's needs than any other plant, but primarily to the peoples of Asia, South America, and some parts of Africa. In some countries, it is considered the poor man's timber, but even the wealthy in those lands make use of the plant in dozens of ways such as food, useful and decorative artifacts, medicine, ceremonial pieces, architectural features and music. Westerners import and use far more bamboo in the form of tinned shoots and artifacts (baskets and chopsticks, for example) than they would believe possible, but remain ignorant and suspicious of the plant and its potential as a diverse economically viable producer. Australia imports millions of dollars worth of bamboo nursery stakes every year (and will probably continue to do so because we can't expect to produce them locally for the price).

As a beautiful, easily controlled garden plant, clumping bamboos are virtually unknown in Australia. In fact, up until 1995, there were more of the small cold-tolerant clumping bamboos such as *Fargesia* in English and USA gardens than there were clumping species in the whole of this country, in spite of the fact that our climate is far more suitable for sympodial bamboos than Britain's or the USA's is!

The picture is, however, changing. People here at long last are showing a strong but cautious interest in bamboo plantations, and an article in the October 1996 issue of

■ **25.B** *An elegant collection of modern Balinese bamboo furniture*

■ **25.C** *The author's wife, Deirdre Stewart, walking beside clumps of gregariously flowering* Dendrocalamus giganteus *in the process of dying in 1995 (Bogor Botanical Gardens, Indonesia)*

the American Bamboo Society magazine is promoting plantations in the USA. Edible bamboo shoots will become an important and viable crop in Australia with at least 150 hectares planted by May 1999. These will provide shoots for both the local market and for export. This will expand during the next ten years as the pioneers prove, and profit from, this exciting new crop. The USA are moving, perhaps more slowly, in the same direction, but the climate there will dictate that most plantations will be runners (moso, etc.) that will take ten years instead of five years to mature. The USA apparently currently consumes more than 30 000 tonnes of edible shoots each year.

The existence of plantations for shoots in both the USA and Australia will supply bamboo poles for the market, not normally available yet. It is highly unlikely that you have ever seen a bamboo pole for sale, but the time will come when many landscape suppliers, nurseries and some timber yards will stock and sell culms in much the same way as treated pine poles. The current lack of a marketing infrastructure is partly because the species now growing and available in both countries are inferior. Lack of interest is also partly because Western people don't know how use bamboo, how to make the proliferation of wonderful items such as furniture, musical instruments, fences, screens and buildings. All those objects are quite easy to make. This book and other information we are putting out will help address this lack of confidence, perhaps even inspire you to have a go!

I believe that the demand for bamboo poles (culms) will grow rapidly as high quality culms become available and are marketed properly with 'how to use' information attached. People will see the results of the increasing few who are now making attractive furniture and other objects from bamboo. People from interstate are now attending

workshops at Bamboo World on specialist subjects like furniture, building, and general knowledge. Already we get more enquiries for culm timber than we can supply. We are using so much of the timber we currently produce both to build and develop our own structures and artifacts, and also for use in teaching groups, that we don't have enough. Additionally, our plantations are young and still being developed (timber takes seven years).

Australia has recently taken a big step forward in forming two constituted bodies for the first time, the Bamboo Society of Australia (BSA), and the Australian Commercial Bamboo Corporation, both designed to promote bamboo and its useful diversity, to distribute information and to encourage a united approach.

During research for my large public sculpture 'Man, Time and the Environment', I was staggered to find that

■ **25.E** *Floorboards being manufactured from moso in a Chinese factory (very labour-intensive)*

■ **25.D** *A Chinese bamboo blind weaving machine*

whilst it took man (*Homo erectus*) many millions of years to reach a population of one billion, it only took 140 years to increase to 5.2 billion in 1993, and it now exceeds 6.2 billion five years later. This is the indication of an endemic out-of-control species (the subject of the sculpture)! Many scientists are now predicting that, due to man's overpopulation and the consequent squandering of resources, the carbon dioxide build up cannot be reversed because forests can't grow quickly enough to create the necessary photosynthesis and carbon dioxide conversion. They are saying we are doomed to a deteriorating environment that will cause massive changes to climate and agriculture within 25 years. I am not qualified to comment on the validity of their claims, but we are all witnessing so many manifestations of this deterioration, with increased reliance on chemical controls, that we must conclude that it is true at least in part, and that we can't afford to wait and see. I believe fast growing clumping bamboo may play a vitally important part in the search for a solution as we inevitably accept the magnitude of our problem. If the world decides it must plant fast-growing biomass plants on a grander scale to cause a reversal of our deteriorating air quality, sympodial bamboo is the obvious and most efficient choice for all mild to warm climates.

Most of the economically viable clumping bamboo species grow many times faster than any forest tree and they produce large masses of luxurious green leaf. They are extremely efficient producers of oxygen from carbon dioxide. With properly organised propagation (such as our current tissue culture production) it would be possible to establish massive forests within four years. These would be forests that also produce large volumes of food and timber within six years.

The plant, properly managed, is annually renewable, producing its timber and food every year in considerable abundance, and without the need of chemical sprays in most environments. Perhaps if such desperate solutions are ultimately required, interplanting with less vigorous (but still very vigorous) biomass producers such as deep-rooted eucalypt trees will lessen possible negative monoculture effects. We are about to become involved in a university monitoring system on such a planting because of the probability that the non-competitive juxtaposition of deep-rooted trees being sheltered by shallow-rooted bamboos will increase tree growth whilst creating an income from the bamboo for the tree farmer. The farmer hence is producing an income whilst waiting the 20 years or more for his eucalypt forest to mature.

In terms of essential vitamins and trace elements, the building blocks within bamboo shoots are impressive when compared to other natural foods. Yet their food and therapeutic qualities remain uninvestigated by the Western world, even though some species of bamboo shoots and plant parts are much valued by Asian medicine. So far they can be grown without using chemical sprays in most places, and such foods are of great value to mankind. In Asia, bamboo leaves are regularly used as a stock food but few Western people are aware that they are approximately 20 per cent crude protein, and possibly higher in bio-antioxidants than any other known plant part (Zhang Ying, 1997). Some research is being done in the United States of America evaluating plantations for producing bamboo leaf for high protein cattle food.

In many Asian countries, bamboo's use is declining because the resource is being overused. The shoots are

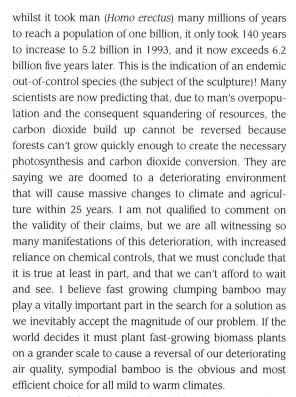

being taken for food and the culms being harvested in such a way that the plants are suffering. This, together with the reduction in both natural stands and established plantations due to increasing population and urbanisation, is causing a reduction of the availability of the resource. India's paper production from bamboo dropped from 73.5 per cent in 1952 to 30 per cent in 1980, partly because of a shortage of the resource and a failure to replace damaged or destroyed plantations and natural stands, and partly because of increased paper consumption. In 1952, India did not need to destroy timber forests for paper. In fact it was using no hardwood for that purpose. By 1980, consumption of pulp had risen from 130 000 tonnes to 1 149 000 tonnes, the 30 per cent bamboo actually being an increase on the 1952 tonnage being consumed, but also having to be supplemented with 507 000 tonnes (51 per cent) hardwood chips! The *Wealth of India* encyclopaedia reports: 'With the expansion of the paper industry and falling supplies of bamboo, coupled with the abundant tropical forests in the country, the industry is forced to use hardwood pulp with bamboo pulp for the production of paper.' If only India had the foresight in 1952 to expand their annually sustainable bamboo plantations, today they would not be destroying tropical hardwood forests to make paper! Apparently there is research in progress that may indicate that adding 30 per cent bamboo chip to wood chip will result in improved quality and strength without having to change the digester machinery, which could be a big step forward in saving trees.

Some countries like India, China and the Philippines are now being forced to develop propagation systems to cope with the need to plant more bamboo, but the shortage of land in some areas has created problems. China has planted more than five million clumps of *Bambusa oldhamii* in one province alone since 1986, purely for local use. Thailand, motivated by export income, increased its plantings of *Dendrocalamus asper* by more than six million plants in three years (1989 to 1992) and is planting another seven million in 1998. Even Costa Rica successfully planted 65 000 bamboos (179 hectares) in three years (1988 to 1991), creating scattered plantations of a *Guadua* species not indigenous to their area. They now have sufficient bamboo to build more than 3000 earthquake-resistant houses per year. India has introduced a replanting and propagation system to try and replace some of the destruction that has taken place, but they have a long way to go before it will make a serious dent. The point is that it can be done if the will to do it and the financial resources are invested. We expect to generate at least 100 000 bamboo plants here at Bamboo World during 1999, and we produced more than 20 000 in 1998.

The people of the Western world haven't yet woken up to the fact that they are spending valuable dollars on tinned edible shoot imports that can be profitably grown in a superior (fresh) form in their own country. When that happens the by-product of beautiful bamboo timber available will inevitably change people's attitude, lack of interest and knowledge of this beautiful plant. Increasingly we are getting enquiries from landscape gardeners for advanced clumping species plants, as they slowly realise that it is not necessary to build a containing box to prevent sympodial species from spreading. I can remember when palm trees were rare in Australia's gardens, and now most gardens have at least one. The time of the clumping bamboo, with the small diameter erect species available, has arrived. They will, I believe, become an increasingly frequent feature in suburban gardens and professional landscaping during the next ten years.

(PHOTO: SIMON VELEZ)

■ **25.F** *An extraordinary and very large bamboo roof with very long eave cantilevers being constructed by Colombian architect, Simon Velez*

■ **25.G** *A beautiful two-year-old* Dendrocalamus brandisii *plant, exploding with new shoots and huge, delicately green leaves— typical of the energy and joie de vivre of bamboo*

Government authorities (local councils in particular) will need to be educated in the difference between clumping and running bamboos. At the moment many of them are reflecting people's aggression towards bamboo generally. They are just not aware that beautiful non-invasive clumping bamboos are available. Already we have supplied significant numbers of clumping bamboos to four of Australia's major botanical gardens, which will ultimately result in more bamboos being planted in parks and botanical gardens. The beautiful, now mature clumping species planted in Brisbane's Mount Coot-Tha Botanical Gardens (near the Japanese Garden) are fine examples of what I am advocating, and our recently supplied plants will further enhance that display.

It is quite possible that the number of Australian local councils moving towards banning running bamboos will increase, and I would support them if they are in a mild climate area, so long as they learn the difference between the two types, and don't ban both. Unfortunately, the prejudice exists even amongst people who claim to be educators. One well-known commercial television show in 1997 ran items calling bamboo a noxious weed without describing the difference between invasive runners and non-invasive clumpers, and didn't want to know when we tried to advise them. I wrote to a Sydney gardening journalist in 1996 responding to her statement 'I'm at a loss to understand how "bamboo trees" polled 10 per cent of the most used plants, especially when it is a noxious weed'. I suggested that she had a responsibility as an educator to acquaint herself properly with the plant and give people a corrected understanding (I also sent her two booklets on the subject); we didn't even get a reply! Twice during 1996/97, reporters visited us (2.5 hours' drive from Brisbane) from a well-known national newspaper at their own instigation, spent time and money on photographs and story writing, read us the article written and told us with enthusiasm that the article would appear within the next few days. Neither ever appeared. The reporters were enthusiastic even after writing the article, but the editors did not like or trust bamboo! Many people in positions of communicative power have made their minds up about bamboo being an undesirable invasive plant, and they don't want to know any different.

Thailand is using woven splits to produce very high quality ply sheets complete with the woven decorative

(PHOTO: SIMON VELEZ)

■ **25.H** *The roof shown in Photo 25F nearing completion*

finish revealed. China is producing high quality flooring and composite beams of immense strength from moso culms, and other Asian countries, plus Columbia, are beginning to produce limited quantities of laminated beam or board. All of those countries, however, have existing plantings of high quality bamboo to draw on, whereas no Western country has such natural stands, nor has taken sufficient interest in bamboo to create the raw material necessary to manufacture these products. The plywood and laminated timber/floorboard factories I have seen are (necessarily) very labour-intensive. Nor do I believe that the Western world will ever embark on manufacturing either paper, plywood, or laminated beams from bamboo in large quantities, certainly not in the foreseeable future. We are told that maturing plantations of eucalypt trees in Australia will, before long, be sufficient to make it unnecessary to continue to harvest timber from our natural stands. That doesn't, however, replace the massive quantities still being destroyed to maintain our export quota of wood chips to places like Japan. When I wrote suggesting the Australian government investigate making paper from bamboo, I received the predictable answer that the cost of establishing a matured volume of bamboo plantations to replace our export and internal usage of wood chip, plus modifying the paper mills to suit bamboo fibre instead of pine and eucalypt, would need to be invested in by private enterprise, and was therefore unlikely to occur. They are right if we take into account woodchip export. They are also right if our eucalyptus forest plantations rather than our remaining natural stands can cope easily with both our timber needs and our local paper manufacturing needs. It doesn't make sense to create bamboo forests simply to replace eucalyptus plantations already created for the same need, but in the light of the world's carbon dioxide crisis, it certainly doesn't make sense to destroy Australia's natural forests for export wood chips! There is a possibility that left over reject plantation culms could be chipped and used as an additive to hardwood chips. But this may not happen until the cost of wood chip increases. Another practical option is converting bamboo chip to fibreboard that could be stronger than any alternative, and the factory process is highly automated.

The edible shoot plantations currently being established will increasingly produce sufficient timber to support a proliferation of craft, artistic and utilitarian uses, but not enough to create manufacturing facilities for plywood, boards or paper. I believe that the market for culms will grow, and will consume most of the supply that becomes available with the help of a little marketing. Already some enterprising people are importing container loads of bamboo culms to sell the wood, something that will be uneconomical as the plantations develop. Aside from some contract fence building and garden buildings such as pagodas, most of the Australian use will be home craft rather than business oriented. The USA pattern will be the same.

Bamboo will become accepted as an architectural feature material rather than as a prime medium of construction. I don't believe it will or should replace timber, stone or other materials currently in use in this country, but the beauty of bamboo features in Western-designed Balinese resorts will catch on here once the quality and supply of the material is assured. It will remain and perhaps become even more popular as a source of cheap home-grown building material for those with the energy to harvest, treat and create their own unique houses. At least now, plants that will produce superior structural quality bamboo are available.

Whilst it has been a slow starter, bamboo will play an increasingly important role in Western culture and economics as a plant, a food, and a usable material. Some Asian countries are already taking significant steps to increase plantation plantings to fill shortages of what for them is a culturally significant part of their everyday lives. The fact that you have read this book indicates that, like myself, you have an affection for this beautiful and much misunderstood plant. I am evangelistic in my efforts, but the message can't be effectively spread by one person. Do you have these beautiful plants growing, or can you plant one? No matter how small your yard, you can still fit in a 1.5 m plant that never will exceed 1 m diameter—for instance *Bambusa multiplex* var. *riviereorum*! It thrives in a pot! Do you know someone you care for enough to give one to as a gift? The best way to impassion people is to expose them to the plant and the beautiful objects that can be made from it.

It's early December here as I write this. The first of the early clumping shoots are leaping out of the ground. This morning we discovered two new shoots on our *Bambusa textilis*, sharp streamlined vertical spears that weren't there yesterday. We also discovered and harvested a beautiful pale green early shoot from the elegant *Nastus elatus*, and ate it raw with our lunchtime salad with a little olive oil and red wine vinegar dressing, serving the salad from a bamboo bowl using bamboo chopsticks. We were lunching, on bamboo furniture of course, in our botanical bamboo species garden overlooking our small lake (stocked with silver perch which we just cooked wrapped in huge *Dendrocalamus latiflorus* bamboo leaves.

Beside us is the giant shoot producer *D. asper*, biding its time before it also will shortly split the earth with its huge 300 mm diameter shoots. Its large leaves breathe out a shimmering whisper in the breeze as accompaniment to the tall culms crooning quietly against each other as they move. The thought that many of these magnificent towering plants were less than a metre tall only two or three years ago, 'babies' collected and brought personally by us from exotic Asian places, is immensely satisfying. There are also the dozens of friends we now have in these countries who have helped us, intelligent bamboo-educated people with a similar passion. Developing Bamboo World and its beautiful gardens has been difficult, stressful and expensive at times, but wonderfully rewarding. There is a peace here in our unique environment that is well worth our years of effort.

Reference List

A Compendium of Chinese Bamboo. China Forestry Publishing House, 1994.

Adkoli, N. 'Employment Generation from Bamboos in India'. Paper at Fourth International Bamboo Congress, Bali, 1995.

Anantachote, A. 'Flowering and Seed Characteristics of Bamboos in Thailand'. Paper.

Austin, Levi, Ueda. *Bamboo.* Wetherhill Press, Tokyo,

'Bamboos Current Research'. Proceedings of the International Workshop, Cochin, India, November, 1988.

'Bamboo in Asia and the Pacific'. Proceedings of the Fourth International Bamboo Workshop, held in Chiang Mai, Thailand, November, 1991.

'Bamboo Towards the 21st Century'. Proceedings of the International Bamboo Workshop, held at Anji, China, 1997.

Book of Bamboo. (Natural History of Bamboo). Asahi Shinbun Press, Tokyo, 1985.

But, Chia, Fung and Hu. *Hong Kong Bamboo.* Urban Council of Hong Kong, 1985.

Cusack, Victor. *Bamboo Rediscovered.* Earth Garden, Melbourne, 1997.

Cusack, V. 'Comparative aspects on management techniques and selection criteria for major bamboo edible shoot species'. Proceedings of the Fifth International Bamboo Congress, Costa Rica, 1998.

Cusack V. 'The Establishment of Commercial Bamboo Plantations in Australia'. Paper given at the International Bamboo Workshop, Anji, China, 1997.

Cusack V. 'Observations on Thai *Dendrocalamus asper* Plantations'. Paper given at the Rural Industries Research and Development Corporation Workshop, Brisbane, Australia, 1998.

Cusack V. 'Bamboo Shoot and Timber Plantation: Comparative Data across Species and *Dendrocalamus asper* — Establishment Costs and Cash Flow'. Paper given at the Rural Industries Research and Development Corporation Workshop, Brisbane, Australia, 1997.

Ding Guohua, Ding Yulong. 'Preliminary Study on the Dynamic of the Auxin in Below Ground Organs of Moso Bamboo'. Paper given at International Bamboo Workshop, Anji, 1997.

Dransfield, S. *The Bamboos of Sabah.* Sabah Forestry Dept, 1992.

Dransfield, S. and Widjaja E.A. (Editors). *Bamboos.* PROSEA, 1995.

Farrelly, David. *The Book of Bamboo.* Sierra Press, USA, 1984.

Fu Maoyi. *Cultivation and Utilization of Bamboos.* Fuyang Research Institute, Fuyang, China, 1996.

Gass, Drusedau, Hennicke (Editors). 'IL 31 Bamboo'. Journal from Institute for Lightweight Structures, University of Stuttgart), 1985.

Hidalgo Lopez, O. *Manual de construccion con bambu* (edited by Estudios Tecnicos Colombianos Ltda. Universidad Nacional de Columbia, 1981. [In Spanish only, but clearly illustrated.]

Janssen J. *Building with bamboo.* Intermediate Technology Publications, 1995

Janssen, Jules, 'Designing and Building with Bamboo' (Comprehensive lecture notes included in 'Bamboo—A Growers and Builders Reference Manual' published by the Hawaii Chapter of the American Bamboo Society in 1997)

Jinsaburo, Oshima. 'The Culture of Moso Bamboo in Japan Part I and Part II'. Paper, 1931.

Jinsaburo, Oshima. 'The Culture of Moso Bamboo in Japan—Part 1 and 2'. Paper from 1931 reproduced in *American Bamboo Society Magazine*, Vol. 3, No.1. 1982.

Liese, W. *Bamboos—Biology, Silvics, Properties, Utilisation.* GTZ, Germany, 1985.

Liese, W. and Weiner, G. 'Aging of bamboo culms'. Paper at Fourth International Bamboo Congress, 1995.

Liese, W. 'The Preservation of Bamboo Culms by the Sap Displacement Method'. Paper, 1995.

Liese, W. 'Anatomy and Utilisation of Bamboos'. Paper at the European Bamboo Society, 1995.

Lou Yiping, Xiao Jianghua. 'Research Needs and Strategies on Long Term Site Productivity of Moso Bamboo Forests'. Paper given at International Bamboo Workshop, Anji, 1997.

McClure, F.A. *The Bamboos.* Smithsonian Institution Press, USA, 1993.

Midmore, Walsh et al. 'Preliminary analysis of culinary bamboo shoot production in Queensland'. Paper, 1996.

Morisco. 'Filled Bamboo Joint Strength'. Paper at Gadjah Mada University, 1995.

Muller, Len. 'Mari Mencoba Sendiri' [Lets Try it Ourselves]. *American Bamboo Society Magazine*, Vol 16, No 2, April, 1998. [A description of making an Indonesian linak chair.] *ABS* has also published many interesting papers by Muller on Indonesian bamboos and customs, and taxonomical work with cell structure analysis.]

Ranjan M.P., Iyer Nilam, Pandya Ghanshyam. *Bamboo and Cane Crafts of Northeast India.* India's National Institute of Design, 1986.

'Recent Research on Bamboos'. Proceedings of the International Bamboo Workshop, Hangzhou, China, October, 1985.

Sumarna Anang. *Bamboo.* Penerbit Angkasa Bandung, Indonesia, 1987.

Sharma, Y. 'Inventory and Resource of Bamboos'. Paper at International Bamboo Conference, Hangzhou, China, 1985.

Shi Quantai, Bian Yaorong andWang Yongxi, 'Study on the Application of Chemical Fertiliser to the Timber and Paper Pulp Stands of *Phyllostachys pubescens* (moso)'. Paper at Hangzhou International Workshop, China, 1985.

Subyakto, I. 'Variation in specific gravity and bending properties of *Dendrocalamus asper* culm grown in Bogor'. Indonesian Institute of Sciences (LIPI) Puspiptek Serpong, Indonesia, 1995.

Surjokusumo, S. and Nugroho, N. 'A study on *Dendrocalamus asper* as Concrete Reinforcement'. Paper at Fourth International Bamboo Congress, Bali, 1995.

Tewari, D.N. *A Monograph on Bamboo.* International Book Distributors, Dehra Dun, India, 1989.

Thammincha, S. 'Bamboo Shoot Industry and Development in Thailand: The Physio-socio Economic Implications'. Paper at Fourth International Bamboo Congress, Bali, 1995.

Tropical Bamboos. Rizzoli International Publications Inc, USA, 1990.

Ueda, K. 'Mechanical properties of moso bamboo, Distribution of modulus of elasticity across the culm wall'. Hokkaido University, 1980.

Yulong Ding. '*Phyllostachys* in China and its Utilisation'. Paper published by Belgian Bamboo Society Newsletter 12,

Widjaja, E. 'A Revision of Malesian *Gigantochloa* (Poaceae-Bambusoideae)'. Paper from *Reinwardtia Journal*, Vol.10, part 3, pp. 271-382, 1987.

Widjaja, E. 'New Taxa in Indonesian Bamboos'. Paper reprinted from *Reinwardtia Journal*, Vol.11, (2), pp. 57-152, 1997.

Wu Liangru, Xiao Jianghua. 'Dynamic of the Endogenous Phytohormones in On-Off year Moso Bamboo Stands'. Paper given at International Bamboo Workshop, Anji, 1997.

Zhang Guangchu. 'Bamboo Breeding: Today and Tomorrow'. Paper at the International Bamboo Workshop, Anji, China, September 1997.

Zhang Ying. 'The Bio-antioxidative Activity of Functional Factors in Bamboo Leaves'. Paper at the International Workshop at Anji, China, 1997.

List of Sketches

Note that the first part of the number represents the chapter where the sketch appears.

Guide to Species Shape

Bambusa arnhemica

Bambusa balcooa
Gigantochloa albociliata

Bambusa blumeana

Bambusa bambos

Bambusa vulgaris cv. 'Wamin'

Bambusa chungii

Bambusa eutuldoides

Bambusa forbesii

Bambusa longispiculata

Bambusa malingensis

Bambusa multiplex

Bambusa dolichomerithalla
Bambusa multiplex cv. 'Alphonse Karr'
Nechouzeaua mekongensis

Bambusa multiplex cv.
'Stripestem Fernleaf',
Bambusa multiplex var. *riviereorum*
Fargesia nitida

Bambusa multiplex cvs
'Fernleaf', 'Golden Goddess',
'Silverstripe', 'Willowy'
Drepanostachyum falcatum

Bambusa polymorpha

Bambusa nana

Bambusa oldhamii

Bambusa oliveriana

Thyrsostachys oliveri
Thyrsostachys siamensis

Bambusa ridleyi

Bambusa textilis

Bambusa textilis var. *gracilis*

Bambusa tulda
Bambusa tuldoides

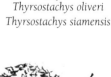

Bambusa ventricosa

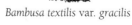

Bambusa vulgaris

Bambusa vulgaris cv. 'Vittata'

Schizostachyum dumetorum

Dendrocalamus sinicus

Dendrocalamus brandisii

Dendrocalamus giganteus

Dendrocalamus latiflorus

Dendrocalamus membranaceus

Dendrocalamus sikkimensis

Dendrocalamus strictus

Dendrocalamus asper

Gigantochloa atter

Gigantochloa hasskarliana

Gigantochloa sp. var. 'Malay
Dwarf Variegated'

*Dendrocalamus asper
Gigantochloa levis
Gigantochloa thoii*

Gigantochloa apus

*Bambusa lako
Gigantochloa atroviolacea*

Gigantochloa pseudoarundinacea

Gigantochloa ridleyi

Gigantochloa robusta

Guadua angustifolia

*Fargesia murieliae
Fargesia spathacea*

*Cephalostachyum pergracile
Dendrocalamus minor
var. amoenus
Gigantochloa wrayi
Schizostachyum brachycladum
Schizostachyum brachycladum
cv. 'Green'
Schizostachyum lumumpao*

*Schizostachyum caudatum
Schizostachyum jaculans*

Schizostachyum sp. 'Murray
Island'

*Guadua paniculata
Nastus elatus*

*Otatea acuminata acuminata
Otatea acuminata aztecorum*

List of Photographic Plates

Note that the first part of the number represents the chapter where the photo appears.

Index

For an alphabetical index of the bamboos species mentioned and described in this book, see Chapter 7 pp. 53–67, Species Descriptions

Page numbers listed below in **bold** are the main reference.